A Wounded Daughter's Survival

A Damaged Life Healed by Hope and Truth

Deborah Leigh Alexander

iUniverse, Inc.
Bloomington

A Wounded Daughter's Survival
A Damaged Life Healed by Hope and Truth

iUniverse books may be ordered through booksellers or by contacting:

iUniverse
1663 Liberty Drive
Bloomington, IN 47403
www.iuniverse.com
1-800-Authors (1-800-288-4677)

Because of the dynamic nature of the Internet, any web addresses or links contained in this book may have changed since publication and may no longer be valid. The views expressed in this work are solely those of the author and do not necessarily reflect the views of the publisher, and the publisher hereby disclaims any responsibility for them.

Any people depicted in stock imagery provided by Thinkstock are models, and such images are being used for illustrative purposes only.

Certain stock imagery © Thinkstock.

ISBN: 978-1-4620-3302-7 (sc)
ISBN: 978-1-4620-3303-4 (hc)
ISBN: 978-1-4620-3304-1 (e)

Library of Congress Control Number: 2011911215

Printed in the United States of America

iUniverse rev. date: 09/22/2011

For my loving, supportive, and ever faithful husband;
for my children and their spouses;
and
for my grandchildren

Contents

Part II
Childhood Healing Begins

Part III
The Dating Era

Part IV
The Functional Era Begins

Part V

Moving to Texas

Foreword

Some have compared the process involved in counseling to the act of peeling an onion. There are many layers that have to be removed before one finds the core. In the case of Debbie an incident occurred in a safe place – her church – that began the unpeeling. However, in her case she knew what her core consisted of.

A Wounded Daughter's Survival is Debbie's journey – beginning with the life-changing incident and travelling back to her childhood. What she uncovered led her to an understanding of the causes of feelings and behaviors related to her family of origin. What made her journey bearable is her profound belief in Jesus Christ.

The unpeeling began with Debbie's realization that her adult feelings in regard to her parents were a direct result of feelings of rejection and unworthiness she had felt as a child. There were many incidents that Debbie recalls that validated those feelings: her intense feelings of confusion when her mother was attacked, when her grandfather accidentally shot someone, her parents' divorce and subsequent remarriage.

Once she was able to unpeel the outer layer, Debbie was able to begin to understand the significance of the events that influenced her relationship with each of her parents. As she continued to unpeel the layers she realized that her family had, indeed, been dysfunctional. And, the dysfunction led to the continued uneasiness she felt as an adult when in their presence.

Debbie has told her story — a story of generational dysfunction — one that could be similar to the stories of others. What makes her story unique is how God has led her through her "unpeeling." The support she has received in her journey has enabled her to complete the process. With God's guidance Debbie has been able to heal her emotional wounds and become the person God intended her to be.

Athena H. Bean, M.Ed., LPC

Introduction

The pond that appeared clear on the surface was stirred, revealing the murky, dirty water underneath. At age forty-six, I experienced a trigger event that brought all the repressed memories from my childhood to the surface. These were memories of survival, and they were not pleasant. That is why I had buried them so far back in my mind; I never wanted to face them. It hurt to be forced to confront the past because of the shame I had always felt. However, I determined to set out on a journey to revisit the things that brought trauma and hurt to my life and to reach a destination of healing and peace. The purpose of this journey, taken completely with God's guidance, is to reveal the truth regarding my childhood. I chose to do this for my family's sake as well as my own.

One of the things I discovered is that I was not alone in my struggles. It's easy to feel like you are the only one experiencing such intense wounds and no one will understand how you feel, but that is false. The reality is completely the opposite. In fact, through much reading, studying, mentoring, and help from people close to me, I have discovered that what I went through as a child is actually more of an epidemic in our society than a rarity. The specific situations a child experiences may be vastly different, but the emotional damage is universal.

All parents need to evaluate the emotional legacy they are passing on to their children. An emotional connection between parent and child that validates a child's feelings is an essential ingredient for healthy development. Many children inherit a lifetime of pain and damage because of the emotional desert they are raised in. As a parent, do your actions and words convey to your children that they are a treasure you value greatly? Or do your actions and words say that you are indifferent and do not really care one way or the other about the child's presence in the family? Or do you convey to your child that you would rather he or she was never born at all? A simple test can bring to light some areas of family life that may require change. Do the prevailing actions of all family members consistently provide your child with an atmosphere of love, compassion, empathy, self-control, gentleness, patience, kindness, faithfulness, goodness, joy, and peace? Or is your family life better described by the presence of one or more of these on a daily basis: strife, anger, discontent, frustration, unhappiness, hopelessness, adultery, harshness, wrath, idolatry, hatred, bitterness, criticism, scorn, or bickering? If these negative traits are more prevalent in your family life than the positive ones, you can be assured that some changes need to be made. If negative traits are a major part of their childhood, your children will reap the damage of a hurtful emotional legacy and inherit a lifetime of pain. If you were a child who grew up in a family where emotional abuse was abundant, you can relate to the pain it brings to your life. If the damaging environment is not eradicated and healing is not allowed to begin for children living in this kind of pain, their chances of going on to lead productive, functional adult lives are slim to none.

In my life, I reached a point where I needed to find freedom from my childhood emotional damage. My husband provided the help and encouragement necessary for me to begin the process. After a time of searching through my childhood and writing down the things that hurt and damaged me, I gained an understanding of the abnormal emotional circumstances of my life. This understanding, in turn, became part of the healing process.

Sharing my experiences of survival, discovery, and healing with others who hurt in similar ways provides hope that a functional future is indeed possible, even for those raised under abusive circumstances. I lived through many damaging and sometimes violent encounters in my formative years, all of which included overwhelming feelings of rejection by both my parents. Facing the past and telling the story brings understanding and healing; it changes the family legacy for the better for future generations. I choose to have a forgiving heart filled with thankfulness. Without the pain, I would have no story to tell or hope to offer. The experiences I lived through made me a better, stronger, and wiser person.

To put the past in the proper perspective and gain functional ways of dealing with the pain and distortion, I needed help from a counselor. In my counselor's professional opinion, because of the many things I experienced in childhood, my life was set up to be very different from the way it actually turned out. Things I lived through are devastating and damaging to a child and usually lead to a very abnormal adult life. According to the norm for my circumstances, I should be on my fourth or fifth marriage, but instead I have been married to the same wonderful guy for over thirty years. I should be addicted to alcohol and/or drugs, but I use neither. No detrimental habits were allowed to take control of my life—I was never even tempted to go there. Instead of all the bad I was headed for, I have experienced a life rich and abundant in blessings and miracles.

I have discovered much on the journey back through my life, and I understand better than ever how vital it is that parents meet their children's emotional and spiritual needs. I hope by sharing my experience with childhood emotional abuse, I can bring healing to people who also hurt from emotional damage. Maybe through increased awareness, some emotional injury can be prevented from occurring at all. The journey I relate has brought healing to my life, repairing childhood wounds from emotional abuse.

In addition to the bad memories, numerous moments of thankfulness throughout the years have been brought to my remembrance. Reminders of many life-changing experiences were magnified, along with the positive impact they had. And there was one prevailing hope I clung to that guaranteed my survival, a truth to life that makes everything about it wonderful and worthwhile. My exploration has brought a renewed awareness of why my life is peaceful, happy, and content. It is no mystery, and I want to shine light on what gives life meaning and purpose and provides hope where there is need.

I share events of my life that are neither embellished nor diminished but are an honest representation of the truth regarding things I felt and experienced.

This is my story.

Part I
The Origin of Emotional Damage

— Chapter One —

My Family's Beginnings

Denying the hurt of my childhood and leaving it buried away seemed to work fine for me through many years into adulthood. My family life after marriage provided the healing I needed to strengthen my damaged emotions. God's presence guided me and gave me peace. I lived in a stable, secure, content, and loving environment, completely the opposite of the one I was raised in. Minor unrest would come only with random visits and encounters with my parents. On these visits, the repressed hurt I'd buried decades before would be disturbed by the emotional digging caused by their old hurtful behaviors. Then, when my parents left, my life felt peaceful, functional, and normal again.

What I did not realize through these years was that just one emotional episode with the power to revive the denied past could happen at a time when I least expected it. A perfect circumstance could send me back to feel all the pain and unbury all the unpleasantness I preferred never to acknowledge. Twenty-eight years after I left my childhood hurt behind, I experienced that one perfect emotional event powerful enough to bring all the bad memories bursting forth, demanding my attention. I was at a place where I had to revisit those repressed childhood days. It was time to face the truth and find real healing from the pain I had carried with me through the years. So my quest into the past began, reliving many experiences that hurt and damaged. The purpose of my journey back was to discover the source of the dysfunctional family patterns and introduce a better way, through understanding and change, for generations to follow. I started this exploration by recalling the things I knew from family history.

The storm in my life began brewing before I was born. It started with the impulsive marriage of my parents one night in May of 1958. When they rushed to marry immediately after Dad's high-school graduation, they were two teenagers not ready or emotionally equipped to enter the adult world. They each brought with them wounds from their own childhoods that led to childish behavior and a lack of ability to cope with adult life, marriage, or children.

As the old saying goes, "Haste makes waste." These words of wisdom can be applied to relationship decisions too. My mother's father did not attend the wedding because it all happened so quickly. He did not get to fill the traditional role of giving his only daughter away at her wedding. Grandpa's absence at the wedding was mentioned casually many times throughout the years. The real truth, though, is that this was a raw emotional wound that could not be healed. There are some once-in-a-lifetime experiences you do not get a second chance at. This hasty beginning for two teenagers, along with the emotional baggage they both carried with them, did not exactly set up this new life together for happiness and success. Unfortunately, more times than not, impatient decisions turn out to be huge mistakes. Impulsive choices can be very costly, not only to the ones who make them but also to the many other people touched by one life or one marriage. The deception comes when a person believes *it is my life, and what I do does not affect anyone but me.* This thinking is false. Many lives can be changed directly and indirectly by just one bad decision of an individual believing that he or she only will reap the consequences.

After my parents were married, my mother was not ready to leave her childhood home. So the newlyweds lived with my mother's parents. Dad worked for Grandpa on the farm doing odd jobs. At some point later, he began working on a ranch, where my mother would visit him. This was the set-up, so I have been told, in January of 1959—when, on one of those visits, I came into existence. Nine months later, in October 1959, I was born in the very small town of Fort Sumner, New Mexico.

After I was born, my mother had a hard time naming me. It seems Dad had no input on the name, just my mother. She claims no name was good enough for me, so the naming process took a while. But I believe she was totally expecting and hoping I would be a boy, and she just did not know what to do next. After a period of failing to come up with a name, a package came addressed to Deborah Leigh. This package was a white christening dress. I prefer to believe that since no decision could be reached in naming me that God stepped in and chose my name. *Deborah* and *Leigh* are both Hebrew in origin; *Leigh* is a derivative of the Hebrew name *Leah*. Anyway, this name was agreeable and became my name. In regard to the white christening dress, as far as I know, I wore it only for a picture. My parents did not attend church. Surely life would have taken a different turn if the gift had led to church attendance.

Significant events in life usually bring reminiscences of the special time and feelings associated with things of importance. The event of my birth was recalled often by my maternal grandma Ada and her son, my uncle Jim, who was ten at the time. Grandma Ada frequently told me how happy she felt when I arrived in the world. She often told me, "With that first glance, you had me wrapped around your little finger." I have heard how my uncle was filled with anticipation and excitement as he welcomed the new baby to the family. He has always remembered precisely how much I weighed and my exact length at birth. My mother's excitement seemed to pale in comparison to my grandma and uncle's reminiscences. My uncle's actions toward me throughout the years have proven that he cares for me. I have always felt a real emotional connection with him. Beginning on the day I was born and continuing through all the years since, this has not changed. My uncle turned out to be the first positive male role model in my life. I have heard numerous times how Grandma Ada and my uncle felt about my birth, but stories of any happiness or excitement about my birth from Dad or my maternal grandpa are missing. However, the absence of any fond memories from Dad or Grandpa regarding my birth is definitely consistent with their lack of participation and lack of involvement in raising me. All these reactions are really no wonder—they were a foretelling of how my relationships with my parents, my grandparents, and my uncle would be throughout my life.

Chapter Two

The Storm

A storm hits randomly, without warning. An environment that was calm and peaceful only minutes before is overcome by uproar and danger. A safe place becomes one of insecurity. The weather minutes earlier was calm and peaceful but now is radically demanding that you seek shelter and protection from its violent force. You cower and cover your head to shield yourself from whatever may go sailing by to assault and wound. Your heart pounds anxiously because your safety is violated. You are unsure if you will remain unharmed as the wind gusts, the rain torrentially slices through the air, and the hail pounds down. You even wonder if something more harmful, such as a tornado, will come sweeping and spinning through to blow you out of this world and out of existence as you sit huddled in its path. You are afraid, and your universe is in chaos. Your only hope is that whatever happens will not hurt too badly. You focus on survival. Then, after a damaging storm blows through, there is usually a path of destruction that requires repair and healing. The damage must be acknowledged and fixed before life can continue on.

Most people can relate to the feelings experienced by those living through a destructive storm, which can bring great harm in an instant. I relate that feeling of helplessness to a child forced to live through endless, random bouts of parental anger raging out of control. My first memory of this parental anger was at age three, and my world thereafter was insecure, violated, and compromised. My mother could go from calm and peaceable to a raging force of upheaval and trauma at the drop of a hat.

It seemed my mother's temper could be set off with the slightest provocation. She would rage and yell loudly, verbalizing her anger with arms flying. Many times, objects in her path would be destroyed, trashed, or stomped. Although never officially diagnosed with anything, my mother displayed irrational outbursts on a regular basis and an overall inability to cope with everyday life. This was all magnified by Dad's extreme narcissistic tendencies and lack of interest in helping out with family demands.

This destructive behavior would be explained away as a family trait—my mother was born with a temper, just like her dad. The type of anger they displayed was unbiblical and destructive. It damaged family, relationships, security, and any hope of living in peace. It was unproductive anger with no purpose but to harm. The Bible says, "Let every man be swift to hear, slow to speak, slow to wrath: For the wrath of man worketh not the righteousness of God" (James 1:19-20). My mother's behavior in this area surely shook the very foundation of security in my world. Experiencing such things from my mother, the one person in the world a three-year-old should always be able to count on, damaged me. A mother is supposed to bring comfort, not anxiety and fear.

These angry episodes brought trauma into my life, which in turn damaged my own coping methods. I went into a survival mode of acting invisible and apologizing for my existence in the world. I was helpless against the traumatic storms my mother regularly caused me to endure throughout childhood. I could only sit trembling, waiting for the storm to blow over.

In working through my past, I have learned there are reasons why both my parents acted the way they did. Both of them had trauma in their own pasts that had molded them and caused them to react to life the way they did. Since neither of them faced their pain or found healing, the dysfunction of the past was ever present to be inherited by their children. It became the legacy passed on from one generation to the next.

Without healing after emotional trauma, people go on living with the damage it causes. They do not acknowledge their injuries. Theirs becomes a life with a distorted view of reality, seeing the behaviors and reactions of others toward them in a false way. This leads to a compromised state of being. Those who are emotionally damaged routinely display irrational, out-of-control feelings. Their life becomes abnormal—moody and angry, with ups and downs, very much like a roller-coaster ride. Living in denial leads to a lifetime of compensating that inevitably leads to more problems. It is not possible to repress the pain of emotional damage; it will surface in many hurtful ways.

Chapter Three

Generational Rejection—The Baggage

My parents' union had many strikes against it and was troubled from the beginning. They brought the baggage of childhood rejection and teenage trauma to their new marriage. Another element providing a negative influence was generational rejection passed from my maternal grandpa to my mother. It became part of my mother's life because Grandpa never recognized, faced, or found healing from his own rejection experiences in childhood.

Not understanding his background, Grandpa passed on the undesirable traits of rejection to my mother. This probably happened because my mother seemed to have a stronger connection with Grandpa than Grandma. Generational rejection becomes a vicious cycle of unnecessary pain and turmoil, of not showing you care, and of hurting the ones you claim to treasure the most. My mother's rejection could have resulted from small things that individually seemed insignificant. But when added together, the sum equaled a life suffering from rejection and arrested emotional development. Her feeling of security could have been compromised to some extent as a child because, out of necessity, my grandparents were devoted to their work on the farm. She was left many times alone at home while they worked in the fields.

Grandma recollected one experience from when my mother was one year old. She cried, and Grandpa continued to spank her until she stopped crying. It had to be difficult to stop crying while being spanked, but Grandpa did not stop. I would guess his temper was out of control. Grandpa's presence could easily instill fear in a child. He did not talk much and rarely displayed positive feelings. His looks and mannerisms could provoke fear. Whether my mother knew it or not, I am sure this spanking experience led her to have an uneasy, insecure feeling about her dad on some unconscious level.

My mother did not grow up in a family that was openly affectionate. Grandpa especially never uttered the simple, emotionally connecting words "I love you" with accompanying behaviors showing proof of a child's importance and value in the family. Love must be communicated to children so they know they matter and belong in the family. These messages must be sent regularly in words and actions for the child to develop a healthy sense of belonging and worth. Instead, during my mother's childhood, the family's general mode of thinking was that these are things you should just know because of your place in the family. Therefore, there was no understanding of the need to repeatedly verbalize and show love.

On a few occasions, when I would say, "I love you, Grandpa."

His response was always, "Aw, pooey!"

Grandpa had trouble giving and receiving love. This led to my mother's lack in paternal, emotional love—an area she desperately craved.

Grandpa did not grasp how very essential emotional connection is. In a functional, nurturing environment, children would never be left to guess about the value they hold for their parents, or that they are loved and cared for. These loving words are extremely necessary—especially when there are so many nonverbal actions speaking very loudly that you are *not* loved; you are a burden; I do not want you here with me; I am so angry and it is because of what you have done. Children are emotional beings. They must hear and feel the words so that in their hearts, they know they are loved. This love needs to be spoken of many times a day. It is vital, too, that love is shown by actions as well. However, a huge barrier arises when parents, due to previous issues and hurts in their lives, have *arrested emotional development*, a condition that hinders normal emotional growth (see Appendix C). Emotionally damaged people many times are just not capable of showing they care. Oftentimes in this situation, it is impossible for them to do what's necessary to build a healthy, emotionally connected relationship or family.

My mother may also have felt rejected because of her gender. Grandpa was a farmer, and he preferred "hay haulers"—males—over females. Boys were better equipped for running the farm, in his opinion; girls were less able to meet the working needs of a farmer. Even though this thinking was more felt than spoken, I am sure my mother picked up on Grandpa's dysfunctional preference, and that led to feelings of rejection, unworthiness, and incompetence. I remember my mother trying many times to prove she was tough and just as able-bodied as any boy. I am sure this thinking also played some part in her disappointment that I was born a girl. Now my mother was unable to present her daddy with a grandson.

A Glimpse into Grandpa's Background

The rejection my mother lived with was very likely related to the fact that Grandpa was rejected as a child. He in turn passed on these rejected feelings to his child. Dysfunction breeds dysfunction; rejection breeds rejection. I believe, from Grandpa's background, that there is a clear reason he placed more value on the male gender. His dad died when Grandpa was fourteen years old, back in the days of the Great Depression. Times were hard, and when his father died, he became the man of the house, responsible to provide for his mother, two sisters, and himself. He worked in the fields from sunup to sundown, receiving only fifty cents a day in wages. This hardship could have very likely caused Grandpa to wish that his two sisters were brothers. Maybe this is where the root of the gender dysfunction began that became a very real part of my family's dysfunction. Since Grandpa's wages were not enough, his mother took her three children and moved in with her parents. Grandpa's mother came from a very large family, and that meant Grandpa had uncles older and younger than himself. All but one of them tormented him and treated him badly. It was an unfortunate situation and one that did not boost the self-esteem of a young teenage boy. Grandpa probably felt that he would not be in his current situation if only his sisters were brothers. Brothers could have helped him earn money to keep the family independent.

Another example of rejection I remember hearing about was when Grandpa began learning to write. Grandpa was left-handed, and the teacher singled him out and whacked him repeatedly with a pointing stick because it was not proper to write with your left hand. This teacher believed that normal people used their right hand to write with. So Grandpa, out of necessity, learned to write with his right hand. After living through this unpleasant experience, Grandpa was able to write with both his left hand and his right hand. However, this was another early experience that led to him living with rejection; at the very least, it definitely did not boost his self-esteem.

The Grandpa I knew was hot-tempered and easily angered, a temperament molded by his unhappy and overwhelming childhood experiences. The rejection Grandpa experienced was passed on, turning it into generational rejection. My grandpa experienced emotional damage that was not dealt with in a way that would have given him a healthy outlook on life. Therefore, he passed a hurtful emotional legacy on to my mother. Because she also did not recognize or deal with the problem, she too became angry, frustrated, and controlling. She then, in turn, blindly attempted to pass this negative legacy on to me.

But I have chosen, with God's help, to face this dysfunction, understand it, and not allow it to continue on into another generation. This is a monumental task that I am unable to accomplish with my own human strength. The bad habits are too prevalent, and the beaten path is full of ruts that make it easy to get stuck. But I know and believe that with God's help, strength, and presence, I can and will change any situation. My determination will prevail only because God enables me. I am not stuck within the confines of the unprofitable, habitual ways of dysfunction. As a child of God, I am able to break the chains of bondage and rejection and live free with a healthy emotional outlook. This is and has been God's will for me since I was saved and spiritually born again at age ten. God has been my strength and guide to do that work which He started in my life as a child. The road has not been easy—drastic change never is—but I am enabled by God, and with this in mind, the possibilities are endless.

Things I Have Learned about Dad's Background

My mother was not the only one with emotional baggage. Dad also came with an unresolved and damaging past, which no doubt was another root cause for a lot of the dysfunction our family lived with. There is a specific tragedy still hanging around from the past to haunt him. This tragedy explains Dad's inability to step up and be an involved husband and father—to grow up and face adult responsibility.

When Dad was a teenager, he had an unfortunate accident he has never talked about. My paternal grandma Bessie told me about what happened to Dad when he was a young teenage driver, before I was born. She said that many years back, when Dad was in high school, he ran over a woman while driving. The accident resulted in the woman's death. He experienced this tragic event when he was about sixteen years old. After the accident, Dad left his home and went to school in a different town. This provided an escape from the condemnation he faced in his hometown and at school. He lived with his oldest sister and her family at this time. However, the residual effects from that tragedy were still hanging around from his past to haunt his future. Growing up and being a dependable dad and husband meant taking a chance and being responsible. Maybe he saw responsibility as a choice too big for him to assume.

Considering this unfortunate incident, Dad's later driving behaviors are difficult to understand. Just a few years later, he got a speeding ticket for driving over eighty miles per hour, at night, with his headlights off. Why did he behave this way? Why was his behavior not consistent with feelings of repentance, and why did it not show evidence that he learned a lesson? Why was he such a risk-taker? Gratitude for not being incarcerated should have been more evident. But instead, he appeared to be heading full speed ahead into yet another tragic circumstance. This speeding ticket was a costly mistake and not one a family guy could afford; my mother was upset and angry with him. To this day, Dad drives so recklessly that my mother chooses to drive them everywhere they go. Maybe this too has some connection to the past. Maybe there is an underlying reason Dad would rather be driven than assume the responsibility of driving himself.

I mostly have memories of Dad acting in childish ways. Instead of expecting better behavior from him, my mother and paternal grandmother made excuses for his immature behavior. These excuses included the obvious: he was just too young to be responsible for his family the way a father should. Another excuse my mother offered for Dad's childish behavior was his birth order—being the baby of his family, he was just Grandma Bessie's baby boy. Maybe this was just my mother's way of dealing with Dad, another way of suppressing the truth. It definitely enabled Dad to never change and grow up. My mother's rationalization gave him an excuse to perpetually resist the need to change.

So what if Dad was the baby of his family? When he chose to get married, it was time to grow up and stop using those excuses as a reason for irresponsibility. I knew for sure life could be different; my uncle Jim was a responsible husband, and he was married at age eighteen just like Dad. Furthermore, he became a father at the same age of twenty. And he also was the baby of his family. But he did not act in irresponsible ways; he accepted his responsibilities in marriage and parenting. In fact, he was very committed to his wife and children and was always there for them. My uncle provided proof that being a responsible husband and father was possible—just not for Dad.

Dad lived in denial of the accident that killed a woman. This was a dark time in his life. It also seems apparent that the underlying emotional damage still causes him to live a compensating life. Dad has kept this emotional pain locked away in his mind for decades, and it is a ruinous secret. Choosing to keep it inside and refusing to acknowledge it happened has deformed Dad's life. This secret has played a major role in the dysfunction of the family I was born into.

Dad avoids serious adult interaction and leaves all decisions for my mother to make. He diminishes any uncomfortable situation or conversation with comic relief and jokes to cut the tension he feels. The human mind is just not meant to harbor secrets of this magnitude, and

Dad has carried this one with him since he was a young teenager. The mind, like the body, can be wounded by hurtful accidents and must be healed from the emotional trauma of such a tragedy. When a person chooses to go on with life after receiving an emotional wound without benefit of healing, dysfunction and a problem-filled life are the results. I know from my own experience that carrying emotional pain around is hurtful and damaging. It changes the person you were born to be. But it is far better and feels much more freeing to face the past and welcome the needed healing.

I don't really know much about Dad; his past is cloaked in mystery. He must live with some terrible things to be the kind of person and father he was. People are fooled greatly if they really believe something of this magnitude can ever be forgotten. Time does not heal anything. These wounds are ever-present, causing dysfunction in your life. But one rarely directly links the dysfunction to its true source, which is the traumatic experience. The trauma and turmoil will always be part of your life until you choose to uncover the secrets, face the past, talk about it, heal from it, and put it to rest. This is where peace replaces unrest, where you can live a normal life free of compensating. The lives of my parents and grandpa are sad proof of what happens when someone chooses to ignore tragedies they have experienced. Without emotional healing, these tragedies cause dysfunctional, compensating lives filled with pain and abnormality, readily passed on to the next generation.

Chapter Four

Family Life before My Parents' Divorce

I was born to a father who had little regard for family responsibility. He was not a "be here now" dad. Little things would frustrate him, and when being at home became too much for him to handle, he would storm out of the house. This happened frequently. Dad was so immature; he was not ready for a family and the responsibilities that came with it.

My mother became pregnant again when I was ten months old, and my brother was born when I was only nineteen months old. Of course, with Dad being as uninvolved as he was, the burden of responsibility for raising two babies was almost entirely my mother's. Grandma Ada helped when she could, but Dad should have been there actively participating in our lives and reducing my mother's stress. From Dad's perspective, though, my brother and I were our mother's children, completely hers to take care of. He did not see himself in a caretaker role at any time. He believed that as long as he had a job and made some money, his duties as a husband and father were fulfilled. Even today, his excuse for being an absent dad, uninvolved in the lives of his children, is the fact that he had a job. He never seemed to understand that jobs do not take up every minute of a man's life.

Somehow, Dad had plenty of time to do the things he wanted to—just not any time for his family. Instead of being responsible, Dad lived as if he was single, free of his duties as a husband and father. Dad was clearly more interested in the idea of marriage than in doing what it takes day in and day out to make a family work. My mother complained many times about how jealous Dad was; he was often suspicious of her for no reason at all. No doubt, his jealousy was inspired by guilt. Situations created by this behavior caused my mother grief, because she was doing nothing wrong. Guess it is an example of the old saying about the pot calling the kettle black. It seems he had no feeling for how his choices affected the lives of his family and cared only for what he wanted. Dad preferred to stay apart from active participation in our family. He did not show the support and care of an emotionally connected father.

Our daily life was mostly separate from Dad and lacking in fatherly support. I remember an incident when Dad was with some of his friends at the lake. He was there fishing, socializing, and waiting for my mother to show up with two toddlers in tow. On our walk to Dad's camp, somewhere on the trail, my mother, brother, and I slipped and fell into the rushing water. She had lost her footing, carrying one baby and holding onto another. We all three fell in the lake, and the water was over our heads. Somehow my mother kept a grip on us and was able to pull us out of the water. This experience has left me with a scary, uneasy feeling around fast-moving water. When we finally reached the place where Dad was hanging out with his friends, we were still soaked, dripping, and shaken by the frightening experience. Dad was quick to ask what had happened to us, but then gave an uncaring, nonchalant response and even laughed it off to show it was no big deal. I remember thinking and feeling that he was not very concerned about our frightening experience. Obviously, he was more interested in continuing his socializing and fishing. This is one of the first times I remember feeling of little importance to him—just an intrusion and an inconvenience to his selfish lifestyle. A real dad would have stopped what he was doing, come to us, and tried to meet our needs in a concerned, caring way. Or even better, he would have been with us walking along and helping so we did not fall into the river to begin with. But I know that even then, my heavenly Father was watching over us. It says so in the Bible: "When you pass through the waters, I will be with you; and through the rivers, they shall not overflow you"

(Isa. 43:2 NKJV). I think of this early experience of falling into the rushing water whenever I read that verse. It is an assurance that God was watching over me then as He has throughout my life. This is one of many times when I know without a doubt that I was in God's care. God intervened when my earthly father was being irresponsible.

I remember another time I felt Dad's uncaring attitude through his uncompassionate response. I was about two years old. There was an air conditioner in the rented house we lived in that had an exposed fan. The blades were moving round and round because the wind was blowing; it was not turned on. Since it was exposed, you could touch the fan blade. The air conditioner was located on the wall by the back of the couch. I was standing on the couch, and the moving blade was within my reach. I remember being fascinated by the blade's movement and watching it for several minutes. I remember thinking: *I wonder if I touched the blade, would it stop?* Impulsively, I reached out and thrust my hand into the moving fan. Needless to say, the result was not as I had imagined. The middle finger on my left hand was cut rather severely—and no, the blade did not stop when I put my hand into it.

Dad's reaction was as follows:

"Of all the stupid things!"

"Well, are you proud of yourself?"

"I sure hope so!"

No consoling words of comfort from Dad; he never seemed to feel anything for anyone but himself. My mother was trying to stop the bleeding while he was ranting. I learned early on there would be no sympathy from him. He stood back in his normal manner as if he had washed his hands of this stupid situation, and it was entirely my mother's problem to fix. I probably needed stitches for my finger to heal properly. I remember my mother suggesting they take me to the doctor. But Dad's response was, "No, she does not need to see a doctor. That was a foolish thing to do. It will heal, and I can't afford a doctor." I still have a large scar on that finger that is extremely painful when it accidentally hits something. But seeing a doctor was too costly and was not an option for me. I certainly was not worthy of medical attention in Dad's neglectful opinion.

My question now, from a parent's perspective, is, "Why was the fan blade exposed?" and "Why was natural curiosity not expected from a child so young?" Dad's behavior led me to the conclusion that this was entirely my fault. I was expected to know better at two years old and should never have had any faith in Dad to protect me. This is the pattern when your dad is immature and more interested in what he wants than in what a child for whom he is responsible may need.

The memories I have from this early time in my life with my mother and dad are not good ones. I remember always wanting to go to Grandma Ada's house; I enjoyed being with Grandma. It must have also been some form of escape from the bad feelings I got around my parents because of their anger and hostility. When Grandma would visit, I remember immediately running to get my things so I could go with her. Most of the time I was able to go to the farm, but there were occasions when it was not possible because Grandpa expected her to help him with farm duties. During this particular time in my life, at age two to three, if Grandma Ada was not busy, I would be with her. I have very few specific memories about being with Grandma during these early years—just that being with her felt happy, peaceful, contented, and safe. There was nothing traumatic to remember during this early time with her. I have read that children of this age rarely remember things specifically unless trauma or violence is involved. My memories of my parents at this time are vivid, very likely due to the trauma involved. Specific memories of time with Grandma Ada are vague, probably because things were good with her and I felt safe. I do remember specifically wanting to be with Grandma more than anyone else. And luckily, I was able to spend a majority of this time in my life with her. It was probably fortunate that I was not around my mother more to get her so mad. My presence seemed to make her so angry.

Chapter Five

The Doll Buggy

A doll buggy I got for my third birthday has significance due to the negative memories it holds, involving both parents in separate situations. These are some of my earliest memories and are vivid probably because of their traumatic and hurtful nature. I liked the doll buggy, but for all the trouble it caused me, I wished many times I had never even seen it. That doll buggy brought about one of the most traumatic experiences of my life.

It was my third birthday. Several family members were present for a family party, including my cousin, Dad's second sister's son. My cousin was about six months older than I, and for some reason he thought he needed to be in charge of my new doll buggy. He took control, and no matter what I did, he would not let me play with my new toy. I remember thinking *who does he think he is, and why doesn't anyone make him behave?* After much protest from me, Dad told me to "let the company play with your things, you need to share." Well, this may have been good advice normally, but only if I had been able to take a look at my new toy or play with it some before my cousin was allowed to take it over. I felt like Dad did not consider my feelings at all, and what others needed or wanted was his priority.

Dad thought a lot of his second sister. It seemed to me that Dad catered to my cousin in order to make points with his sister, no matter who got hurt or put down in the process. I felt he cared only about impressing his sister. He did not care about being fair to me or how I felt. This incident is one of my first memories of Dad treating me as something of little value and showing his loyalty to others. This became a pattern throughout my childhood.

Soon after I got the doll buggy, my mother's anger and wrath brought "the storm" to my life in an unforgettable and damaging way. This incident is very significant in my memory. It is the first memory I have of feeling terrified, alone, and in danger. But at three years old, I had no choice but to let it play out as it would. It was a traumatic incident that led to a pattern of behavior I would experience many times. Before this day, I remember being happy as I played with my new doll buggy; it was fun to put my dolls in the buggy and give them a ride around the house. We lived in a small rented house at the time. There was not much room for children's toys or play. On this unfortunate day, I made the mistake of pushing my doll buggy into the kitchen and getting it in my mother's way. She went into an uncontrolled rampage and stomped my doll buggy until it was like a pancake on the floor. I remember feeling terrified and small, hoping she did not choose to do that to me next. She looked like an angry monster yelling and screaming and stomping. This is my first vivid memory of my mother in full-blown anger. I felt guilty, thinking I had caused it because I knew I had left my doll buggy in her way. This incident also was my first terrifying memory, because I felt in danger for being the one who had made her so mad. I felt like she hated me and anything that had anything to do with me. I related myself to the buggy. This was the beginning of feeling afraid, lost, and alone. It was obvious I could not count on my mother for love and support. After she calmed down, my mother never comforted or reassured me. She did nothing to repair the damage she had done. Even now, as I write this decades in the future, she has done nothing to repair the damage.

This single act caused me to withdraw and was responsible for choices I made never to provoke my mother's anger and rage ever again. My conclusion from this experience was that I could make things better if I left no evidence that I existed. I knew for sure I did not want to feel responsible again for this kind of rage. Experiencing my mother's anger and wrath definitely changed the person I was and shook the foundation of trust that my mother was someone I could count on. I remember deliberately keeping myself and my things out of her way after this encounter. My security and self-confidence began to diminish at this time. This traumatic incident was the first in a pattern of behavior my mother displayed. Unfortunately, it proved to be a sneak preview of things to come.

It seemed that my mother was angry every day. Although she never received a diagnosis to explain her frequent irrational outbursts and inability to cope with everyday life, it was probably related to arrested emotional development, which leads to repressed anger and narcissistic tendencies. In addition, she had two small children by a husband who chose to do just about anything but go home where he belonged. It is no wonder my mother responded with anger, resentment, and frustration. There was no evidence Dad had a real emotional connection with my mother, and he never even attempted to connect with me on an emotional level.

The anger my mother routinely displayed was her response to frustration. Her anger also came from an inability to deal with everyday family life and children. She therefore would blame others when she got angry, not realizing that anger is a chosen response. Blaming others for one's anger is unfounded. Choosing to respond in anger only reveals what is really inside a person. It reveals the presence of a bigger problem underneath and is a sign that something detrimental is lurking inside.

At some point after four or five years of marriage—because of all the anger, hurt, irresponsibility, turbulence, and pain—my parents decided it was best to get a divorce due to irreconcilable differences.

Chapter Six

After My Parents' Divorce

After my parents divorced, I lived with my maternal grandparents and my uncle. My brother went to live with my paternal grandparents and Dad. We all lived in the same town, with the exception of my mother. I was happy and content with Grandma Ada, and my uncle also had a tremendous positive impact on my life.

I continued to experience turmoil and problems with my mother, dad, and maternal grandpa. These three had a common link. They each possessed emotional damage from serious, life-changing experiences in their earlier years. Their dysfunctional pasts were never dealt with, talked about, or allowed to heal in a way that would lead to a healthy emotional outlook on life. Their bad actions and attitudes were the by-product of their emotional damage. The unfortunate things they had lived through clouded their basic coping methods for life. Since their coping skills were abnormal, they reacted to life in abnormal ways, causing a continuing trail of dysfunction.

Adults with this kind of baggage bring the toxic effects of their negative life-changing experiences into the life of a child in their care. The toxicity becomes a family legacy when damaged parents do not recognize they have a problem that requires attention. The underlying problem surfaces and produces undesirable behaviors, such as uncontrollable fits of anger, inability to cope with life in general, childishness, and selfishness. They really cannot care for anyone but themselves. They are constantly seeking their own significance because of unmet needs. Therefore, they are incapable of meeting the needs of a child. Their interpersonal relationship skills are inadequate to promoting stability in their home. They have great difficulty caring for another human being, even when that person is their offspring. They behave in irrational ways they would not normally display if the emotional damage had been allowed to heal. Children reared by caregivers with past dysfunctional baggage are usually affected negatively and do not grow up in an emotionally nurturing environment. The parents are not capable of meeting basic emotional needs. Love, if present at all, is mostly conditional.

During the time after my parents divorced, it felt like life was just one unfortunate incident after another. The divorce years were full of chaos and turmoil; damage came from both parents and Grandpa. These disturbing experiences came with no explanation. It felt as though both parents were free of me and any responsibility they had for me, and that is how they preferred it. Neither of them was available. They were in and out of my life with no stability or time to talk about anything that concerned me. That is why I learned to count on Grandma Ada, and I looked to her and trusted her as my mother figure and stable adult influence.

Following the divorce from Dad, my mother left town and lived with friends almost two hundred miles away. She got a job in civil service at an air-force base in Albuquerque. Visits from my mother were weekends only and felt more like visits from a big sister than someone in a parental role. She chose to detach from my life and knew very little of how I felt or what I experienced during the divorce years. I would have died during this time if I'd been dependent on my mother to meet my needs. The reality of my situation is that I was a child abandoned by her mother. I trusted Grandma to consistently meet my needs, and she did not get mad or yell. Grandma filled the position of mother in my life as a trustworthy companion, teacher, and caregiver.

On one occasion during the divorce period, I went to Albuquerque to visit my mother. This trip provided a good example of how abnormal the interaction was between us. I do not remember why I went, but my memories of this time are very uncomfortable. I went with Dad's friend;

I did not know him very well and felt uneasy traveling with him for three hours during the night. I also remember that, when we arrived, I did not feel like my mother even wanted me there—no hugs, no touch, no welcome greeting. She felt cold and distant. I even remember her telling me not to touch her. I did not feel like I belonged there, even though I was with my mother. She showed no joy or happiness in seeing me. I felt more like a burden than a blessing. At this time in my life, my mother should have been working on building a loving relationship with me. But instead, I felt pushed away, unwanted, and abandoned. My mother did not instill feelings of security.

My pre-divorce memories of my mother were mostly of her anger, which brought great fear to my life. After the divorce, my mother's presence was very limited and had no characteristics of one filling a mother's role. The attachment, caregiving process never happened for me with either parent. That is why they have both always felt so foreign to me and are mostly uncomfortable to be around. I have tried to remember back to a time when I felt any love toward my mother. But any such feelings are extremely vague, intangible, and disconnected. I do feel genuine love, though, for Grandma. I knew without a doubt that she cared for me unconditionally, and she brought no bad feelings into my life. I received my support completely from Grandma Ada and my teenage uncle. I felt at this time in my life that there was no one other than these two whom I could really count on.

My mother, dad, and grandpa should have been responsible, dependable caregivers—but they contributed only life-changing, painful, traumatic, and emotionally damaging experiences to my life as a preschool child. They each were responsible for additional emotional damage during the divorce period. They provided no empathy or understanding, only a constant feeling of possible tragic news in a life void of peace and contentment because they refused to acknowledge God. In divorce, there are no winners, and children suffer most.

Chapter Seven

Grandpa's Attitude

While living with my maternal grandparents during this divorce period, I sometimes had to be around Grandpa. As I mentioned earlier, he did not say much and was not welcoming and warm. I felt very insecure around Grandpa. Just a look from him in your direction could be frightening because you did not know what he was thinking. Since he displayed anger like my mother, I was anxious around him, hoping I did nothing to make him mad. He was notorious for getting out-of-control angry. These episodes brought back memories of how I felt when my mother got so angry before.

There was no one-on-one interaction between Grandpa and me; he mostly did not acknowledge my presence. He was cold and indifferent. It seemed he thought of me more as an object than a person and felt no obligation to be involved with me. I never believed I had any special significance to him; it was more like I was nonexistent as far as he was concerned. Grandpa should have been a significant role model in my life, but he caused me to feel I did not belong, that I was a burden and an intrusion. There was no love, caring, or emotional connection available from him. He caused me to feel very unwelcome.

Maybe Grandpa's lack of involvement with child rearing came from his delusion that just because he was a male, he was free of that responsibility. Even though this was a time when men were not as involved with actual childcare, their responsibilities for emotional development were not relinquished. Even if Grandpa took no part in meeting my physical needs, this did not mean there should be no relationship, connection, or interpersonal interaction. Grandpa should have shown he cared in some capacity, somehow. It felt like he believed he owed me nothing, which is exactly what I got. His life would not be inconvenienced or changed just because some kid had moved into his house. It seemed in this man's way of thinking, the position of "grandpa" meant nothing. But grandpas, because of their family position, are potentially able to make a great, positive impact on their grandchildren. Sadly, this was impossible from my grandpa, because he chose to live in his own world and not let me in to learn from him, or know who he was, or find anything lasting from him that I could take forward in my life. Thinking back, there is really nothing I learned from him personally. His contribution to my life was more harmful than helpful.

My appearance may have been an instant barrier to Grandpa's affection. It could have been the source of an instant dislike he had of me. It was my uncontrollable downfall—I looked too much like Dad and not as much like Grandpa's side of the family. In Grandpa's opinion, looking like an Indian was something that made a person special. I guess that is where he got his sense of value and self-worth. He seemed to be very proud that he was one-quarter Cherokee Indian and his grandmother was a full-blood. The look that comes with this heritage is dark hair, dark eyes, and a certain face shape. Grandpa placed high value on a person with these characteristics and interpreted this as an enviable family trait. My looks were very different. My hair was cotton-top blonde, and although I have brown eyes, I did not possess the darker look of an Indian. Grandpa referred to me as "Blondie," which never sounded like it was meant in a positive way but rather like he was pointing out a fault. I certainly did not have the look he preferred.

Grandpa's attitude toward me never promoted self-worth. I felt inadequate around him. Because of Grandpa's anger, it seemed wise to be as little trouble as possible, and again I felt a need to apologize for my existence. I believe Grandpa had little to no respect for Dad, and I was just a constant reminder of Dad and his disappointing behavior. So Grandpa probably felt justified in treating me as insignificant and unimportant. My presence was a constant reminder of the pain he was experiencing on his daughter's behalf because of the divorce and Dad's bad choices.

Therefore, from a young age, I remember feeling very afraid of men in general. This was probably due to the fact that most of the men I had known so far had not given me a reason to trust the male gender. I was glad when Grandpa left the house and went to work in the fields on the farm. It was much more comfortable to do housework with Grandma and not have to deal with the feeling I got from Grandpa. These feelings probably also stemmed from my experience with Dad and how he caused me to feel devalued. I was also fearful of my paternal grandfather, who came across as a grouchy old man. My early experiences with males were mostly negative.

However, my uncle Jim probably had something to do with helping me feel more comfortable around males. He was my friend, and he would spend time with me and talk to me. At fifteen, he was at the perfect age to tease me relentlessly just like a big brother—but at least he was giving me attention, and this said to me that I mattered to him. I have always held him in high regard and still feel only good things when I remember my uncle and our relationship. One of my uncle's friends also provided a positive male influence. He was a gentle, caring young man who had a knack for making a child feel special. His name was David. Looking back, I am thankful for my uncle and his friend. It is sad that the other male role models who should have been making a difference in my life, mainly Dad and Grandpa, were by choice uninvolved.

During this period, Grandpa was present in my life almost every day, but he chose to live in his own world and never let me in to build a relationship with him. From my perspective now, I understand that Grandpa's behavior was his problem, rather than there being anything wrong with me. Another fallacy I recognize now was the value and importance placed on the Indian look. Being part Cherokee Indian meant nothing special. I learned that the world's view of Indian ancestry was not the same as Grandpa's. It definitely was not so valuable as to become a reason for lifelong family dysfunction.

── Chapter Eight ──

Dad's Contribution

The year I was four could be described as living from tragedy to tragedy. I received my only support through these life-changing experiences from Grandma Ada. Many of these bad times originated directly or indirectly with Dad. They also came without explanation or comfort from him. Most of these unwelcome experiences could have easily become more positive with just a little communication and caring from Dad. Instead, he chose to deny my existence.

When my paternal grandpa died, it should have been a time when I could count on Dad for support. But he was so wrapped up in his own situation, he somehow forgot he even had a daughter who might be touched by this experience and need his reassurance. This was the first time I had experienced death. It was very confusing and also created more feelings of insecurity. I attended the funeral with Grandma Ada. I saw Grandpa lying in the casket; he looked like he was sleeping, but it was a scary sort of sleep. He was so still and was not breathing. During the funeral, I remember sitting in the congregation with Grandma and seeing the paternal side of the family, including Dad and my brother, sitting in the reserved area. This also was confusing to me, since I thought I was part of that family too. Another thing adding to the strange feelings on that day was that Dad never came to me or said a word to me about anything that was going on. He should have at least made an effort to talk to me, but again, I was not his priority. Dad never even acknowledged I was there. He felt like a real stranger to me that day.

Even though I was only four years old, I remember very well how this strange experience felt. Grandma Ada did explain to me what a funeral meant and that my paternal grandpa was dead. I understood what she said as best a four-year old could, but it still would have been good for Dad to show me he cared too. This was another one of numerous instances where Dad proved again, things were all about him.

Another incident in this tumultuous year was when Dad shot his leg on a hunting trip with a friend. He was childishly playing with the gun in the vehicle as they were traveling on a bumpy country road, and the gun went off. He did not realize he was shot until the streaming blood made it obvious. Dad was lucky his leg was all that received a bullet. When he was in the hospital healing from the consequences of his foolish behavior, Grandma Ada took me to visit him. His leg was bandaged, and he was not very mobile. Dad made light of it by laughing it off. It always seemed easier for Dad to joke about serious circumstances than face them. That was how he dealt with this accident and just about any other serious situation in our life.

Many of Dad's behaviors make little sense to me. He was hospitalized because of his childish, foolish behavior. But just a short time prior, he would not take me to the doctor for stitches when I cut my finger in the air conditioner because of *childlike* behavior—not childish and foolish, but childlike. Then Dad plainly said, "No medical attention for doing something so foolish." Dad's actions often made me feel devalued.

There were several times Grandma Ada took me to visit Dad throughout the divorce period, trying to keep me connected. When Grandma and I went to town, we dropped by Dad's workplace just to see him briefly. However, my memories of these random occasional visits reinforced the fact that seeing me meant very little to Dad. He never once greeted me with a hug or seemed glad to see me. In fact, I have no memory of him hugging me at all during my childhood. He kept his distance always.

While my parents were divorced, it was normal for Dad to be absent during the time I was supposed to spend with him. A visit with Dad meant I went from Grandma Ada to Dad's girlfriend's house. One of his girlfriends had sisters much older than me. Time I spent with them was supposed to be time I spent with Dad. I did not like being with these people. But visits with Dad meant his girlfriend would babysit me; Dad rarely showed up. I knew at age four that Dad did not care to be with me. He manipulated the timing of these meetings in his favor so that he could disregard his fatherly responsibilities. Dad had more important things to do than be with me.

The worst memory I have of Dad's girlfriends was when Dad took me to the lake with some woman and her daughters. This was an extremely uncomfortable experience. I got a taste of how Cinderella felt. This woman was mean and did not care about me at all. I remember her hateful attitude and how put-down I felt around her and her daughters. She took every opportunity to treat me with disrespect and make it known what little angels her daughters were. She even scolded me for going back to the vehicle from the lakeshore to get my sunglasses because one of her daughters tagged along with me. It was no surprise that Dad sided with the woman against me. I do not know why I was even subjected to this sort of thing. Dad never cared if I was around or not; he never tried or wanted to build a relationship with me. I strongly felt he only had me around occasionally for his convenience to claim as his child. It was some sort of ego trip for him. His actions and behaviors often spoke loudly that he cared nothing for me.

Being around these random women and Dad was upsetting and emotionally damaging. Where was my mother, and why were these women moving into her place? This time of divorce was tumultuous, damaging, and hurtful, and my parents did not talk to me about what was happening or explain how things and relationships would inevitably be different after a divorce. My individual interest was not considered significant enough to require an explanation. Again, I was left to find my own way through it all. As with every other trauma my parents introduced into my life, I felt they screamed at me, "You are on your own, child. Do not expect any support, guidance, or help from either of us. We are too involved in our own pain and needs to consider what this is doing to you—suck it up and be tough. That is the only advice I have or am able to offer you." This made the establishment of an emotional connection between us impossible. They could not give something they did not understand or possess.

Chapter Nine

Billy Jeff

It was a sunny day in September 1964. Autumn was approaching, and the annual event of birds flying south for the winter was in progress. The fields of the farm were sometimes black with birds taking a break from flight to eat the seeds lying in the hayfields. Since a farmer does not want seeds pirated from his fields, Grandpa took steps to rid the hayfields of the pests. His normal procedure was to drive to various points on the farm where the birds were heavily congregated and fire his shotgun to scare them away. On this particular day, Grandpa had a companion. His second cousin Billy Jeff was helping rid the farm of the unwanted intruders.

After a productive and fun-filled morning accomplishing their designated task, they took a break for lunch. My grandparents and I had lunch with Billy Jeff, and our conversation centered on our guest. Being only eighteen, Billy Jeff was a young man full of hope for the future. As we ate, he talked about his life plans. He had graduated from high school just a few months before. He talked about girls but had no steady girlfriend yet, and maybe plans for college at some point. The discussion centered mostly on Billy Jeff's future and the things he planned to do with his life. I also remember Billy Jeff talking to me personally, and I felt like the interaction was comparable to that I had with my uncle. He acknowledged my presence and treated me as significant, not as an object like Grandpa did. I liked him; I felt comfortable around him even though I had known him only part of this one day.

After lunch, Grandpa and Billy Jeff continued with their mission of eliminating the birds. Since they were driving around the farm, it was not unusual for them to stop by the house randomly. They had done this several times throughout the day. When they made the last stop at the house, I was playing outside in the yard by the porch on the side entrance to Grandma's house. Grandma was inside the house. I was digging in the dirt and playing with toys. I noticed when the pickup pulled up and stopped in the driveway.

I had heard shotguns fire all day; it was not unusual to hear gunfire. But the shot I heard at this particular moment felt different. They had just driven up, and the shot was fired too soon for them to have gotten to the field by the house. The shotgun discharged as Grandpa was removing it from the gun rack in his pickup. After I heard the loud, booming blast, I remember inhaling the gunpowder smell common when a shotgun has just been fired close by. I was playing only a few feet from where the shot went off. I recall being aware of these unusual events and getting an uneasy feeling immediately.

When I looked up, I saw Grandpa running to the door and screaming in a panicked voice that he had just shot Billy Jeff. Seeing my grandpa react to something in this way was frightening. Unless he was angry, he normally showed little emotion. He was obviously extremely frightened. Grandma met him at the door, and he told her he had killed Billy Jeff. She tried to reassure him by saying, "Maybe he is just hurt and will be all right."

Grandpa responded by saying, "No, he will never be all right again."

Grandma went to Billy Jeff to see for herself that indeed there would be no reviving this young man; he was, in fact, clearly dead.

The events that followed were chaotic to say the least. Grandpa was in shock and hysterical. He was talking in a high-pitched voice I had never heard him use before and never heard from him again. Grandpa went inside the house and began fumbling through the phonebook. He could hardly hold the book, much less find a number or even function enough to know whom he should call. Grandma took the phonebook from him and began notifying the appropriate parties of the accident and emergency. There were many phone calls to make, including the difficult one to Billy Jeff's grandparents, Grandpa's aunt and uncle.

While Grandma was busy on the phone and Grandpa was incoherent due to his emotional state, I went to investigate the situation myself. I found Billy Jeff lying on the ground on the passenger's side of the pickup, and understandably the image I saw is something I will never forget. He was shot in the head by a 12-gauge shotgun, which had discharged no more than three or four feet from his head. There was human debris scattered everywhere. He was lying in a pool of blood with his brains strewn in every direction on the ground. I remember at least one of his eyes looking blank and staring up. The pool of blood grew into a stream of blood that ran down the dirt driveway to the ditch. The chickens gathered to peck his remains. This view was more than traumatic for a four-year-old. I can still see the shirt he was wearing; it was maize-colored with some dark blue in a distinct pattern of plaid and checks, a unique material for the 1960s. It too was soaked in blood. No one ever realized that I had seen Billy Jeff after he was shot, much less the damage I lived with afterward. At the actual time of the accident, the only people present were Grandma, Grandpa, me, and of course, Billy Jeff.

After Grandma made the necessary phone calls, many people came to the farm, either in an official capacity or to lend a hand. The emergency crew came to pronounce Billy Jeff dead and to do what they could for Grandpa. The sheriff came to file a report. Billy Jeff's grandparents came in addition to numerous neighbors, friends, and relatives. It was quite chaotic, and this became a normal occurrence for many days and weeks ahead as a deluge of people visited regularly to bring support, help, and food. When the chaos waned, still no one talked to me; no one thought I could have possibly been affected by any of it.

The fact that I had gotten to know Billy Jeff that day and knew he was someone I liked made the tragedy even harder to deal with. He clearly would never talk to me again. I look back on the lunchtime memories and am overcome with tremendous sadness realizing Billy Jeff was living out his last few hours on this earth. All the dreams he shared had abruptly come to an end. This experience gave proof to me at a very early age of the brevity of life—how one second you are alive and fine and the next you are dead and gone. Grandpa probably shared these views. He had an extremely hard time getting over this tragic accident. For several days, he could only groan, and his words were few to none. It felt like he would never return to normal again. There was a point, weeks or months in the future, when Grandpa seemed to be back again. But he was never the same.

Remembering this time, I have to wonder why my mother never thought it necessary to inquire about the negative impact this experience could have had on me. It never occurred to her that I could have been affected by the traumatic incident. My mother was living in Albuquerque when the accident happened. My uncle was also in Albuquerque, attending the state fair and visiting my mother. They both got the news and headed home. When my mother arrived at the farm, she was totally absorbed in Grandpa's condition; my pain and confusion were invisible to her. Her attention, concern, and focus were only for Grandpa. She was emotionally unavailable to help me face this kind of damage, which only caused more dysfunction for me to deal with alone. This too was added to the rapidly growing list of unpleasant things we just did not talk about.

But there were repercussions in my life from this heartbreaking time. This experience gave me an unrealistic view of death. Death became something I feared, even to the extreme point that it became an irrational fear. This distorted perception of death became overwhelming at times; it was very likely a form of post-traumatic stress disorder. For years to come, I regularly had to rethink situations to get back to a rational mindset in order to cope normally. To get a healthy perspective on death afterward required a lot of work. It took many years and God's intervention to accomplish.

There were many years of torture no one knew of but me. I remembered the horrible image of how Billy Jeff was disfigured beyond recognition. Being present at the moment he violently departed from this world left an indelible imprint on my young mind. It presented abnormal things in my life to deal with and caused thoughts I would never otherwise have had. Seeing someone full of life one minute and dead the next, with his earthly remains scattered everywhere, makes you feel insecure and shatters a part of what you thought you could always trust. I witnessed the fragility of life, and it left me with an uneasy, insecure feeling about losing people close to me.

Throughout my childhood, because of this unresolved incident, I suffered every time family members went hunting. I related hunting and guns to accidents and death, increasing the possibility of witnessing another accidental shooting. In later years, I was very uncomfortable when Dad took my husband and oldest son hunting. Death became big and fearful. I had to come to terms with the irrational fear by knowing I could not have faith and fear in the same body—"For God hath not given us the spirit of fear; but of power, and of love, and of a sound mind. Hold fast the form of sound words, which thou hast heard of me, in faith and love which is in Christ Jesus" (2 Tim. 1:7 and 13). These Bible verses became great power for me to cling to. The knowledge that faith and fear could not co-exist became great comfort and gave strength to overcome the irrational fear of death planted in me the day Billy Jeff died. With God's help, I have learned to rely on faith to know He is in control of everything, and I do not have to worry anymore. The feeling of fear and loss continued well into my own marriage and became livable for me only when I truly believed that God was in control of everything, including the people I care for. In the beginning, I had been left to face it all alone, to work through my feelings and rationalize on my own. Then, with God's intervention, I found healthy thinking and a rational mindset. God gave me a normal perspective on death.

Sadly, it was more than forty years before my parents even had a clue what all this meant in my life. This was after the trigger event when I chose to speak up in spite of the secretive conditioning I had been raised with. However, I got very little caring or compassion from either of my parents when I told them about the death of Billy Jeff and the negative repercussions in my life. They still do not seem to have the capacity to feel anything for what I lived through as a child. Their attitude is more along the lines of, "Yes it happened. So what do you want from us now? Why do we have to think about all this dysfunction from the past?" They never understood or had any compassion for me as a child, and there is still none for me now. They seem to prefer to continue on, keeping the dysfunctional past swept under the rug, never dealing with it and therefore never healing from it either. But they also want to have a place in my life, as if none of this dysfunction ever existed and life was normal. That will no longer work, because I am at a place in my life where I cannot go on denying the pain of the past. Without my parents' active participation in fixing the hurt and acknowledging it all happened, they will always represent pain and continue to bring unrest and hurt into my life.

Grandpa's shotgun, the one responsible for Billy Jeff's death, has a history that bears telling. This 12-gauge shotgun had accidentally fired before and had a history of being undependable. It seemed at times to fire at will, and a hole in Grandpa's bedroom ceiling proved what it was capable of doing. But Grandpa kept this gun because it was the only earthly possession he had that belonged to his dad. That fact alone made it hard for Grandpa to give up the gun. After Grandpa died, because of Dad's interest in the gun, Grandma gave it to him. Dad knew of the gun's history and that it was not dependable. The gun proved this yet again when Dad and my brother had the gun inside my parents' house and it went off unexpectedly. My mother came home to find a section of her carpet shot out, and the wall, the freezer, and a cabinet all showing evidence of buckshot. This incident got Dad's attention, and he removed the firing pin, something that should have been done long ago before an eighteen-year-old paid with his life. My mother has been known to say that "once in a blue moon," Dad would do something right. In my opinion, this was one of those rare instances.

When Billy Jeff was a small child, his father was shot and killed in a hunting accident. While sitting around a campfire, a gun discharged, and that became the fatal shot for Billy Jeff's dad. Then Billy Jeff grew up without a father, only to have his life end in a similar way. It is sad, especially for Grandpa's aunt, losing a son and a grandson in the same senseless way. However, Grandpa's aunt and her husband gave support to my grandpa in his time of despair. Considering their circumstances, Grandpa's aunt and uncle were compassionate and revealed few feelings of bitterness or anger. They mostly conveyed sadness for their loss and empathy, sympathy, and compassion for Grandpa, which is what he needed. He felt bad enough on his own for what had happened.

I was only four years old when Billy Jeff was shot, and I would go on to experience much more emotional damage in childhood. This was an extremely traumatic day of upheaval and chaos in my life. Even after living through this life-changing experience, though, I am not an advocate of gun control in America. I *am* an advocate for safety and wisdom when handling guns. Being responsible by not using a faulty weapon would have prevented Billy Jeff's death. Again, life is all about the choices we make. Grandpa could have chosen to remove the firing pin from the shotgun before Billy Jeff died, eliminating the possibility of the accidental shooting. People's irresponsible choices are not a reason to make firearms illegal; that would remove a basic right of all Americans. If guns are outlawed, then only outlaws will have guns. That would be un-American!

Chapter Ten

Grandpa's Addiction, Denial, and Emotional Disconnection

For Grandpa, the consequences of the accidental shooting were deadly. It was the beginning of a long, slow death for him. He began drinking whiskey; he told friends he drank to get Billy Jeff's face out of his mind. His drinking increased throughout the years—the changes and things the family lived through were sad, heartbreaking, and destructive. Grandpa lived for another eight years and four months after the shooting took place.

One of the signs of alcoholism, I have heard, is that the person drinking will hide his alcohol. Grandpa hid bottles of whiskey in various places around the farm. My brother and I found many of them and took them to Grandma. She would pour them out, but that did not stop Grandpa from buying more. He would go on drinking binges—loud, rambunctious, and very free with his money. It was like the rational person he could be disappeared and was not even present at all. Often, he would not be physically present either; he would leave for long periods of time.

On one of Grandpa's binge-drinking trips, he left home and did not return for days. He would usually travel from the farm to his sister's ranch about ninety miles away. On this trip, he was not at his sister's, and there was no way to trace where he had ended up. But Grandpa finally showed up, and he had a story. He told us he was sleeping in his pickup by the side of the road and some unsavory guys stopped to go through his belongings. Since Grandpa had been asleep, he decided it was in his best interest to continue as though he was still sleeping. He felt that if he awoke, they would very likely shoot him. These guys did end up stealing some of his things, including a 30-30 rifle. Grandpa could do nothing but let them steal and continue on their way. His only defense was in their possession, and he did not choose to be shot with his own gun. This was his story—however, I had known Grandpa to exaggerate or stretch the truth. I had witnessed him changing the real story rather than face the consequences of what actually happened. This was the period when he frequently went on drinking binges, and that was very likely the reason he ended up in this precarious position.

Another of Grandpa's wild, probably alcohol-related adventures happened when he was driving his sister's pickup home one night. While he was driving down a wet and rainy road, the brakes went out. He was approaching a highway intersection with an eighteen-wheeler truck coming fast down the highway he was approaching. He had two choices: one was to turn sharply and hope he did not turn the vehicle over; the other was to give it the gas and hope to get across the highway before the truck hit him. He went with choice number two, but the problem with that was a steep embankment on the other side of the road that went up to a railroad track. So when he made it across the road without the truck hitting him, the other side went down into a depression and quickly up toward the railroad tracks. Needless to say, the end result was damage to the pickup and Grandpa. The impact caused several broken ribs.

Grandpa had to be in bad shape to consider going to a doctor; however, he did decide to get medical attention this time. My mother and I were present with Grandpa for this visit. When the doctor asked him what happened to cause his condition, Grandpa said, "I fell off a windmill!" It was obvious the doctor did not believe this. His eyebrows were immediately raised as if to say, "Really!" I never understood why Grandpa chose not to be honest with the doctor. It never made sense to me. Grandpa said he did not want the doctor to report the vehicle accident to the police, because the authorities had no record that it had ever happened. I believe he should have been honest with his doctor.

There was no reason for the doctor to report anything to the police. I guess it was just another example of suppressing the truth for me to witness. Do not face the truth at any cost. Grandpa was not the best role model. It is no wonder I could not talk about all the dysfunction in my life for so many years. I was taught to repress, suppress, and deny from numerous situations I experienced growing up.

But lives lived in repression and denial backfire when the truth comes out. One Sunday night, more family secrets surfaced in a most unlikely place. When my mother, brother, and I went back home from the farm, Grandpa went with us. He had an appointment with our family dentist the next day. Grandpa wanted a sloppy joe, so we stopped at Oleta's roadside diner in Melrose, New Mexico, along the way. The waitress recognized Grandpa from years ago before he married Grandma Ada. She proceeded to reminisce and brought up details of Grandpa's life that had been previously hidden to us all. She talked of Grandpa's one-year marriage to a woman named Ruby. This family history, completely secret before, was suddenly revealed. Grandpa acknowledged that what the waitress said was true, but he did discourage the woman's conversation. We got Grandpa's sloppy joe and continued home. My mother never asked Grandpa one question about what we had just learned. And Grandpa's only comment after leaving the diner was, "Why did they put a darned wiener in a sloppy joe? Whoever heard of such a thing?" His previous marriage was a shocking bit of news to learn randomly at a small roadside diner. I anxiously waited for my next visit with Grandma, and she filled me in on the details about Ruby. It seems the truth always surfaces eventually.

There was another binge-drinking incident one night when Grandpa ended up at a local bar—or maybe I should say, saloon. While he was there, he took out his shotgun and began shooting up the bar. On still another occasion when Grandpa had been out drinking, one of my boyfriends stepped in to help out by bringing him home. Grandpa had lost his keys and his wallet. My friend was aware of Grandpa's need, so he drove Grandpa home. My friend later told me that he took care of Grandpa as a favor to me. I appreciated this, but it was very embarrassing for me as a teenage girl to have to discuss this sort of thing with a boyfriend. There are many other stories I could tell about the gloom and dreariness that alcoholism brings into the life of family and friends, but there is another aspect of all this I want to turn to.

As I have said before, I believe that Jesus the Savior and God the heavenly Father are the answer to all life's problems, no matter how complicated they may seem. My grandpa was crying out for help every time he drank. He was trying to repress and deny the truth again. What he really needed was someone to talk to—someone to give him hope, reassurance, and a reason to go on and get through this horrible time he faced. His alcoholism was an outward sign of the pain he was experiencing inside and the torment and torture he endured every day after the fatal accident occurred. He would go to friends and neighbors to talk of his pain and tell of what he was experiencing; the friends told Grandma about this after Grandpa died. But no one that I know of gave him the hope and answers he needed at the time to be able to turn it all over to Jesus and live in peace after such a tragedy. Our family never talked about the accident. The general thought was that if Grandpa was having a minute's peace from thinking about the accident, why would anyone bring it up to remind him of the pain? The answer to that is simple: stop sacrificing his sanity for the family's comfort and communicate with him. The man needed to talk. That is how you get rid of the pain. But family members out of touch with their feelings will avoid emotional encounters at almost any cost, no matter how desperately they need to face a traumatic situation and find healing.

I believe fear prevented the family from opening up to Grandpa about his grief. A simple talk initiated by a family member did not have to be lengthy to be helpful. It could have been as brief or as long as Grandpa wanted or needed—but to never initiate the talk was not stepping up to do what was best for him. Talking could have provided comfort and let him know someone close to him cared. He could have rested in the reassurance that his family was there for him whenever he needed help. Talking could have given him more peace and comfort than the presumed peace he *might* be having through ignoring and denying what was truly happening. Talking brings healing, but no one took a risk to speak. The worst-case scenario would have been that he did not want to talk about the incident and how it was affecting him. I believe ignoring the pain and choosing not to talk to him was a cop-out. I wish I'd had more spiritual maturity and boldness at this point in my life to speak up and not let the false thinking of other family members keep us all mute on such a serious subject that desperately needed to be addressed. It is so sad. Help was all around Grandpa, but all the mouths were closed—I think more for their comfort than for Grandpa's, as he was dying before our eyes.

Talking about spiritual help for someone else's benefit was not a normal mode of operation in our family. Real Christian faith and mature spiritual boldness were not present in our family during this time. I believe since Grandpa's life too was touched by rejection from childhood, such a devastating incident would be even harder to overcome, especially when silence can mean disagreement. Grandpa may have interpreted the family's silence to mean they thought badly of him and blamed him for what happened. His self-talk probably added to his pain—since people were saying nothing, he filled in the blanks in his mind. A rejected person will fill in those blanks in a self-destructive way. No one was reassuring him that they still loved him, that it was not his fault, that it was an accident, that he did not do it on purpose. He needed to hear people, especially his family, say those things—and he needed to know there was hope for him because Jesus could heal his wounds and would always be his friend. Jesus could have been his help in the healing process rather than alcohol, which eventually killed him.

For those who have survived a life-changing incident like this accidental shooting, healing comes through talking and support—not through silence and leaving a rejected mind to fill in the blanks of what his family thinks. A Christian counselor is more likely what Grandpa needed to sort through the guilt, shame, and blame he felt. Since it was highly unlikely that Grandpa would seek that kind of help, the family should have been available to talk with him to help ease his pain. But the truth is that Grandpa did not lead the family in a way that encouraged spiritual growth. I mentioned earlier that Grandpa would become out-of-control angry. During these fits of anger, he would use profanity, which usually included taking the Lord's name in vain. The Bible says, "Thou shalt not take the name of the Lord thy God in vain: for the LORD will not hold him guiltless that taketh his name in vain" (Exod. 20:7). I am not saying specifically that this caused Grandpa's grief, but I believe it is clear from God's word that this behavior is unacceptable. There is a high possibility that Grandpa's use of this unnecessary language contributed to his problems. If he had been the Christian, fatherly influence he should have been for his family, someone from the family possessing a Christian background would have been able to help him through this traumatic time with boldness in knowing what they were doing was right. Then again, if he had lived a Godly life, this fatal shooting might have never happened at all. God protects those who seek Him. I know this is true because of the profound difference in my pre-saved life compared to my life after salvation. Living with God as your Father is like living in day instead of night. Living in God's protection always yields the best life, a life that is peaceful, productive, and meaningful. Without God, life is lived from one tragedy to another. With God, there is peace and protection.

Chapter Eleven

My Mother's Secret

During the divorce period, there was one very memorable visit my mother made to the farm. This visit sticks out from all the rest because she showed up with obvious bruises and a black eye. It was apparent that something bad had taken place. One look at her and Grandpa said, "My gosh, babe, what happened to you?" Her response was to throw a newspaper down in front of him so he could read what happened to her. Grandma also read the newspaper. Reading the story caused both of them great emotional distress. Whatever it was obviously troubled them both immensely, because they too were feeling the pain of my mother's experience.

I was only four years old and could not read yet, and no one read the words from the newspaper aloud. No one thought it necessary to tell me what was happening. If the purpose was to protect me, that reasoning was absolutely wrong. At my age, I would not have understood specific details of such a violent act. However, the way they handled this was very upsetting and frightening. I had no idea what my mother had been through. I had no idea how bad she was hurt. But I could tell from their reactions that whatever happened was terrible. With no reassurance or inclusion from these three adults, I only felt more horrible and helpless. Someone could have at least reassured me instead of leaving me to deal with my confusion alone. I felt I was on the outside looking in, and no one acknowledged my presence. I needed to hear that everything would be okay, and life would remain constant. But they were wrapped up in their pain at this time and totally excluded me. I was treated no differently than if I was that proverbial fly on the wall. This subject was too adult to discuss with a child.

This became another example of how my mother never realized I had feelings too. I know she was hurting badly. But I just wonder at what point parental responsibility would become a consideration. The "big sister" had returned home needing attention, and I was shoved aside again. Normal parent–child feelings were never present between her and me. In most situations, my mother was too needy to care how I felt. This turned into a pattern of behavior I expected from her.

Even four years later, it was clear that my mother was determined to keep this story under wraps. She became very forceful and irrational at the slightest mention of the incident. Her unfortunate experience happened several years before my uncle got married. But sometime after he was married, his wife mentioned something insignificant about my mother's past to me. I made the mistake of telling my mother what she had said. It appeared my uncle's wife knew a little but not much. At this time, I was around eight years old. I still had no understanding about what happened to my mother or why she kept it a secret. When I mentioned what my uncle's wife had said, we were in the car heading home from the farm. My mother was fuming; it was obvious that she could not wait to get me home to discuss in detail what I was talking about. My brother was in the car, and she did not want to talk about it in front of him. He knew nothing of our mother's past until he was grown and married.

When we arrived home, my mother ushered me into the bathroom, locked the door, and demanded I tell her exactly what was said about her past. I had already told her everything that was said, and I had no more to say. I was anxious and upset by this interrogation and still confused about what had actually happened to her. I sure did not understand why she was behaving so irrationally. She finished the conversation with a warning to me: "You are never to talk about my past to anyone at any time. No one ever needs to know anything about it."

Through the years, I learned more about the incident as my mother and grandma revealed bits and pieces of the circumstances randomly to me. There was a man who had been stalking my mother and watching her apartment, keeping up with her every move. He learned that she lived alone and was an easy target for his purpose. Then one night, when my mother was home alone, she saw a man outside her door and became filled with fear as an engulfing feeling of heat flooded her body. The sliding-glass door suddenly shattered. After a loud crash, the intruder was inside the apartment, with the intent to attack and rape my mother. And he did just that, telling her that he had been watching her for days. Afterward, he made it clear that if she told anyone what he had done, he would come back and kill her.

Before the rape occurred, my mother had attended a meeting at work with her co-workers at the Air Force Base Exchange. The purpose was to give advice and tips on how to handle the situation if you were ever raped. They recommended not fighting or resisting; doing so could bring more harm or death. At the time of the rape, my mother said, she remembered the advice and thought it may have been beneficial in saving her life. During the attack, she did not fight; without the previous counsel, she felt that she probably would have resisted and fought back, which according to patterns of these situations would have made the attacker more angry, forceful, and violent.

Other women accused this man of the same crime, and the case against the rapist went to trial. My mother and the other women were present to testify. However, since this rapist had his wife take the stand and testify that he was with her on all the dates in question, there was a reasonable doubt. The rapist was released, now free to do the same thing to other helpless women. This was another time when a member of our family needed the help of a Christian counselor. It became yet another tragedy swept under the rug, where the pain and dysfunction grew and changed the lives of my mother and her children. Emotionally damaging situations have to be talked through before victims can get to a place of healing and stop the negative effects.

Over forty years later, as I began working through the years of damage, one thing became very clear: I had been programmed to keep things inside and not talk about unpleasant or embarrassing things that happened. Acknowledging these events was just not acceptable, and things of this nature were better left unsaid. In my opinion, this is why I have been able to deal with the past only by writing. Talking to my parents—my mother in particular—has never worked because of her emotional outbursts. Denial is a damaging and hurtful way to live.

My mother recently told me that I should have talked more about the pain of the past, been more open, been more like her and not kept things inside. Her statement clearly took me aback, because it was such a contradiction—it was in my mother's very nature to deny things. Her new advice, compared to her reaction to the rape, when she warned me to keep things secret, is a true oxymoron. How much more could your statements conflict? When she did talk, it was only angry words, venting steam and causing more harm. It added nothing productive, nothing capable of repairing the dysfunction in a productive, healthy manner.

I would not describe my mother as someone who was able to talk openly about problems. Her definition of "not keeping things inside" is venting in anger, a behavior I have witnessed from her all my life. "Being more open" or "letting things out," for her, did not mean having a controlled, productive discussion with a purpose to mend. The way she let things out was only a symptom of repressed deeper problems—that is, the trauma she lived through that is still locked deep in her mind, ever present to spill forth in fits of anger. Out-of-control, irrational anger does not constitute being more open. My mother taught me to keep the hurt inside and not talk about the pain.

As a point of clarification, anger is a normal emotion when kept in check. But what I am talking about in the descriptions of my mother and maternal grandpa is anger that is out-of-control, irrational, and damaging, manifested as a symptom of repressed traumatic experiences. My mother's input, years later, provides an ironic twist. Her advice and summary of *my* situation was to inform me that I was not open enough—I was not like her. Just because I do not use anger to let things go, she interprets that to mean I am not open enough; I do not talk enough or deal with the pain correctly. I do not do it right like she does. I needed to get things out, like she did, and not hold them inside. Conversely, from my perspective, I purposely controlled my temper because I had witnessed the damage that an out-of-control temper will inflict. I personally choose to believe that giving way to anger and temper is bad advice. And if she thinks I held too much inside, she needs to take a long hard look at her life and see where I learned that behavior. I was taught from her to deny and repress unpleasant things, acting like they never happened. Honestly! It can be very hard to see the forest for the trees, especially when denial fogs your vision.

It would have been better for our family and for all concerned if my mother had faced the truth back when the assault took place or as soon after as possible. I wish she could have known that it is emotionally healthy to live your life in truth. Hiding life-changing secrets only holds you hostage to those secrets. Living in truth ends the power of denial. There is freedom when you choose to live in complete truth. Hiding truth only comes with bondage to the secret, and causes dysfunction and damage to prevail. Our family paid a high price for my mother's choice to deny her pain.

Chapter Twelve

Rationalizing Reasons to Relive the Dysfunction

My two-year-old brother lay motionless in a hospital bed; he had been injured very seriously. Grandma Ada and I were checking on his condition after the accident. My brother's eyes were closed as if sleeping, but you could not wake him up. We talked to him, but he did not respond. He could not talk and did not move. By all indications, he appeared dead, but I noticed he was breathing. I was told he would be okay. At age four, however, I had a difficult time distinguishing between the possibility that he would always be in this lifeless condition and the hope that his motionless body would at some point revive to be the little boy I could talk to and play with again. This visit was yet another unsettling experience during the time of my parents' divorce.

The accident happened when my brother and Grandma Bessie took his little puppy for a stroll. My brother walked on a retainer wall built around the courthouse yard. Since the courthouse was on a hill, the walls were rather high in places. Then unexpectedly, the dog ran under my brother's feet, causing him to fall off the wall. He was unconscious after he hit the ground. He was taken to the hospital, where it was determined he had a brain concussion.

My brother remained in an unconscious state for an extended period of time. It was long enough to cause great concern about the possibility of his recovery, since it did not seem he was getting better. There came a time, however, after many days, when he finally began to revive from the comatose state. This happened when our mother and Grandma Bessie were both present. My brother reached for Grandma instead of his mother. This became a defining moment for our mother and was probably her first indication of what was going on with her son. He was attaching to Grandma, the one giving him day-to-day care, and there was little or no attachment to her, his mother. This incident caused my mother to reconsider her circumstances. She did not like what she witnessed and decided it was time to somehow maneuver back into her son's life. The thought of him connecting with someone else gave her reason to explore the possibility of remarrying dad.

However, my mother had more than one reason for thinking about remarriage. Another was the unfortunate rape experience, which my mother refers to as a "sign from God" that she should get back where she belonged and reunite our family. I do not believe God is ever responsible for causing something as terrible as a rape to occur just to get someone back on track. I do believe, however, that when a born-again believer is living outside of God's will, God could allow bad things to happen—the key word is *allow*, not cause or plan. If someone has willfully chosen to live in disobedience, God's protection would not be present the way it is when someone chooses to obediently live within His will. You can get yourself in a mess, but that does not mean God had anything to do with putting you there; you get where you are by choice. God is always faithful to help you out of your circumstances, if you only repent and ask.

Another reason my mother mentioned for considering reconciliation was as a rescue mission for Dad. He planned to marry another woman, who was pregnant with another man's baby. My mother believed it was her responsibility to save her former husband from impending matrimonial doom. She also knew that if he did go through with another marriage, her hopes of reuniting her family would be lost. So my mother talked to Dad and prevented the marriage. Then, for a time afterward, she played aloof and would not commit to re-tying the knot as quickly as Dad was expecting.

It seems from all these different angles that my mother was really, in essence, trying to talk herself into doing something she perceived she should do, but not really what she felt in her heart. I have learned that if you are doing something just because it fits a preconceived mold of belief, you need to step back and reevaluate, because "should be" can bring some of life's biggest burdens. Just because something should be, according to a certain person's standards or your own internal dialogue developed from a lifetime of collected behaviors and beliefs, does not necessarily make it the right thing to do. Making life-changing decisions based on these thoughts and beliefs can bring more problems because they are not always based in truth. These important life-changing decisions can only be made appropriately within God's perfect will for your life. If you truly seek Him, He will guide you in what is best for you.

Chapter Thirteen

Memories of Grandma Ada

During my first five years of childhood, there was one constant in my life amid all the turmoil that hit me from every direction. With Grandma Ada, I learned of a functional life and a loving relationship. In those early years, she was the one I could count on for stability, security, love, and nurturing. The foundation she provided became a critical anchor for my future existence. These memories I recall of my time on my grandparents' farm are all prior to Billy Jeff's fatal shooting which happened the month before I turned five.

Memories of Grandma Ada are warm and comforting. I never felt like an intrusion in her life. She was glad to have me with her. Being with her was always my preference over being with my parents, because time we spent together was about emotional connection and building a relationship. Grandma focused on teaching me, guiding me, and getting to know me while I got to know her.

After my parents divorced and I moved to the farm with Grandma Ada, I do not remember feeling as though much had changed. My parents' absence felt normal, not like a loss. As long as I was with Grandma, I really cared very little about where my parents were or what they did. Neither parent explained the divorce and how it all affected me anyway. Being with Grandma was a very normal part of my life, and the turmoil I experienced with my parents became a distant memory when I was with her.

Day to day life on the farm was filled with activity. Grandma was very busy, and I was privileged to be present for it all. I went everywhere she did. I learned a lot from her. Grandma talked to me and treated me like an important person she valued. I always felt like I belonged when she spent time teaching me. Cooking was one area where I benefited greatly from her knowledge. Even though I was only four years old, Grandma never let that stand in the way of making me feel capable and competent to learn and help her and work right alongside her. She taught me at this young age how to make the perfect skillet of cornbread; how to make pungent, spicy gingerbread; and how to create the favorite family cookie, moist and rich with the sweet smell and taste of vanilla. Grandma was also very proficient at making candy. One of the most fun types of candy we made was vinegar taffy. It was delicious—lusciously sweet vanilla with a subtle sharpness added by the vinegar. Pulling the taffy was the fun part; this transformed it from a clear syrupy consistency to a mound of snow-white fluff. Also, fried apricot pies was a recipe we made often—pie dough enclosing a sweet and tangy apricot filling, fried to perfection with a flaky brown crust oozing with goodness. Yummy! Wonderful sweet memories of Grandma's kitchen blended with the security, love, and acceptance of functional emotional health growing in my life as a very young child. That is the recipe for wonderful, coveted childhood memories. Grandma grew my self-confidence through the many things she taught me, and I knew from her encouragement that she believed I could do anything I chose to. I became competent to help her, and we were a team in the kitchen and many other places of activity on the farm.

The main farm crop Grandma and Grandpa grew was alfalfa hay. When you live on a farm and raise animals, there are many daily tasks to perform. The animals have to be fed and watered, the cows have to be milked, and the eggs have to be gathered. Other farm chores included burning irrigation ditches, planting and irrigating fields, and cutting and baling hay. These tasks were involved and time-consuming because modern-day methods had yet to make their way to my grandparents' farm. Memories of irrigating and muddy fields, the smell of freshly cut hay, the lazy summer river complete with lines of cottonwood trees, dirt roads, and walking barefoot in a cool, damp, just-plowed field take me back to my childhood on the farm and make the country song "Almost Home" by Craig Morgan rich with experiences I can completely relate to.

As a young child, all this did not seem bad; it was all I had ever known, and it was just our way of life. Grandma tried to keep me as comfortable as possible through all these episodes of farm duty. Sometimes I would sleep in the pickup if the field was far away from the house. Or sometimes Grandma would let me sleep at the house and meet her in the field in the morning when my uncle was available to take me to her. On the mornings when it was just my uncle and me, we would have Trix cereal for breakfast. Eating Trix with him was always a treat because normally, we had a huge breakfast of eggs, bacon, homemade biscuits, and gravy. This was Grandpa's expectation every day; he claimed that anything less was not substantial enough to get you through the morning work to lunchtime. Therefore, cereal was a rarity and a treat. After breakfast, my uncle would take me to Grandma in the field and start his day with either work or school.

During these times in the hayfields, I would usually play with my dog. He would go with me everywhere. He was a friend I spent a lot of alone time with. He had a blond coat of long hair and a friendly smile. I loved my little rat terrier dog named Dusty J. He was my loyal companion for the frequent lonely times on the farm when all the adults had to be busy. My little dog and I would run in the hay fields together and climb up stacks of hay. He also was a very good listener. He and I had many secrets.

There were days when Grandma Ada and I would stay close to the house, focusing on domestic chores. I really enjoyed anything I got to do with Grandma. On ironing and sewing days, my job was to play the music. I kept the record player going with Grandma's favorites, such as "The Locomotion," an instrumental called "Green Onions," or the Bob Wills album, plus many others. It was fun because the music would keep Grandma singing and humming throughout her chores. Sometimes she would even dance, too, which she playfully referred to as "cutting a rug." I usually joined her, and we danced through many days of chores. Being with Grandma Ada was the best!

Another aspect of farm life was that trips to town were a rare occasion. We bought groceries to supplement what the farm produced. One of the things Grandma would buy for me was soda pop. In my opinion, soda pop definitely was an important reason to make the trip to town. Grandma's Dr. Pepper floats were yummy! Another memorable part of buying soda pop was the noise of the clinking and rattling soda-pop bottles vibrating together as we drove through the valley on the not-so-smooth country roads. The sound of pop bottles rattling was a distant noise on both the trip to town and the trip home because back then, soda-pop bottles were returnable for deposit.

However, one of the things I most enjoyed about our trips to town was getting to visit the neighbors on our way home. Farm life could keep you very isolated, and for weeks at a time, the only people I would see were Grandma, Grandpa, and my uncle. Visiting with neighbors provided a nice change of pace. It was a lot of comfortable, country-style socializing. Grandma knew almost everyone in the valley, and we would stop in to visit many friends as we made our way back to the farm. There was no definite purpose for stopping at each house other than to visit and catch up on how they were doing and have something to drink—usually sweet tea. Listening to my grandma's conversations with her friends was something I never tired of. The subject was always something interesting about their daily life, usually some kind of farm experience. I also became acquainted with grandma's friends through our visits, and they became my friends too.

Grandma could tell endless stories of her childhood, and I learned much about how her life was before. Her history was rich, and she was willing to share her feelings and emotions about her experiences as well. Unlike my mother, who would share very little about herself, Grandma was always very open to sharing her feelings. Although Grandma's parents, Mr. and Mrs. Chapman, were dead before I was born, I did meet four of her six brothers and sisters. From Grandma's stories, I felt as if I knew them all before we ever met, especially her younger sister, Ollie. Ollie took an interest in family roots and traced their family tree back to a man named John Chapman from Ohio—better known as Johnny Appleseed. There were many interesting facets to Grandma's family history.

I loved hearing all about Grandma and her family; this too created an emotional connection between us. I knew who she was, what she thought and felt, and many noteworthy details of her life. She also never left it to chance or made me guess how important I was to her and how much she loved me. Grandma would on many occasions tell her family back in Oklahoma, through letters and phone calls, about me and all the things we did together. Even though I was very young, Grandma had a knack for making me feel special and like I was a big part of her life. Her love was manifested in her actions of caring, concern, understanding, and guidance. She encouraged me. She gave me her time, her history, her thoughts, her experiences; she shared herself with me. Grandma valued the person I was, and she believed in me. She was interested in what interested me. And I, in turn, loved, cared for, respected, obeyed, and honored her. I also felt I was a blessing to her just as she was to me. Life on the farm with Grandma Ada was the best time of my childhood. There was no emotional damage here—only healthy emotional growth. It was a period that gave me stability and resilience.

In addition to family history, Grandma told me many fictional stories. There was usually a bedtime story, or sometimes Grandma would sing a song. Grandma loved music and dancing, and since recordings were rare for most of her life, she memorized the lyrics to songs she especially liked. She had a pretty singing voice, and I very much enjoyed listening to her sing her versions of "El Paso" or "North to Alaska," among many other popular country or rock-and-roll songs from the fifties and sixties.

I had learned from Grandma how a functional life should feel. Even though she worked hard, she included me and had time for me. She built a foundation early in my life that later gave me something positive to draw from. Grandma gave me a reason to believe in myself and know my life was worthwhile. And even though she was not always able to be physically present in my life, I knew she was always there to care, in spirit, throughout my childhood. I always knew she was on my side. Grandma gave me the feelings of belonging, acceptance, worthiness, love, competency, and security in my early years. These are all necessary for a person to feel emotionally whole. Since I did not get these feelings from my mother and dad, it was therefore understandable that I built my childhood attachment to Grandma rather than either of my parents. Grandma was never selfish or childish. Her adult presence brought security and confidence to my life. She was always there, always supporting, always giving of herself and showing her love concretely and functionally.

Grandma taught me many things, and she never showed anger. She was always calm and in control. This was a great comfort to me, especially after I had experienced the upsetting episodes of anger in my mother's care. My mother had very little patience, but my grandma had an abundance of patience without a trace of a temper. That was a real blessing in my life.

However, Grandma's patience would wear thin with me on a few occasions when I did things she had told me not to—like getting muddy when playing in the snow or getting oil all over my clothes from playing in the oil left from an oil change. On these occasions, I remember getting "the elm switch." Since I had disobeyed, Grandma was compelled to discipline me. She really hated doing it, but she did it because she said she would if I got into the oil or the mud one more time. She went to the elm tree, broke off a switch, and swatted me several times. It stung, and I cried. But I knew for sure by looking into Grandma Ada's eyes that it really did hurt her more than me. I knew for sure Grandma was not hitting me because her anger had taken control of her actions. It was not at all like I felt when my mother whipped me with a belt. Most of what I learned, I learned from Grandma Ada. I learned from her in loving discipline and in everyday work.

Gladly, though, we did not work all the time. I also learned from her while doing fun things, like playing card games or putting puzzles together. We also watched cartoons and cooking shows. My personal favorites of all the shows we watched were the westerns, such as *Rawhide*, *Bonanza*, *Daniel Boone*, *The Lone Ranger*, *The Big Valley*, *My Friend Flicka*, and many others. Today when I watch a western show or movie, it rekindles memories of Grandma Ada and a wonderful, secure time long ago on a ninety-acre farm when childhood felt good.

Most days, farm life was filled with activity, but cold winter days sometimes dragged by. Usually Grandpa was outside doing chores around the farm. But on days when the daily high was in the single digits, he would stay inside by the fire. He fed his animals but quickly returned to the house because of the bitter cold. On these days, Grandma Ada would hang blankets up to partition off the living-room area from the rest of the house. The farmhouse was drafty, and unless you were in the room with the butane heater, you would freeze. I found these days to be extremely boring. Grandma Ada would cook our meals and then do things that kept her busy, such as sewing, quilting, or reading. I would usually find some way to entertain myself.

One of the things I would do was just sit and watch Grandpa from across the room as he read his favorite book about Billy the Kid. Grandpa's eyes would grow wide with excitement as he was transported to a different time, experiencing in his imagination the shootouts and narrow escapes of a youth on the run turned bad because of a damaging relationship with a hurtful stepfather. I watched as Grandpa became one with the adventure. It was intriguing to see Grandpa react as he read, probably because he normally displayed little feeling unless it was rage. I always wondered why Grandpa was so interested in the outlaw Billy the Kid. But after growing up and reading about Billy the Kid myself, I understood Grandpa's interest in the life of this young desperado. Learning of this famous outlaw's life is captivating because it is filled with escapades of great adventure and engrossing suspense.

I have also realized now that Grandpa was reading about the very farmland he possessed. Grandpa's farmhouse sat on land Billy the Kid passed through numerous times during his short lifetime only eight decades earlier. My maternal grandparents' ninety-acre farm was located in the Fort Sumner Valley, just a short distance from the banks of the Pecos River—a river Billy the Kid traveled along on many trips to various New Mexico towns.

If I had known this at the time, sharing Grandpa's interest in this young outlaw could have been a bonding experience for us. I enjoyed watching western shows with Grandma; I know I would have shared Grandpa's interest too. This could have become a point of connection if, on just one of Grandpa's many trips to town, he had taken me along. There were many Billy the Kid points of interest to see along the way in our fertile valley, rich in Old West, American history. Grandpa could have shown me the very house where Billy the Kid drew his last breath after Pat Garrett fatally shot him. Then, just up the road a short distance from the famous house, we could have stopped to visit the military cemetery where the Kid was buried. Back then, before the tombstone was stolen, it cost nothing to visit the grave. The tombstone was clearly visible from the road. Grandpa and I could have talked about the notorious outlaw who made our town famous, and how people traveled from all over the country just to see the grave we drove by regularly.

Emotional connections happen through sharing common interests. Grandpa and I could have explored how this famous figure of bygone days probably traveled through our farm many times during his twenty-one years. We could have mapped and walked the exact steps very likely taken by Billy the Kid years before. I know Grandpa would have thought this all to be nonsense he had no time for. However, there are some very simple things in life you cannot afford to miss. I could have easily shared Grandpa's interest in Billy the Kid, but this just became a lost opportunity because Grandpa was unable to open up. The American history Grandpa read about had great relevance to the farm we all loved. Sharing it could have made a difference and become something Grandpa and I had in common. But instead, Grandpa's interests, life, and feelings were a closed, inaccessible book.

It was good for me that Grandma Ada had a completely different way of communicating with people than Grandpa did. She shared and cared openly. It was no surprise, due to Grandma's disposition and her life's portrayal of the fruit of the spirit, that she was a born-again Christian. She talked to me about Jesus; she said that she read and believed in the Bible. Grandma's maternal grandfather was a Baptist preacher known for preaching about hell, complete with descriptions of fire and brimstone. Her sister and nieces verified Grandma's salvation experience when they came to visit toward the end of Grandma's life, at the time she was sick and dying. They told us of her baptism, done the old-fashioned way in a river in Oklahoma. These relatives were amazed at Grandma's strength as she approached death. Remembering her salvation experience, they concluded that Jesus was positively the source of her strength and peace in the face of terminal illness.

However, during the years of her life with Grandpa, serving the Lord was not obviously her priority. Grandma did not stand up to Grandpa concerning her need to serve God, since it did not appear that Grandpa shared her beliefs—or maybe it was just that he did not see it as necessary. Grandpa was very controlling, and he also controlled Grandma. Grandpa was not prone to place his trust in God; rather, as a farmer, he trusted the *Farmer's Almanac* and faithfully watched the weather forecast each evening. It is easy to identify the source of turmoil in Grandpa's life. Without God, life is chaos.

But in spite of Grandpa, my grandmother let her Christian light shine. She gave me security and built my trust in the world. She always encouraged me. Without the foundation I got from Grandma, what was to come in the years ahead with my parents would have been even harder to endure, greatly decreasing my chance of having a functional life. She had given me knowledge of what was good and right in the world and how it was to feel normal. When I lived with Grandma, I was able for a short time to know unconditional love, support, and caring on a daily basis without the turmoil, anger, and fighting. Grandma Ada helped me build the emotional foundation necessary to survive the storms ahead.

When I lived with Grandma, she drew pictures of horses for me; she knew that I loved horses. I kept those pictures she drew and took them with me when I had to leave the farm. They became something tangible to hold and feel to revive the good memories of Grandma when I had to live with my parents. I kept those pictures in a box, and I slept with that box containing the horse pictures Grandma drew for me. When my life hurt, I would take out the pictures and look at them. They reminded me of the good side of life I experienced with Grandma, and I cried because I missed her so much. I could retreat in my mind, going back to the love and security with Grandma Ada that was missing in my current life with two immature, childish parents. These memories provided my escape and helped me endure the years I faced in my parents' home—a home filled with rejection and sin, a home void of God's presence.

Grandma Ada was caring and emotionally connecting. She and Grandpa were opposite in the ways they related to children, this I had learned firsthand. My mother and Uncle Jim were also different in this area. To me as a child, Uncle Jim felt more like Grandma Ada and my mother felt more like Grandpa. In my opinion, there were reasons for their differences. My mother attached to Grandpa. He was the one she looked up to and desired to be like. She gave more weight to his guidance and seemed to want to please him above anyone else. Therefore, this circumstance easily passed on Grandpa's dysfunctional past of rejection and pain to my mother, and that turned her into a person very much like himself. In addition, Grandpa's lack of faith in God only magnified his dysfunctional tendencies.

However, Uncle Jim attached to Grandma Ada, growing and learning mostly from her in human relation skills. Grandma could best be described as a functional, Christian woman very much in tune with her emotions and the emotions of others. Therefore, Uncle Jim became more like Grandma with an ability to feel and care for those around him and grew into a mature adult and loving father.

Chapter Fourteen

Good-bye Security—Hello Dysfunction

I have heard mothers in general, including mine, speak of bonding with their children as if it is some sort of magical encounter that creates a feeling of mutual love and eternal togetherness. This statement confused me, because this elusive experience of love and belonging never happened between my mother and me. I wondered, *What is the definition of this bonding experience?* I found that bonding is an experience mostly for the mother. Mothers bond and children attach. In psychological terms, the bonding experience is more for the birthmother's benefit, because it happens in the first few moments during the first visit between mother and newborn. It is brief, and the infant has no remembrance of this event of bonding, which explains why I naturally never felt any closeness due to bonding. What follows this experience, however, is the attachment process, when the child grows a relationship with the person who gives her security, love, and belonging—the person the child can count on to meet her everyday needs. Sadly, I never felt close to my mother because of attachment either. Attachment has a lot to do with emotional relating, an area my mother seemed unable to understand or grasp.

Throughout my first five years, I attached to Grandma Ada, not my mother. My memories and feelings of a maternal relationship were all intertwined with Grandma. It is also noteworthy that the first five years of life are critical formative years for a child. The person with whom they attach during this period is the one they feel comfortable trusting for their needs. The personality is also formed during this time, and my mother did very little to contribute to the formation of my personality. Grandma was there for that task as well. She was the one I trusted to care for me physically and emotionally. Unlike my mother, Grandma wanted me with her.

Because of the divorce decree, I believe my mother equated having custody of me with ownership. She seemed to think that custody and ownership automatically created attachment. I was supposed to magically attach to her with no work done on her part just because she was my mother. This mindset may have made her miss the fact that I had attached only to Grandma. My mother provided no opportunity in my very early years for me to grow any sort of relationship with her. She seemed to believe there was a real relationship between us just because she had control as the custodial parent.

My mother made me feel guilty for attaching to Grandma. Since my mother did not invest the time or present the warm, welcoming motherly demeanor that is required for attachment to form, I did not feel close to her or know her. Attaching with children takes work, and my mother did not put forth the effort during this critical period in my life to ever make me feel comfortable, welcome, or cared for by her. She spent her time being angry, scaring me, and pushing me away; it felt like I was a burden to her. Therefore, during the divorce period, custody was the extent of any relationship shared between my mother and me, and even her custody was subrogated to Grandma.

Then came the upheaval, when my parents showed up at the farm announcing they were getting back together. My parents said they believed it was best for all concerned. My mother stated three reasons for the remarriage, but none included me. My brother was living with Dad and my mother wanted him back; he was a reason for the remarriage, but I was not. Dad was going to marry another woman, and my mother did not want that to happen; that was a reason for the remarriage, but I was not. My mother had lived through a traumatic experience during the divorce; her feelings were a reason for the remarriage, but again, I was not. Any reasons for reassembling this dysfunctional family were unrelated to my existence. Either parent wanting *me* was never mentioned as a consideration. My mother often stated she wanted her son back, but Dad never once said he wanted his daughter back. It was as if I had no place. I was not considered individually. My existence was never mentioned as any compelling consideration in this life-changing decision.

My world was secure with Grandma. The thought of leaving Grandma and moving back into the turmoil and dysfunction my parents provided was an unsettling and unhappy one that led to more insecurity. Moving meant I would see Grandma very little, and she would not be there for me like before. This thought made my stomach turn into knots. My parents had a great lack of concern for my feelings. They had no empathy for my emotional pain or for how I was affected by their decisions. Moving back with them and leaving Grandma was a fearful prospect to me. I felt very uneasy about having to be around Dad at all, and I also knew the anger my mother was capable of. I would be living with and depending on two people who felt more like strangers than parents. My earlier memories of living with my parents were hurtful and frightening. I did not want to return to that. I was happy with Grandma. Therefore, this news meant my life was taking a turn for the worse, and I faced the future with great skepticism.

My parents, in their emotionally damaged state, could never detach from their own neediness long enough to understand the hurt and pain they imposed on my life. I felt alone, confused, and insecure. I was frustrated because all the old pain was back again. Furthermore, I had not been given a vote or even a chance to voice my feelings about being put back into this all-too-familiar, hurtful place. Not being considered in major decisions that affect your life makes you feel frustrated and helpless. I was never talked to about the divorce, I was not included in the decision about the new house, and my mother prevented Dad from marrying a woman whom I had never met. It came out of the blue that my parents were getting back together. These decisions affected me too. There was no assurance from either parent to help me through the turmoil—no thought given for my feelings and emotions. I was left to process all this change alone.

It must have been more comfortable for my parents to deny any feelings but their own. I was just property they owned—no different from a piece of furniture to move at will. So I would do as they said, and they would not be considerate enough to help me with my feelings of misplacement, rejection, and fear. Not talking about something this big can only leave major wounds and emotional pain. A child needs security and reassurance. But at five years old in my parents' home, I was left to cope alone with no parental support. However before I left the farm, Grandma tried to reassure me by pointing out a few positive aspects. She made sure I knew that she would be a part of my life as often as possible.

Because of the way my parents handled their divorce and remarriage, the effects were life-changing. I was just along for the ride. They would do what they wanted with no need to consider me—after all, I was just a pawn at their mercy. It seemed that they played with my feelings, and I would just have to adjust to whatever was best for them. They expected me to do as I was told, not because it was best, but only because they said so. And I was the compliant child. This inconsiderate parental behavior sets a parent–child relationship up for failure. Children lose trust in and connection with parents who choose to treat them disrespectfully. The lack of communication and lack of consideration for my feelings had a direct effect on my relationship with my parents. With no attention given to my emotional needs, this lifestyle became part of the emotional abuse inflicted by both my parents.

I now was at the total mercy of my angry, raging mother and my childish, self-centered dad at a very vulnerable time in my childhood. I had not one dysfunctional parent but two. Each contributed to lifelong problems in a unique way, and collectively they contributed many different types of dysfunctional, toxic parenting behaviors to my childhood. My mother's parenting style was controlling, intrusive, and domineering. Dad's style, without question, was neglectful and distant. They rarely worked from any other parenting style. Any discipline from my mother was motivated more from anger than love. Dad never cared enough to discipline me. The element of parental love was clearly missing in interactions between us. My mother also never apologized for her hurtful behaviors.

I would often be repulsed by people telling me after my parents remarried, "Well, at least your parents got back together." They just did not understand the dysfunction in this situation. My parents had previously divorced because of irreconcilable differences. She didn't remarry Dad because she suddenly realized she was in love with him and could not live without him. Because of this decision, my parents, my brother, and I were all forced to live through the consequences in a family reunited for all the wrong reasons. My parents did not repair or heal the damage before trying marriage over again. It was a damaged family during the first marriage, and it continued to be an even more damaged family in the second marriage. The remarriage may have looked like good news and a blessing on the outside to people not living it, but in reality, it was a nightmare to endure. I had to learn survival techniques to make it through an environment of damage and harm that could be healed only through God's divine intervention.

Chapter Fifteen

Living in Confusion and Chaos without God

Why were no boundaries set prior to remarriage? There were things tolerated before that should never have been allowed to return the second time. Remarrying without repairing the damage and changing expectations is like running a marathon with a broken leg. My parents each needed a deeper understanding of their pasts and time to recover from their emotional pain—steps that would allow them to recognize and fix the things in their lives that had caused the turmoil and led to divorce in the first place. But they remarried without healing from prior damage, and our family continued on the dysfunctional path. Why would anyone assume they could build a happy home without mending a broken marriage?

How had irreconcilable differences magically become reconcilable with nothing done to fix the underlying problems? My parents needed God, counseling, and healing before remarriage should have even been an option. They could have benefited greatly from a neutral, unbiased person giving them a healthy perspective on their trauma. They each possessed personal hurts and damage one cannot unload without professional help. Their children became living proof of how they passed on the baggage rather than found a functional method to rid us all of the pain they carried with them. Even though counseling was not as readily available then as it is today, it was accessible for those who chose to recognize their emotional damage and seek a better way of life. Church was always an option then also.

Although I never heard Dad say he wanted me back and our family reunited, he wanted my mother for sure—he said that many times. This reveals the heart of the problem regarding this dysfunctional setup; it did not include a dad who was plugged into family responsibility. It never felt to me that he cared if I was in his life or not. Dad was a selfish parent. *Selfish* and *parent* are two contradictory terms. A parent cannot be selfish and do what is best for their child. The very meaning of *parent* and the nature of parental responsibility are all about selfless giving. Selfish people are just not equipped for the job. Dad's narcissistic tendencies created an even greater need to draw boundaries before remarriage was considered. But when my mother forfeited her chance to dictate changes, Dad—being just like a little kid with unreasonable demands—got his way again. He was right back where he wanted to be with no changes expected and no work done. How lucky could he be?

Getting just what you want with no price paid almost always leads to a life of ingratitude. And that's exactly how Dad behaved—ungrateful and unthankful for the family he had. If Dad would have had to work to get his family back, he might have appreciated the position he was privileged to return to. But instead, he took it all for granted and brought his abusive ways back into our life again. If my mother did any bargaining, Dad did not comply. But she did not like being divorced and preferred to be married, even if it meant she would be living a life worse than before. So with no changes necessary, the remarriage happened. The best reason Dad gave to me for it all was that I would have my own room in the new house they bought. Considering how I felt and what I faced, having my own room meant very little to me.

Many years later, in talking about the dysfunctional past, Dad described the divorce period as the most miserable time in his life, so he was happy about the remarriage. But for it ever to work functionally, Dad needed to change the person and father he was. He needed to become a responsible family-oriented dad, and my mother was the only one who held the key to making Dad change. But Dad did not change. If the divorce period was in fact such a miserable time for Dad and he really wanted his marriage back, gratitude should have caused him to work at making our lives better.

I guess things can be so simple, but people choose to make their life difficult. Denial of the true circumstances was at work here. Some people just do not want to face the truth and change for the better. Change is frightening. They like their dysfunctional lifestyle just the way it is. It becomes a comfort zone no matter what the cost to themselves and those around them, and they fear the unknown. The kind of change our family needed was only possible and available from God, but my parents did not acknowledge God.

Without God and Christian counseling—and with the denial of the truth and an inability to face the need for healing—absolutely nothing was different the second time around. However, more pain evolved from hurtful events during the divorce period. These events were denied but ever-present, despite my parents' desperate attempts to ignore their existence. Life went on, simply on the pretense that if you did not acknowledge the bad things that happened, they would somehow miraculously cease to exist. But denial only increases the problems and the pain.

My mother could not realize on her own, with no outside neutral counsel, that the decision she made to remarry was absolutely not in the best interest of her young children and their development, especially emotionally. My mother was so controlling with her children; why could she not be just as controlling with Dad? For our family's benefit, Dad needed control and specific expectations to follow. He needed to be accountable somewhere in his life. And with this second chance at marriage and a new start, it was time for him to grow up, be responsible, and put his family before his selfish, juvenile wants and whims. He needed to behave as a responsible husband and father—no more breaking marriage vows and no more childish behavior. He needed to support my mother and be involved in his children's lives. And most of all, our family needed God to overcome the dysfunctional mess my parents had created. If Dad could not commit to this standard, then there should have been no second chance. Dad needed to earn his way back into our lives, not just get it all back with the same lack of conditions and carefree setup as before. There are times in our lives when boundaries have to be drawn and expectations agreed upon, especially when raising children.

I also know that even though my mother claimed to be a born-again Christian, she lacked the spiritual wisdom to make the necessary family decisions. This led her back to the same bad situation. This is why church attendance and growth in a personal relationship with God is so important. It enables people to stand firm and make decisions that are best for all concerned. God is strength, truth, and wisdom for anyone who will let Him lead. My mother could have made a huge difference for us all by standing up for what was right—beginning with putting God first. Instead, she tried by her power only to make things work and pull it all together alone. Thus, she had no peace, and her anger and wrath continued to grow unchecked.

It is so ironic. All people want to be happy and content, but they choose to run from the only answer that would make it possible to achieve that sort of life. They view obedience to God as something to avoid like the plague, all the while seeking their own way to happiness and contentment. Then life without God always comes up short and brings great disappointment and turbulence. My mother did not grasp her great need for God's guidance, especially being married to an unsaved man. She lacked spiritual wisdom. There were other forces in play, too, that made it improbable for her to stand firm on what needed to happen spiritually. She had been raised by a controlling father who did not obey God. She had not left her childhood home emotionally by cutting the necessary emotional ties. With these ties still intact, she was not free to live life as an adult, making her unable to stand up for her rights as a wife and mother. Adults must set boundaries and enforce them for a functional life to follow, especially in such life-changing matters as marriage reconciliation. But this decision will prevent old problems from resurfacing only when these expectations are set with God as the foundation.

I have lived on both sides of this basic life decision, which is of the utmost importance, and without reservation I happily and gratefully choose God's way. I know that when God is all you have, He is all you need. I also have experienced personally the comfort God gives freely, and I would never choose to live life without His guidance, protection, and provision. He truly is the very best friend you can ever have, and He will never let you down. Living without God is choosing hell on earth and then hell for eternity. Choosing God is choosing peace, happiness, protection, and contentment on earth and then heaven for eternity. No Jesus, no peace—but when you know Jesus, you know peace. Clearly, our family needed God's guidance to live functionally and happily.

It is ironic that my parents started their second marriage in a new house that was located only a short distance from a little white Baptist church. We could walk out the back door of our house and be at the church door in a few minutes. God was speaking, but they were not listening. He was saying, "Here I am. I have made it easy for you." But they both responded by ignoring God, His convenient church, His blessings, and His better way for our family. They continued on in their childish, narcissistic behavior, reaping the consequences of hurt, disappointment, and trials for both themselves and their children.

Chapter Sixteen

Lack of Qualifications

It is interesting from my upbringing how I was programmed to view our family problems as my mother's to fix and expected little from dad. This unveils a large part of the dysfunction present. The husband is responsible to lead the family, but Dad was no leader. Leading our family fell on my mother's shoulders and became one of many ways Dad dishonored his wife. Dad needed to become a husband and father of morals and integrity, live his life as an adult putting aside childish ways, and become the understanding family leader we needed.

After my sister and I were married, my mother told us over lunch one day of Dad's unfaithful behavior. She said that she always dreamed of a marriage like the ones my sister and I had with our husbands, but it never worked that way for her and Dad. Dad remarried my mother and continued to mistreat her. One of the many ways in which Dad dishonored his wife was by being unfaithful.

Sex outside of marriage is never acceptable. It is an act of disobedience and always leads to pain and heartache—not only for the spouse but for the children as well. Any sexual act outside of marriage is no different from robbery. You allow another person to take what belongs to your spouse—or, for unmarried people, your future spouse. Marriage vows are a commitment to give yourself *only* to your spouse. Sexual promiscuity and adultery are the total opposite of freedom; they always put your life in greater bondage. A right to sexual freedom is a lie that multitudes of people have gullibly swallowed. It is a deadly sin for all concerned.

Sex within marriage is one of God's most precious gifts to mankind, good for you in every way. Sex outside of marriage is hurtful, permanently damaging, disobedient, deadly, and wrong. The hurt of adultery ruins marriages and causes children to reap the consequences of an adult's decision to be selfish and immoral. Dad's sexual sins were a damaging behavior he inflicted on our family. His sinful choice in turn led to some of the most hurtful things he did and said; it was like a heavy weight he carried around. The guilt it must have caused was most likely the catalyst for some of the direct damage he inflicted on his children. Mostly, Dad was uninvolved in our lives, but when he was present; his actions were scornful, bitter, and cruel.

If living without my mother after they divorced made Dad so miserable, why did he find it so difficult to remain faithful? He seemed miserable after remarriage as well. Where were the loving and caring behaviors of a husband grateful to have his family back? Rather than love and appreciate my mother, Dad stomped on her feelings. Sin causes needless pain. Allowing God to guide and protect shelters one's life from the damage of sin. Dad did not let God guide his life. He went to sin's cesspool and lived in the stinking destruction of sin.

Did something happen in Dad's childhood to cause him to be so impulsive in the area of sexual sin? Grandma Bessie told me that Dad's father was unfaithful; she said there were many women he had adulterous relations with. Was Dad exposed to Grandpa's despicable behavior at a young and tender time in his childhood? Did he witness something damaging? It seems reasonable that the sins of the father are a possible answer for Dad's bad decisions. This in turn became a blight on my brother's life as well. It was as if a curse was in place to plague the family for generations. However, there are no more males in this family to be plagued. My brother had no sons to carry on the name. For at least three generations, this infidelity was allowed to inflict hurt, pain, and disconnection on the families involved. This selfish decision of infidelity did not affect only the ones going astray—it hurt everyone close to them and sent ripples of dysfunction into future generations, until there were no more sons to carry the burdensome torch.

Having grown up in a family damaged by adultery, I can state without hesitation that the hurt experienced by the children is monumental. The adult's life is full of emptiness and inner turmoil caused by feelings of betrayal that they choose to inflict on their spouse and family. This becomes an endless cycle that manifests in abusive language and abusive treatment inflicted on a child by the adulterous parent, no doubt coming from their intense feelings of guilt. This senseless hurt can end. There is peace and contentment in living life on a firm foundation of doing what is right. Adultery and sex outside of marriage are wrong; this is inclusive of single people as well. The perpetual damage can hurt for decades and infiltrate future generations.

In large part, this mindset of sexual freedom is imbedded by Hollywood. The movie industry tends to glamorize the sin of adultery and sex outside marriage, to make people think it brings happiness, wealth, and success, and makes you more whole and complete. However, in reality, it does exactly the opposite. If the actual lives of those used to spread this propaganda and those choosing to live in sexual sin were exposed for what they truly are, we would see that they are full of discontent, pain, heartache, alcoholism, drug abuse, and death. They would be lives lived in a less-than-whole state with little to no direction or real purpose.

Finding and living the truth brings freedom and contentment, but living the lie of sexual freedom deteriorates and injures. This destructive behavior and belief unleashed on society destroys families. And when families are destroyed, society as a whole is headed for destruction also. Another lie associated with this is believing that no one will ever know. This too is false, because God knows everything—and those practicing sexual freedom know of their sin as well. Their conscience is damaged, causing them to live a compensating life of guilt and turmoil. At some point, they will realize that God knows all, and in the end, it will be clear they should have cared all along what God knew about them.

Dad did not seem to grasp the real meaning of family responsibility. When he remarried my mother, he was asking for her to have faith in him a second time. But the way he handled family life both times, it was as if he was applying for a job he was not qualified for. He lived the husband and father roles in title only, oblivious to the core meaning of his position, job description, and responsibility.

Men need to grasp that as husbands, they are promising to be loving, faithful, and committed leaders of their families. Dads need to be involved and in tune with all aspects of child growth and development— just providing money for necessities does not make a man an adequate father. I do realize that *functional* dads do not do everything right (after all, they are human), but they are at least present and involved. They make an effort to know their children and have an active role in molding their children's lives. Parenting is a partnership between a husband and wife. It is not a job ever to be totally delegated to your spouse. And it is essential that God is reverenced, honored, and obeyed by all family members. That spiritual relationship provides a safety net for the family when parents, out of human weakness, fail to meet all needs.

Dads who do not live up to the qualifications and behaviors symbolized by the terms *dad* and *father* present a false face to society in general. When people mention their dad to another, it should evoke common feelings and good memories of love, security, stability, caring, commitment, and all the positive things that *dad* should commonly mean. But, when *dad* means the opposite of all it should, there is a breakdown in communication and a distortion of the term that should never be allowed to happen. To one person, *dad* can mean detachment, hurt, pain, rejection, and damage because of a dysfunctional childhood. But to another, *dad* can mean warmth, love, caring, and security when blessed with a Christian dad of integrity and confidence. In that case, *dad* means what it is supposed to. Dads choosing to raise their children in dysfunction do a disservice to dads choosing to do what is right and expected in their position as father.

My feelings toward my parents are evidenced by an example that comes to mind. Through the years, when I would buy greeting cards for my parents for various occasions, I would for the most part steer clear of the cards declaring great admiration for all their sacrifice and love, because these cards said things I just did not feel. I did buy a few of them when I believed it was what I should do, but then realized that if I did not feel it, there was no sense in saying it. So cards I bought at this point carried a vague message. This was one of the first indications that something was amiss in the relationship between my parents and me.

Chapter Seventeen

Old Problems Resurface

I have memories as a small child of a time when I thought a lot of my mother and of a time when I even looked up to her. I wanted to be just like her. I would enjoy watching her get ready to go somewhere, trying on her shoes and wishing I could look just like her in the clothes she wore. These feelings and actions could have led to attachment between my mother and me. However, that period in my life was very short-lived. The pattern my mother almost always portrayed was of disgust and an unwelcoming spirit, which made me feel like an intrusion in her life. She did not encourage me to be close to her, and the predominant memory I have of her was coldness and pushing me away. It felt like I bothered her greatly, and my presence was a burden to her.

The intense rejection I experienced diminished any desire to imitate my mother's appearance and later evolved into a strong mindset that I did not want to be like her at all. I was unable to spend my preschool years building a relationship with her. During the school-age years, even though she was physically present in my life, her actions prevented any closeness from developing, which also made it unlikely that an attachment would be built. The potential joy of a normal, functional relationship between my mother and me quickly diminished into hurt and wounding and faded away into feelings of rejection and neglect. I felt like an unattached object dangling outside the family circle with no sense of belonging.

Dad's family role did nothing but compound the problem of dysfunction. His main contribution to my life was monetary. He had a job to provide only the very basics of food, shelter and clothing. In Dad's mind, holding down a job completely fulfilled his obligations as a father. This left me no chance to grow any sort of relationship with him. It also offered no opportunity for Dad to instill other necessities of a healthy life, such as security, stability, or emotional, spiritual, or social growth. Providing only the things necessary for physical survival leaves several other equally necessary realms of child development totally unattended to. However, even the basics of food and clothing for our family were provided partly by my maternal grandparents. There were several years in which Grandma Ada bought all my school clothes. In order for us to have enough food, my grandparents gave us meat, vegetables, and milk produced on their farm. One time, the only food in the house was rice and milk. The milk from the farm was at least a week old and had spoiled. Dad was gone for the day, and the rest of us ate rice and bad milk. That night, like clockwork, we all in succession developed a stomachache. First it was my mother, then me, then my brother, and finally that night, even our dog got sick.

Money was tight, and we enjoyed very little entertainment. But there was one night when Dad decided we could go to the movie theatre. *Mary Poppins* was showing at the walk-in theatre on Main Street. On this specific night, my cousins were with us. Dad's second sister was in the hospital. My parents were babysitting her two children—one of these cousins was the "doll buggy" boy. I believe had it not been for my aunt's kids being with us, Dad would have never had the idea to go to the movies. He did not do things like that for us. We sometimes went to the drive-in movies—it was one charge per car. But we did not go to the walk-in movies because they charged per person.

Whatever the reason for us going, I was extremely excited. I really wanted to see *Mary Poppins* and could not believe I was getting to go—and it was even Dad's idea. We got to the ticket booth, and even after taking money from his coin collection, Dad did not have enough money to pay admission for my parents, my brother and me, and my two cousins. Seeing *Mary Poppins* was still a dream as we walked away and went back home. If my cousins were not along, Dad would have had enough for our family to see the show. But if my cousins were not along, we would not have gone anyway. Either way, I was not to see *Mary Poppins* at this time. I have seen the movie since, but am sure it will never have the intrigue and memorable excitement it would have had for me at six years old in the movie theatre.

As with entertainment, eating out was something our family almost never did. Each year, Grandma Bessie gave my brother and me five dollars for our birthday. I decided one year, when I was about seven, that I wanted to spend my birthday money at the drive-in. Since I was not old enough to go alone, if I wanted to eat out, I would have to buy dinner for the whole family. With five dollars today that would be impossible, but in 1966, five dollars was worth something. I was able to buy burgers, fries, and drinks for our family of four with only five dollars. We ate at a local drive-in called The Dog 'N Suds. My experience from this decision was that giving to others could be a real blessing. It was a great treat, and one I will always remember. Even at a very young age, I was very interested in this type of restaurant. Since God gives His children the desire of their heart, maybe this experience is partly how my husband and I, years later, came to own and operate two McDonald's restaurants of our own.

In spite of doing what I could to find some enjoyment, everyday life with my parents was mostly unpleasant. It was not long after the remarriage that the dysfunction from before began to crop back up. Dad returned to his old ways of womanizing and being uninvolved with our family. I believe this was the reason that money was tight. Dad did what he wanted, and again my mother was left to deal with the entire burden of raising a family. She should not have been the only one trying to make our family work and was extremely angry with no real wonder why. My mother was doing everything regarding raising my brother and me, and Dad only earned a paycheck. He was in no way a dad to us. My mother could not handle this pressure and remain sane. She was able to continue on by using denial as a coping method, not realizing that denying the hurt she currently experienced coupled with the entire past trauma only led to bouts of uncontrollable anger.

Denial used as a coping method for past and current trauma is a dangerous way to live. Denying that things happened only skews your perception and outlook on life. The past is always there waiting for you to acknowledge its presence. This is apparent in every reaction you have to life. One reaction to denial and repression is anger. Even though my mother was the one most likely to display fits of anger and rage, Dad was not immune to exhibiting his own repressed feelings. His anger would be targeted mostly at my mother, usually blaming her for his shortcomings. They would fight loudly and abusively, displaying much wrath between them. I remember one night, when I was around seven years old, they were so loud that I could not sleep. I got up to steal an undetected peek, only to see them sitting in the living room with a gun on the armrest. I ran back to bed terrified there would be another experience like when Billy Jeff was shot. The anger and yelling continued for a while, and then there was silence after Dad stormed out of the house, slamming the door as he left. At least they were both alive. These outbursts of anger happened often. However, this is one I remember in the most detail because of the gun and the language I heard with this fight. It felt like they could be mad enough and out-of-control enough to shoot each other.

With these incidents, I felt the hurt and loss more intensely of being ripped away from the security of Grandma Ada into this new living arrangement with my parents. I was school-age at this time, and I not only had to move into a hostile, angry house with a lot of fighting, but I had to start a whole new phase of life with the beginning of first grade. In the mid 1960s, most children did not attend kindergarten. At this time, kindergarten was more like a babysitting service and was not required. Starting school also prevented any attachment from happening between my mother and me. She continued to push me away rather than try to keep me close.

Feeling secure at home and knowing there was support at home no matter what I faced in the world was always missing for me. Grandma was not a part of my everyday life anymore, and I had to learn to deal with all these new experiences with no one to come home to and receive support from. There was no one I felt a connection with. My life consisted of going to school and being in bed by eight p.m. every night. There was no time to build an attachment with my mother, not that she felt it was something of vital importance anyway. She did not seem to notice there was nothing ever built between us. Possession and ownership or just being my mother did not build attachment and relationship. With no effort on her part to care emotionally, attachment never happened for me. She did not try to make me feel loved, secure, or stable. I never believed there was a soft place for me to land or a place to receive unconditional love.

I also felt like my brother got the better deal since he was two years younger and did not have to start school yet. He spent time with our mother, which was something I never had an opportunity to do. But this gave our mother what she had been working for—a chance to connect with her son. She did get my brother back and fought to begin fixing the attachment problem with him. It even seemed from her actions and things she said that she wanted her son back more than she really wanted for our family to be reunited. She got her son back, but she never really got her daughter, at least emotionally, the way she thought she did. Throughout the time she spent mending things with my brother, she never noticed that I too was not attached to her. For me, things were very different, with my school routine continuing on day after day, month after month, year after year. I never felt close to my mother, and my relationship with Dad was virtually nonexistent. There was rarely a time that he was a source of support or even offered a feeling of security; he was a disengaged parent. Dad lived as he pleased. He was not accountable to God, or to my mother, or to his children. He lived in rebellious disobedience, causing hurt, damage, and pain to those he was responsible to protect, care for, and provide for emotionally, spiritually, socially, and physically. Dad neglected our needs to meet his own.

Chapter Eighteen

The Worst Part of Childhood

The most unsettling, hurtful, and damaging period of my life came between the ages of five and ten. Even though I had experienced many traumatic circumstances during my first five years of life, I could count on the emotional support of Grandma Ada to help me through the turmoil. But now it was different. Living with my parents again felt no different from moving in with two strangers.

After leaving the security of Grandma and the farm, I moved with my reunited family into a new house in a new neighborhood in a different city. It was a neighborhood common in the 1960s, consisting of rows of houses that all looked basically the same, with only minor distinctions between them. Our house was the first in a row of six. My memories of growing up in this house were mostly unpleasant and unhappy. It is not a place I have ever longed to return to or a past I wish to recollect. The best thing about that house was its location—the church I would later attend was nearby. Really, all I looked forward to during this period of my life was visiting Grandma on the farm.

My parents' behavior led to many problems in my young life. The human contact was impersonal; I never felt important to them. Healthy talk and nonverbal communication between us was greatly lacking, but probably just as damaging were the absence of security and any feeling of stability, warmth, and love. Neither parent was capable of showing affection to each other or to their children. Hugs were mostly nonexistent. Parents need to promote feelings of emotional connection, essential for attachment and healthy growth of their children. I felt disconnected at home, and to make the emotional upheaval even worse, I had to start school at this time of great disruption and turmoil. My foundation was less than secure in my home life, and I was sent off into a whirlwind of new experiences, new people, new schoolmates, and new challenges that I was not ready for. It felt like the proverbial rug had been pulled out from under me. Without Grandma as part of my everyday life, I had to learn to deal with all these new experiences with no one to count on for understanding, empathy, and love to help me through the misplaced feelings I experienced daily. But I coped with it all as best a five-year-old could.

In addition to the struggles at school, there was an extremely unpleasant bus ride. Our stop was the final one on the way to school because our neighborhood was new. The bus was loaded with kids of all ages from grades one through twelve. When the bus finally arrived for us, the seats were all full, and if there was a seat, it was only because someone had saved it. I knew none of these kids, so no one saved me a seat. High-school students filled the seats while the grade-school children stood during the long trip to school.

I made this unpleasant bus trip daily, only to get to school and face the anger and unfriendly disposition of my first-grade teacher. She could be demanding and short on patience, and in many ways was very similar to my mother. For now, home life, the schoolroom, recess, and the bus ride were all extremely unpleasant, and all provoked a knotted, twisted, sick feeling in my stomach. This kind of transition from the security of Grandma to my current plight would be hard even for an adult to make, much less a five-year-old. I had access to no one capable of listening with compassion and empathy to the feelings generated by these new upsetting circumstances. My mother seemed unable to understand my needs or feelings. There was no soft place for me to land and nowhere to receive unconditional love.

There was also a particular friend who came into my life during this tumultuous time. She began first grade the same year and was in my classroom. Her dad and mine were acquaintances; her family had moved into the same neighborhood we lived in. With this girl, I use the term "friend" very loosely. She was really in no way a true friend to me. I needed a real friend, and this girl was only happy building herself up and putting others down. She came by this behavior naturally—her mother built her up so high no one could compare or come close to what she thought of herself. She reacted by exercising her perceived superiority over others she came in contact with, especially anyone younger than her. And I happened to be younger—only fifty-two days younger, but younger nevertheless, which gave her reason to gloat. In her opinion, being fifty-two days older definitely made her wiser and better. She was such a poisonous influence that later in adulthood, her younger sister had to deal with emotional problems partly due to this girl's actions. As a child, I remember thinking how glad I was that she was not my sister. At least I could get away from her, but her poor sister could not.

This narcissistic girl, influenced by her mother, believed she was God's gift to the world and no one could measure up to her. But behind her back, people often told me how much they disliked her and asked why I was her friend. I truly felt that being her friend was not my choice; I had no part in making that decision. Our parents were friends, and we lived in the same neighborhood. This friendship was forced on me without regard to the toxic influence it brought to my life. My parents thought it was such a perfect setup, but it was not. This girl brought another aspect of damage to my childhood. However, strangely enough, while at school I did find a very small sense of security in her presence, just because she was someone familiar in the crazy, hurtful world I was experiencing.

On one occasion when this girl visited my house, my mother watched secretly as we played. This girl told me, "You are a stupid head."

I said, "I am not."

She replied, "You are if I say you are."

And my mother let it go at that. She never came to my defense or reassured me that I was not stupid. But my mother did relate this exact conversation to me after I was grown. I needed her support as a child, not when I was an adult. Her observation and silence did nothing to give stability to my emotions. My mother was not my advocate. She let this girl call me names; she watched and never said a word. Why did my mother do nothing? Why did she allow me to be treated disrespectfully? As my parent, she had an obligation to protect me, especially after personally witnessing the damaging interaction.

My mother missed a golden opportunity to build an emotional connection with me. She needed to tell me at a young vulnerable age that I should not believe this girl's lies. I am sure this conversation was hurtful because I know how my "friend" affected my emotions and self-image. My mother did nothing to counteract the false thought planted by this girl who perceived she was such a superior being. I know for a fact that my self-esteem would have been better developed had I never known this person. I had a nickname for her, over four decades ago, before the computer age. Then, the nickname was nothing bad and all in fun. But my husband finds it amusing that in today's computer world that nickname now means worthless, unwanted e-mails.

Uncomfortable, emotionally damaging experiences happened at school as well. My first-grade teacher was very similar to my mother, with an out-of-control temper. Her hot temper would surface at the slightest provocation, just like my mother's. One day, during the first few weeks of first grade, my mother gave me ten cents to spend at the candy store during recess and failed to mention I should go *after* lunch. At age five, there was no difference between ten a.m. recess and lunchtime recess. So a friend and I went to the candy store during the ten a.m. recess. We bought two grape snow cones. We had not even returned to the playground when our teacher met us on the street and slapped the snow cones out of our hands. The whole first grade and the people who worked at the candy store watched as the snow cones splattered on the street. The teacher scolded us for not knowing better than to go to the candy store at that time of day. The "friend" who lived in our neighborhood could not wait to tell my mother what happened. Guess it made her feel so smart—she was notorious for putting me down to make herself look good. My mother said, "Oh, I should have remembered to tell you to go to the candy store *after* lunch, not before."

From this experience with my first-grade teacher, I deduced it was normal for women around my mother's age to act angry and frustrated. This irrational behavior seemed to hit me from all directions. I wondered, was anyone except my grandma gentle and loving?

This first-grade teacher could be very frightening, especially to small children. She would paddle us if we could not begin reading in the correct place during reading time. If she called on us and we did not know exactly where to start reading, we would have to come up in front of the entire class, lean over, and receive a spanking. This was one thing I never let happen to me. I was terrified of having to go in front of the class for a spanking and made sure I never lost my place in reading. I did not like it when my mother spanked me, and I sure did not want a public spanking by the teacher. I remember feeling greatly stressed during reading time. School felt like home. I was thrown into another group of strangers who did not really care for me and were incapable of understanding the hurt I was living with. At age five, I did not know why I felt like I did or understand that not everyone felt frightened and insecure. Nor did I comprehend how bad my circumstances were or that what I was feeling was very abnormal.

The start of school came with another childhood ritual I disliked immensely: bedtime at eight p.m. Maybe eight p.m. is not that extraordinary for a young child's bedtime. But I probably hated it so much because of how intensely I felt Dad used it as a way to get rid of me rather than caring for my welfare. It was Dad's rule imposed only for his convenience, not for my good. This was a no-exceptions rule—another rule for parent control and preference. I believe if I had felt secure, loved, and cared for, I would have gladly complied. But I did not agree happily to this rule. I was not ready to go to bed that early, but my protests did little good. Dad was very adamant about his rule, which I later learned was so important because he wanted to spend time with our mother without the kids around. Remembering how I felt then and now knowing the underlying circumstances, the following sums up perfectly Dad's demeanor: "Suck it up, kid! I don't care how your world hurt today, I don't care who hurt you, and I don't care how you feel. I just want to have sex with your mother, and I want you out of the way at eight o'clock." My mother complied with Dad's wishes; she too cared nothing for how I felt. If I dared to disagree about bedtime, I was threatened with the belt. But Dad never spanked me even once; this is consistent behavior for an uninvolved, undisciplined dad. God chastens and loves His children. It should be no different with a loving earthly father.

After the eight p.m. turmoil, I went to bed each night feeling sick inside about facing the next day. There was a cloud of dread that loomed over me for several years. I cried a lot during these times, most times silently but other times with loud screaming and yelling. Just to get me to shut up, my mother would finally come to my room for a while. But because of Dad's plan to get me out of the way, this made him even madder. I think it made him hate me even more. It also probably did nothing to endear my mother to him. He regularly seemed disgusted by the whole situation. When my mother would come "console me," she just looked at the ceiling. Seems like it could have been the perfect time to talk about how I was feeling or what I needed. But again, her nonverbal message seemed to be, "Suck it up and go on—you are a human dead to feelings. I have no feelings, and you should not either." I could not trust my parents for any affection, comfort, or understanding. They were more comfortable being uninvolved and attending to their own desires than ever considering my emotional needs. I needed emotional connection not feelings of further abandonment from my parents, but bedtime at eight p.m. became a convenient excuse they hid behind.

Dad's rule for bedtime was about the only way he was involved in my school years. Dad never attended a school function for me while I was growing up. He never even drove me to school once. But Dad's brother who lived in California drove my brother and me to school at least one time. My high-school graduation was the only school function Dad showed up for.

The Unbalanced Social Life

Weekends brought more of the same disconnection from both parents. My feelings and needs did not matter; Dad would rather socialize with people I did not know. He often had company over for card games, cigarette smoking, and sometimes drinking, which continued late into the night. I felt pushed aside and thrown away, and when I protested, Dad seemed to despise me for existing. He did not tolerate my presence and would ask me to leave, saying, "This is not where you belong." I never felt included in Dad's life. He would rather feel young and irresponsible and did not want to be reminded of his responsibilities. Dad was committed to selfish priorities and had no empathy for me; he did not care how I hurt through it all. Both parents regularly caused me to feel abandoned. I wish they had put some effort into a relationship with me the way they did with strangers. I wanted to belong instead of feeling like excess baggage being shoved aside. But my protests changed nothing; there was no place for a child at these social gatherings. I was not Dad's priority. Strangers he probably does not even remember now were more important to Dad then than me.

I cried because my parents made me feel unimportant, rejected, and thrown away. Why were they so uncaring? They only wanted me to be quiet and sleep, giving them peace to play cards with their "friends". But I was clearly in a state of confusion and hurt. The turmoil should have been an indication that there was a real problem they needed to deal with. Instead, their reaction was rage, anger, and hatred because I did not cooperate with their wishes. And I could not cooperate because they did nothing to acknowledge or meet my needs.

Since I had not developed an attachment to either of my parents, there was nothing normal or emotionally healthy about my life at this time. I felt I was aimlessly floating around with no purpose, no stability, no caring, no love, and no security. My parents damaged my emotions, and I was intimidated and hurt by people I had to deal with daily at home and at school.

One Friday night during these years of turmoil, my parents decided to go partying. They could not take me and my brother with them because they were going to a bar or dance hall. So that night, Dad and one of his friends at the time took me and my brother to Grandma Ada's house. On the sixty-mile trip, Dad drove eighty miles an hour, putting the lives of his two children in danger simply because he was in a hurry to have some fun and get rid of the kids. By God's grace, we made the trip safely, but then when my parents set out to get us from Grandma's, the axle broke on the car when Dad turned a corner before leaving town. Some things seem to happen to serve the purpose of a wake-up call. Dad should have been thankful the axle did not break when he was speeding. You'd think this close call would have caused him to feel some gratitude. But even this did not change his reckless behavior. Having fun was his priority over being a dad who cared for his children. Nothing seemed to change his self-centered attitude.

In these early years, both my parents smoked. Our house was filled daily with the disgusting smell of cigarette smoke, especially at the weekend card games my parents hosted when they both smoked excessively. Their friends usually smoked too. In recent years, I have heard Dad say, "An adult should have their head examined that chooses to smoke around a child." But he makes this statement now with no thought that my brother and I were children exposed daily to his house full of cigarette smoke for most of our childhood. The thing I hated most about the cigarette smoke was having a cold and being shut up in a car with one or both parents puffing smoke; it felt miserable. I also despised it when my mother would take a puff from her cigarette, place her mouth on my nose, and blow the smoke up my nose. Yuck! My memories of my parents smoking definitely prevented me from ever developing the nasty habit.

My mother started smoking, in her early teens, with Dad before they were married. Grandma Ada pleaded with my mother not to smoke because of health concerns. My mother behaved rebelliously and heartlessly and refused to consider Grandma's pleas. She probably also thought smoking was acceptable because Grandpa smoked. In years ahead, on several occasions, Grandma mentioned this situation to me. Remembering it brought great sadness and disappointment to her life because of her concern for my mother, who had suffered with pneumonia several times as a child.

The dysfunction continued with Dad's irresponsible behavior and unwise choices. For a time, Dad "helped out" some friends from his hometown. These friends were several teenage boys who frequently came to our house on Friday or Saturday night during my early grade-school years. Dad would leave with them and return a short time later. I asked my mother why Dad left with these guys. She said he was just visiting with his friends. I later learned that Dad was buying alcohol for these young men who were minors. There was one fateful night when these boys had gotten their alcohol and did not make their sixty-mile trip back home. They had been drinking, missed a sharp curve on the road, and died in a fatal car crash. Lucky for Dad, they had not come to him this particular night for their alcohol; he had not provided their booze this time. Dad never talked about this incident, as was the case with so many other tragic things that happened. But I always held out hope that the consequences he could have faced were real enough for him to change his behavior. Dad knew the teenage boy who was driving and his dad very well. The boy's dad was grief-stricken and probably never recovered from the agonizing experience. Sin and "fun" have eternal consequences. As our preacher Stan White used to say, "Sin will always take you farther than you wanted to go, keep you longer than you planned to stay, and cost you more than you ever intended to pay." This was another incident that made an impression on me—another young teenage boy, dead from a preventable cause.

Lack of Boundaries, Lack of Security

For a child in my parents' house, there was little assurance of your possessions remaining secure. With no consistent boundaries to protect your things, others commonly used them without your permission. My most treasured possessions in my preteen years were my record player and my Glen Campbell record albums. However, my mother often used my record player without permission. She liked to play records for my cousin when she would babysit. So when I was in school, they played my record player and the baby would go through my records. This seemed perfectly normal as far as my mother was concerned. Many of the things I purchased with money I earned from babysitting got used without my permission. If I spoke up, I was made to feel selfish. However, it is normal and healthy to respect the possessions of others.

One should not have to apologize for this functional expectation of boundaries drawn.

My mother no doubt learned this dysfunctional attitude toward others' possessions from her dad. Without regard for ownership, Grandpa would control things as he pleased with no communication or consideration for the feelings of others. When I was five or six, Grandpa gave me a horse—it was a small Shetland pony. The horse was silver in color, and I named him Silver, just like in the TV show *The Lone Ranger.* I had always wanted a horse; it was like a dream come true. I had the horse to enjoy for a short period of time and then one day, when a friend of Grandpa's was visiting the farm, Grandpa sold my horse to him. The man loaded up my horse in the backseat of his car and left with it. I was heartbroken. My horse was gone, and there was little I could do about it. I dared not complain to Grandpa about anything I was feeling. Grandpa never explained what he was thinking or why he had decided to sell my horse so unexpectedly. I did learn, many years later, that Grandpa sold the horse because he heard of a small girl dying when her pony took a quick turn under the clothesline and she was fatally hurt when she fell. Grandpa should have told me why he sold my pony; at least I would have gotten a hint that he cared for me. But he was in control and could do as he pleased with no regard for the feelings or emotions of a grandchild. This is where my mother must have learned to be emotionally disconnected.

Dad, however, was not so different. Music was important to me, and it brought a form of healing to my life. Sometime before I turned ten, Dad bought an eight-track stereo player for our car. We had many eight-track tapes that I enjoyed listening to. The time came when Dad needed money more than he needed a stereo, so he sold it to my Uncle Jim. I cried and begged Dad not to sell the stereo, but he coldly, without any regard for my feelings, sold it anyway and said nothing. My uncle could see how much the stereo meant to me and consoled me by saying, "You can listen to it anytime in my pickup." My uncle always showed that he cared and had compassion, but Dad as always looked out only for number one. My feelings meant little or nothing to Dad.

Dad often threatened my brother and me with getting rid of our things. He barely tolerated our possessions and openly showed his frustration with our bicycles, dolls, and toys. He referred to our "dern bicycles" often; they were in the way of *his* things. Dad's actions taught us nothing about mutual respect. I did not particularly like looking at Dad's reloading equipment or his guns. In my opinion, these things were unnecessary and ugly to look at.

I also felt a need to protect my possessions from my brother. He often accused me of hoarding sweets—but if I did not stash some away, my brother would eat them all, and I would get none. I did not like sweets as much as he did, and he would eat everything in one day and save none for later. I constantly felt like I was in survival mode if I wanted to get certain kinds of food with my brother around. I believe this situation could in part be due to our abnormal beginnings; some of the normal, mutual respect for each other was missing. My brother many times took things that were rightfully mine and faced no consequences. And I am sure there were things I did that he was not so fond of either. There were no consistent guidelines in place to promote feelings of security.

Facing these defining circumstances from my past has uncovered underlying reasons for my behavior in regard to possessions. I sometimes have an inappropriate need even now to hold tight to my things and make sure they do not get ruined, lost, used up, or taken away. Families can pass on dysfunctional behaviors even in regard to personal belongings because of control issues and lack of structure. But understanding the reasons and defining circumstances that created those feelings about possessions makes it easier to overcome the dysfunctional behavior and move into a more truthful mindset.

Problems with Interpersonal Communication and Social Behavior

It felt many times as though I was being raised by kids. My parents often behaved immaturely. Dad often acted without regard to consequences that could and likely would follow. It also seemed on many occasions that my parents were just plain uncomfortable being who they were or living normally in the world. My mother did not seem to realize that I was not an integral part or an extension of her.

When I was a child, my mother would silence me often and make me feel inadequate to talk and speak out. Time and again throughout my growing-up years, I would be stopped in mid-sentence by my mother because she did not agree with what I was saying. This creates a learned behavior, and that is to be silent. It's embarrassing to be talking to someone and have your mother disagree and stop your conversation. She was controlling and thought she was always right. These episodes were about putting me down to lift herself up. I mostly over time would just clam up and keep everything in. It just was not worth the effort to talk; whatever I had to say was wrong in my mother's eyes. I began to feel so uncomfortable talking in front of her that somewhere along the way, the real me was mostly hidden to her. This process started after I left Grandma Ada and began living with my parents at age five. I remember the difference distinctly; I was very comfortable talking to anyone around Grandma. She encouraged me to speak and socialize and wanted to know what I thought and felt. I enjoyed growing in this social area around her, but my mother stifled me and my social growth. I believe this was due to her own insecurities, hang-ups, and need for personal significance.

Dad's immaturity also brought uncomfortable moments. One night, my parents, my brother, and I were at the grocery store. I was about six years old, and I noticed a woman with an abnormally extended abdomen. I asked my parents, "What is wrong with that lady?" Dad laughed like a kid. He seemed embarrassed, making me feel like I had asked a stupid question, and now I was embarrassed for asking. I had never seen a pregnant woman before and was depending on my parents to give me some common information. Dad was uncomfortable and so was my mother, but she finally said, "Oh, the woman is going to have a baby." They both made me feel as if I had committed a terrible sin just by asking an innocent question. Mature parents would not react to such a common question about life in this manner. I felt guilty for asking. With this reaction from my parents being more the norm than the exception, I continued to become more introverted. My parents were both uncomfortable with the topic of sex. With their behavior, you would have thought I asked them to explain the birds and the bees right there in the grocery store. And it is also ironic that at age six, I would never have connected sex with this woman's condition. Dad's embarrassment because of a pregnant woman spoke volumes about his thoughts on the subject.

Clearly, teaching was not a strong point of Dad's. He could make you feel stupid with his inappropriate laughter or nonverbal gestures. He was more into laughing and making fun rather than sharing what he knew through teaching. If I did not know something, I developed a learned behavior never to admit it to dad. This was abnormal, since I was young and learning. I should have been able to trust dad; it was his responsibility to teach me the things I did not know, not laugh at me. Maybe it made him feel smart or boosted his self-esteem, or maybe he just did not have much information to pass along. Dad could be so very childish. After many uncomfortable situations trying to learn from Dad, I withdrew. I avoided his ridicule of negative gestures, head shaking in disbelief, and humiliating laughter. He was not someone I was comfortable learning from.

I was living with hurting, immature, needy parents who were too wrapped up in their own needs and emotional deprivation to be able to give a child the basic things necessary for personal development. Therefore, the cycle of dysfunction continued. My parents still cannot see that this pattern of behavior exists as a result of their past experiences, which caused emotional wounds in their lives. They deny this truth, and therefore their past hurt continues to bubble up, begging to be resolved. Choosing to deny their emotional wounds makes healing impossible for my parents. It has become their undesirable emotional legacy, passed on to cause future hurt, pain, and wounds.

Other Hurts

My parents weren't the only source of painful experiences in my life. One of these distressing situations—involving my dog, Dusty J—happened when I was about seven years old. When I left the farm at age five, I also left behind the dog that I loved. I had attached to him because he was my completely trustworthy friend, confidant, loyal companion, and playmate. I loved him so much because he was always there for me when I lived on the farm. But my life had changed, and I missed Grandma Ada and my little dog every day. I visited them randomly.

On one visit to the farm, I was met with some of the saddest news ever. My little dog had been killed by an intruder. A big dog came to the farm one night, and Dusty J tried to defend his home. My little dog was no match for the big German shepherd. As they fought, the big dog slashed Dusty's throat. Grandpa was going to bury my dog right away, but Grandma Ada asked him to wait until the weekend. Grandma told Grandpa that I needed to say good-bye to my little dog and friend. I remember crying when I got the news. I went to where Grandpa had Dusty waiting for me. I remember the permanent snarl on his face; he definitely had died fighting. I told him good-bye, thanked him for being my friend, and said how much I would miss him. I touched him one more time. And then Grandpa and I buried him on the farm, near the fields where my little dog and I used to run and play. It felt like life was just becoming one big hurt after another. I would go on to have other pets, but I never let myself love them so deeply or get so attached to them as I was to Dusty J. I never wanted to feel this way again.

Chapter Nineteen

Emotional Pain Becomes a Physical Illness

Living in my parents' home away from Grandma Ada brought great anxiety to my life. The mental feelings of gloom, dread, and anguish that haunted me nightly came mainly from a fear of facing each tomorrow. After almost three years, this emotional abuse became a physical illness. By the age of eight, when I was in the third grade, I began to have stomachaches regularly. They would appear at times that were inconvenient for my mother, and she accused me of making it all up. She said I just did not want to go to school. It seemed real funny to her that it was always school time when I was too sick to continue on. Well, I'm sure that is how it appeared—but these feelings were very real, and I was in a lot of pain. As I have described, my home life, school, and the bus ride were all very stressful, and the anticipated stress would trigger the physical pain.

Somehow Grandpa heard that someone in our family was sick. He mistakenly thought it was my mother. So he and Grandma Ada drove to our house one night. He got there only to realize it was *just me* who was sick, and my mother was fine. He rarely drove at night, especially sixty miles. It was a big deal that he came, but I doubt he would have made the trip if he knew I was sick, not my mother. There was never any proof that he cared for me like that.

As time progressed, my condition worsened. My mother still leaned toward believing I was faking the pain, but it reached a point that even she could no longer deny there was a problem. Therefore, to my parent's dismay, doctor visits became necessary. I went through many X-rays and upper GI tests, which meant drinking great volumes of ice water and a white concoction containing barium that made things inside more visible on an X-ray. The tests were supposed to reveal a reason for the pain. But through several bouts of testing, the doctors found nothing.

The pain continued; my mother became more and more intolerant and frustrated. To her way of thinking, I should be as controllable as any inanimate object that she could manipulate however she pleased. My behavior in response to the pain was becoming out of control for her. I remember refusing to go to school because it hurt so badly. Almost anything would cause the pain to surface. Eating would sometimes make the ache so severe that I could not stand up; I would roll up in a fetal position just to endure the pain. Stressful situations also were an obvious contributor. My mother's response as she threw me around in the bathroom was, "You just need to make up your mind that you will go to school, and stop imagining this pain. They did not find anything wrong with you, and you just need to get on with life." But my pain was real. I was only eight years old, and my mother—the one person in the world who should be on my side—did not believe me. She chose to believe I had the capacity to be so conniving at this young age that I was capable of making up something so serious. It would indeed have been a great acting job for a child of eight to have made all this up and acted out the pain and torment I was living through. She did not believe me, and in response to my pain, her touch was rough, her words were harsh, and I continued to be sick. She also did not hesitate to inform me that this was a great financial burden on the family, saying, "You do not know what you are causing us to deal with." All I knew for sure at this point was that I hurt, and again she did not acknowledge my pain. She was incapable of showing empathy, understanding, or caring for how bad I felt. My parents as usual viewed this situation as all about them and focused on the problems I had created for them. They had no ability to see that I needed their help. Neither one had anything to give. In their eyes, I was a bad kid for being sick. I was bringing them hurt, pain, and stress—I should just suck it up and get over it.

Dad never once asked me how I was feeling or if I was getting better. He showed no empathy and no compassion. I got a strong feeling that he never believed I was sick at all, and it also felt like he did not care. All he cared about was how much money I was costing him. Dad's behaviors and actions conveyed his true feelings in general about me, which were: "You are no good. You are an expense to the family." I also felt many times that my parents both were nonverbally screaming, "We didn't want you anyway. You need to stop causing such a financial problem in our lives." The ironic thing about all this is that if they had cared for me as they should have, I would not have had this physical illness at all. They blamed me for being sick. But I did not just dream up this illness. My parents needed to face the truth: the damage was real because of their abnormal parenting, lack of emotional connection, and inability to feel. They chose to live in denial of it all. They left me alone to deal with the hurt they inflicted, with no parental support or comfort. I got no emotional help from them to feel better about all the turbulence and hurt I faced every day.

The turmoil continued, and I ended up back at the X-ray office going through the same terrible, uncomfortable tests as before. One day during these tests, I had reached the maximum I could handle, and sitting in the waiting room full of patients waiting for my next test, I got sick. I'm sure my mother did not appreciate this either. Then, after days of testing, they finally found what was making me so ill: I had a bleeding duodenal stomach ulcer. The day they finally found it, I remember feeling near death. I was close to unconscious from throwing up and not being able to eat, I was drained from all the tests, and my memories at this point are of feeling like I was in a cloud with blurry movement all around me. At this specific time, I really did not care what happened anymore. I could have just drifted off, and it would have felt really great. However, God was not ready to call me home at this time. When I got to the hospital, they started an IV, and I began to feel better. I was glad to hear they had finally found what was causing the pain, and there was hope that I would feel better. I also learned that the difficulty they had in finding my condition was increased because they were not looking for a bleeding stomach ulcer in an eight year old child. That was a condition usually found only in adults living stressful lives.

I was in the hospital for one week. I took medicine around the clock and had to drink half-and-half regularly night and day. Being awakened throughout the night, poked with needles, and fed an ulcer diet that was very bland was not my idea of a fun time—even though Dad said many times I was on vacation at his expense.

Dad came to visit only once during the entire hospital stay, even though he worked in town and had plenty of time to visit. Again work was his excuse for ignoring my needs, but I probably did not need him around anyway. All I remember from his one visit was the way he complained about how much my hospital stay was costing him—and that he did not think I looked very sick at all. He saw me after I had been there a few days, and then I *was* feeling better. Dad always made me feel so devalued. Those words of his still stab and wound like a knife in my chest that he twists.

This makes it very clear why two years later, God came to me, saved my soul, and became my Father. Dad lost the privilege of that position in my life because of his selfish, unconnected actions. In the future, God would heal my emotions. Even though I did not feel that Dad wanted me, God wanted me, and He wanted me to live in truth and be whole.

While I was in the hospital, I had at least two uplifting visits from the preacher of the little white church by our house. I had attended Vacation Bible School the previous two summers and knew this kind man from church. He brought words of encouragement, prayer for my healing, and also some children's books for me to read. This visit made me feel much better after Dad's visit had been so wounding.

My mother took home movies of me in the hospital. Through many years to follow, whenever these movies were viewed, Dad's comments were invariably, "She sure does not look sick, just laying up there in the hospital costing me money like she's on vacation or something." He just never got it. The money Dad cared so much about was money he intended to use to meet his selfish needs; again, he cared nothing for me. He preferred to act as though the daughter God had given him was nonexistent. I was in the hospital with a bleeding stomach ulcer because the emotional pain had manifested into a physical condition common to a person living with great stress. The fact that I was resilient and a survivor was the only reason I was still alive; it was not because of any parental support or empathy. I was living through this emotional and physical pain because Dad was not a supportive father who gave me security in life. I was very sick, but Dad preferred to believe I was just acting selfish and bad. When Dad visited me that one time, I had been in the hospital for several days, and my stomach was not constantly irritated by food; I was on an IV and taking medication around the clock. At that point, I felt much better. Dad never saw me during the worst part, so he had no point of reference for any opinion at all. His comments labeled him as a fool and were consistent with the fact that he knew nothing about me and what I was going through. Once again, the greatest truth is that he just did not care anyway. All he cared about was his money; it was never my physical or emotional health. My parents were not able to understand or feel anyone's pain but their own and coped through blame and denial.

My mother had her own version of denial to explain why I had the adult condition of a bleeding stomach ulcer at the young age of eight. She was always so good at rationalizing things and placing the fault on someone else instead of taking responsibility for her own actions. She chose to believe that I had developed an ulcer because of the teachers I had to deal with at school. She stated that they were old maids and could not understand children because they had never been married, much less had any experience with children of their own. This theory was not reflected by my grades. I had gotten almost straight As with the exception of only a few Bs each grading period. My ulcer was discovered in early May of my third-grade school year. When my mother went to my teacher, concerned that I would not be able to attend school anymore that year, she was told I had already passed the third grade a long time before because my grades were that high. My mother's other theory was that I had an "acid system" like Dad's, and it had corroded my stomach just as it had done to my teeth. I did have a few cavities. However, this was because of not brushing my teeth regularly, not an acid system. My son, who is a dentist, verified this in later years. It was too painful for my mother to face the truth about our home life. I am sure she really did not see the truth of how dysfunctional our home was. Denial was how she coped. She certainly was disconnected from my circumstances and probably never even had a clue about what I lived through.

To this day, my parents choose to deny the reality of emotional abuse becoming a serious physical condition. They are so out-of-touch with emotions and live in denial to the point that they never let themselves face what was true. They did not have the capacity to ask or care how I felt. They would not let themselves face the reality of the mental anguish present in our dysfunctional home that led to my physical condition of a stomach ulcer. Even if they do understand some of it, maybe guilt is keeping them mute on the subject, and living in denial is still more comfortable.

This was all happening in the late 1960s. It was a time when child abuse and neglect were not acknowledged as they are today. I believe my pediatrician should have referred my entire family to a counselor. It would have prevented much turmoil from continuing on into future years. There is no doubt that everyone in my family needed counseling. There was too much hurt, pain, strife, denial, and anger present for anything about our family to be called normal.

Many years later, when the time came to face the past so I could continue on in a healthy fashion, I met with my parents to discuss the things that had surfaced. My husband and counselor were also present. When I brought up this subject about my stomach ulcer and described it as one of the most hurtful times in my childhood, my mother's only response was, "It was a hard time for the whole family." She still had no compassion or empathy for me as an eight-year-old child in her care. It should have come as no surprise to me that even now, over forty years later, there was still no empathy or compassion for what I had lived through back then. It was clear that they were still more concerned about themselves; they probably still have memories of the financial burden they believe I caused them. I told Dad I believed he was so concerned about money then because he wanted extra cash to go to bars and pick up women. He looked down and gave no response.

There was no evidence of empathy, understanding, hurt, or pain that a mother and dad should feel when I explained how I felt as a child and that their dysfunctional home was the reason I had developed a stomach ulcer in the first place. It is so sad that they seemed to place a price tag on my life, and it was not even worth a ninety-seven-dollar hospital bill. I did not develop a stomach ulcer at age eight because of teachers or an acid system—it was because of the pain and rejection and dread I felt every day of my young life from ages five to eight. The stomach ulcer grew because of worry and dread over what I faced daily at home and at school. Both my parents seemed unaffected when, for the first time in my life, I was able to tell them what I lived through. I told them how I felt and explained the true cause of my stomach ulcer and how much it hurt physically and emotionally. Many times over the years, when they referred to this "ulcer" period in our lives and rationalized it away with their excuses, I would feel misunderstood and devalued. They seemed to care more for themselves than for me. It felt like they would not even try to understand, and after so many years, nothing has changed. My parents continue to believe I made up the illness. Again they live in denial of the truth. And their current stance only adds more emotional damage to the mountain of pain that continues to exist.

One thing I know for sure: childhood problems, pain, and trauma are not as hurtful if the child has a caring adult she can count on to soothe the pain away. Unfortunately, when Grandma Ada was not a constant part of my life, that stable adult relationship was nonexistent. My parents resembled immature children unable to meet a child's emotional needs, and most of the emotional abuse I experienced was inflicted by them. The emotional abuse happened because of past traumas my parents each experienced but never faced or found healing from. A great deal of their unacceptable behavior stemmed from arrested emotional development causing repressed anger, and they continually lived with hurt and lack of forgiveness. Also, their parental behavior could be categorized as childish, and their needs were more of a priority than those of their children. Having their own children with needs only frustrated them both. My parents passed a great deal of pain on to me. Emotionally, they seemed to live in their world and I in mine—we might as well have been on different planets. I felt left alone, void of adult support, and forced to get along the best I could.

Chapter Twenty

Fourth-Grade Abandonment

After the hospital experience with my ulcer, autumn arrived, school started back, and the fourth grade began. During this time, I still felt the turmoil of dysfunction. I felt pushed away by my mother, and having to go to school made it all worse. At the beginning of the year, I was having a problem in math, figuring volumes of cubes, cones, and cylinders. This was a subject I had trouble grasping. At home, I got no support or help to figure it out. Again, I was on my own to fix my problems, with no choice but to face them every day. I was teased at school because I had gained weight from the ulcer diet I had been on for several months. The friends I liked to spend time with were not in my class that year. At almost nine years old, I needed security and stability, comfort and reassurance— anything to make my life feel better and relieve the daily turmoil. My mother seemed incapable of comprehending or meeting my needs. Feeling alone and pushed away by my mother, combined with Dad's lack of involvement, made learning how to cope with life in general very difficult. The alone feeling with no help available made my stomach hurt, and the knots and churning inside prevailed again.

To deal with these upsetting feelings, I coped sometimes by withdrawing or retreating. These episodes could be triggered by hurtful words spoken by Dad or the all-too-frequent bouts of anger and rage put on by my mother, or just at random times when I felt a great need to get away from it all. My mother accused me of pouting, and she would say that I was acting just like Dad. Pouting is an act committed in order to gain recognition. "Pouting" never described me at all. I never withdrew to gain any sort of recognition from anyone. I withdrew to get away from those around me, not to solicit their attention or intervention in any way.

When life became overwhelming, I would mentally detach myself from the present situation and withdraw. I would either go to my room or just mentally go to my own world and shut everyone else out. When I had to surface, I was usually greeted with some derogatory or hurtful comment from Dad, or I would be greeted with nothing at all—just as if I did not exist. I know they were trying to show me that my behavior was totally unacceptable, but that was just their opinion. I say now that the way they emotionally abused me was totally unacceptable, and a child raised under normal circumstances does not feel the need to emotionally retreat. But in my life, there were plenty of reasons I felt a need to escape and get away from the turmoil. However, withdrawing was really just avoiding the problem; it didn't fix anything but did provide momentary peace. And the ulcer symptoms continued regularly.

All this led to more doctor visits and more stomach tests, more X-rays and more barium. I continued to live in turmoil. Emotionally, I was not healthy; I was always looking for some kind of connection, but continually received no support from either parent. I still cried out for my mother's love and attention but got nothing positive in return. I guess she just did not have love and support to give. Dad chose to be completely uninvolved, contributing zero to my emotional well-being.

During the first weeks of the fourth grade, I would regularly end up at the doctor's office. The ulcer was healed but still aggravated by the anxiety I was feeling every day. I had yet to learn this was just a lifelong condition I now had, and would have to learn how to manage it, to avoid the pain. Further tests revealed nothing new; there seemed to be no reason for my current sickness. Finally, my doctor met with my mother alone. The explanation she passed on to me regarding my condition was that there was some abnormality with my intestines causing the pain. She presented me with some pills the doctor gave her that would do the trick and make me better. I know now that these must have been sugar pills, which did absolutely nothing for my stomach. I also know our family needed Christian counseling. Life can never go on normally with so much repressed hurt, pain, anger, and traumatic life-changing events swept under the rug and denied.

I have a vivid memory of one day when I did not want to go to school, and my mother insisted that I go anyway. I was still trying to achieve a meaningful relationship and a stable adult presence at home, especially since this period of my school years caused me to feel so alone and disconnected. I just wanted to feel of some significance or importance to my mother somehow, some way. On this particular day, it had become late enough that I missed the bus. So my mother said in a controlling tone, "You will go to school today; you are not sick enough to stay home." She showed no regard for my feelings. The important thing to her was that she won, and I would go to school. Her favorite thing to say was, "I'm the parent, you are the child." Control was important to her. Anyway, she believed I was making up all this sickness, so she would take the bull by the horns, and I would do as she said for my own good. So she drove me to school, promising to walk me to class when we got there. But though she did walk me inside, it was partway only. She then disappeared.

There were a lot of people in the halls, and she slipped away before I got to my classroom. At my classroom door, I realized she was nowhere around. I trusted her to do as she promised. But she had abandoned me in the crowd and was gone; all I could do was cry and say, "I want my mother." I felt like she just wanted to be rid of me, and whatever measure was necessary to get that accomplished was what she would do. This situation prevented our class from beginning school that day in the usual manner. My teacher got another teacher from across the hall to watch our class while she went to talk to the principal. When the other teacher was there, I continued to scream and shout, "I want my mother." I remember the sixth-grade teacher telling me, "I want my mother too, but she is dead." As far as it felt to me at this point, my mother might as well be dead too. I realize now that I did not simply want my mother's presence that day. I wanted a mother who would really *be* a mother and care about me and give me security, love, acceptance, value, and belonging. I was lacking in all those things from the person who called herself my mother.

After my teacher met with the principal that morning, he called my mother and asked her to come back to the school. The principal was a kind man. I liked him, and I felt he cared about my situation. He talked to me with my mother present. He promised me some things as far as school went. But he could not give me what I really needed; he could not fix the dysfunction I was living with. Always, after this encounter, the principal was my friend. I felt a real connection with him because he cared about how I felt. I think he perceived something was going on in my life beyond what he could see on the surface. He seemed to know it was something way deeper, a more serious underlying problem than what he was being told. He showed an interest in me years after I left grade school. He even got acquainted with my future husband during our dating years. I had made a connection with a caring adult at school, and this did a great deal to heal what I was living through. My mother even said, "That one visit with the principal did more to get you better than all the doctor visits that year combined." Well, she was right about that. But without knowing what she was saying, she gave credibility and proof to the fact that my condition was due to emotional abuse causing a physical ailment. The help I got from the principal was emotional healing, not physical healing. I ended the fourth grade with an A in math. I got only two Bs on my report card the entire year, the rest were As.

Another bright spot in this year was the healing that music brought to my life. I especially liked Glen Campbell. With money I earned from babysitting, I purchased many of his albums and spent many hours listening to those records. I also watched *The Glen Campbell Goodtime Hour* every Sunday night. This was the time in my life that I developed an infatuation for guitar players. Glen Campbell was especially talented, and I loved watching him play. I also joined his fan club and received an autographed glossy eight-by-ten picture and a guitar pick with his name on it. I had always loved music, but it became even more important to me this particular year in my life when I was nine years old. I found it to be very healing for my emotions, and I could escape to wherever the songs traveled—Galveston, Phoenix, Wichita.

I dreamed of seeing Glen Campbell in person. And many years later, in March 2010, my dream became a reality when I attended a concert in the Dallas-Fort Worth area with my husband and sister. Featured at this concert was none other than Glen Campbell, along with the Beach Boys and B. J. Thomas. It took me back to the days when I listened to those old familiar songs as a child. I know this was another blessing God allowed me to live out for real!

Chapter Twenty-One

More Experiences of Emotional Abuse

Dad was cold, unapproachable, and hurtful during my childhood, with the most damage being done between the ages of five and ten. He has told others in recent years that "if you would have known me during this period in my life, you would not have liked me either." There are many examples of his actions causing pain and damage to my brother and me as young children when we needed his comfort but received only his wrath. He said things that no parent should even think much less say to their child. It did not appear to be Dad's goal to raise children in a manner that gave them security, stability, belonging, love, acceptance, or structure. He was handy to throw around words that hurt but never acted like a father by setting healthy boundaries and providing guidance for his children. Dad knew little about nurturing healthy emotions. Children are a gift from God, and a parent should not look at them with contempt and scorn because they have dared to invade a parent's selfish world. Loving fathers do not look at their children the way Dad looked at me.

There were times when Dad told me and my brother at the dinner table, "I'll be glad when you kids are grown and gone, so I won't have to feed you anymore." This statement coming from your dad really removes any feeling of belonging and takes away any importance you needed to feel in his life. Recalling the way Dad's choice of words made me feel as a child made a definite difference in the way I chose to relate to my own children. I consciously made it very evident that they were wanted, and it would be a bittersweet day when they grew up and moved out to begin their own adult lives. I wanted my children to know without a doubt that I loved them and they mattered to me. I focused on conveying that message to them, and there may have been times where I overcompensated because of how my childhood felt. Through the years after I was married, whenever my parents have been at our house eating with us, Dad's comments made years ago have crept into my mind. With them comes a sick feeling of hurt and disgust—and, now, an awareness that these things need to be faced and healed rather than left to cause random pain. Dad never seemed to be aware of the pain he caused and has yet to acknowledge it and bring healing to those he hurt. In those bygone days when everyday life as a child hurt unnecessarily, the pain was due in great part to Dad's opinion that no one mattered more than him.

Dad had a lack of compassion for sickness. One day when I was sick with a cold, Dad dished out more scorn than caring. I made the mistake of coming to dinner with a runny nose, which was aggravated by the cigarette smoke always present in our house. I had sniffled only a few times when Dad said, "If you can't stop that, then you can get on out of here." I went to my room without eating lunch that day, and neither Dad nor my mother seemed to care. Guess that just left more food for Dad. They never checked on me the rest of the day. Where was the caregiver here? I have no memory of ever receiving comfort from Dad when I was sick or otherwise; he made no time to care how I felt about anything. It felt so many times as though Dad was just disgusted because he even had to tolerate me being around. He showed no love and was usually hateful and uncaring. There was no emotional nourishment from him. I truly believe during this period in my life that if I had dropped dead on the spot, Dad would have celebrated, at least to himself.

Another time I experienced Dad's hurtful actions, his lack of understanding, and his inducement of willful hurt had to do with the torn and scratchy kitchen chairs we had. All the kitchen chairs needed repair with the exception of one. I made the mistake of sitting in the good chair—it was at my place at the table. Dad told me that I needed to make sure my mother got the one that was not torn; it was for her, not me. So I traded chairs with my mother. My mother stood up, took the chair, and never said a word. Again, there was no sense of value given to my existence. I dared not feel worthy enough to think of sitting in a chair that was not ripped and scratchy. I really had not even picked the chair on purpose, but Dad made me feel that I was being inconsiderate of my mother's needs, and he devalued me in the process.

Another bad memory I have that happened regularly after dinnertime was Dad forcing me to wash dishes while he sat at the table and watched. He would say, "Your mama should not have to do everything." He sure never lifted a finger to help her out around the house. Guess he thought he was making points with her by making me do the dishes. I believe if he wanted to make points with my mother, he should have tried being faithful to her. I believe he used me as his scapegoat to ease his guilt. It also would have been better for the emotional health of us all if he had done the dishes sometimes. I never respected him for being so uninvolved and thinking he had any right to be a dictator with me. His demands and rules were never for my good; everything he did was for his selfish benefit in some way. And if he wanted me to do the dishes, why did he have to sit and watch? I never rebelled or talked back; I was a compliant child. However, I still feel hurt to think about those times, and I really hate to do dishes to this day. Now, in my own life, I realize that doing dishes is really not such a bad job, but I'm doing them for my family—not Dad. Still, though, sometimes when I'm doing dishes, the sick memories revive and rekindle unpleasant feelings.

Dad's actions were many times inappropriate and damaging, and the things I remember him saying were offensive and hurtful as well. Some direct quotes from Dad to me were:

"Are you proud of yourself?"

"You think you are something special, don't ya?"

"Think you are hot stuff, huh?"

His tone of voice would add to the insult. My answer to Dad regarding all these questions was "*No!*" I regularly got the feeling from Dad that I was nothing special. During my growing-up years, he gave me no reason to believe in myself. Things he should have said, just for example, are:

"I'm proud of you."

"You mean a lot to me."—But, these feelings were not in dad's heart.

Dad regularly called my brother a "hoop-dee-doo feller," and the way he would say this was sometimes very degrading. I am sure this did very little to build my brother's self-esteem and self-worth, but it did a lot to increase his self-doubt. I guess Dad was so uncomfortable with himself that he had to bring others down too by saying hurtful things.

A caring, loving father's presence is essential to a healthy family. But loving and caring did not describe my dad; he was absent emotionally. His influence contributed nothing to help me reach my potential. Dad was prone to spend his extra time, effort, and money on others outside the family. Women called our house looking for Dad. With the selfish lifestyle he lived, it is no wonder he was so mean and cruel. Through actions, attitudes, and behaviors, Dad proved his family was not his priority.

The Things Dad Did Not Say

Dad never told me I was pretty or mentioned any other positive affirmations back when I was a child who needed to hear those words from him. Since Dad never took an active part in my life or showed that I mattered to him, I was left to fill in the blanks on my own. The blanks I filled in were that I had little value in his eyes, I was not worth his time, he did not love me, he thought I was ugly, and he did not want me in the first place. When he looked at me, his reaction felt more like one of disgust than admiration in any form. Years in the future, I saw him look at his granddaughters this same way.

I was almost grown before Dad showed any real interest in my life. But his change of attitude was too little and too late. The day I graduated from high school, he finally seemed proud of me. After all, I was wearing the gold cords and graduating with honors, ranked seventeenth out of 523 students in my graduating class. My high-school graduation was the one and only school function Dad ever attended. At this time, I was dating my future husband, who I would marry five months after graduation. Dad's minimal attention finally came at a time when I really needed very little from him anymore. Years later, Dad did finally tell me I was pretty. But it came with an inclusion of my sister—he said, "Oh, my beautiful girls." The problem then was, first of all, how long it was in coming; and second, the fact that it was not personal for either my sister or me. Also at this time, my sister and I were not his responsibility any longer. We both had been married for several years.

My childhood was a time when Dad should have been seizing the opportunity to teach me many things. He should have been actively participating in my life in general. He should have been exploring the many different aspects of life a dad can share with his daughter. Dad should have been getting to know me instead of making me feel he was ashamed of me. However, it does seem when looking back that there was only one goal he did have for me: to get married and move out of his house. I got the feeling many times from him that I was not ideal and would have problems attracting a guy who would want to marry me. Throughout my childhood years, I was left to grow up without his involvement, learning as best I could with no guidance from him. Then, however I turned out, he hoped it would be good enough to "catch" a husband. For me, childhood was not spent dreaming about my future because I was only trying to survive my present.

Dad did not believe in me or encourage me to pursue worthwhile goals. He just wanted to be free of his responsibilities. Then he would no longer have to foot the bill for my existence. It is sad that there were no feelings toward me coming from a dad's caring, loving heart. It never felt like Dad thought much of me. But I happily discovered that Dad's opinion of me was not the norm; I had many male friends who thought a lot of me. Dad did not realize his opinions were in the minority. However, I believe it is unacceptable for a young girl to have to guess about her self-worth, especially when her dad is physically present in her life. It is confusing and dangerous for a teenage girl to have no anchor of protection at home.

Dad's lack of interest in my life continued when dates arrived to pick me up. If Dad was even around, his only communication when I introduced them was a grunt and a nod, and then he would look the other way. He was not in the least bit concerned with who I dated, nor did he care to take the time to learn anything about the guy. It felt more like he thought, *I have no interest in Debbie, take her on out of here. Do what you will with her, it doesn't matter to me.* My husband said his first meeting with Dad was very uncomfortable and noncommunicative, and dad's disinterest was very noteworthy. To me, this behavior showed I was not valuable to dad. Again, the words whirling around in my mind from years earlier, which he had spoken to my brother and me, were, "I'll be glad when you kids are grown and gone, so I don't have to feed you anymore." These words, along with Dad's behavior in regard to me dating, validated my impression that he thought very little of me and really did look forward to the day when I left home.

There were many other situations in which Dad did not act like an adult, caring parent. Often during the years, Dad failed to defend me but should have. At our house, I parked my car in the front yard where I was told to park. One day, Dad's sister came to visit. She said to Dad, "I am sure you have a lot of trouble getting your grass to grow with kids parking their cars in your yard."

Dad said "Yeah, it is pretty difficult with so many kids parking around here all the time."

I parked in the yard because Dad told me to. But Dad did not defend me; he took his sister's sympathy and put me down. His response was in line with his previous pattern that kids bother him, and once again he probably thought, "I will be glad when they are grown and gone." I could not even depend on Dad to defend me to his sister when I was doing what I was supposed to. He acted as though I was doing something wrong because that is how his sister perceived it. An adult would have stood up for how we did things at our house and told his sister I was doing what he gave me permission to do. Instead, he agreed with her that I was doing something to cause him trouble and let her console him with his problem, just as a child would do. He never stood up for me like a real father would.

Dad had a friend with a daughter my age. This friend often compared me to his daughter. She was very skinny, and I was not. When Dad's friend talked to other neighbors, he summoned his daughter and me over so he could compare us in front of the neighbor. He would say, "Can you believe they are the same age?" and would add that his daughter was even a little older than me. I was bigger than her, but I was not bigger compared to my classmates in general. His daughter was too skinny, and I do not know why he was so proud of it. I also do not believe such things are relevant at all. Dad's friend, pointing out our differences, had a negative effect on me. I should have been able to count on Dad to protect me, not push me off with people who were only interested in building themselves up by putting me down. Dad should have been more involved in what I was experiencing, but he was uninvolved and unaware of how his friends treated me. Even when he did witness this behavior, he was silent. My self-image was being formed, and Dad's positive, functional involvement in that process was almost nonexistent. Dad did not defend me; as usual, I was not worth his effort. This also said to me that this man's friendship meant more to Dad than I did, and however his friend treated me was okay with Dad.

Years later, after I was married, Dad's friend and his wife were in their forties and expecting another child. I commented about how old they would be when the child was grown, and Dad strongly reprimanded me for what I said to his friend. This hurt again because he never reprimanded his friend for the way he put me down as a child. Again, Dad clearly cared more for other people's feelings than mine. Dad seemed to think I had no right to live and breathe or have an opinion but his friend did.

Then more years into the future, when Doug and I and my parents met with my counselor, Dad told of how he did not hear the words "I love you" from his dad, but he knew that his dad loved him because of how he would fight for him. Dad said that if anyone talked bad about any of Grandpa's kids, he would fight. I never saw Dad fight for me, ever. I told him that he did not fight for me or stand up for me, and Dad could not argue that fact. The truth is that Dad was too uninvolved to know what was going on with me, much less know if I needed him to defend me. So Dad never said he loved me and never showed it either. Throughout my childhood, I cannot recall even one memory of Dad hugging me.

I could not depend on Dad for support and stability. I had no confidence that I could count on him at all. He acted like a child and ran from his responsibilities as a dad. I could not trust him for comfort and reassurance. He let me down instead of supporting me. He was sand, and I needed a rock.

Dad's Siblings

In addition to the hurt Dad brought into my childhood, there were many situations when his second sister added to the confusion. This sister seemed to think her kids were superior to me and worked her manipulative ways, preventing me from getting too close to Grandma Bessie. One time, she asked me to go to the rodeo with her family, but then prevented me from going by saying my clothes were too dirty. Grandma Ada had definite reservations about letting me go anywhere with my aunt and was glad when she called with the flimsy excuse of my clothes being too dirty to go with them. Grandma Ada quickly came to get me and found that the "dirt" on my clothes was just one small spot of ketchup, which was not even noticeable on a navy-blue shirt. It seemed that asking me to the rodeo was just a gesture by my aunt to make herself look agreeable, but then she had to come up with a reason to withdraw her invitation.

There were a few rare times when I was allowed to spend time with Grandma Bessie without Dad's second sister around. I liked Grandma, and we could have connected and built a real relationship, but my aunt would never allow that to happen. From her actions, it seemed she believed that Grandma Bessie belonged only to her children, and I had no business interfering with that. She treated me like a second-class relative and always promoted her children over me. But there were a few times when I got to attend church with Grandma Bessie—just me and her. In fact, she was the first person in my life who told me about Jesus and how I should trust Him. Grandma did not drive and walked everywhere she went. She and I walked up the hill from her house to church together. This is a great memory I have of Grandma Bessie; she would hold my hand as we walked along. She talked to me and treated me special when it was just me and her. These times were very different from the times when my aunt was present with her manipulative ways.

During one visit to Grandma Bessie's, when my aunt and her children were present, my aunt said, "You are lazy and fat, just like your dad." She continued on, trying to give the impression that she was saying this out of concern for me. But I know it was just because she did not like me being around Grandma Bessie. She took every opportunity to put me down or belittle Dad to me. I have been told by professionals that her input could have caused me to become anorexic. But I really believe there was no danger in that, due to the fact that I thought very little of this aunt. It really did not matter to me what she said or what her opinion was about anything.

Every year our family had to spend some time during Thanksgiving and Christmas at her house—no surprise, this was Dad's decision. At these family gatherings, I would witness Dad buddying up with his second sister. They would regularly make announcements to the family and brag amongst themselves about how perfect they were. They said they were the only perfect ones and felt bad for others who were not perfect. There was a behavioral pattern here with this aunt; she thought everything should revolve around her, and no one else was as important as her. For some reason, Dad felt obligated to build her up and feed her false assumption. Guess it was some weird type of bonding between them. But as a young child, I found this announcement of perfection from them to be strange, and from my perspective their statements were totally false. I knew for sure she did not believe Dad was perfect at all, though she'd only say that when he was not around.

This aunt obviously had many problems and hang-ups of her own to behave the way she did. It seemed she had some great insecurity and a need to control Grandma Bessie in an unhealthy way. When Grandma Bessie died, Dad's second sister stepped in to claim all Grandma's possessions, even though Grandma had three other children. I do not feel cheated by the material aspect of it—if my aunt wanted to take the stuff, I say let her have it. But I do feel greatly cheated because this aunt was allowed to prevent the growth of a real relationship between me and Grandma Bessie. I was her first granddaughter.

I have often wondered if this manipulative aunt was part of the reason for Dad's arrested development and dysfunctional family behavior. Dad had three siblings—two sisters and one brother. I found my other aunt, Dad's oldest sister, to be a great friend and a loving support. She was a hairdresser by trade, and she was the one who cut my hair throughout my childhood. I never went to a beauty shop to see anyone other than my aunt until I was married. Most times, however, my aunt would cut my hair at our house when she visited. I would ask her to trim my hair, and Dad would scold me for asking. But my aunt would tell Dad to leave us alone, and she would always cut my hair. My aunt knew haircuts were something Dad did not have money for. Dad's oldest sister was someone who I did emotionally connect with. She treated me with respect and showed an interest in me as a person. She never made me feel like an insignificant kid.

I also liked Dad's brother. After his high-school graduation, my uncle left the small town of Fort Sumner, New Mexico, joined the Navy, and eventually ended up living in California. His return visits back home were very infrequent. As a young child, I do remember feeling very intimidated by his presence, but as the years passed, he became a real caring support also. This was the uncle who took me to school one day when I was in third grade, which was one more time than Dad ever took me to school. Dad was home every day but never took me anywhere, and he felt for certain he had no time to drive me to school.

During my uncle's years in California, he too was a business owner. He knew the frustrations of the job. There was one time when I was upset with some of the things I had to deal with at our McDonald's restaurants, and I talked to him. This turned into a blessing, because my uncle could relate to me and cared about how I was feeling. He gave more empathy and understanding than I ever got from Dad. My uncle said to me, "Your employees only think they know what is best for them, because if any of them had to spend just one day in your shoes, they would be dead." Owning a business and dealing with employees is a task most people just do not comprehend. My uncle's comforting words and sage advice really did help me a lot. That is why I can still recall his exact words from that night.

In experiencing the good feelings and caring responses from my aunt the hairdresser and my uncle, Dad's only brother, I have to wonder what happened to make dad and his second sister so different. There is a definite inconsistency in their behavior. But it seems the answer will remain a mystery unless Dad decides to face the truth of family dysfunction and analyze the situation from his knowing perspective.

My Mother's Effect on My Self-Worth

I believe that children should feel comfortable communicating with their parents, and parents should always strive to be open and welcoming with their children. Parents must convey without question to their children that "you matter to me," "you are important to me," and "I love you." Children need to know that what they have to say does matter to their parents and that the parent wants to listen to them and be a part of their life. I say these things wishing that my mother had shown she cared about me and how I felt or shown an interest in what mattered to me. Instead of letting me know she cared, her verbal and nonverbal messages to me were:

"You are not welcome in my world."

"What is important to you does not matter enough to me that I need to listen to what you have to say."

"Your presence annoys me."

"I will get angry at the drop of a hat."

"Don't provoke me with your childish behavior."

"I don't have time for you."

"I'm the parent; you're the child."

"Never forget that I am in control here."

"When you speak I will disagree and correct you in front of others, to the point of making you feel inadequate and unworthy of giving information or opinions."

"Your conversations embarrass me because I see you as an extension of myself—a clone of me."

"I believe what you say is mostly wrong, so I will preserve myself and silence you so I do not look bad to others."

"You are a child, incapable of doing anything up to my standard."

"I believe if you want the job done right, do it yourself."

"I have no responsibility to teach you with patience."

Some of these are direct quotes from my mother, some are not. But I felt this all intensely from her actions and her words. Her patience wore thin most of the time, and she acted like I was an intrusion rather than a blessing to enjoy, teach, and love.

I never felt comfortable resting in the assurance that my mother wished me well. It usually felt, from her disposition and attitude, that she did not want my life to be any better than hers. Anything I accomplished seemed more like a personal threat to her rather than an occasion to celebrate. My academic victories never felt like anything she was genuinely happy about. They were my ticket to a better life, but she did not want me to be better than her—I should not rise above her circumstances. She had trouble encouraging me or celebrating my achievements. She was a controlling, depriving mother. She did not have fun, so she did not want me to have fun. I never remember her telling me to have fun when I went out with friends. My mother's position, in relation to my life, seemed to be, "Do not step out of the predetermined family mold—this is how our family operates, and you have no right to come in and change it. Do not get ahead academically, and do not have fun along the way." I felt that my mother preferred I remain in the family status quo, living a life possibly equal to her but definitely not better.

I learned what I know about running a home from Grandma Ada. She taught me many things. My mother never had the patience to let me learn by trying. For example, when I knew for sure I could cook chili because I had done it at Grandma's house, my mother told me I'd better not try because I might ruin the hamburger meat. When I asked my mother to teach me how to sew, we bought a pattern and material, but she never let me try. When I was gone from home, she cut out the material and had the clothes sewn before I got back. She never taught me a thing about sewing. She did not trust me with trying, so I learned very little from her. If it was not for Grandma, I would have had a hard time as an adult.

Many times encouragement, approval, or compliments I received from Grandma Ada were met with resentment by my mother. It felt like she did not want Grandma to boost my self-esteem in any way. My grandma told me regularly that I was beautiful. She told me that my blonde hair and brown eyes were an attractive and unique combination. I know my grandma loved me, and I know she thought I was pretty. I intensely got the feeling that my mother did not appreciate the attention I got from Grandma or the relationship of love and attachment that I formed with her. It seemed my mother believed her family position was threatened in some way just because Grandma openly showed how she felt about her first grandchild. Instead of feeling stability and comfort from my mother, I felt competition and strife. As a child, I felt that I had to protect myself from the competition all around me. I had falsely believed that feelings of competition came only from children my age. I now realize that most of the competition I felt was from my mother.

When I was born, my mother was not ready to enter the adult world and give up her place as a child in order to meet my needs as her child. The attention I got from Grandma was one of the main fuses for the dynamite in this area. The competition started there and continued throughout the years. When Grandma would give me positive recognition for anything I had done, I often felt scorn from my mother. Maybe the help, encouragement, and attention I received from Grandma made my mother feel left out somehow. My mother was not open with her feelings and they were usually subtle, but I felt them just the same. I believe that is why she could not tell me "I love you" or "You are pretty." And it is the reason she had trouble giving me encouragement or input in any way that would positively contribute to my self-esteem, self-worth, and positive emotional growth. I believe this was due to the fact that her own emotional needs were not met; therefore, she was incapable of meeting mine. The responsibility she had to me as my parent did not override her deep-rooted needs that I believe still continue to go unmet. I was raised by a *child*, still full of unresolved childhood hurt of her own. I was trying to learn how to get along in the world from an immature adult who had not found her way either. Sadly, this "immature adult" description fits Dad as well. Having no true adult presence in either parent, I was left to figure life out on my own with sporadic, positive influence from my grandma.

The Compliant Child

In my childhood home, I lived my life under a shell, pretending to be what my mother expected. I was not a rebellious child but a very compliant one. The "true me" was never totally revealed to my childhood family. I learned at age three, with the first memorable fit of rage I witnessed from my mother, to behave like she wanted me to and hide anything about myself that would set her off. I had learned at a very young age that I never wanted to be responsible for triggering my mother's temper again. As a teenager, this thought was ever-present in my subconscious mind. I also strived to live obedient to God's way—at least, as much of it as I had learned so far. I know God guided me through this time in my life; I felt His voice gently leading me away from harmful choices that I could have made. So I caused the family no problem, and they went on thinking everything was fine and normal as far as I was concerned. God became my Father. He protected my life during my vulnerable teenage years, and through His power I was able to get along and avoid the trouble of parental strife.

My brother's methods of surviving the family dysfunction were different. He did not hide how he felt or who he was and acted as the detonator for many out-of-control episodes of anger from our mother. He became known as the bad guy for always being so contradictory. But really, much of the conflict happened because my brother's ideas were simply different from our parents', our mother's especially. Though he was described as hard-headed, stubborn, and rebellious, it is clear now that he was just reacting to our dysfunctional circumstances. During this period, the focus was mostly on my brother and not me while my parents were busy dealing with all the *trouble* my brother brought into their lives.

I wish I had supported my brother more. Back then, though, I realized that compliance was something about me that my parents were finally pleased with. I therefore did not support my brother much because my parents were many times unhappy with his behavior. I just agreed with their assessment of my brother's behavior and sympathized with their trials. I know now that his irrational episodes were just manifestations of the hurt, rejection, and incompetent feeling he had from the family dysfunction. My brother was only guilty of trying to be himself. When he faced contradiction from our parents, he reacted in frustration.

I know now that I just did not understand the real problem in our family. I chose to deny my true self and cause no problems. I did not see this as just another way of compromising the real me by becoming what my parents wanted me to be—a daughter who was no trouble for them. My brother and I were responding in our own way to the family dysfunction we lived with. My brother was surviving in his way, and I was surviving in mine. But if I had to relive this turmoil again, I would at least be true to myself and not conform to their control. And if my mother reacted in anger, I would inform her that her anger was irrational and caused emotional damage. I also would explain to both parents how dysfunctional and abnormal our family's life of denial really was. I could stand firm because now I know the truth—a truth both my parents have yet to face.

Part II
Childhood Healing Begins

Chapter Twenty-Two

The Beginning of a Time that Felt Better

I now began fifth grade and the year of change. Every day of my fifth-grade year started out with a seemingly uneventful routine. Our teacher, obviously a woman dedicated to her Christian beliefs, began each morning with the pledge of allegiance to the American flag, then the pledge to the New Mexico flag, and then the most noteworthy part, the Lord's Prayer, which was recited without fail. At age nine and ten, I did not understand the magnitude of this routine. However, looking back, this daily habit was something that provided peace and comfort and had the potential to impact the lives of a young group of children for the better, even years into the future. I know it positively impacted my life, and I am grateful. Prayer to God is necessary for guidance in avoiding the pitfalls of everyday life. It is no coincidence either that this year was when my life started to feel livable, hopeful, and more peaceful. It was a turning point for my entire future; positive things began to occur, and I give credit to daily prayer. I believe my life improved totally and completely when I learned to pray each day, reciting this prayer verbatim collectively with each member of my fifth-grade class, led by our teacher:

Our Father which art in heaven, Hallowed be thy name.
Thy kingdom come. Thy will be done in earth, as it is in heaven.
Give us this day our daily bread. And forgive us our trespasses,
as we forgive those who trespass against us.
And lead us not into temptation, but deliver us from evil:

For thine is the kingdom, and the power, and the glory, for ever. Amen. (Matt.6: 9—13)

After learning in later years about legislation passed previous to this school year of 1969-1970 that made it unlawful to pray in school, I believe that Mrs. Evelyn Francis was a true hero, because she prayed with us anyway. She simply prayed the Lord's Prayer each day, which gave us direction and guidance on how each day needed to start with God's presence and help. She did not preach to us about her personal beliefs, she just magnified God. Knowing now the impact this daily routine had on my life, I can proclaim that my fifth-grade teacher is without a doubt a hero in my eyes. I am not saying that breaking a law makes you a hero. But I am saying that when the law enforced on the God-fearing nation of America is so unjust in relation to its founding roots and the intentions of our founding fathers, defying such a law and doing what is morally right is the best decision for all concerned—not to mention the fact that prayer is for the common good of all people.

Man's law can never override God's law. The following is a quote by George Washington, issued to all state governors on June 8, 1783: "I now make it my earnest prayer that God would have you, and the state over which you preside, in His holy protection ... that He would most graciously be pleased to dispose us all to do justice, to love mercy, and to demean ourselves with that charity, humility, and pacific temper of mind which were the characteristics of the Divine Author of our blessed religion without an humble imitation in these things, we can never hope to be a happy nation." I believe that banning God and prayer from our public schools today has led us to reap unhappy experiences as a nation and as a people. It was an enormously wrong decision, and the consequences in current times speak for themselves in regard to the violence in public schools—public schools that have chosen to reject God.

Here is a quote from another founding father predicting what would happen without God's presence in our public schools. Dr. Benjamin Rush, a signer of the Declaration of Independence and author of the first chemistry textbook, is noted as the father of public schools. He predicted the following: "In contemplating the political institutions of this United States, I lament that if we remove the Bible from schools, we waste so much time and money in punishing crimes and take so little pains to prevent them … For this Divine Book above all others, favors that equality among mankind, that respect for just laws, and those sober and fugal virtues which constitute the soul of our government." This warning by Dr. Benjamin Rush in 1791 has come to pass in America today—the Bible and prayer are removed from public schools, and we are punishing crimes rather than using the tools God has given us to prevent the pain and loss. Those essential, preventive tools are God's priceless gifts of the Bible and prayer. Without God, there is no peace. Prayer to God is essential for peace to exist in one's life. God created every human to have a relationship with Him; when that is ignored, chaos ensues.

Having been afforded the privilege of beginning each day of the fifth grade with prayer, I found my life enriched with new meaning. Prayer brought wonderful results, far-reaching and immeasurable in nature. One immediate change happened when, at age ten, Christ became the center of all future Christmases in my life. It is sad but true that any Christmas in my life prior to this year had no mention of the true meaning of Christmas. Christ had no part in our Christmastime— Santa Claus was the center of it all. My mother seemed to think the idea of Santa was magical and was the reason for the Christmas season. All our presents would be from "the man in the red suit." I believed this falsehood until I was ten years old. It is amazing how trusting children can be, to the point of believing something as completely unrealistic as the adventures of Santa every Christmas Eve simply because your parents say so.

But this Christmas when I was in the fifth grade, the brilliant truth that Jesus is the true and only reason for the season of Christmas completely overshadowed and outshone the fallacy of that fairytale. I must give Dad credit for one of his best moments. He asked my mother, "Don't you think it is about time we told them about the true meaning of Christmas?" My mother's answer was negative; I guess she was not ready to give up the fantasy. But at this point, the proverbial cat was out of the bag, so they had no choice but to tell my brother and me what Dad was referring to. Really, though, all that followed was a conversation about how Santa was just an imaginary character; I still did not get an in-depth discussion about the story of Jesus. I eventually learned about that at church and school, not at home. At least Dad tried to set the record straight for two young children ages eight and ten who up until that point had experienced little of the true meaning of the Christmas season. I did not believe there was a Santa Claus anymore, because children at school had begun to plant that thought and then Dad settled the mystery.

My parents still said nothing to me about Jesus and how He came to earth as a baby to save all people. But my fifth-grade teacher told us the true Christmas story, and that made more sense to me than the idea of Santa. My knowledge of Christmas that year went from falsehood to truth. I learned the true meaning of Christmas told in the Bible in Luke 2:1–20. God gave mankind the greatest gift ever by sending His son to earth to become a Savior for all people. Christmas is a celebration of the birth of Jesus Christ. Once I learned this truth, Santa Claus lost his mystique. I developed my convictions about celebrating the true meaning of Christmas. Now there are things that I avoid purposely as part of my Christmas celebration because of the worldly value they represent. One of those things is Santa Claus.

Knowing now what I should have been able to know as a child, it feels as if Christmases during those early years of my life were wasted believing a pagan fantasy. It is sad and disappointing to see so many people focus on Santa and materialism instead of grasping the truth that has the power to change their lives by filling them with hope, happiness, and contentment. Santa is a tool used by Satan to take the focus off Jesus, who is the real help and peace for all and whose birth is the reason for Christmas celebration. Have you ever noticed that the word *Santa* can be turned into *Satan* without adding or taking away one letter? Just by moving the *n* from the end to the middle. Then Satan moves *n* to Christmas through Santa, and people unwittingly welcome him there. How would you feel if your family celebrated your birthday every year by honoring your worst enemy instead of you? "The man in the red suit" has a mission to divert attention away from the peace, love, and joy of Christmas, which comes when Jesus is your reason for celebrating. Christmas is a special time to give, and care for fellow human beings. Christmas is not about what you get, it is about what you give out of a caring heart. It is a celebration of the matchless gift God gave to us—His one and only begotten Son. God gave His only begotten Son, Jesus Christ, so that through Him all of us can have the gift of eternal life in heaven through forgiveness of our sins.

This year of truth and revelation brought many other positive changes in my life. I attribute these positive changes to God's provision, protection, and presence through prayer. One good thing was that Dad took a new job that required him to be out of town during the week. He was home only on weekends. This gave me a feeling of freedom and peace, because when he was gone, his unreasonable demands and attitude were not present either. My mother was also a lot less angry when Dad was absent. She seemed to take comfort in settling into her weekly routine without him around. However, when the weekends came, the turmoil returned with Dad. Another blessing that came to our family during this year was the anticipated birth of a new baby. The thought of a new little person joining the family was a joy; it relieved tension and pressure by adding a renewed focus. I also got straight A's every grading period this year without the same strife, worry, and struggle as before. I know the many different positive things that happened at this time were no coincidence.

In reflecting back, I believe it all happened because of prayer—the daily prayer in my fifth-grade class by a teacher who stepped out in her faith. Never underestimate the power of prayer, and never underestimate the power of one individual who chooses to stand up and do what is right. The positive things that happened for me were the fruit of daily prayer; prayer changed my life forever in a positive way. I wonder if there are similar stories that the other students of my fifth-grade class could tell; I believe there are. Prayer and God belong in the schools of America. God belongs in our public schools, because without Him the future is bleak. As God's people continue to proclaim God's word and stand firm on this foundation, they can rest assured that their future is bright. Our children are our future, and we need to give them a hope they can grab onto. Without access to God through prayer, that hope is lost.

My fifth-grade year began just as the years before, but this year progressively got better. I was not a born-again, saved Christian at the beginning of the fifth grade; before the school year ended, I was. I found salvation, a definite positive fruit of daily prayer. I met Jesus—he was real to me, and knowing him made all the difference in my life. This became my real hope in surviving the emotional abuse and damage that I lived with daily from my parents. I got emotional resilience from Grandma Ada, but what I needed to survive the childhood I faced was more than a human can draw from within. The support I required to survive could come only from God and my faith and trust in Jesus Christ.

Chapter Twenty-Three

The Best Experience of My Life

When the life you live is all you know, your reality seems to confirm that this is life and there is nothing different available or possible. As a ten-year-old living with my parents, I did not necessarily feel that a better, happier life was feasible. I had lived where I was for five years. On occasion, during infrequent visits with Grandma, I still knew and felt the comfort I had experienced almost daily in my earliest years. But the idea that my everyday life could be filled with peace and contentment was very abstract. With the emotional abuse I lived in causing damage to my spiritual and emotional well-being, I needed healing to repair my injured psyche. And at this point in my life, I was unaware of my need.

Then one day, my opportunity for help came unexpectedly when a friend at school invited me to a church revival. Choosing to go was a decision that affected my entire future. It led to my best experience ever and the best decision I ever was to make. In April of the year I was ten years old, I met the best friend I would ever know when I met Jesus. After finding salvation through Jesus Christ and becoming a child in God's family, my entire outlook on life and my emotional health all took a positive turn. Everything felt new and clean and fresh. My parents still behaved the same as before, but inside me was a renewed hope that can be given by no one other than the Savior. And now God was my Father and Jesus was my Savior and I became a child of the King of kings guided by the indwelling Holy Spirit. The wonderful renewal of life I experienced was because God was now my guide, friend, protector, provider, and companion. He fulfilled all the things that were lacking in my life. He began healing my emotions and protecting me from the hurt. God was close to me and I felt Him with me everywhere I went. Now as His child, I was cared for far better than my earthly dad was capable of. A new door opened for me, and God became real to me. I was redeemed.

Even though I could not physically see God, I felt His closeness, caring, and protection in a very tangible way. The previously missing security, stability, love, contentment, peace, and hope were now present in my life through God's love. With this change came a desire to learn more about God and how I could live my life in a way most pleasing to Him. The more I learned about Him and committed to being obedient, the more blessings He sent my way.

The church my friend Melinda invited me to was the little white church just a short walk from our house. I will always be grateful to her for extending to me such a valuable invitation. As it happened, my parents were also invited to the church revival by a neighbor and attended the service as well. It was a Friday night in April 1970, and the church was packed. I was sitting with my friends across the church from my parents and toward the front. When the sermon was over and the invitation part of the service began, I felt an overwhelming sadness and a need to act in some way. I wept and had no idea why; I cried, and it was not silently.

I learned later that many were praying for me, asking God to help me make the most important decision of my life. I needed to walk up the aisle and meet the preacher at the altar. There I needed to pray for salvation and accept Jesus as my Savior, repent of my sin and receive His forgiveness. But I was confused in regard to the connection between my feelings and the action I needed to take. I had never experienced this feeling before and did not know immediately that God was calling me personally for salvation. I really did not realize that on this Friday night, it was Jesus gently tugging at my heart and calling me to Him. That is why I cried, and that is why I felt the overwhelming need to respond. My heart felt as though it would burst from the emotions involved. Jesus made me aware of my need; I needed salvation from my sinful condition, and Jesus flooded my being with His unconditional love. That night, I walked out of the church not realizing why I cried, what I needed, or what I should have done. On the way out the church doors, the preacher said to me, "See you back Sunday." I felt this to be a prompt, compelling me to return Sunday. Upon leaving with this decision unsettled, I felt great unrest and incompleteness, a nagging burden that I must resolve. I had a decision to make; I could not ignore the greatest invitation I had ever been given. One of my favorite songs is "Cryin' in the Chapel," the version sung by Elvis Presley. Hearing this song takes me back to the night I was crying in the chapel and beginning to understand the truth of the song's message about trusting God completely for salvation and for help with life's burdens thereafter.

The Bible states, "For all have sinned, and come short of the glory of God" (Rom. 3:23). No one is immune from needing the Savior's forgiveness. I personally realized my need during the sermon. The sadness I felt came from awareness, for the first time in my life, of the lost condition I was in. I was living in a world of sin with no hope. Finally, I realized that Jesus was the hope I needed to set me free from the bondage of sin. The tears came when I felt His love, when He called me to Him with the hope that only Jesus could offer. Jesus's loving presence touches deeply, reaching and convicting the inner spirit and soul. The King of kings was caring for me personally. The one who created me, formed me, and gave me life was drawing me to Himself, extending hope through His invitation for salvation and freedom from sin. There is no more important or deeply emotional experience a human can undergo. When a person has the privilege of this experience, he or she can respond in one of two ways—to *accept* or *reject* the loving offer your creator bestows. (See Appendix A.)

Previous to this night, I knew about walking the aisle and being saved at the altar only on an intellectual level. I had been to church before and witnessed the event of people being saved. I also had been instructed on the necessity of knowing Jesus and accepting Him as my Savior by my paternal grandmother. The procedure was familiar, but I had never before known how it felt in your heart. I didn't understand that what I felt was Jesus inviting me to accept His gift of salvation. It was clear looking back that the knowledge of salvation had traveled that space from my brain to my heart. I actually felt Jesus's presence rather than just intellectually knowing about it. This "head knowledge" had transformed into a feeling that penetrated my heart and caused me to know the action I needed to take. A statement I have heard many times since then is, "Sadly, some people miss out on life's greatest gift because of a twelve-inch span, which is the distance between their brain and their heart." The knowledge never travels from intellectual to heartfelt, resulting in a destiny of hell rather than heaven. No one can reject God's son, Jesus, and end up in heaven. The heartfelt experience of repentance of sins is necessary. It is a personal experience between a person and Jesus; it does not have to be done inside a church. You can pray the prayer of salvation anywhere, but at some point, confessing Jesus before others also needs to be part of the experience, and then following through with baptism as a public profession of faith.

In my life, family dysfunction prevailed, and my church experience was no exception to that pattern. My parents added their own brand of pain to my salvation experience. They were present at the revival when I began to cry during the last part of the service. Since my mother said she was saved at church camp around age twelve or thirteen, she must have known what was going on with me. The hurtful thing, though, is that after I cried during the invitation part of the service, my mother never said a word to me about what I was experiencing. She never offered me help so I would know what I needed to do. She was my mother; she claimed to be a saved and born-again Christian. But when I needed help working through my own salvation experience, my mother was silent. She said absolutely nothing to help me understand what was happening or to make sure I knew the gravity of what I was facing with my decision. Dad also said nothing. That, however, is more understandable, since Dad was not saved until long after I was married and had left home. But regardless of their background in this area, they both did understand the magnitude of the decision I faced. After all, Dad's mother was the first person to explain salvation and Jesus to me. I am sure she had also talked to him too.

Advising and guiding in this experience for me should have been my parents' number-one priority in child rearing. But sadly, the eternal destination of my soul did not seem to have the significance it should have, which was evidenced by their actions or lack thereof. As with almost everything else in my life up to this point, I was on my own to work it out and decide what I needed to do. I was without the assistance of adult parents to give advice and direction. I also felt very strongly that my parents were embarrassed because I was the one crying in church, and they were more comfortable ignoring my needs. Because of their silence, I felt they were ashamed of me and would have preferred I had not cried at all. They most likely wished it would all go away and not become something they had to be involved with. The seemingly unconcerned reactions of people around me made this a very lonely experience. But I had already decided what my plan of action would be. I would go to church on Sunday, and when the invitation started, I would head to the altar without delay. God wanted me to be His child, so He led when my mother and dad were silent.

As I had determined, I was at church this important Sunday, April 19, 1970. Some friends were there, but no one from my family went with me. The same evangelist was speaking. When the invitation hymn began, I wasted no time going forward to meet Jesus. I prayed with the preacher and asked for forgiveness. I confessed that Jesus is Lord and received Him as my Savior. Then I experienced the greatest feeling of freedom. I knew the peace that salvation brings. This was the most wonderful feeling I have ever felt. It was one of overwhelming peace and abundant joy that nothing on this earth can compare to. Your soul is released from the bondage of sin, and you are pardoned and redeemed by the only one capable of saving your soul: Jesus Christ, King of kings and Lord of lords.

I have wondered from a human perspective how I knew exactly what to do. However, it really is no mystery when you know the Holy Spirit is always present to draw the unsaved to God when they are willing to accept Him. My brother was also saved during the revival, so he and I were baptized the following week, on April 26. Being baptized was a wonderful, memorable experience. It was an obedient act that symbolized death to the old life of sin (going under the water) and being raised in newness of life (rising out of the water). It was a terrific warm feeling, and it seemed as though all the bad stuff in my life was washed away. My life was changed for the better beginning at that revival in April 1970 at a small Baptist church in Clovis, New Mexico. This is when and where I met God, which was in His plan all along. Then, through obedience on my part, it was accomplished according to His perfect will. I am so thankful that God drew me to Him, making salvation possible, because I was a child who had no resources to find my way alone. This one decision gave direction and healing to my life that only God as my Father could provide. At age ten, when Dad was not fulfilling his parental responsibilities, God became my Father. It did not matter so much anymore that Dad did not want me. Now I knew for sure that God and Jesus did, and that made everything in my life feel better.

My mother's common behavioral pattern is to never talk about things that she denies or wants to forget. Therefore, it is no wonder that she has never spoken about the night I cried in church. It does seem strange, however, that I went to church on Sunday, got saved, and joined the church, and my parents were not there to witness it or be a part of it. I do not understand why they chose to distance themselves from the most important event in my life and to say absolutely nothing about what was obviously going on. God drew me to Him, and I found my way with no help from my parents. They never even showed any joy or happiness for me at this most important time in my life.

My spiritual condition had changed forever, but my physical circumstances remained the same. We were still a hurtfully dysfunctional family. My brother dealt with it through rage and rebellion. I dealt with it by turning it inward. During this time, most of my memories of Dad in day-to-day life were of him being hateful and uncaring. He could be so mean. On Sunday mornings, after my brother and I were saved, Dad would tell us we better get ourselves to church. This demand would be accompanied by a piercing stare across the breakfast table at my brother and me. There was no love in his heart for his children—at least, it was not apparent. My brother and I did not need Dad's demands to get us to church. Dad had no intention of going to church with us, and I do not feel he cared particularly for our spiritual growth either. It felt more like he just did not want us around.

We never attended church as a family. But, after I was saved, I attended church regularly. Many times I went alone, but often my brother and I would go together. I attended the same little white church until after I was married. Several years after I was saved, my mother did begin going to church with us. I do not remember Dad ever attending church with us on Sunday mornings. He mostly did his own thing when we were in church. On rare occasions, Dad would go to revival meetings. He was very uncomfortable going to church, and when the invitation hymn began, he would behave like a cat on a hot tin roof. God was gently calling him, and he was rebelling. It was very obvious. I prayed for Dad on many occasions, that he would find the peace of salvation and stop running. There was one revival meeting where a friend and I, who also had an unsaved father, went to the altar to pray for our dads. It was a great revival, but it was obvious that much more praying was necessary for Dad to stop running.

After my mother started attending church, there was a special weekend meeting at our church. One of the college students who was part of the program stayed at our house during the event. A prayer meeting was hosted in our living room on Saturday morning. The room was filled with church people. Dad came home and entered the house, unaware of the prayer meeting. He was asked to join us, and he did for a few minutes. I guess the tug on his heart became more than he could handle, because he left soon after he had arrived. He was emotional when he left the house, obviously being convicted by the Holy Spirit. Dad ran from God for so many years. Therefore, in my life, sharing spiritual growth in church with Dad was never a possibility.

In the years previous to my salvation experience, I was unknowingly on a journey in which God was at work on my behalf. Even during the time I was pulled away from the security of living with Grandma and moved to the house that happened to be just a short walk from the little white church, God was changing my circumstances for good. I have no doubt that God provided the house we moved into, because of its perfect location in relation to the church where I was saved. That church was the place I would begin the most relevant and important relationship of my entire existence. God knew and cared about the turmoil and pain of my childhood, and He also knew He would be there to help me through it.

God is ready to guide anyone's life away from pain and heartache; all that is required is a willing spirit. For God's perfect will to be accomplished, one must be open, tender, moldable, and obedient, with a non-rebellious heart. I can only speak from my experience, but since being saved, I have had a heart that is open to God's instruction. I have not always been perfectly able to hear His voice when I should, but I know it. I believe my prayers as a hurt child fell on God's ears, and He had compassion for a little one who had faith in Him. He helped me through my damaging circumstances and was there for me as no one on earth ever could have been. Looking back on my years from age ten to present, God has provided protection for my life, and that happened only because He is my Father.

I believe God has always watched over me. But after I was saved, His presence felt more real. God has been there for me and molded me and healed so much of the pain I felt as a child. He has protected me from many things. Through the years, I have developed a relationship with Him that is based on His word, the Bible. I have enjoyed many experiences, blessings, miracles, and Biblical promises because I am a born-again believer and God is my Father. In reflecting back and writing about my life, I have realized countless times that God has been the one who healed the pain, turned the dysfunction into function, and always protected and guided me through every moment.

Chapter Twenty-Four

Major Life Changes for the Better

In the summer of 1970, many things in my life began to change for the better. Since these changes started to happen at the point when I became a born-again Christian, a new member in the family of God, I look back and believe the positive changes were no coincidence. God became my Father and took care of me in ways I had never experienced before. I know Dad was not taking his parental responsibilities seriously, so God in a sense "fired" him and assumed that position in my life. I knew one thing for sure: everything was much better this new way. My parents were no different, but many things were rearranged, and my emotions felt more normal. God brought people into my life to begin the healing process that I so desperately needed. I also began to recognize truth; therefore, many fallacies were unmasked.

In July, I was blessed with a sister. One night only a few hours after we had gone to bed, I was awakened with the news that it was time to go to the hospital. We all piled into the car, and Grandpa drove to the hospital. On a Wednesday in the middle of the night, while Dad was away working, my baby sister was born. It was a thrill to see her only moments after her birth. I will always remember that special night when I received God's priceless gift of a sister. I have loved her ever since. Her presence has brought much happiness into my life.

I mentioned before about my mother's difficulty in picking a name for me when I was born. Even though my mother had chosen a girl's name and a boy's name this time prior to the birth, she still had difficulty naming my new baby sister. It seemed once again she had been really hoping for a boy. She wanted so badly to use the boy's name that she tried making it into a girl's name. If my sister had been a boy, the name was to be James Nicholas, so she was almost named Jamie Nicole. I watched as my mother struggled again to name a daughter. She finally gave up the ridiculous idea of naming my sister the altered boy's name and went with the more appropriate girl's name she had chosen weeks earlier.

My baby sister was a genuine blessing in my life. Her presence brought changes to many aspects of our family life. Our mother was too busy taking care of a new baby to be as controlling with me and my brother. Also, a new baby always brings a special kind of joy to a family, no matter how dysfunctional that family is. Dad had a new job and was gone from home a lot, and his absence most definitely brought more peace to my mother's life. For that reason, her temper was not as quickly triggered. Since my sister was born in the town where Grandma Ada lived, we were able to spend most of that summer at Grandma's house. This circumstance brought cherished time with Grandma, which I was always very grateful for.

During this period, God regularly brought people and circumstances into my life that boosted my self-esteem and grounded me with purpose—all independent and separate from my parents. Beginning here, my parents had little to no input over many aspects of my life. It felt as if their control had greatly diminished.

When school started in the fall, I was in the sixth grade. I was chosen to be a member of the school patrol. This was an honor, because only students with top grades and good citizenship were considered to participate. It was an organization created and directed by the school principal, and he conducted our regular meetings. The school principal was my friend from before—the same man who helped me through the fourth-grade trauma. Being in the school patrol was good for me and was a real fun job, since many of my very close friends were involved too.

My sixth-grade teacher was also a real boost to my emotional state. She was young, only twenty-three, and her name was Mikki. She was a freestyle, unrestrained lady who knew how to make learning fun and was a teacher that sixth-graders could really relate to. Her dress and appearance leaned more toward the hippie type; she had very long hair and drove a VW Bug. She also had a six-year-old daughter our class got very well acquainted with. Mikki would let us listen to the popular rock music of that era. One song I remember in particular was "Joy to the World" by Three Dog Night. This became one of my favorites then. While I was in sixth grade listening to Three Dog Night, my future husband was in Oahu, Hawaii, also listening to Three Dog Night. He personally attended one of their concerts, at which Chicago performed as the opening band. They were not very well known then and were booed off the stage. No one wanted to hear Chicago, just Three Dog Night. My husband told me this years later, around the time we paid several hundred dollars to attend a Chicago concert in Minnesota.

My sixth-grade class also included the narcissistic "friend" from my younger years. She still was hung up on how wonderful she was. But this year, I realized that what this girl believed about herself and what others thought were in contradiction. Our very hip teacher did not seem to like her very much and subtly put her down whenever she would try to act so smart. I saw this as a truth being clearly revealed. I could finally see what this girl was all about. She thought no one could ever measure up to her; she believed she was perfect. And it was comforting for me to see that others I looked up to saw the real truth. No longer could she or her mother make me believe their lies. I had been enlightened and could now heal from the damage they had done to my self-esteem. Many girls and boys who had been my friends for several years would ask me, "Why are you friends with her?" and then add, "I do not like her."

I then wondered why this narcissistic person had to be my friend— just because it was forced on me by my parents' circumstance and convenience? The answer to my question was that I no longer had to be friends with anyone whom I did not choose to. Just because her parents were friends with mine did not mean that I had to be saddled with her. She clearly had been costing me real relationships. It was time to cut the ties with her and stop giving my friendship to someone who cared nothing for me. God revealed the truth in regard to this fallacy I had been allowing to drag me down for too long. I realized with God's guidance that this friendship my parents encouraged was not good for me or my self-esteem. Parents need to take every aspect of their parenting position seriously and protect their children in every way. They need to be aware of the effect their children's friends have on emotional well-being. My parents did not protect me in this area, and again, God stepped in to fix this situation in my life.

Often I experienced other bad feelings inflicted by my mother. She had very little empathy for me. Many things that happen as you grow up in a state of emotional abuse are not easily forgotten. It is harder to rationalize these situations that are more easily shrugged off in a functional situation or as an adult. Two examples follow of how insignificant I felt to my mother. She routinely minimized my feelings and treated me, more times than not, as an intrusion and a burden. What I felt and needed was ignored routinely as she would give more weight to her preference of others over me.

It was the summer after sixth grade, when I was eleven and my baby sister was about one year old. My sister, mother, and I were returning to our house from the farm. The car had seat belts, but we did not use them. During the sixty mile trip home, my mother drove as my sister lay sleeping with her head in our mother's lap, which positioned her feet perfectly to reach my leg. As usual, I was wearing shorts in the hot summertime. My sister was wearing high-top walking shoes, common back then for babies just learning to walk. Her baby shoes dug and gouged into my bare leg. I tried to ignore how uncomfortable this was and keep quiet. My thought was just to endure; we would be home soon. As my sister was sleeping, she would move her feet, pushing them up against my thigh. I could not move far enough away to escape the soles of her shoes bearing down into the exposed side of my leg. My skin was becoming red from the friction. Finally, I could no longer keep quiet. But it became apparent quickly that I should have followed my first plan and just endured. Obviously, I knew my mother better than I thought.

When I complained of my uncomfortable situation, I was equally or more upset by my mother's lack of understanding. She told me, "You are so much older and bigger than your sister. How can such a little person cause you such a problem? You need to act your age and give a little. She can't be bothering you that much. You should be ashamed of yourself. Leave her alone and let her sleep. She is tired."

No surprise there; this is what I was told often. It was my mother's common advice for my problems. Just endure! Once again, she offered no empathy, no understanding, no compassion, and no ability to care about my feelings at all. It was not an option to negotiate and balance the situation for both my benefit and my sister's. I must always be the bigger person and *endure*. I have no memory of my mother ever taking my side. She seemed to enjoy making my life hurt. Someone else's needs took priority over mine as far as my mother was concerned. It never occurred to her to even try to understand my feelings … ever!

Often I felt more like an intrusion into my mother's life than a daughter welcomed by her. She had a knack for making me feel like I should be anywhere but with her. This is a rather crude example, but I believe it is relevant to how my mother was mostly annoyed by my presence. When my sister was an infant, I made the mistake of believing I was welcome to go with my mother to my sister's baby bed to help change her diaper. When I followed them, my mother turned to me and said, "Are you afraid I am going to fart, and you will not be there to smell it?" I looked at her in disbelief and left. This was one of many examples that caused me to feel my mother did not want me near her. There were many more times throughout my childhood when my mother suggested I keep my distance than times she made me feel welcome.

This was the point in my life when I began separating my feelings from the hurt my mother often inflicted and seeking a more comfortable emotional state. I did not have to feel hurt emotionally on a regular basis anymore. With these revelations of truth about old things I had been living with, my parents had less and less control over my emotions and how I felt about life in general. Many positive things were coming into my life, allowing me to focus my feelings and emotions on things that made me feel good about myself. I was also learning that there were people who really liked me and people who thought I was pretty. Experiencing more positive influences slowly brought about change for the better, in spite of the programming I had gotten from my parents. When your parents treat you ugly, you believe you are unattractive physically and also to the very core of your being. This thinking is hard to overcome, but not impossible. God, my Father, was sending people into my life to deprogram this fallacy.

After sixth grade, junior high began, which was a very new experience. Class was not in just one room for the entire day anymore. This new adventure brought excitement, new friends, more responsibility, and more escape from home. I joined clubs, attended junior-high and high-school football games, cheered at pep rallies, and enjoyed the general overall feeling of newness. I liked having seven different classes every day and seeing friends every time classes changed. I liked my teachers and made friends with them too. I was chosen to be student-helper for a few favorite teachers and enjoyed being able to help out the teachers I especially liked. It was at a junior-high football game that I met Dee, one of my lifelong very best friends. She and I are still friends and keep in touch regularly. Several years later, on my wedding day, Dee was there supporting me as maid of honor.

I cannot talk about the people who positively influenced my life during this time without giving credit to my uncle's wife, Judy. She had her problems, but she was always a true friend to me. Even though I did not always give her credit, she continually boosted my self-esteem. There was a nine-year age difference between us, but that did not matter to her. She genuinely liked me and enjoyed spending time with me. She was a kid at heart and was good for what I was missing emotionally. She always showed an interest in what was going on in my life with friends, boys, and school. She complimented me on my looks and intelligence. She provided a much-needed escape from my home life, and even though she and my uncle lived sixty miles away, she visited regularly. We had fun together. She took me to town; we visited her family. We went to the movies on many occasions. She talked to me about things I was interested in during the preteen and teenage years. I helped her take care of her daughter and son, who were also my cousins. She enjoyed going places and doing things, and I liked being with her. We went to the lake and swam in various places throughout the Fort Sumner Valley. She bought me things like magazines and clothes. My aunt was one of the few people I spent a lot of time with and also felt comfortable enough around to truly be myself. She provided a lot of what I needed emotionally during my childhood.

Although my mother tried to warn me about spending time with my uncle's wife because of the potential bad influence she might have on my life, I feel that the relationship I built with my aunt was good for both of us. Visits with her gave me much-needed freedom from my parents, and in turn, my influence on her was greater than my mother could have ever imagined. There was one conversation I had with Aunt Judy when I was approximately age twelve. She was giving me advice on dating and warning me about some of the pitfalls I would most likely have to deal with—one in particular being that kissing boys could lead to acts I should know about and were probably inevitable when the kissing "got hot." My response to her was, "Jesus will be with me always, and I know I will be able to avoid that temptation." I also reassured her that I believed this with all my being, and I was not worried about those kinds of things. My aunt responded to the conviction I voiced with tears and a look I will never forget. My words had touched a spiritual nerve, and she was impacted by the confidence I put in my faith. I was true to my conviction in the dating years to come and never slept with any of the guys I spent time with or dated except the one I married. I feel like I had made some spiritual things real for her that she previously had not grasped so well, and she in turn helped me by increasing my confidence. It was a win-win relationship. She boosted my self-esteem and gave me freedom; I stood firm on my faith and convictions and set the moral tone when we spent time together.

However, it was disappointing at times when my aunt did things that I disagreed with. She could be boisterous and do things that were not always right. But however she chose to act did not change the fact that I liked her and I thought a lot of her. She was my friend. When she joined our family, she was only sixteen. She did many immature things, which often frustrated my grandparents. Grandpa would storm around the house in a rage, complaining about the newest infringement, hurt, or conflict that daughter-in-law had created. Other family members had plenty of opinions about her behavior. Regrettably, I too would join in with them sometimes. I was a fence-rider. I was listening to people I looked up to and learned from as they said things they should not be saying. I was young and had not figured out much about loyalty, or that my family was not displaying family trust and loyalties in these gripe sessions. Some of the things my aunt would do frustrated me too, but I now know that I should have remained loyal to a friend and kept silent during these times or defused the situation rather than adding my two cents.

Aunt Judy was my advocate, which was something I had not grasped at this time. Judy thought very little of the narcissistic "friend" I have mentioned; she did not think this person was good for me to hang around with. My aunt was very much on target with this assessment. Maybe my mother should have warned me about that bad friend rather than warning me about Aunt Judy. My aunt was supportive of me and helped me experience the fun side of life. Unlike my parents, she also was never a fan of people who treated me badly.

Looking back to this time now from a very different perspective and realizing some of the dysfunctional family dynamics that were in place, I think my aunt was only trying to survive a controlling influence by drawing boundaries for her family. My uncle had a 160-acre farm just across the road from Grandpa's 90-acre farm. Grandpa had helped my uncle get his farm, and since he was the patriarch of the family, his control was no doubt very strong in the lives of my uncle and aunt. Grandpa would get mad; Grandma would try to keep the peace, no matter the cost; my mother was forever loyal to her daddy. And my uncle did exactly what he should have done—he remained loyal to his wife always.

Cherry Pie

There was a family dinner scene that truthfully depicts the dysfunctional environment we all lived with. One day at lunchtime, also known as dinnertime on the farm, Grandpa tried to give Judy's daughter cherry pie. Since the girl had not eaten her dinner, Judy did not want her to have pie. Grandpa continued to dish out the pie, completely ignoring Judy's wishes. Judy told Grandpa, "If you give her the pie, I will take my daughter and leave." Grandpa continued as if oblivious to her warning and set the pie down in front of my cousin. My aunt grabbed up her daughter and left. My uncle got up and followed them home. It caused quite a family scene. From grandpa's point-of-view, he had done nothing wrong and blamed *that* irresponsible daughter-in-law for the entire unreasonable incident. He also focused on the cherry pie, and why would she refuse her daughter some pie? He said, "What's wrong with her? Why can't the baby have some cherry pie?" But it was not about whether or not the baby got cherry pie. It was about Grandpa's controlling intervention and trying to override a parent's wishes. This was not Grandpa's decision to make. He needed to back off and let Judy be a mother to her child. He had no business trumping my aunt's wishes. It only caused more family dissention and problems.

I say that my uncle was right to follow his wife out and support his family. I know that for sure now, but I was very confused back then as to how it all should have been handled. I see now that Grandpa was wrong. He also was the one who taught my mother to be a controlling parent, and in addition instilled in her the belief that she had every right to be that way. I realize now that this family scene was the dysfunction in action—something I could not grasp at the time in my preteen years. It was a dysfunction I would go on to experience in my life when my controlling mother would act very much like her own daddy with my children.

In spite of Grandpa's control, my uncle Jim was forever faithful to his wife, Judy, and always stood up for her. It was sad for him when she passed away in July 2007 at age 56. I know that he still loves her and misses her, and always will. I miss her too, and will always be grateful for the friend she was to me during some of the most difficult years of my childhood.

Grandpa's Heart Attack

During my eighth-grade year, on January 28, 1973, my maternal grandpa had a heart attack at age fifty-nine and died. It was on a Sunday afternoon. We had gotten a phone call earlier that day—Grandma Ada was letting us know that Grandpa was not feeling well and was on his way to the hospital. We were only an hour's drive away, but when we got to the hospital, Grandpa had just had another attack and the doctor was with him. As we were sitting in the waiting area, the grim news came that Grandpa had passed on. I will never forget my grandma's face when these words were spoken to her. I do not remember another time when she looked so hurt or her tears flowed so freely.

My mother was very disappointed that she was just a few minutes too late to be able to talk to Grandpa one last time. I remember Grandpa's still and lifeless body on the hospital bed just minutes after his death; his eyes were still open. My mother went to him, touched him, held him, and closed his eyelids as she cried. She also said many times that now there was no one in the world who understood her, because Grandpa was the only person she could ever relate to. This was probably very true, since they both were notorious for their controlling ways. My mother had learned from the master in this area of life.

It was sad, and I missed Grandpa, but I mostly missed him more for Grandma than I did for myself. Just days before Grandpa died, he called our house, and as usual my mother talked to him; he never wanted to talk to me. I was doing my eighth-grade English homework in my room, and my mother began calling me to come to the phone. I took my time, because Grandpa had never wanted to talk to me before. She called again and I said, "In a minute." A little later, she said "Grandpa is not going to hang up until he talks to you." I guess he must have known he was going to die soon. I did finally get on the phone, and he began talking to me about a dance our family had attended at the Fort Sumner Community House over the Christmas holidays. Grandpa stayed home instead of going to the dance, but he talked to me about what Grandma Ada told him regarding my dances with some of the guys there. He basically just made small talk about what he thought interested me, but

I believe it was his way to tell me good-bye, especially since he had never wanted to talk to me personally before.

Grandpa's funeral was sad. I hope he was saved and knew Jesus as his Savior but I really do not know for sure if he did. Because of the funeral arrangements and other business to take care of, my brother and I missed about a week of school. We also spent time with Grandma so she would not be left alone immediately. One of the saddest, most heart-tugging memories I have is of leaving Grandma alone and going back home after it was all over. I hurt for her and did not want her to be alone; I knew it frightened her. I was comforted, though, to know that my uncle and his family were only a short distance away. Grandma was strong, and she was okay, but the thought of her being without Grandpa's company was something that bothered me until the time Grandma passed on almost twelve years later.

Part III
The Dating Era

Chapter Twenty-Five

The High-School Dating Years

The era in my young life that came with the most freedom was the high-school dating years. I had many friends and got to know a lot of guys through dating and other social opportunities. I spent time with friends I had known since first grade, but most of my time was spent with two girlfriends I became acquainted with in junior high. They became my lifetime best friends; we still keep in touch almost forty years later. We experienced a lot together and grew in our newly acquired freedom, mostly in responsible ways. We really did very little during our high-school years that anyone would consider to be bad; the worst was skipping school and drinking alcohol. We regularly enjoyed dating but were never considered promiscuous and were respected by the boys we knew.

Up to this teenage period in my life, I had conflicting experiences with alcohol—was it bad or not so bad? Should one drink or not? My thoughts regarding alcohol had evolved from confusing, mixed signals. I was never told by either of my parents not to drink. Alcohol was not off-limits, and I started experimenting more than I ever should have in my parents' presence. As I have shared, Grandpa became a heavy drinker after the shooting accident, and alcohol became a regular part of spending time with Grandpa. For example, my mother drove Grandpa to a cattle auction, and Grandpa brought whiskey and 7UP to drink along the way. As he was drinking, Grandpa was glad to pour drinks for my brother and me as well; in fact, he even encouraged us to drink.

My mother sat silent as Grandpa gave us alcohol. Grandpa could do no wrong in my mother's eyes, and she would never question him. At this time, I was about ten, and my brother was two years younger. Grandpa made our drinks somewhat diluted, but my brother and I still got a little giggly and tipsy.

A few times at home, my mother let us have margaritas—a drink she liked. Dad bought her tequila from Mexico when he worked in the Las Cruces/El Paso area. They would have friends over, and my mother would make margaritas for all. Another time, when my parents were not present, I had beer at my uncle's house. It was plentiful there. I tried it the first time when I was around age nine.

On other occasions, I had witnessed my parents' overindulgence in alcohol. One New Year's Eve around 1968 or 1969, my parents went with some friends to a dance hall to bring in the New Year. They left my brother and me with the neighbor next door. The following day, what I remember most was the dull, dreary, depressed atmosphere at our house. There were no good feelings, because both my parents were hungover, and my mother spent the day throwing up in the kitchen sink. They both must have had a real good time the night before and were experiencing the consequences of it on New Year's Day. The problem was that my brother and I felt the depression that invaded our house as well.

A few years later, on New Year's Eve in 1974, Dad was with a friend who had to bring him home because he got falling-down drunk and could not function. Dad managed to accomplish this all before nine p.m.—drinking eggnog. He got home at the same time my friends and I were leaving for town. Dad could not even stand up, and his friend had to help him into the house. Dad only stumbled and laughed—he was so drunk, that is all he could do. I was only fifteen and very embarrassed for my friends to see this. Their parents did not even drink. In my world, though, alcohol was not forbidden and was never something I was taught to avoid.

I had acquired some thoughts and feelings of my own, though, after living through my childhood years exposed to alcohol. I knew for sure that it did not taste good, and it also made my stomach burn.

Drinking was something I should have totally avoided because of the stomach ulcer that burdened me since age eight. I witnessed the effect alcohol had on my grandparents' lives—a lot of pain, heartache, discontentment, and bad health. I also believed it was the main reason for Grandpa's premature death, leaving my beloved Grandma grief-stricken and alone. I had witnessed the depressed atmosphere it brought into our home through hangovers and self-inflicted sickness. Drinking was never something I enjoyed or purposely set out or planned to do. I did not like the way it made me feel afterward.

Still, at this point, I had not developed any strong convictions about alcohol one way or another. I had not put together what it all really meant—the cause and effect of it all. Probably how I would have been categorized during this period in my life would be a very random social drinker. Drinking was prevalent in a lot of places I went, including at home and with family. Most of my dating experiences were alcohol-free, though there were some exceptions. Those who got to know me best understood and respected that I did not really enjoy drinking. But I just had too many confusing and mixed messages about alcohol to be able to stand firm as a teenager for what I thought was right. I went along with no real convictions to define on which side of the fence I should stand.

Even though I drank on occasion, I can honestly say with God as my witness that I never have had even one experience with illegal drugs. This was a strong conviction and a promise I made to myself while in junior high. It was then that I learned in health class about drugs and all the negative effects they can have on the human body. This class taught me about the harm drugs can cause with procreation and birth defects. I planned to have children someday and was not willing to take a risk with drug use, not even just once, knowing it could potentially harm my future children. A policeman came to our class and talked about some encounters he had with people using drugs. This was also the time in my life that I read a book called *Go Ask Alice*, written by an anonymous author. This book shows how drugs send one's life down into the gutter. And I knew for sure that drugs were wrong. I also know that God was, as always, present in my life, keeping me strong and enabling me to do what was right, helping me prevail when under my own strength I would have fallen.

I had my first date when I was only fourteen years old. To make this situation even more inappropriate, the guy was twenty-one. I had met this hometown boy when I was thirteen. He resided in the town where I was born and was well acquainted with my family. This is the guy who took my drunk Grandpa home that night; he also attended Grandpa's funeral. He was respected by and friendly with my family—everybody except Dad. That was only because Dad was not around enough to provide input about anyone I dated. However, Dad did have rules. He said I was not allowed to date before I was at least fifteen and able to drive on my own. But he was just not around enough to enforce his rules. So my mother liked this guy and allowed us to date, thinking Dad would never know anyway, which turned out to be true.

Since this boyfriend lived in the town where Grandma Ada resided on the family farm, she was the one around most when he would pick me up for dates. This first dating experience was good for building confidence. The guy was kind, respectful, and considerate, and he appreciated spending time with me. It was fun. He was a perfect gentleman, honorable and careful not to breech the trust my family placed in him. The family I speak of here was Grandma, my uncle, and my mother. This was the beginning of God's watch and protection over me during my dating years.

In between this first experience with dating and getting my own driver's license was the annual event of sophomore initiation, the first social experience of my high-school years. This practice is no longer allowed, but in 1974 it was an annual event. After midnight, two "kidnappers" arrived at my house and took me away wearing only a T-shirt and underwear. This was very skimpy attire for a cool September night. During the night, we were exposed to many humiliating activities. Then, at the end of the initiation in the wee early-morning hours, they took us to Sambo's for breakfast. This would have been much more pleasurable with adequate clothes on. The waitresses and the patrons at the time all got a good laugh at our expense. The overall experience was not that bad. The initiation was all done in fun and did get you acquainted with a lot of older classmates with all your defenses taken away. It was the right of passage to enter the great Clovis High School.

After sophomore initiation, I experienced many more things that were a lot more pleasurable. Also, God continued to protect me during these vulnerable years in ways that were not apparent to me at the time; looking back now on my teenage years, I can see that He was always there watching over me wherever I was. I got my drivers' license when I turned fifteen. I went to school each day with my two best friends, Kim and Dee, as well as hitting the drag with them on weekends. Basically, we drove up and down Main Street—this was the teenage routine to socialize, meet potential dates, and have fun with your friends.

During one of my first experiences with dragging, I met my future husband for the first time. I was with Kim and Dee when some guys who called themselves the Main Street Demons motioned for us to pull over. At this particular time, I had an interest in someone else and little excitement for talking to these two guys. But we talked to my future husband and his friend anyway. I do not remember this encounter as vividly as my husband does. This was the only time I would be around him for about two years. I would see him on the drag and maybe even pass by him in the halls at school, but there was nothing at this time that drew us together. I look at this period as God's protection, which held out for more perfect timing in the future. God knew neither of us was ready at this time for what He had planned for us later on. Getting too close at this earlier time certainly could have spoiled what was to come. I had a lot of growing, experiencing, and dating to do at this point in my life (as did my future husband) before I was ready to settle down with one guy. All the things that happened in between our early Main Street encounter and the time we began dating would only help me grow into a person much more thankful and appreciative of the wonderful husband God would give to me later.

I stayed busy through my high-school years, spending time with friends, meeting many boys, going on a lot of dates, and making many good memories ... and only a few not-so-good memories. The high school we attended was considered a big school, and the "draggin'

Main" crowd consisted of high-school boys and some older guys who had graduated. Even with hundreds of possibilities, there would always be one guy a girl would target. This guy for me was the one who had my attention the time I first met my future husband.

In my opinion, this guy was one of the cutest I had ever seen. He drove a Camaro with a mural painted on the hood. I will call him William. He was shy and so was I, which made it remarkable that we ever even dated. He attended a Baptist church where my two best friends went, and he asked them about me. I had previously noticed him too and thought he was definitely someone I would like to know better. William asked my friends to introduce us the next time we saw each other downtown on the drag.

At the earliest opportunity, my friends obliged, and William and I met face to face one night on Main Street. I probably was not very encouraging because I was so nervous, and he could have perceived it as disinterest. Grandma Ada had always told me to never act too interested in a boy no matter how you felt about him. "Always keep them guessing," she said. Well, I probably did a real good job of that. My friends and I got in his Camaro and rode around—up and down the drag—talking and listening to a newly released eight-track tape by Paul McCartney called "Band on the Run." I liked William even more after meeting him. He was sweet and even cuter up close—a real dream of a guy. During our ride together, an older guy who drove a Mustang challenged William to a race. So we went out on a country road and raced the cars. The Camaro beat the Mustang. The race was exciting and added some adventure to our drive that night. William was a thrill-seeker and extremely cute. Needless to say, I remained hooked.

A few months passed by, and during this time, I would see William in the halls at school as well as downtown. Then one night in February, we met on the drag. I was with my friend Carol, and William was with his friend Rocky, who drove a new Chevy van. Carol and I rode around with them. This night in February 1975 was magical and one that became my top memory of dating, until I began dating my husband.

There was alcohol, and even though William liked to partake of the spirits, he was not so interested this particular night. He was happy to be with me. We drank some but mostly talked. William knew I did not care much for drinking. He and I remained sober, which was a good thing for Rocky since he needed someone to drive his new van for him.

That Friday night was too short; I did not want it to end. But William asked me out for the following night. I had a date the next night with the special guy. It felt like a dream! I mostly floated through the day Saturday with excitement and anticipation of the date coming up that night. Saturday night was a cold night. William arrived for our date right on time and seemed very happy to spend time with me. We went to a movie called *Blazing Saddles*, a very peculiar and strange film. But I was more interested in the company than the content of the movie.

During the date, William gave me a key to his car—the Camaro. It was all rather ambiguous. Did it mean we were going steady? He did not say. I did learn after our date that there were a lot of girls who liked him too. At school the next Monday, my date was the talk of the girls in every class I had that day. They wanted to know what he was like. Was he as nice as he was cute? Were we going steady? I also learned that some girls were upset by our date and chose to send mean looks or obscene gestures my way. I just rationalized their juvenile behavior by knowing for certain why I was the one who dated him and they only wished they did. William and I continued to see each other for several months afterward, but there were no commitments and I dated and spent time with many other guys in between.

On one occasion when William and I were together draggin' Main, we were listening to an eight-track tape by Black Sabbath. I voiced my opinion that I did not particularly like this group nor did I like their name. William immediately took the eight-track out of the player, pulled the tape out of the cartridge, and threw it out the window. He said now we would not have to worry about listening to that tape again. I was impressed that he would do that for me. I told this story to my youngest son who loves music, especially music from the seventies. He shook his head and said, "What a waste. I like that group; wish I had that eight-track."

I continued to have a special affection for William, and the feeling seemed to be mutual. He was the one guy who I would have committed to before I began dating my future husband. William always treated me with respect and cared about me. Some of our dates included going to church together; this too was something I liked about him. And thoughts of marriage had obviously crossed his mind. One night we were listening to a song called "I Can Help" by Billy Swann. Some of the lyrics are, "Does your child need a daddy? I can help." William asked me, "Debbie, does your child need a daddy?" My reaction to this comment was one of surprise with very little encouragement. I say this comment came with thoughts of marriage because after knowing William for some time, he never indicated his intentions were anything but honorable. And an offer like this would only come after marriage.

William confided in me about his childhood, which was also filled with some very sad, unusual, and extremely traumatic events. Since we both had lived through a dysfunctional childhood and both had damaging scars from the past, a relationship for us most likely would have been a disaster and would have contributed to the divorce statistics at some point. Neither of us would have been able to give more than we had, no matter how much we might have wanted to. I thought I loved him, but I believe now it was only infatuation. And if I did love him, God had already determined another path for my life. Because of my childhood background, my future husband would need to be someone who could give me more support than probably would have been possible from William. I really liked William, and I believe he felt the same, but God guided my life for my good. God knew my husband needed to be Doug. Doug had a stable childhood home, under the leadership of his stepdad. This made him emotionally capable, despite his dysfunctional, biological dad. He also was secure because he had never been abandoned by his mother.

Even though William and I ended up getting together many times over my early dating years, there was no magnet that pulled us together permanently. Circumstances putting us together just never worked out, and more often they pulled us apart. Looking back, I never gave him any real encouragement. He made many moves that I responded to in ways that would never move things forward. My responses never revealed how much I liked him and how I really felt.

About five months before I began dating my future husband, William got married. This was not a particularly happy day for me, and I even thought very briefly about talking to William regarding our feelings for each other before he took the plunge. This action was not led by God and was something that I quickly understood would be a mistake on my part. So I kept silent and let things happen as planned. The timing and circumstances were always off for the two of us. I look back and am thankful to God for His perfect timing, for things that did not work out, and most of all for my failure to push anything to work out the way I thought I wanted it to. I chose to be patient and wait for God to give me the husband he knew would be best for me. I have no regrets about letting God lead my life at this time or at any other time in my life. This has proven to be a very wise choice, since Doug, the wonderful man I married, has far exceeded any image or dream I ever had of a husband. Doug is everything I ever needed and more. After I married Doug, William got a divorce. Doug and William were also friends from high school. They saw each other in town one day and William verified that Doug and I were married. They continued to randomly see each other around town and talked some during the years we lived in Clovis. I too would see William around, but we never talked.

After William, there was another special guy who I had several memorable dates with. He also was very respectful and mentioned marriage, but I am sure it was only a humorous jest, or maybe just to test the waters. This relationship never had the traits of anything permanent—it was mostly just for fun.

Although several guys asked me to go steady, I never committed to only one guy. I found it more fun to have the freedom to partake of opportunities as they presented themselves. I enjoyed many friendships during this time of dating and experiencing teenage freedom. On one occasion, I was with the guy I mentioned earlier who drove the Mustang and lost the race to William's Camaro. His name was Steve. When he inquired about my philosophy on marriage and saving myself for my husband, his response to my answer was, "Your husband is going to be one lucky guy." He too was a friend who respected the person I am and what I stand for. I hope with all the people I knew and all the lives I touched during my dating period that I succeeded in shining God's light somehow to some along the way. Giving me mutually beneficial friendships was another way in which God boosted my damaged self-esteem.

In all, I dated over forty guys from my first date at age fourteen to when I began dating my future husband, Doug. That was plenty of experience with the dating scene, so I would know for sure when I got married at eighteen that I wanted only one man in my life from then on, and that man was Doug. Looking back at this period in my life, I know for sure that God was with me through all my dating years and all my dating experiences. He was present and provided protection for a naïve teenager that even an engaged earthly father would not have been able to provide (if I would have had one). I was a virgin when I began dating Doug at age sixteen. With all the guys I had met and spent time with, that was a miracle, especially when you consider my background of dysfunction, an absent father, no paternal relationship, very little parental guidance, and very little education in the ways of the birds and the bees. I know there was a protective boundary placed around me, which most guys just did not even try to cross. That boundary was God's presence. I had a relationship with God, and I had convictions in this area, which meant that "going all the way" was just not an option I even considered. There were many guys I knew who could be referred to best as an octopus, but the guys who behaved this way were *not* ones I chose to see again. I preferred the guys who respected me.

God has always been there for me all my life, and the dating years were no exception. God provided for my emotional needs when my parents failed. He protected me from potential disaster with guys who would not be a permanent fixture in my life. He protected me from the heartache of making a choice that could have cost me a relationship with the most wonderful man in the world for me. I stayed pure and untouched because God was my Father and He protected me and guided me through my dating years when my earthly dad was uninvolved and detached. I asked God to guide my life when I was a child, and He was faithful to answer that request. As described in a prior chapter, when talking to my aunt four or five years before my dating period, I had voiced my conviction of God's faithfulness regarding my future dating years. God has always taken care of me, and as I work through writing the details of my life, one prevailing purpose seems to be that God wants me to know specifically how He has guided me, and how He has always been there protecting me through it all. Knowing this truth provides a feeling that nothing else on earth can match. God's love is unique and wonderful and something to be shared with others so they too can know personally of God's goodness.

There are some identifiable times when my faith was evident to those around me. Carol was a friend of mine since the beginning of school. We always got along and liked doing things together. She was a little more on the rowdy side, and some of her choices were not congruent with my convictions. We had been friends for so long that we tolerated each other's choices, though; we had been friends when we were too young to have convictions yet.

One night when Carol and I were draggin' Main, her sister and some friends invited us to a party. I knew this would be a "smoking" party and was not interested in going; it was an activity I chose not to partake of. But I could tell Carol wanted very much to go to the party. I told her to go ahead. She was concerned about leaving me, but I told her it was fine with me and that she should go—really. She said, "Well, if you are sure, I'll go." She then said, "I just want you to know, you are a saint; how you have the determination to turn down such an invitation and stay true to what you believe!" Her comment meant a lot to me and gave me encouragement to continue doing what I knew was right.

Friends can make a huge difference in your life. They can bring healing to damaged emotions. Friends truly are one of God's most precious gifts. I had many friends, including my two best friends, Kim and Dee. They both brought healing into my life through their enduring friendship. They made a difference for me through the time we spent together and in the many experiences we shared. I was given the privilege to observe their parents in action and see that functional families with involved fathers really did exist. We attended church regularly together and sometimes even made an adventure of it by visiting different churches in our city. Sharing time with them and building memories with them was a gift. And today, spending time with them again is also a gift because we can relive the memories and reminisce. Friendship is truly one of God's wonderful blessings.

Chapter Twenty-Six

The Beginning of a Forever Love

It was a Sunday night, August 29, 1976. I was with Michelle, a friend since day one of first grade. She and I were draggin' Main, looking for Grant, the guy she was dating. I had no specific guy at this time and was available for whatever came our way. We had made one or two runs up and down Main Street, and then my friend's purpose was accomplished as she saw Grant's metallic-lime-green Monte Carlo approaching. She yelled at him to follow her home and then took off, driving fast as she always did when a guy she liked was in pursuit. Grant had a friend with him, a guy I recognized as an acquaintance but knew very little about.

After reaching Michelle's house, the four of us spent the next few hours in the den talking. It seemed the feeling between Grant and Michelle was mutual; therefore, the awkward silliness was present between them both. That atmosphere dominated the conversation, making them the ones in the spotlight. Grant's friend and I needed no formal introduction; I knew he was Doug, and he knew my name. Doug and I were there providing support for our friends and enjoying a comfortable, relaxing evening.

Grant was a fun guy and had a talent for remaining totally serious when he was pulling your leg. He would go from laughing and cutting up to completely straight-faced in a split second. I summed up his behavior in one word: "monkey." This term may or may not have led to the one very memorable event from this night. Maybe Grant did not like being called a "monkey," even though he did not seem to mind it—and I called him that many more times in the future with no consequences. Maybe Doug just wanted an excuse to do more than talk. Anyway, upon leaving Michelle's house, Grant and Doug cooked up a plan to turn on the garden hose and spray us with water. Doug claims he had to do it because I needed to be cooled off! For me, it is a great memory, and nothing about the experience was the slightest bit negative.

I recently learned what Doug was really thinking on this night over thirty years ago. He said it was necessary to hose me down because I was so *hot,* as in good looking. And I thought all those years that he thought I was *hot* as in mad about something. Mystery solved; I never could figure out why he thought I was mad about anything that night. Selective perception coming from one's life experiences really does cause a wide variety of personal interpretations. I was programmed in childhood by my parents to filter input about me personally in a negative way. But Doug had meant it only in a positive way. He liked me and thought I was cute, and I perceived there was something about me he did not like. This special night at my friend's house marked the beginning of a special relationship.

About twelve days later, on a Friday night, Michelle and I went with a group of friends to a Clovis High School Wildcat football game. We all yelled throughout the game for our team—a team with a winning reputation established over decades of victories. This night also was sophomore initiation, and we participated in that as well. Because of Friday night's activities, I woke up on Saturday morning with laryngitis. This is memorable because Saturday night would mark a new beginning for me, and I was not at my best for the life-changing occasion.

My first real date with Doug was on September 11, 1976; it was a double date with Grant and Michelle. We went to the Curry County Fair. Thankfully, Doug seemed unbothered by my laryngitis, even though communication between us was somewhat hindered. It turned out to be a fun-filled date. Doug and I rode many carnival rides together, but the most memorable was the tilt-o-whirl. For some reason, the guy operating that ride decided we needed an extra wild ride. Our turn on the tilt-o-whirl went longer and faster than usual, which pressed us together and plastered us to the side of the car. It was such an abnormally wild ride that I was thankful I had no supper earlier. We still laugh every time we see a tilt-o-whirl carnival ride. For our next adventure, Doug played one of the carnival games and won a stuffed elephant dressed in patriotic attire, which I still have today. With all the fun, it seemed to get late quickly, bringing the evening to a rapid end. We took Michelle home first. While Grant walked Michelle to the door, Doug and I remained in his car. This was the moment we first kissed. I remember the kiss as tingly, loving, and tender—a kiss that could definitely lead to future dates. I thought Doug was a very special guy. Our first date was fabulous, our feelings were mutual, and our dating era began that night.

Since Doug played bass guitar in a band, his weekends were usually reserved for band engagements. Therefore, our dates were almost always on Sunday nights or weeknights. During the week, Doug worked for a sign company that built and repaired signs, a regular eight-to-five job. It was not unusual to see Doug at various places around town high up on a ladder working on signs. Doug also lived alone in a house he purchased only a month prior to our first date.

Doug and I began dating regularly; soon we were together as often as possible. Most of our early dates did not involve meals out but were usually a movie, bowling, pinball at the Laundromat, or just driving around town. Since he was a bachelor living alone, we often went to the Laundromat to do his laundry. It became very obvious early on that we just liked being together no matter what we were doing. On one of these laundry dates, we folded a particular T-shirt from an event called The Crater Festival. Doug explained that this was a music festival held in Oahu, Hawaii, in Diamond Head. He described it as a once-in-a-life-time experience he would someday tell his kids all about. This comment gave me a very strange, unexplainable feeling at the time. However, as our life events unfolded, I remembered back on this night and probably got such an odd feeling because his kids would be my kids too.

Because I had never committed to any one guy as a steady, this was also the way things were with Doug in the beginning of our dating period. We dated regularly and exclusively for about two months. Then sometime in November, Doug was busy playing a gig with his band for the entire weekend. I was downtown with some friends and saw a previous boyfriend who wanted to talk to me. I had a necklace of his, and the actual purpose of this meeting was to return the necklace. I had never been that interested in this guy. Then the next night, while Doug was still busy with his band, another old boyfriend called for a date. But this guy was one I was unsure about; I thought I might still like him. So with Doug occupied, I went with this guy to his sister's house and played a board game. Ironically, the board game we played was Risk.

My parents and siblings were out of town this weekend visiting Grandma at the farm. I talked to my mother on the phone and told her of my date plans. She was not at all supportive and criticized me for doing such a foolish thing. I guess the family talked plenty about my foolish decision on their way home Sunday night, since my brother came in the house telling me "Boy, Sunny, you really blew it this time." (Sunny is what my brother called me.) His comment was referring to dating someone other than Doug.

I never understood why I could not get support and encouragement from my parents. This was a life-changing decision I was working on, and if I was unsure of one previous boyfriend, I did not feel it was fair to commit to Doug with doubts. Why could they not support me in finding out what was best for me? It seemed my mother was on Doug's side and only wanted me to do what she thought was best.

However, after this one date with an old boyfriend, I knew exactly what I felt and how to continue. The date ended up only proving to me once and for all that Doug was the one. The proof I needed was all in the kiss. All the doubt was erased, and I knew for sure. Doug did not know about this date, but I told him because I wanted no secrets between us, and I wanted to be the one he heard it from. He was not happy at all that I had a date with someone else. After the old boyfriends intruded, it took a while for things to get back to normal between us.

A few weeks later, an opportunity presented itself to get our dating relationship back on track. One afternoon, I noticed Doug working on a sign at a convenience store not far from where we lived. I saw him from the front door of our house. My mother said I could invite Doug for dinner on Friday night. So I asked my little sister to go with me over to the Circle K for moral support. It took no persuading to get her to go; she liked Doug a lot. So we walked to the store and asked Doug to come to dinner. Although his attitude was a little chilly, he agreed to come and eat with us.

Dinner that Friday night was a bit uneasy for me; I was nervous and could not even roll the canned crescent rolls correctly. The menu was roast, mashed potatoes, gravy, rolls, salad, and a family favorite we called cream-cheese corn. Doug liked the corn, and as he got a second or third helping, my little sister commented, "Boy, Doug, you sure do like that cream-cheese corn," for which she was reprimanded by several people all at once. She still remembers that situation and says, "I thought I was being nice. I didn't know I was saying something wrong." Doug thought it was funny.

After dinner, my little sister sat on Doug's lap and talked to him about things that were important to her while I helped with the dishes. Then Doug and I went to town. Our relationship was repaired, and there were no more problems with old boyfriends. Doug said he was glad I had settled the matter for good in regard to the old boyfriend. From this time on, I never desired to date anyone else ever again. Our unspoken setup had suddenly turned into one of unspoken commitment.

That unspoken commitment between us became evident one morning when I was on my way to school. I happened to see Doug working; he was repairing a road sign for a local restaurant called The Snazzy Pig. He waved, and I waved back. Strangely enough, at this exact time, there was a song playing on the radio that went like this—"I don't want to have to marry you … I don't want to have to say 'I do.'" It was a country song by Jim Ed Brown and Helen Cornelius. This particular moment is very memorable, because it was exactly when I knew I would one day marry Doug. The song somehow verified that inevitable fact. But this was a scary thought for me at this time. We had been dating for a relatively short time. How could I know this for sure? I cannot explain, but while more of me was saying "I don't want to have to marry you," there was a small part of me that knew it would happen one day. This thought made me more ready to run than commit. The examples I had witnessed of marriage thus far did not convince me that peace and contentment were a possibility. Wedded bliss seemed only a fairytale dream. I also believed that marriage was a lifetime commitment and not something one should ever take lightly. And since I was only a teenager, this made a lifetime promise of marriage seem even longer.

I did know at this defining moment that my feelings were following the song playing on the radio more than dreams of marriage. But since God's voice had whispered to me on this particular morning, giving me an assurance of His gift and the blessing He had prepared for my future, it also felt as though our wedding day would inevitably come. At seventeen, I had yet to figure out that when you are God's child, He will put your life together in perfect order. I had nothing to fear—I only had to trust and let God work things out in His perfect time. I was not to get impatient and make things happen on my own. Nor was I to drop out and hide because the thought of marriage was fearful. All I had to do was let God work, which is where you will always find life at its best, full of blessings and contentment. Marrying Doug became one of my greatest, richest blessings in life. With what I know now, the thought of *not* marrying Doug is the scary thought—a real nightmare, in fact.

So needless to say, our dating period continued, even with the possibility of commitment looming over us. The first time Doug took me with him to a band gig was at a local dancehall. I really enjoyed the entire experience. Doug was a lead singer and bass player for the band. He sang many songs I liked, both country and rock. The special treatment band guests received made it even more fun.

Another special band memory was when they played at Clovis High School for our pep rally when I was a senior. It was a great experience to get to hear my boyfriend's band play for the entire school. Afterward, Doug met me and walked through the halls with me to my next class before he had to go back to work. On our walk to class, many of my classmates wanted to meet my boyfriend. It was a unique memory, and one I will always treasure.

Even though we had been dating for several months, I still waited for Doug's phone call to determine if we went out or not. This could be challenging, since we had only one phone line at our house with two phones connected to it—one in the main living area and the other in a more private location in my bedroom. My younger brother, also a teenager, would call his girlfriends and stay on the phone *forever*—always when I was expecting a call from Doug. He would use my phone and sit on my bed. This could be very frustrating, but I guess it was just a normal teenage problem during this era with two teenagers in the same house before the days of call waiting, answering machines and cell phones. Eventually, Doug would grow tired of getting the busy signal and come to my house without calling, especially after he understood the situation.

When we finally made a connection in spite of the phone arrangements, one of our favorite things to do on a date was go to the movies. Doug and I saw many movies together. Some of the popular movies of the time that I remember seeing were *Saturday Night Fever* with John Travolta, *A Star is Born* with Barbara Streisand, *Rocky* with Sylvester Stallone, *Lifeguard* with Sam Elliott, *Car Wash*, and a Disney movie about football called *Gus*. Our town had two walk-in movie theatres and two drive-ins. There were many times during our dating period when we had seen every movie showing at all four locations.

One Sunday night date sticks out in my mind, not because anything out of the ordinary happened, but mostly because it was just a simple, uneventful evening. Doug and I were doing nothing special, just driving in the night. I laid my head on his shoulder. The lights coming from the car dashboard were soft, and the winter air outside was cold, making the heater inside the car feel cozy. I believe this was the exact moment when I totally and completely fell in love with my wonderful, loving companion with whom I had spent so much time over the previous months. This moment, I fell in love with Doug, and I have been in love with him ever since. We continued to feel that the more time we spent together, the more we wanted to be together.

Another special band date was New Year's Eve 1976. The year 1977 would prove to be very memorable for us both. Doug's band was usually booked for New Year's. This year, they played for the Officer's Club at Cannon Air Force Base. This became one of the best band engagements I attended. There was all kinds of food; you could eat all you wanted. It was nicely decorated, and they served champagne. It was an elegant military-officer's social affair. Not that I'm prejudiced, but the music was the best part; it was fabulous. The only problem was that Doug was unavailable for dancing. But I looked forward to the band's intermissions.

Then on New Year's Day, Doug and I went horseback riding with some friends at Palo Duro Canyon near Amarillo, Texas. It was a cold, freezing day but a very memorable time of fun.

When Christmas break ended, I began my final semester of high school. School began each day at seven-thirty a.m. with a zero-period computer class. This was when computers were run by punch cards, and the computer took up an entire room—way before the days of small laptop computers. Also on my schedule were three core classes and a student-helper period working for one of the principals. Each day lasted from seven-thirty a.m. to shortly after one p.m. I would then go to my newly acquired first real job at a local accounting office. This made for a very long day, especially considering the very late nights I routinely spent with Doug. It is odd, however, that I was not overly tired and never came close even once to falling asleep in class. I was very happy with every aspect of my life during this time; it seems that teenagers can go through life with little sleep as long as they are doing something they enjoy.

At some point after the New Year began, Doug started looking for a better-paying job. I was unaware that he was making some immediate plans that included long-range preparations for the future. His current job was adequate for a bachelor living alone, but Doug wanted a way to provide financially for a family that seemed very likely to be in his future. Therefore, during the first week of February 1977, he started working for the local Coca-Cola bottling plant as a route salesman. He was paid by commission, and many weeks his pay was triple that of his previous job.

That year we celebrated our first Valentine's Day together. Doug bought me a card with kisses all over it and the words, "The passionate kisser strikes again." Doug believes this Valentine's night is when he fell in love. It definitely was a romantic date of dinner and a movie. Things continued to move in the right direction as we became more and more emotionally attached with each and every date.

Then April 1977 came around, and with the warming of the weather, Doug seemed to change. All of a sudden, he required space and time away from me. I did not like it, but I let him have his space. There was a very short period when we did not see each other as much. I think he was feeling too close to commitment and still needed to feel in charge but was really only running from the obvious.

One night I was totally expecting to have a date, but Doug called and said, "I think I will do something else for a change. I want to shoot pool with Grant."

I said, "Fine, go ahead and spend some time with Grant. I have to take care of my brother; he has a migraine headache."

Doug told me, "He will be fine, just give him an aspirin."

I explained that when my brother got one of these headaches, it was not that simple. But anyway, Doug went with Grant, and I stayed home. My parents were out of town with Dad's second sister at a cousin's basketball game. My brother became worse as the night went by. His pain got so intense that he thrust his fist into a brick wall and broke his hand. I ended up taking him to the hospital; a neighbor went with us. It was a very stressful night, and I was very thankful for the neighbor friend who helped me out.

When Doug heard how my night went, he said, "I'm sorry I was not there for you." But he had even more to feel guilty about when I learned that he and Grant picked up some girls that night. However, it seemed this was a defining moment in our relationship for Doug. After that night, he never even hinted that he wanted his space again. In fact, it was quite the opposite. It was more like he did not want to be apart anymore. Since it was springtime and Doug had a house to care for, there were household chores and yard work to do. He explained to me, "There are some things I need to do that might not be as fun as a formal date, but you can be there with me at my house if you want—that is what I prefer." So we worked on the yard and cleaned things together.

April 1977 also happened to be the month I met his mother, stepdad, and little brother. It was a Sunday, and we were introduced over lunch at Sirloin Stockade. They lived in Albuquerque, and this was the second time they had visited since Doug and I began dating. The first time was too soon for Doug to think of introducing me to this mother. Over the months together though, Doug told me a lot about his family, and I looked forward to meeting them. It was an enjoyable Sunday lunch with Doug's family, and I got only good feelings from our first visit.

My last year of high school was quickly coming to a close, with mid-May starting senior activities, beginning with the prom on May 13. The prom was extra special because Doug and I actually got to dance together. The prom theme was the song "I Only Have Eyes for You." After prom was Senior Week, when seniors were given time to socialize before graduation day. Senior Week consisted of bowling, an all-night showing at the local drive-in theatre, swimming at the YMCA, a trip to the lake, and picnics—all to enjoy together before high-school days officially ended. Then, just ten days after the prom, in May of 1977, I graduated from Clovis High School. My brother played trombone in the high-school band, and he performed "Pomp and Circumstance" over and over as our class of 523 marched in for graduation.

After graduation, Doug installed an FM converter to my AM radio. Now I could get my favorite radio station that played all the great seventies music. I really appreciated Doug's gift and that he had taken the time to install it too. Later on, my car battery went dead. Dad seemed glad to blame Doug for the dead battery because of how the converter was hooked up to my radio. Afterward, Dad regularly put Doug down for doing such a bad deed. Dad's attitude was scornful, and he seemed to think he was the only one capable of doing anything right. After hearing enough of Dad's criticism of my future husband, I told Dad, "You have criticized Doug enough, and you need to know that I love him. I don't want to hear anything else negative from you about him." This became the first time in my life I had drawn a boundary with Dad. I could not bear to hear any more of his corrosive talk. He probably did not stop his bitter, scornful criticism, but at least I never had to listen to anything else he said about Doug again.

I was very certain I had found my forever love in Doug. All the guys I dated previously, with whom I could have considered a commitment, were just not right. But it was different with Doug; he was the perfect fit for my life. Everything about our relationship felt comfortable and right. We were custom-made for each other by God, and there were no adjustments or compromises necessary. With this feeling, it only seemed appropriate to draw a boundary with Dad where my future husband was concerned. Besides, my car battery was easily fixed.

Our lives continued bonding through many different experiences. In June, Doug's maternal grandparents would be celebrating their fiftieth wedding anniversary in Tucson, Arizona. Doug asked me to go with him, so we made the 1,200-mile round trip over one weekend. Doug was born in Tucson, and most of his family still lived there. I met many of them on this trip. It was clear they all thought very highly of Doug, especially his grandmothers. After meeting the family, it was on to the anniversary celebration. The celebration was a very elegant affair hosted by the children at a beautiful local hotel. The food was exceptional, and the ambiance was refined. It was a fabulous experience and a fantastic trip. Traveling with Doug bonded our relationship even more.

Another connection was built when we purchased our white AKC registered German shepherd, Sugar Baby. We both loved our dog, and she was a living thing we cared for together. However, because of my previous experience with my dog Dusty J, I never let myself feel as deeply for another dog.

In July, Doug's band played in Fort Sumner, New Mexico, for an annual celebration when the community goes back in time to celebrate its old western roots. Doug's band performed on a new tennis court built in the historic area of the Fort Sumner Valley. They played late into the night under the stars at a location that happened to be one of my favorite places in the world. It was the valley where I spent the best years of my childhood with Grandma Ada. It also was a bonus this night that Grandma attended the celebration. It was a wonderful, memorable night on which I was afforded the privilege of sharing my favorite place with my favorite guy—my one and only love, Doug.

Clearly, with Doug's presence, my life had begun to take a more functional turn. I had been spending time with someone who cared about me and who was able and unafraid to show it. I mattered to him, and there was no doubt that I cared deeply for him in return. During the previous ten months, we'd started building a lasting relationship of mutual caring and trust. A real, essential emotional connection was present, and love was blossoming between us.

Chapter Twenty-Seven

The Worst Decision I Ever Made

Doug was the one I had been dating for over ten months, and he became the one I fell in love with. I trusted him; I felt comfortable with him, and I truly believed he cared for me and loved me in return. There was something different about him. A real connection was felt by us both and being together was all either of us desired. I had never felt this way about a guy before. Then all that had built up between us after many months of dating culminated in the inevitable. Despite many opportunities over my dating years with other guys, I had resisted until now. Resisting before had been easy compared to this power of emotion that existed with Doug. I finally gave in and no longer was a virgin. I had no legitimate justification for behaving so recklessly and putting myself in a position of great vulnerability. The only explanation I had to offer was that I was in love, and I knew Doug was the one guy for me. But being in love is not a legitimate reason to justify premarital sex. God says sex before marriage is wrong, and God's laws are in place for our good. Ignoring His protection comes with consequences that damage your being and your emotions. "Sexual freedom" is nothing but a form of bondage; there is nothing about it that resembles freedom. Sex outside of marriage will bring damage to your life in some way, no matter how brainwashed you may be by the world to believe otherwise.

As time went by, I began having unusual pains that I had not experienced before. These sudden pains felt similar to cramps, pinches, or a sharp stick. It was not clear what was wrong, but with persuasion from my boyfriend I decided to see a doctor. I had not missed a cycle and did not relate the problem to pregnancy. During the appointment, the doctor informed me that what I was experiencing was most likely a pregnancy. He asked, "Have you been exposed?" I said, "Yes." He told me to come back in a few weeks because it was too early to do an accurate pregnancy test. This was 1977, and current methods of pregnancy testing were not available then. The visit, to say the least, left me feeling very uneasy. However, I did not feel alone in this situation. My boyfriend told me we would be married. Our plans for that event were about two years into the future, though. I knew he loved me and would not desert me, even if there was a baby on the way. But at this point, a pregnancy did not seem real likely. I was living in a state of denial, which was the normal mode of my upbringing.

Living with the thought of a possible pregnancy for several weeks was a heavy load for one so young, at the tender age of seventeen. I am sure there were many instances when I was moody and behaved unlike myself. I continued working for the accountant and spending the rest of my time with Doug. He kept busy with his steady job and band gigs, which sometimes would last for an entire week at a time. I either went to these performances or spent time with my girlfriends prior to starting college at ENMU in the fall. It was difficult waiting to find out about the pregnancy. Then came the time for my cycle to begin, and it was late. This added more anxiety, because it became very clear that I did not need a test to tell me the truth.

At some point before my next doctor's appointment, my mother picked up that something was amiss and insisted I confide in her what was wrong. I had not planned to tell her anything, but she pressured me by asking, "Are you pregnant?" I could not keep from telling her the truth with this pointed question, even though I did not want her to know. From my perspective, it made more sense to know for sure before I told her anything, but as always, she controlled the situation and found out anyway.

When the time came to see the doctor again, I went with Doug ... and my mother. The doctor verified what we already knew: we had a baby on the way. The doctor communicated options. We could either keep the baby *or* we could end the pregnancy with a procedure called an abortion. This seemed to be the option the doctor favored—it appeared he thought an abortion was the only choice for an unwed mother to make. Although he mentioned keeping the baby, abortion was the only alternative he advocated. I had never heard of this choice before and really did not understand the whole concept in relation to the physical as well as the emotional aspects. But Doug was raised by a very liberal mother and had been taught that abortion was a feasible choice. He had also been taught about this "acceptable and safe" method of terminating pregnancy at the more liberal high school he attended in Oahu, Hawaii. My doctor explained abortion to me as a safe procedure that would be quick and easy. He did not talk about what would actually take place. I was uneasy with this choice and could not make that kind of decision so quickly, especially since I still did not feel I understood exactly why I should do this. I was only a few weeks along in the pregnancy, and the doctor told us we had some time to decide what to do—but we should not tarry too long. I was also informed that because of my age, I would have to get a parent's signature for such a procedure to be performed. That meant if we decided to go through with it, my mother would have to be present to sign paperwork. So we left with the news, the options, and the knowledge that whatever choice we made would be life-changing.

During this time period, the Roe v. Wade decision had been in force for only three years, and abortion was not talked about as it is today. It was unusual to hear anything about this so-called "safe procedure"; it was not in the news like it is now. It was certainly never mentioned in the church I attended and was not talked about in any form at the public schools I attended. I had no understanding about this term or what it really meant to have an abortion.

However, I did understand that I had made an unwise decision that came with life-changing consequences. For the first seventeen years of my life, I had been living with the dysfunction of emotional abuse dumped on me throughout my childhood as a result of bad decisions my parents made. Now the bad decision was one I had personally made. Although I have always chosen to take full responsibility for this wrong decision, in reality it does stem in many ways from my upbringing, through my parents' deficient involvement in my life—which, in turn, caused me to reach out for what was lacking. As a child growing up, I was never afforded the stable comfort and security of an earthly father's presence along with the assurance it brings to a daughter's life. To be a daughter loved, cherished, and guided by a caring, involved dad was always an elusive desire for me. Just to know the actual feeling of a male presence I could count on in the basic ways a daughter requires was not a possibility. It is a miracle and a result of God's protection that I was spared the heartache of living in excessive sexual promiscuity, which is a common result for girls experiencing a similar home life to mine. However, I had made a bad choice for a very brief period with one guy—the one guy I would marry for life. Together, we were facing the consequences of our poor decision. We desperately needed wise Christian counsel, which is easy to see now but sadly not so obvious then.

So now what does a seventeen-year-old do when faced with this kind of decision? Since my doctor recommended the option of abortion, trusting him led me to believe this was a viable choice. Doug was frightened concerning our future of being pregnant and not married. And with his background and upbringing, he did not see a problem with having an abortion. My mother was not helpful in giving any sort of input or reasons to *not* go through with this deadly choice—her input was very minimal and non-persuasive. She mostly would wring her hands and say, "I don't know about all this."

Today, after sorting through my past, I have come to realize there was a lot in play here in relation to my emotional health and strength of which I was unaware at seventeen. I had, for all my life, been rejected by Dad; I had been devalued, controlled, and pushed aside by my mother while others in the family seemed to count on me for some form of stability. I could be trusted to do what was right and did not do things that caused trouble to others. But I simply was not strong enough emotionally to face whatever would come from the family if the sense of trust I felt they had in me was shaken for any reason—especially over some bad decision I had made. Reaping the consequences of my actions publicly was just not something I was emotionally able or strong enough to live through. From the history of my childhood, I doubted that any form of support would be there for me if I let it be known that I had messed up. So I reluctantly went along with the advice of my doctor and my boyfriend to have the abortion. Our current situation could be *fixed* quietly, and no one would ever have to know.

The only people who knew at this time besides Doug and I were my mother and one friend I confided in. But it really matters little what people know; it only matters what God knows. And the fact is that God knows everything. There are no secrets in your life from God. At the time, this was a secret my mother had promised to tell no one else, not even Dad. I did know my mother was good at denial and keeping secrets. However, I learned later in life that she was good at keeping secrets if they were her own secrets that covered up *her* pain and trauma. *My* pain and trauma became fair game for her to share with others, even though I asked her not to. After all, I was the child and she was the parent; she could make up the rules as she saw fit. She was in control.

I am not blaming others for something I chose to do. But I really doubt that I would have arrived at the same decision to have an abortion without input from significant people of influence in my life. I know for sure that if I knew then what I know now, I never would have chosen to snuff out the life of the first baby I conceived. Today I cannot even grasp what I could have been thinking to allow such a thing to happen and become part of my life. As a mother of three beautiful, gifted adult children, it just makes no sense to me now that I would even entertain the thought of having an abortion, much less actually go through with it.

This consequence of my impatient decision was fixed quietly and permanently. It also came with a lifetime of regret, pain, and irreplaceable loss. There is a side to the abortion process that is not communicated by the so called "pro-choice" advocates. The majority of abortions are performed for young ladies who are in their teens or early twenties. This is an age when the whole concept of what this choice really means in a life-changing way cannot be grasped by one so young and inexperienced in the journey of life. It was not until two years into the future when I was married, pregnant again, and holding a newborn baby belonging to my friend that I truly understood what it meant to have an abortion. It was a moment when I came to feel the overwhelming reality of it all. Somehow, the little newborn girl looking up into my face gave real meaning and an identity to the baby I would never hold and look into the eyes of.

Abortion should never be a viable option for birth control and convenience. At seventeen, when I walked into the abortion clinic, I was confused and not totally convinced that this was really what I wanted to do. The clinic staff knew what I was feeling because I told them. But rather than giving good and helpful counsel that represented the pros and cons of each choice, they were totally pushing and convincing me that the abortion was the only choice for my own good. I felt like a lamb led to slaughter; I felt coerced into this option. I did it because people who were supposedly "in the know" were telling me it was the right thing to do. It was not what I felt to be right in my heart, but no one offered me a strong reason to change the destructive path I was on. There was no mention of the benefits of giving birth to the baby inside me; it was as if the baby was an object, a thing to dispose of because of the inconvenience it *might* bring. There was no wisdom speaking of the blessings I would definitely lose—my mother did not even mention those.

The day before the abortion, the process was started with a seaweed implant that was put in place to dilate the cervix. This made it possible to aspirate the contents of the uterus with a device similar to a vacuum cleaner. During that night, I felt disoriented, dizzy, confused, and light-headed. All I wanted to do was sleep. The next morning the dilation was complete, the implant was removed, and my baby was sucked out into oblivion as if it never existed and was nothing to value or cherish. I was put into a room for recovery—my boyfriend and mother were allowed to be with me there. I cried uncontrollably. I remember feeling as if something of great value had been stolen from me, and I had little say in the events. I do not remember a lot of physical pain, but I do remember that the emotional torture was overwhelming. The physical pain came later. I was released with antibiotics and pain pills to go home and recover, leaving my baby behind.

The abortion clinic failed to tell me of the profuse bleeding I would experience in a few days. When this happened, it was extremely frightening. The pain was torment, and the bleeding was excessive. I called the clinic, and their reply was, "Oh, did we not tell you to expect that? It is normal; do not worry. See you for your check up next week." They spent their time convincing me to do something I should not have done and not enough time telling me what I needed to know. I was okay, but at seventeen, there is so much you just do not know, and life is scary at best without experiences of this nature to cause more fear and apprehension. I returned for my follow-up visit the next week and by God's grace, everything about my physical condition was normal and healthy.

Abortion clinics are full of brainwashing and lies, telling frightened teenagers, "It is just a safe procedure; there is nothing to it." These lies and deception are robbing our country of our youth and our future. The real truth is that abortion clinics are a place where lawful murder is committed daily, and no one cares about the rights of the unborn baby. I believe with all my being that the choice is made when the woman chooses to have sex. When conception ensues, the choice has already been made. Therefore, if you do not want to have a baby, do not choose to have sex. There is nothing moral, right, or ethical about abortion. I unfortunately speak from experience. I also wonder how many women who claim to be "pro-choice" have personally experienced an abortion themselves. I daresay not many, otherwise they would be transformed from the repercussions and pain of it all.

Any woman who has had the unfortunate experience of an abortion is a victim of our society's convenience. It is my strong opinion that abortions should not be accessible. A young girl is just not equipped to understand all the life-changing ramifications involved with this sort of procedure—and no matter what a woman's age, it is emotionally damaging to have your baby killed.

Most importantly, God says, "Thou shalt not kill" (Exod. 20:13). This is the universal overriding reason to end this heinous practice that represents a black mark on our culture. Just because man has made a law declaring abortion to be legal does not make it right. How can a moral wrong be a civil right? The Bible says, "The truth of the Lord endureth forever" (Ps. 117:2). God's truth does not shift with popular trends or changes in cultural whims. God's truth does not change because man chooses to write and enforce a new earthly law. God's law overrides all of man's pathetic laws when a controversy exists. God's law and truth are constant and forever enduring. His law is the same today as it was thousands of years ago. What was wrong then is still wrong today—no matter what sinful man chooses to believe and attempts to change in order to cover up his sins and ease his guilty conscience.

Through the years since my abortion, I have never been able to forget the pain and sense of loss. Not that I think of this loss constantly, but when triggers bring this past to mind and I do think of the baby I will never hold on this earth, tremendous sadness comes over me. I also experience the feeling of missing out on a once-in-a-lifetime blessing that God had for me. I know for sure, however, that one day I will meet the baby I was unable to cherish and care for here on earth, because that baby is in heaven with God, my Father, where I too will be for eternity. I also know for sure that God has forgiven me for the abortion, which was the worst choice I have ever made. In spite of that regrettable decision, and only by God's grace, I am privileged to enjoy the blessing of looking into the eyes of the three children God gave me after marriage. I have also told each of my children at an appropriate age about the unwise decisions their dad and I made years before, with the goal in mind of communicating our shortcomings to prevent them from experiencing the same pain and heartache their parents live with. The three children my husband and I have been blessed with provide proof of God's forgiveness for the poor choice we made as teenagers.

The pain all began because premarital sex is wrong, which led to another bad decision, the abortion, which also was wrong. Premarital sex is sin. Again the wise words of Pastor Stan White apply, "Sin will take you places you never wanted to go, keep you longer than you wanted to stay, and cost you more than you ever intended to pay." Pre-marital sex may seem okay by society's standards, but it is *not* okay in reality or by God's standards. Humans try to deny God's standards, but whenever they choose to go against God's law, which is in place for our protection and good, there is inevitably a high price to pay for the disobedience. Speaking from experience, abstinence is the best choice. Just wait until you are married. It is better for you physically, emotionally, and spiritually—which is what God knew all along.

What I Lost Forever on August 18, 1977, through Abortion

I believe the baby I will never know on earth was a girl. Her birthday would have been around April 12, 1978. Her name would have been Emilee. I know almost exactly what I missed, because she would have been similar in looks, beauty, laugh, smile, mannerisms, and personality to the daughter I have had the privilege to raise, know, and love. She, however, would have been a unique individual like no one ever born before or since. Her one-of-a-kind qualities are something I will never experience, enjoy, love, or appreciate. I have missed out on ever knowing the joy of being her mother—loving her or feeling her love in return. She would have been similar to her siblings but unique in ways that would have created her own special self. I long to know who she would have been and the special joy she would have brought to my life. I know her dad would have loved her too, because I have seen the special place he has in his heart for the daughter we were blessed to have and love. Why we chose to let go of such a gift is something I will never understand.

I ache to think of leaving my baby in an abortion-clinic aspirator. A helpless small heartbeat was snuffed out before she had a chance to live. How cold, how lonely, how desperately wrong, and how inhumane is this "safe procedure of convenience." It is solely for human comfort and ease—for those who choose to go their own way, make their own rules, and wipe out the consequences of their bad choice by death to the innocent. It has to begin with death to your own feelings; this is the only explainable way a conscious human mind could even be able to think of permitting the deadly procedure or allow such a damaging wrong to occur. This convenient decision of choice ultimately ends in death to an innocent life, death to a baby's small beating heart, and death to what is morally right. This immoral procedure begins with a thought, is conceived into an act, and finishes with the death of your own flesh and blood, sucked away and catapulted into eternity before its time.

My little baby girl was aborted on August 18, 1977. My first child conceived died on this day. My first daughter, Emilee, would never feel sunshine on her face, know the warmth of her mom and dad's love, taste chocolate, laugh, walk, run, swim, or play ... so many things are never to be when one's life is ended before it is allowed to begin. She would never graduate from high school or college, never fall in love, find "the one," get married, and have children of her own. Her dad missed out on walking her down the aisle and giving this bride away. And I missed the wonderful bonding experience of planning her wedding as the mother of the bride. There are so many things we will never experience or do with her. What uniqueness did this daughter possess that the world will never know and will forever miss out on completely?

I love all the things that are wrapped up in the meaning of being the mother of a daughter. I was blessed to experience it all with the daughter I have and love. I threw away the privilege I had to do it all twice. I forfeited the ride and adventure of a lifetime and even gave very little thought as to what it all really meant. At seventeen, you are just not old enough to make such a decision.

An experience I had one day validated to me that my baby I will never know on earth was a girl. In 2004, after we had sold our first home, I was looking through old receipts to add up improvements we made to the house we sold. Among the receipts, I found one from the abortion clinic, and it was dated August 18, 1977. August 18 was the date our daughter, Amanda, was born in 1985—eight years later. At the exact moment I found this receipt and was reminded of the date, my phone rang. I was already crying when I answered the phone; it was my daughter on the other end. She said, "Mom, what's wrong?" I told her what I had just discovered. (Understandably, the date of the abortion was not one I chose to remember, and I needed a reminder from the receipt to put it all together.) My daughter, then age nineteen, knew of the abortion, and I told her I just found that it had been performed on her birthday. I continued to cry and was overwhelmed by the newfound realization. My daughter was comforting, supportive, and reassuring as always. At this moment, I felt God's presence, along with a strong feeling of certainty that the baby aborted was a girl. My daughter's phone call at this moment was no coincidence, which also came with the feeling of God's total forgiveness in such a hurtful circumstance.

I do not believe in reincarnation. I believe my first baby girl is in heaven enjoying peaceful bliss. I also believe that God wanted me to know that the tragedy that occurred on August 18, 1977, was transformed into a day of rejoicing, forgiveness, and gratefulness when August 18, 1985, became the birthday of the precious daughter I have had the privilege of being a mother to. God wanted our daughter involved in leading me to that revelation by her very timely phone call ... *maybe* while our other precious daughter, Emilee, watched from heaven!

I am at peace with forgiveness from God; He has shown me undeniable proof that He forgives me for the worst decision of my life. However, I must explore the root of what I feel regarding this decision. In addition, I must examine what caused me to allow the procedure that will always haunt me because it took the life of my baby. Why was life harder to face by telling the truth about my unwed, pregnant condition than by killing an innocent baby? Especially since I knew that my boyfriend was ready and willing to marry me with or without a baby involved. I felt I could not face the world as a teenager who had made a mistake and gotten pregnant. Why was that so? I believe the answer to that question can be found in the fact that I felt very worthless and unwanted as a child. I did not understand the value of a child because my parents did not value me. And I did not feel I could face more rejection for a bad decision I had made.

My parents were childish; they did not face life head-on as adults do. Up to now, I have taken the full blame for the abortion, with no blame placed on my parents at all. But I think it is time that I realistically revisit what was going on in my life and place some of the blame where it is due, with my childish parents. My parents were very uninvolved and unable to give adequate parental direction along with love, acceptance, reassurance, and stability. Without a real, functional dad figure in my

life, it is a miracle I remained a virgin until I began dating my future
husband. A daughter lacks many things when she has no dad to guide,
direct, and teach as well as just be a good example for life in general.
There is also great comfort in a father's protection that gives stability,
security, and strength to a daughter's life. Dad was unable to provide
for his daughter's basic emotional needs. I believe that if I had gotten
the things I needed from Christian parents in a Christian home while
growing up, especially from Dad, that I would not have faced such a
decision as abortion at all.

When I did become pregnant at seventeen and faced the decision
of abortion, I knew, if I told Dad, I would only get ridicule, scorn,
wrath, and judgment for screwing up my life. Maybe if he had been a
father to me, I would have felt he had a right to give his opinion—but
since up to this point I had survived on my own with no involvement,
guidance or direction from him, I chose to tell him nothing about me.
I had no relationship with him, and I would not talk to him about this
either. Since Dad's behavior had always been childish, when something
big came along, I had no evidence to believe he could give support or
guidance. He had never supported me before, and I could not believe
he would support me now. I also did not want to give him one more
reason to despise my presence, be annoyed with me, and hate me.
What I needed from him was love, support, guidance, and an adult's
perspective; instead, I knew I would get bitter words that I could not
deal with in the state I was in. I needed to know I belonged with no
possibility of further rejection—something I knew Dad could not offer
me.

Although my mother did know about my pregnant, unwed
condition, her reaction conveyed little of what I needed from her. She
just went along without giving her feelings, advice, help, or reasons
why I should not have an abortion. I believe that a parent's consent
is required for a seventeen-year-old to have an abortion because that
parent giving consent has a responsibility to be accountable to give
advice and direction. She never gave me reasons to reconsider the
decision my doctor recommended or to imagine another perspective as
to why I should not go through with the murder of my unborn baby.

She never helped me grasp the fact that I would regret never knowing my baby and that I would regret never knowing the joy of being my baby's mother. I believe she probably did not talk to me about this angle because it was a place she did not understand or come from herself. All I remember her saying as she signed the papers is, "I don't know about all this." That really helped me a lot! I needed a mother's advice; I needed a mother's conviction that came from living life and gaining experience that made her qualified to explain the real meaning of all this. I needed her to tell me why I should not go through with it and why I would regret it all terribly the rest of my life. I knew nothing about what it all really meant, what I would feel years later, and why as a mother I would come to regret the whole decision as the worst choice I had ever made in my entire life. Her signature came with no wisdom or advice that I could grab on to and use—nothing to make anything better for me or my baby. I believe what she needed to give me that day, she did not possess. Love and emotional connection were not things my mother has ever felt or grasped.

Now about me—what was that scared, insecure seventeen-year-old thinking as she permitted such a horrible destructive injustice to happen to herself and her innocent baby? I believe in some part, denial was definitely in place. I had been taught so well by my parents' example to ignore your feelings and be numb and go on with life ignoring the truth. That had to be at the heart of this entire horrible ordeal. I felt so rejected already, I did not feel as though I could live through my family's reaction to me being pregnant and unwed. I also know that I felt worthless and devalued; these feelings had been ingrained into my thinking by both my parents' actions throughout my childhood. I believe I had felt so devalued by my own parents that it enabled me to abort my own child. Since I had little value placed on me, I had not yet learned the irreplaceable position and enormous worth of a child. My life was not worth much, and I was taught that children were a burden, an imposition on one's life, and a consequence caused by sinful behavior. Something Grandpa quoted often was "If you play, you will pay," referring to being pregnant; it is what he told my mother when she told him she was expecting my baby sister.

All of this human thinking and conclusion is completely opposite of the message God gives to us in the Bible. God's view is that every person is valued so much by God that according to the Bible, "For God so loved the world, that he gave his only begotten Son, that whosoever believeth in him should not perish, but have everlasting life" (John 3:16). God loved and gave to us through the life, death, burial, and resurrection of Jesus, His Son. Jesus gave His life so I could live in heaven one day in spite of the sins I would commit; all I had to do was put my faith in Jesus and in what He did for me. Jesus died for me so He would not have to live without me. There is no greater love than that, and I am worthy because of what Jesus did for me. Every life has value, no matter what message your family may convey in contradiction to that.

If I could go back in time, this is one thing in my life I would do differently for sure. I would choose to abstain in obedience to God's law, because He knows what is best for me. I am confident the outcome could have been different and better. If I had to face being pregnant and unwed again, I would have my baby, no matter what others might think of me in their false and unfounded beliefs. I would never again consider abortion as an option. Abortion is wrong and should never be offered as a choice to legally kill your baby.

Part IV
The Functional Era Begins

Chapter Twenty-Eight

A Proposal of Marriage

Many times throughout our life together, Doug was led by circumstances that pushed him toward making the right decision. It is unclear at what point Doug would have actually decided it was time for us to get married. However, it seemed that the abortion, being such a hurtful and damaging ordeal, did somehow provide the catalyst. On August 22, 1977, Doug proposed to me on bended knee, as he placed a diamond ring on my finger. And knowing for sure there was no other man for me than Doug, I quickly accepted with "Yes," a hug, and a kiss.

Life then rapidly turned into a frenzy of activity, giving attention to the necessary preparations and planning of our wedding. All these activities would have to be worked around school, which was to begin the following week at Eastern New Mexico University. And since I was still working for the accountant, my job also took a share of my limited time. At this point, there were two things we decided about our wedding: the colors were light blue and white, and the exact date was to be October 29, 1977, only days after I turned eighteen. That gave us only two months to plan our perfect wedding day.

The great demands on my time became very stressful, causing the emotional damage from childhood to surface again. So much to accomplish in such a short time became overwhelming because of the limited coping skills I had acquired up to this point in my life. There was a time, after several weeks of planning, that I was unsure if I even wanted to get married at all. I was very emotional at times, especially when Doug was away playing in the band or college demands were great.

Doug knew there was a problem, so he went to talk to my mother for advice. She told him that my actions were normal in this type of situation. I am sure she based her input on her own emotionally damaged life. The next time I saw my mother after Doug had spoken to her, the advice she had for me was to quit school, quit the job, and marry Doug. That was basically good advice, but why did I have to forfeit my career and education just because I decided to get married? It had always felt to me that my mother did not want me to get a college degree; she wanted me to be a housewife, just like her. Why couldn't she just support me and encourage me, if only for the simple reason that it was what I wanted to do with my life? Instead of telling me that I could succeed and I was completely capable of doing all these things and doing them well, she told me to quit and give up. I did not quit school; it was important for me to continue. And I certainly did *not* give up on the best relationship I had ever known. I really only required some help with getting a proper perspective in regard to all the newly placed demands on my life at age seventeen. I am sure, too, that the emotional damage from childhood made life harder, in addition to the abortion weighing on my mind, causing more emotional trauma and problems with coping. But I fully intended to marry Doug. Therefore, the wedding plans continued. It was what Doug and I both wanted.

If I needed to give up something, it did seem that the job was the most reasonable thing to let go at this time. A few weeks passed after the emotional encounter that had prompted Doug to talk with my mother. I was still feeling overwhelmed by all the things that were requiring my attention. I was on my way to work after lunch and was to be the only person working in the accounting office that afternoon. I drove by Furr's Supermarket on the way. This was one of Doug's stops on his Coca-Cola route, and he happened to be standing in the parking lot by his truck. I stopped, intending to only say hello. But we began talking about the stress and our wedding demands. I was to be at the office at one p.m., and it soon became one-fifteen. I had to leave.

When I arrived at the office, my boss had had a change of plans, so he was there. Since I was late, I was glad to see he had been there all along, and the doors did not remain closed because of my absence. This man who gave me my first real job was very empathetic and understanding. During the time I had worked for him, we had developed a mutual respect and friendship. And as it turned out, he was more in-tune with my feelings than I was. He met me as I came into the office and inquired, "How are you doing today?"

I replied, "Okay."

He asked, "Are all the things you have going on now getting to be too much for you?"

I reluctantly agreed, "Yes, I guess they are."

He then asked how he could help. I told him that it seemed the time had come for me to stop working for him. I really did not want to quit. I loved working at the accounting office. The work I had done there was what led me to choose accounting and business as my college major. I told him, "I really do not want to quit my job. I enjoy doing this type of work, and I like working for you."

He responded, "You do not have to quit forever; you can return at a future date, when it fits better into your life." He added, "Maybe you can come back after you have graduated."

I liked that possibility, and I was glad to see that he did not want me to leave. So at this point in time, we discussed what I needed to accomplish before I quit. I continued working for a time until all the projects I was personally working on were finished. Then I left my job and concentrated on college and wedding planning.

Our most important wedding plan was to meet with my preacher. Doug and I visited with him and talked in depth about the decision we were about to make. One basic question he asked was whether Doug was saved or not. Since he was my preacher, he knew I was saved but needed verification as to Doug's spiritual condition. This question is of the utmost importance when a Christian has decided to marry. The Bible gives guidelines regarding Christian marriages: "Be ye not unequally yoked together with unbelievers: for what fellowship hath righteousness with unrighteousness? And what communion hath light with darkness?" (2 Cor. 6:14). This was the root cause for the dysfunction in my childhood home—my mother was saved and Dad was not. A Christian choosing to disobey God's guideline for marriage leads to a life of pain, damage, and turmoil. Before deciding to marry Doug, I knew he was a born-again Christian. I was determined not to make the same mistake my mother had made. Doug told the preacher of his salvation experience and confirmed that he was a born-again, saved child of God. We were then given the preacher's blessing to marry and began talking about the ceremony and other arrangements in regard to the church's participation in the wedding event.

Next we met with our photographer to discuss specific poses. The photographer suggested one photograph in particular—of Dad and me when we entered the church as the wedding began. Our photographer would wait next to an end pew, and Dad and I were supposed to pause for a moment and look at each other as the picture was taken. Then we were to continue on down the aisle. (The picture did not happen this way; I will explain in the next chapter.) Our pictures would become extra important because there were no videographers back then, and VCRs had not been invented in 1977.

I had little trouble finding the perfect wedding dress and veil. Doug rented his tuxedo. The drummer in Doug's band was his best man, and my friend Dee was my maid of honor. We had two flower girls; one was my little sister, the other was my cousin close in age to my sister. My five-year-old cousin, the flower girl's brother, was our ring bearer—he called himself the "ring bear." Together Doug and I, along with my mother, made most of the necessary wedding arrangements. Dad was not involved at all and knew very little about anything regarding the wedding. But he did complain several times during the planning process about "all the money" we were spending. Just as always, money was his priority, not my needs and happiness.

The final event before our wedding day was the wedding rehearsal. Our wedding had several candelabras—one was very big and heart-shaped. Doug's little brother had agreed to light the candles. He felt confident that he could handle the job because he participated in candle-lighting at church many times. Doug's mother often tells of his little brother's overwhelmed amazement when he said, "I have to light all those candles! I thought there would be just a few!" That was the biggest revelation at the rehearsal.

Then it was off to the restaurant for our rehearsal dinner. Doug's parents chose a local steakhouse that had been in Clovis for many years. Doug's stepdad's preference was prime rib. It was a delicious dinner, and the prime rib was excellent. The dinner was obviously a significant expense. But the feeling I got from my future stepdad-in-law was that it was never about how much it cost. It was more about a feeling of emotional connection and genuine caring for Doug and me, which was opposite to the way Dad had always made me feel. After the wonderful rehearsal dinner, all the events prior to the wedding day were complete. I was looking forward to beginning my future with Doug and building a family free of all the hurtful things I had lived through as a child.

October 28, 1977, was the last day of my childhood—a childhood that hurt so bad I would one day need counseling to live through the repressed memories of the past that inevitably would be triggered in the future. That day, I left behind my childhood home under the authority of an unsaved Dad who did not worship or reverence God. And I also left behind all the pain, turmoil, trauma, hurt, emotional damage, and dysfunction that living under the authority of an unsaved dad had brought to my life. The worst era of my life now ended.

My brighter future would begin tomorrow. It was thrilling to think, we were only hours away from our *big day!*

Chapter Twenty-Nine

Our Wedding Day

"...put your hand in mine sweetheart; together we shall go; along life's path, a dream fulfilled because I love you so."—A quote from our wedding album

Our wedding day began when, in different homes, Doug and I woke up at precisely the same time of 8:43 a.m. Doug was at his home, soon to be our home, and I was at my childhood home. Grandma Ada was there and was appropriately present for my final night in my parent's house before embarking on adulthood. I started this special day talking to Grandma; I always loved spending time with her.

Even on my wedding day, I was not immune to the hurtful feelings our family dysfunction continued to bring. At some point during this morning, I looked out the front door and noticed Dad's best friend walking up to the house. He was there to see Dad and had no idea I was getting married or that Dad had a wedding to attend this day. It seemed that again, whatever was going on in my life had little to no impact on Dad's routine. I told Dad's friend I was getting married today and he said, "Oh, I did not know. Congratulations!" Such an important day in my life, and Dad did not even tell his best friend. Once again, I was reminded that anything happening in my life, even my wedding day, was not significant to dad. The hurtful dysfunction was ever present in my parents' house. I watched as Dad's friend walked away, and I thought, *I will change my name today. I will leave behind all this mess and start fresh.* This really was the first day of the rest of my life, and I knew for sure it would all be better than it ever had been before.

I quickly changed my focus and went back to the happiness of the day. The wedding ceremony was to begin at two p.m. We were to be at the church, fully dressed and ready for pictures, by noon. I planned to dress at the church, so I gathered some things and began the short walk to the church. I am not sure of the exact time I arrived at the church, but I know it was well before noon. As I entered the back door of the church, Doug was standing inside the doorway. He was fully dressed in his white tuxedo, and upon seeing me, he quickly vanished. He was determined we were not to see each other before the exact moment I began walking down the aisle. I was surprised to find Doug already at the church and ready for pictures. He had developed a reputation for lacking promptness. I, however, was pleased; if he chose to be on time for something, our wedding was a good place to start. My groom had beaten me to the church! That told me he really was excited about getting married, and I could relax. There was no need to worry about Doug being late today.

I went back to the appointed room and began putting on my wedding dress. As part of getting dressed, I included the traditional something old, a pin from Grandma Bessie; something new, my wedding dress; something borrowed, a gold bracelet belonging to my maid of honor, Dee; and something blue, my garter. I also wore pennies in my very tall shoes, minted in the year of my birth and in the year of Doug's birth. I needed tall shoes, since Doug is nine inches taller than me. I was assisted in getting dressed by Dee, the flower girls, and a few other friends. As soon as I was ready, the photographer took all the pre-wedding pictures possible without me crossing paths with Doug. There was a moment during the picture-taking with my parents that became emotional. This was the first memory I have of them telling me they loved me. These words were not spoken in our house. And at this point in my life, they felt very awkward—like words that were supposed to be spoken because they seemed appropriate during this day of change, not because they were backed with real feelings.

The ceremony began at exactly two p.m. Doug's little brother did a great job lighting all the candles. The many candles glowing amongst the blue and white flowers and greenery provided the main source of light inside the church. Doug, the preacher, and the best man were all in place at the front of the church. The music played as the first to walk down the aisle was the "ring bear," carefully carrying his lacey pillow with Doug's ring firmly attached. Then the maid of honor proceeded to the front of the church. Then my little sister and cousin walked in, spreading their flower petals from the baskets they each carried, preparing the way for the bride to come. Dad and I were ready to proceed down the aisle as soon as the flower girls made their way to the front.

Then came the emotional surge when a small moment of silence was broken by the energy and feeling that accompanies the familiar beginning of the bridal march, to which Dad and I entered the church. I was carrying my very heavy bridal bouquet made of tiny white roses and blue carnations accented with baby's breath and greenery, along with my Bible covered in white satin decorated with lace and ribbons. I was desperately trying to hold back tears as I focused on Doug, my groom, my one and only love, as he stood waiting for me at the altar. I felt God's presence and knew for sure everything about this moment and this decision was right and completely in God's perfect will for my life. Feeling all this intensely, I started down the aisle heading to the altar and to my groom where God and the preacher were also waiting. In this moment, I totally forgot about a picture that was supposed to be taken with Dad looking at me. I never even saw the photographer waiting inconspicuously behind the pew, posed for the perfect picture of daughter and dad. It somehow really did not disappoint me later that this picture was missing. God was with me and also with Doug as he waited. We proceeded down the aisle, and I continued to fight back the tears.

Now began the wedding ceremony when I married Doug before God. Each word in the ceremony has meaning and is part of beginning and building a solid marriage. My marriage began the functional, happy era of my life. These words taken and lived seriously by both Doug and me were the healing foundation God brought to my life. Therefore, because of its significance, I will share our entire ceremony.

When we reached the steps to the altar, I stood with Dad as the preacher began speaking:

"Marriage is God's first institution for the welfare of the human race. In the quietness of Eden, before the forbidden tree had yielded its fateful fruit or the tempter had touched the world, God saw that it was not good for man to be alone. He made a helpmate suitable for man and established the rite of marriage. His word teaches that marriage is to be a permanent relationship of one man and one woman, freely and totally committed to each other, as companions for life. Our Lord declared that man shall leave his father and his mother and unite with his wife in the building of a home, and the two shall become one flesh."

Doug stepped down to meet us.

Then the preacher asked, "Who gives this woman to be married to this man?"

Dad replied, "Her mother and I do."

Doug took my hand and led me to the altar beside him. Then our wedding song began as a longtime friend played the piano. The friend who sang was the maid of honor's mother and my former English teacher from junior high. The song she sang was "We've Only Just Begun," a song made famous by The Carpenters. Then the preacher continued:

"Marriage was ordained by God in Eden and confirmed at the wedding in Cana of Galilee by the gracious presence and miraculous blessing of Jesus Christ. It is a sacred, unbreakable union of one man and one woman who dedicate themselves to the loving service of God, each other, their children, and their neighbors.

"Marriage unites two hearts and lives, blending all their interests, sympathies, and hopes. It involves mutual forbearance, loving sufferance, unwavering confidence, lifelong trust, and happiness that is found in making each other happy.

"Such a solemn linking of destinies should not be effected lightly, but reverently, prayerfully, soberly, and in the fear of God. In contrast with all other earthly compacts entered into for mutual protection, advancement of interests, or hope of gain, marriage is a holy contract uniting man and woman for the establishment of a home that shall endure through all the storms of life.

"Whether, then, the oncoming flood of years from out of the unknown future bring joy or sorrow, health or sickness, prosperity or adversity, sunshine or shadow, hopes fulfilled or dreams shattered, husband and wife are pledged to be true to each other forever, finding in mutual love life's greatest treasure and God's generous gift.

"The home is built upon love, which virtue is best portrayed in the thirteenth chapter of Paul's first letter to the Corinthians: 'Love is patient and kind, love is not jealous, or conceited or proud; love is not ill-mannered, or selfish or irritable; love does not keep a record of wrongs, love is not happy with evil, but is happy with the truth. Love never gives up: so faith, hope, love abide, these three, but the greatest of these is love' [a rendition of 1 Cor. 13:4–7 and 13].

"You, Douglas, and you, Deborah, having come to me signifying your desire to be formally united in marriage, and being assured that no legal, moral, or religious barriers hinder this proper union, I ask you to join your right hands.

"You are exhorted to dedicate your home to your creator. Take His word, the Bible, for your guide, give loyal devotion to His church, live your lives as His willing servants, and true happiness will be your temporal and eternal reward.

"Douglas, will you take Deborah to be your wedded wife, to live together after God's ordinance in the holy state of matrimony? Will you love her, comfort her, honor and keep her, in sickness and in health, and forsaking all others, be true and loyal to her so long as you both shall live?"

Doug answered, "I will."

"Deborah, will you take Douglas to be your wedded husband, to live together after God's ordinance in the holy state of matrimony? Will you love him, comfort him, honor and keep him, in sickness and in health, and forsaking all others, be true and loyal to him so long as you both shall live?"

I answered, "I will."

"The wedding ring is a symbol of marriage in at least two ways. The purity of gold symbolizes the purity of your love. And the unending circle symbolizes the unending vows that you are now taking, which may be broken honorably only by death.

"Douglas, you will give the ring and repeat after me: 'Deborah, with this ring I thee wed, in the name of the Father, and of the Son, and of the Holy Spirit.'

"Deborah, you will give the ring and repeat after me: 'Douglas, with this ring I thee wed, in the name of the Father, and of the Son, and of the Holy Spirit.'

"Will you both now repeat after me: 'Entreat me not to leave thee, or to return from following after thee. For whither thou goest I will go, and whither thou lodgest I will lodge. Thy people shall be my people and thy God my God.'"

Two Candles Become One

"Because of the vows that you have taken, you have become one flesh, one in thought, intent, and hope in all the concerns of the present life. Therefore, Douglas and Deborah, you are no longer two independent persons but one, for by the laws of this state and as a minister of the Gospel, I now pronounce you husband and wife. What God hath joined together, let not man put asunder."

Doug and I then lit the unity candle together with individual candles and blew out our smaller candles.

Home Dedication

"It makes our hearts glad that you desire to dedicate your newly established home to God. I trust that you will at all times honor it by His continual presence and daily leadership. Make certain that you have a family altar that will honor Him and deeply enrich your lives in His work together. Homes may crumble about you and life will not always be easy, but with God as your foundation, you will be able to withstand the storms of life and build a home to His glory and to your deserved happiness. If this is your desire, will you please kneel?"

Doug and I then knelt at a prayer bench we had placed at the church altar and bowed our heads. The preacher said a prayer that dedicated our home, our marriage, and our lives to God, our Father and asked for His blessings and guidance as we began our new life together. After the prayer, the preacher said, "And now, Douglas and Deborah, go forth upon your journey of life to bless the world and glorify God. *The groom may kiss the bride.*"

Doug gently lifted my wedding veil and gave me a very memorable kiss. (Prior to this moment, Doug had told me there would be no short peck on the lips that you see so many "just married" couples do for this special kiss. So he warned me to be prepared.) Doug did as he promised; the kiss was representative of Doug. "Mr. Hot Lips" was true to form.

Then we turned together and faced our church full of family and friends as the preacher introduced us as husband and wife. The church was filled with happiness and clapping as my husband and I proceeded down the aisle and out the church. The photographer took a picture as we were headed out the front door, and I was completely overjoyed and fighting back tears accompanied by huge smiles of radiant bliss.

Next was the reception immediately following the ceremony, which began with the receiving line consisting of Doug, me, and our parents. It was a great part of the wedding when we greeted and spoke to all our wedding guests. Both Grandma Ada and Grandma Bessie attended the wedding. Uncle Jim and his wife, Aunt Judy, were there; their children participated as flower girl and "ring bear." Doug's maternal grandparents from Tucson also attended—I am especially glad they were able to be with us on our wedding day, because I know without a doubt that Doug's grandma prayed for us regularly throughout the years. There was also a host of family and friends to follow. A memorable part of the receiving line was when, from all the hugs, my veil would not stay attached to my hair. As it came off one final time, Doug took it and placed it on his head. The photographer was quick to get a picture; it happened for only a brief moment. This picture is extra special because it was taken when Uncle Jim was shaking Doug's hand.

A special part of the reception was my dream wedding cake—a tall five-tier masterpiece beautifully decorated with blue and white candy flowers lacing and winding throughout each tier. The cake topper was an upside-down glass brandy snifter encasing a miniature bride and groom. Absolutely beautiful cake! According to tradition, we fed each other wedding cake and toasted from our "bride and groom" goblets containing a delicious recipe of non-alcoholic, blue punch.

During our wedding day, my little sister was very emotional and cried a lot. I am sure the entire wedding experience felt like chaos to a seven-year-old. I later learned that she did not want me to leave and felt like she would not see me anymore. During a time before the ceremony when she was upset and crying, Doug's stepdad talked to her. He said, "Are you upset because they would not let you wear your sneakers today?" That made her laugh. She still remembers him caring about how she felt and the now infamous question he asked her.

After changing into our going-away outfits, we proceeded out of the church. I could see Doug's car from the door; it had been decorated. I learned later that my brother and some of Doug's friends were involved with this decoration ploy. Mounds of puffy shaving cream covered the windows. As we walked out the door, we were heavily pelted with rice. I remember my brother was the one who got in my face and hit me the hardest. That really stung! There is a picture of him throwing rice at us. We made our way to the car with eyes partially closed to shield us from the deluge of stinging rice. Doug turned on the windshield wipers to remove the shaving cream and clear his view to drive. We then headed downtown to Main Street, with friends following and horns honking and "Just Married" written all over the car.

In thinking over how the wedding event had gone overall, the only thing that was forgotten was cream for the coffee—absolutely *not* a tragedy. Amazing! There were many friends who jumped in and helped out during the final crunch time when everything had to come together at once. Nothing about the day turned out imperfect in any way. All the plans and all the frustrating moments had worked out to our advantage, and we had a blissful, blessed, and perfect wedding day.

We enjoyed a short honeymoon at a hotel in Carlsbad, New Mexico. We stayed in the bridal suite, which had a huge sunken bathtub in the shape of a heart. It was romantically unique. We woke up the next morning to a breakfast of steak and eggs, and then we toured Carlsbad Caverns and spent time by the Pecos River, the same river that flows by Grandma Ada's farm. After honeymooning for two days and two nights, we returned home to move my belongings from my parents' house to the new official residence of the newlyweds. We moved in together on the night of October 31, 1977, the first night in *our* home. My new beginning started off in the arms of my Christian husband. Tonight I began the rest of my life—the best part.

Here seems the most appropriate place to describe some of what I was to experience with my one and only, my faithful and true love of a lifetime husband, Doug. "Knight in Shining Armor" or "Prince Charming" are inadequate to describe the wonderful fairytale marriage Doug and I would go on to live. You could read or watch the world's most moving romantic love story, and I guarantee it would pale in comparison to my real-life love story with Doug. There is no element I have ever discovered in any romantic saga that outshines my true-life day-to-day romance of everlasting love. Doug is much more than the man of my dreams; until I met him, I never knew men like him even existed. He is caring, loving, and always giving. His goal for our life together is to make today better than yesterday. When we said our wedding vows to each other on October 29, 1977, Doug took them to heart. For each of us, the vows became a part of our very being. I know and feel every day that nothing but God is more important in Doug's life than me, our marriage, and our love. It is a "won't let go" kind of love that has weathered many trials of life—even so strong as, by God's will, to overcome death. All I can say as I stand amazed and in awe of the most wonderful gift God ever gave to me, second only to my salvation, is "Thank you, Father, for blessing my life with Doug, and for the love you put in his heart for me alone." When I call Doug "my one and only," I mean just that; there has been no one else for me ever. I have had physical relations with no one but Doug, and furthermore, I have never even been tempted in this area of life to do otherwise. Some people may think it is boring to have only one sexual partner for a lifetime, but I count it as a peaceful, wonderful blessing. It is a gift from God, a definitive strong point of my life that I take great pride in. After over thirty-three years, this is still my stance. I believe it is living in obedience to God's plan for my life, and I know it is a reason that I enjoy the blessings and miracles I do, along with God's special protection.

Continuing your Christian walk throughout life with your one and only spouse solidifies marital love and stabilizes a marriage, filling it with security, love, peace, trust, and a thrill for life found in no other relationship. A Christian marriage, where God is honored first and obeyed, truly is a "heaven on earth" experience. Life is not perfect—it never is. But for Doug and me, our life together has been one I would sign up to live over and over and over again. I love Doug, and I know that God is guiding and protecting us in every way.

Chapter Thirty

God Provides a Safety Net for Life and Marriage

Our wedding ceremony was based on God's principles for marriage. It was the beginning of a strong marriage built on a sturdy foundation. In our wedding ceremony, we did not say the words "I do"; instead, we said the words "I will." It seems to be more of a continuous commitment that way. "I do" seems to be just one point in time—as in right now, maybe not later. "I will" states intent to continue on with the commitment. Our ceremony was this way by the advice of our preacher. I believe it was wise input.

Many people today choose to get married in a ceremony that leaves out God and His guidelines for marriage. This is foolish. In today's modern world, many marriage ceremonies are only words written by the bride and groom about their feelings for each other. These words are used in place of the guidelines God recommends for a wedding ceremony and are void of God's presence, blessings, and divine leadership. This only sets up the new marriage for failure. There is no substance or power in what they are saying—it is just words they each are humanly powerless to perform. It is like trying to build a home with no foundation. Nothing in life has substance and meaning without God's presence and blessing. This is the most probable reason that many marriages fail. They crumble as sand, but the Christian marriage built on and lived by God's principles will stand firm because marriage and life are both built on "the rock."

Most marriages fail when God is left out. Marriage is a relationship that can never reach its full potential without God's guidance. Marriages that try to succeed without "the rock" are usually the ones that crumble. And if a couple is determined to stay together in a marriage without God, it often becomes an unhappy union of strife, discontentment, and bickering without peace and mutual respect. This is an accurate description of my parents' marriage. I know from my childhood how damaging and harmful a home can be when God is abandoned.

However, for Doug and me, our marriage has worked and been the source of much love, happiness, joy, and peace over the years. This is only because God is the foundation of the life we have built together. Life is not perfect, and there have been some difficult times in our relationship together. That is expected, because life is life and hard times are part of life. But with God's presence and guidance, hard times do not damage but only strengthen a marriage and family. Unfortunately, Doug and I have also experienced a few times when we were not on track spiritually and were not as close to God as we needed to be. These times were mainly in our early adjustment years together. We have learned, though, that difficult times can be overcome. Living the Christian life every day is the key. Building a relationship with God will make your entire life better and more meaningful. Christian growth and maturity is a desirable goal. It is important that *both* husband and wife have a strong foundation and relationship with God and *both* are seeking His will. Then the marriage will be solid, immovable, and permanent, just as it was meant to be.

Whether you are single or married, living life without God's leadership will always leave you empty, with a constant nagging feeling that something is missing. Without God's guidance and enabling, the empty void will be present, leaving you vulnerable and open to some very costly mistakes. This can be a reason that marriage vows are broken or a cause of other bad decisions that bring hurt and damage. Seeking peace and contentment anywhere other than God will always leave one empty-handed, lonely, and injured. True peace and happiness are unattainable without God's provision. More times than not, bad decisions will inflict pain and suffering on innocent people. Spouses or children also reap the consequences of bad decisions made without God's protection.

For Doug and me, our faith in God and our determination to put Him first has made the difference in our marriage and in our lives. There are many statistics pointing out that few marriages have a chance to make it through an entire lifetime. According to Jennifer Baker of the Forest Institute of Professional Psychology in Springfield, Missouri, "Currently, the likelihood of a first marriage succeeding is 50 percent; which means one out of every two, first marriages fail." And if this were not worrisome enough, I recently heard on the radio that couples who married in the 1970s have a lower chance of succeeding than the norm. Marriages performed in this period have less than a 50 percent chance of keeping it together for twenty-five years or more. With these statistics in mind, and considering that my husband and I got married in 1977, along with the fact that he was twenty years old and I was eighteen, beating the odds for our circumstances, in worldly terms, would have been considered a long shot. When I got married at age eighteen, if I had known these facts, I could have been frozen by fear to never take a chance on lifelong happiness with the one true love God had sent to me. After living through a childhood of turmoil and pain, I determined I would marry for life—divorce was *not* an option. I would not raise my children in a broken home. Considering the marriage statistics, deciding to marry at age eighteen in the year 1977 could have been a scary decision to make, let alone believe I would be able to see it through for a lifetime. But depending on God and faith overrides worldly circumstances.

Doug and I are in the less-than-50-percent group married in the 1970s who have kept it together now for over thirty years. God can make the difference and use lives dedicated to Him to disprove manmade statistics. My marriage started out God-centered, and it is still God-centered. Without faith in God, my husband and I would have probably ended up as one of these quoted statistics. I believe with my entire being (and I believe this because I have lived it) that no marriage relationship can be truly happy and fulfilled, experiencing contentment and peace, unless the man and the woman *both* are born-again children of God, *both* are totally committed to serving God, and *both* give Him the ultimate authority to guide and direct their lives together. When you put your faith in God, statistics or anything else gleaned from worldly wisdom do not impose fear or unrest because they do not touch a life dedicated to God that is under His protection. When I chose to get married at age eighteen, I was stepping out on faith, doing what God was guiding me to do, and trusting Him to take care of the rest. Having a God-centered marriage for over thirty years has proven to me yet again that God's guidance is always far superior for my life, in spite of what the world may say is normal or try to dictate. God's abiding presence has again blessed Doug and me with another miracle. We enjoy a long-term, happy, contented, and peaceful marriage despite worldly odds that were not in our favor.

There will always be times in life when storms come your way. However, with God as the divine anchor for the husband, wife, and marriage, it is possible to weather any storm. Divorce rates are so high today because people mistakenly believe they can live without God's guidance, presence, and protection. With this setup, families are damaged, lives are hurt, needs are not met, and marriages fail. I have lived the damage from being raised in a home where God was left out; it is destructive. I also know the other side from choosing to make a Christian home with my husband where God is honored and obeyed. Life this way is far superior; it is better than any dream you could ever imagine. Marriage is at its best when God is present through the faith, trust, and love of a couple committed to obediently seeking and living His perfect will for their life together. When you choose to willingly give God His rightful place in your life and marriage, everything else will naturally fall into place. "Seek ye first the kingdom of God, and his righteousness; and all these things shall be added unto you" (Matt. 6:33).

Chapter Thirty-One

Newlywed Adjustments

Getting used to married life and learning the give-and-take required in marriage began to cause old feelings of rejection to surface. My husband has always been the kind of guy to give above and beyond the minimum required to anything he does, which is not a bad thing and one of the many qualities that I truly admire about him. On any job he has ever had, he works to the best of his ability—above and beyond the norm. After all, Doug is an Eagle Scout, and that fact alone says a lot about a guy's work ethic. That work ethic has always reaped great rewards for our lives, but it also meant he worked long hard hours at the sales/delivery job he had then. And in addition to his more-than-full-time job, he also played regularly with his band. Being a popular dance band in the community and the surrounding area, they were booked almost every weekend. The band had to practice, too, as is required of any musicians to perform at their best. Blending his schedule with my schedule of full-time daily attendance at the university thirty miles out of town left little time for us to be together.

The band added other inconveniences to our daily life as a newlywed couple adjusting to living together. Doug and his three band members practiced at our house, which made studying for school very difficult because of the noise level. Band practice should not have been a problem on the night I attended night class, which usually let out around ten p.m. However, when I got home at this late hour, the band was still practicing. Our house was located at the end of a cul-de-sac, which meant parking was at a premium. So I would drive home late at night, tired from being at class all day and night, only to find there was no place to park. It was usually about an hour before they finally would break it up and go home. My new husband and I lived with this arrangement for months after we were married. He would always listen to my concerns and do what he could to make things work more smoothly. The band even began to practice at another member's house instead of ours.

Since Doug and I began living together after marriage, we faced a lot of adjustments and changes to work through. I knew of Doug's band responsibilities before marriage, but as long as we were just dating, the day-to-day impact on my routine did not surface. Since I married my husband knowing full well that he played in a band, it was difficult to speak up about how all this made me feel. I married him for better or worse, and the band had definitely become part of the worse.

As newlyweds, we needed time together. But with work, school, studying and the band's demands, time together was rare. Although the money from the band was nothing to dismiss lightly, the time required in practice, setup, and sometimes travel left little alone time for the two of us in our early months of marriage. I knew that my husband enjoyed playing bass guitar with the band, and that it was more than the money to him. Money was just a bonus he received while doing something he loved. I felt guilty for how hard all this was for me to adjust to. I wanted what was best for my husband but had difficulty reconciling how the band could really fit into the family life we envisioned. I also had no idea that the dysfunctional environment I experienced as a child was the reason I felt and behaved the way I did. Lack of coping skills seemed once again to be in the forefront of my problems. This caused me to need more reassurance, more presence from my husband, more of him than was available when he was putting his extra time into a band. We had our relationship storms, partly because we were getting used to living together, partly because we were both spiritually immature and the dysfunctional past was present, but mostly because we were not attending church regularly where we both could grow spiritually together. I especially needed to be in church regularly to heal from the emotional abuse I had experienced in my childhood. Therefore, since this was not happening as it needed to, strife was present to a greater degree than was necessary.

I kept occupied with school, studying, and spending time with my two best friends from high school. But it often felt that not much changed after marriage, except now I felt extremely unwelcome at my parents' house when I visited alone. On several occasions when I visited my parents, they made me feel like I was intruding, especially my mother. "Why are you here?" was the message she relayed to me nonverbally—and sometimes verbally. These visits on weekend nights were so uncomfortable that I stopped visiting unless Doug was available to go with me. Doug was always welcome, and he seemed to be my ticket to a normal visit with my parents. Otherwise, I did not bother with seeing them when I was looking for something to do during Doug's busy nights. They still seemed to push me away.

As a child and into my adult years, my parents were not the same people to me that other people saw. To others, they wore a mask and covered up the person underneath, denying their true selves. My parents seem likable; that is what they put forth. Without living with them, you could not know them. To the world, they behaved the way they think they should instead of living in truth. They worked hard to conceal and cover up their compensating life. My mother does not control, possess, and throw fits of raging anger around other people. Her normal behaviors were not revealed outside our four walls. My mother's anger was her secret; she would have been embarrassed for anyone to witness her true personality. In fact, the mother I knew was mostly unknown even to her parents and brother. And Dad could be open, welcoming, and friendly to other people but displayed opposite behaviors to his family. Dad could appear amiable when other people were around but quickly reverted to his normal scornful, unwelcoming demeanor with us. Our neighbors had a very different view of my mother and dad than I did; their true self was covered up and compensated for. For company, they put on their best and most beautiful emotional attire. Their ugly, emotionally damaging ways appeared only to our family when no one else was around. My mother could change moods at the drop of a hat if someone came visiting. Dad always looked out for number one. So I saw my parents even less after I was married.

Nights alone while Doug and his band performed well into the night were the worst, and this was not my idea of marriage. After several months of trying to suppress my feelings, one night it all came to a head. I was at the end of my rope and had lived with enough inconvenience because of the band's needs, and so the explosion happened. Doug came home extra late from practice one night, and that became the final straw for me. I told him this was not working, and I felt frustrated by the band's demands. He tried to talk about more things he could do differently to make this workable. But I was fed up with the situation and proceeded to act without thinking. I pulled my wedding ring off and threw it across the house. I threw it from the couch where I was seated in the living room. It flew into the kitchen across the floor and slammed into the baseboard around the cabinets at the far end of the wall below the kitchen sink. At this point, we both realized that something had to change. My husband got up and retrieved my wedding ring. He lovingly put it back on my finger and said, "I will quit the band tomorrow."

This decision made me feel bad and empty inside. I did not want to give him an ultimatum or be the reason he gave up something he loved doing so much. The thought of him quitting the band gave me some peace, but it also came with a nagging feeling of discontent and sadness. Doug told me he really was fine with the decision, and that I and our marriage mattered more to him than performing in any band ever could. The way he told me he loved me with words and even more the way he showed me with the sacrifice he made was an extremely meaningful defining moment for me. I had never been loved like this before. It was clear to me, I had married someone who I undoubtedly meant something to, and I was even valuable in his life. Although I could see that he really would do anything for me, I chose from this moment on to be extra careful not to abuse the dedication he had to me. I have concentrated more on thinking and trying to do what I can for his good than to abuse his willingness to do whatever I ask him to.

There is a power in the love my husband has for me, and I always will strive to use it for our good rather than manipulate it for what I can get. His willingness to give up something that meant so much to him only strengthened my love for him and made me even more thankful for the wonderful husband God had given to me. Doug's sacrifice naturally compelled me to feel more giving and loving toward him.

I have since realized that the struggle I felt because of this experience was God's presence helping me get to the place He wanted me to be and become the person He made me to be. I would have to overcome a lifetime of wrong programming from my parents and choose to live in and return the love Doug was offering me for our future. Doug's choice in this moment had shown me a better way. The struggle I felt was because I was behaving like my childish parents, and I knew I wanted to be different. The turmoil this caused was part of the molding process for me to become a better, more caring, and more giving person. Doug was showing me love instead of further wounding. He cared how I felt, and he made that tangible to me through his actions and decisions. I knew I did not want to be like my parents, displaying the irrational behavior I had learned from watching them throughout the years. Also, I knew I had never seen Grandma Ada behave out of control with little ability to cope with life in general. This struggle became the starting point for the better path I chose for my life. I was determined to be more like Grandma Ada and more loving toward Doug, just as he was being to me. It also became a choice of putting my life on a more functional path, to live more like Jesus and be a person worthy of Doug's unconditional love and find my ability to love him unconditionally in return.

As I have said before, the band was not all bad. I had many magical, fun evenings attending the functions where they performed. Because of the band, we went to places that I would not have gone otherwise, and I spent time with people I would not otherwise have met. It also was an enviable thing to many that I was with the cutest guy in the band. It was fun—but the fun and perks were not worth living through the interruptions to our normal life that band life brought.

I also believe now, knowing what I have learned about myself after facing the childhood turmoil and dysfunction, that I am a stronger, more mature person. If I could go back to this time, taking with me what I have learned, I believe I could handle whatever my husband needed me to. However, in retrospect, it was best for our family overall in the years to come that the band was not a part of our life. Frequenting bars and being around alcohol was not where God wanted us to be or how He wanted us to spend our time on this earth. It also was not a lifestyle to introduce into the lives of the children who would join our family later on. Looking back from where I am now, our life together would have taken a different turn had we continued with the band life. Golden opportunities we were presented and partook of would not have been available if we had not let God lead us away from the band.

In August 1978, a few months after Doug quit the band, I became pregnant again. I was only a few weeks along when I had a miscarriage in late September. This brought many questions into our lives at the time. Because of our much-regretted decision not to have our first baby, would we not even be able to have children at all? Losing another baby, this time through miscarriage, brought many feelings of uneasiness and a deep wondering. Would our worst decision ever ultimately come with permanently surrendering our chance at parenthood?

Doug's Parents

I liked Doug's mom and stepdad from the beginning. Through the years, they have both been a real blessing to Doug and me and our marriage, and I have an emotional connection with them both. They are able to achieve the proper balance of being part of our lives without being controlling. This was one characteristic of Doug's mom that I noticed right off; considering where I came from with my family, it did seem odd at the time. But I have realized through the years, it is a quality I do admire and now try to emulate with my own children. Doug's mom was involved in our life but never intrusive or controlling.

Doug's stepdad feels like a father should; he has definitely earned the title of *dad*. He is caring, kind, sharing, loving, and always ready to help. He is a humorous storyteller with an abundance of tales collected through his life experiences while serving in the US Air Force. Visiting with them is always enjoyable. When Doug and I married, there were many things I had not been afforded the opportunity yet to experience, and one of those things was tasting lobster. Doug's dad took us to a fancy restaurant in Albuquerque and encouraged me to try lobster. I liked it, and it became one of my favorite things to eat. Every time I have lobster, I think of Doug's dad.

Another thing I had never done was flying in an airplane. Doug and I had been married for less than a year and were visiting Doug's parents in Albuquerque. Doug's dad is a pilot and had his own airplane then. Piloting an airplane was something he always loved to do. One day back in 1978, Doug's dad took me flying in his airplane. It was my first flight and was an unforgettable experience. I even got to fly the plane for a short time as he let me take the controls. One thing I recently learned about Doug's dad is that he gets really excited at the sound of military jets taking off with their standard deafening sound. We were near a military runway, and it was music to his ears just to hear the extremely loud *whoosh* and thunder of the jets flying in close proximity. Doug's parents made a real difference in his life as a boy and also in our lives together after we were married.

Doug's Biological Dad

Most of the time, Doug's biological dad could best be described as a father who was uninvolved and emotionally detached. He was very similar to my dad, a selfish parent who did what he wanted. Doug's biological parents divorced when he was six years old. His dad continued to be mostly uninvolved in Doug's life, just as before. This man had only one child but he could not overcome his selfish tendencies long enough to ever become a real part of Doug's life. Throughout our marriage, Doug's dad rarely visited, called, or even remembered Doug's birthday. There was little opportunity for Doug, as a child or an adult, to build any type of relationship with him. That is how things remained until Doug's dad died in February 2003.

I find it interesting that on some of those rare times when Doug's biological dad visited our family, he and my dad made a real connection. They enjoyed pursuing activities of mutual interest. It appeared they had a lot in common which unfortunately included their deficiency in paternal responsibilities. And just as it was with my dad, many people thought Doug's dad was such a *nice* man.

Chapter Thirty-Two

A Memorable New Year's Eve

Slightly past noon on Saturday, December 30, 1978, Doug and I set out on a trip to spend New Year's weekend with Doug's parents in Albuquerque. The trip would normally take three-and-a-half hours, but the weather this weekend was nasty; the roads were covered with ice. An older, wiser couple would have turned around and gone back home in such weather. But at age twenty-one, my husband must have felt invincible, so we continued on our icy journey north. Fort Sumner was a town we passed through on the way, so we drove down into the valley and stopped briefly at Grandma Ada's house. She was surprised that we were heading to Doug's parents' house under such adverse conditions. She shared her reservations about us continuing on but realized Doug was determined to go on anyway. So she loaded us up with her homemade chocolate-covered cherries and other goodies to have on hand for snacks in case we got stranded in a snowbank.

We pressed on, traveling extremely slowly on the icy road, making it to I-40 as the sun began to set. The stretch of road on I-40 between Santa Rosa and Albuquerque was busy, as always, in spite of the icy conditions. We trudged on, traveling between twenty-five and forty miles per hour and observing many motorists darting by us and then sliding off the road and disappearing into the snow. Because of the fog and the snow flying, other cars on the road were visible only by their lights. A steep, huge hill around the Clines Corners area was lit by miles of taillights revealing its location. It was quite a sight and looked a lot like the interstate was decorated for Christmas. Many of the taillights were from cars that had stopped on the roadside while the driver installed chains before attempting the drive up the steep hill. We passed what felt like hundreds of cars as we made our way up the hill in our 1969 Ford Thunderbird with no chains. It seemed that if we could only keep in motion, we would make it up the hill. After many anxious minutes, we safely topped it. The next part of the road we were concerned about were the foothills and winding mountain road as I-40 entered the city of Albuquerque, the area also known as Tijeras Canyon. But that too was no problem as we continued on—slow and steady, the key combination to safely make it through the wintry conditions.

Around midnight, after about eleven hours of snaillike travel, we made it to the doorstep of Doug's parents' home. Doug's mother was almost in tears to see us safe and sound. We had called her before we left our house, but that was many hours earlier. Knowing the treacherous road conditions, all she could do was very anxiously wait for our arrival. Cell phones had not been invented yet—in 1978, phone calls were made only from stationary locations.

Our trip was definitely stressful and draining. We were both very tired. After we visited for a while with Doug's family, and I called Grandma Ada to let her know we had made it safely, we got ready for bed. We thanked God for a safe trip and drifted off to sleep. The next morning was December 31, 1978, the end of another year. The day became memorable for much more than this reason alone, however. Upon waking that morning, I had an overwhelming desire for Doug to hold me. The night before had been frightening and distressful, and I needed his comfort. The bedroom we slept in had twin beds, so I made a "come here" motion to Doug. He came over to my bed, and his comfort became much more than just a mere hug. It seems unexplainable, but before the day was over, I knew I was pregnant.

We did nothing special for New Year's Eve, just stayed at the house and welcomed in the New Year of 1979 with Doug's parents and little brother. The next day, we had to leave because Doug had to be at work on Tuesday. The weather had not changed much and was not any warmer. The roads were still icy, but at least the blowing snow and fog were gone. We left with plenty of time to allow another eleven hours for a usual three-and-a-half hour trip home. The journey back was very similar to the trip there, but better because we traveled exclusively in the daytime. As the time progressed this day, I felt more and more nauseated. The morning sickness had set in almost from the moment of conception. During our drive back home, my husband and I discussed the likelihood of a baby. The thought brought happiness, and we were both thrilled with the possibility. New Year's 1979 became a weekend I will never forget!

Looking back to this New Year's excursion, it is clear that my husband and I were completely covered by God's hand of protection. His presence was obvious because of how we made such a trip with no incident at all, either way. God had also provided this special circumstance for our son to be conceived, this perfect time in His perfect way. However, at this point, only time would reveal the great extent to which we had been blessed during this weekend. This day it was all beyond our comprehension.

Even though feelings of queasiness were ever-present, I began my fourth semester of college mid-January 1979. I took a full load again to make certain I would be halfway through college in May, if a baby was really in our near future. As time progressed, it became obvious that the next step should be to see my ob/gyn. My appointment was on a Wednesday afternoon. Wednesdays were one of the days I was out of town attending college most of the day. My mother decided it was her duty to go along for the appointment. I was expected to stop on my way back from school and take her along. So I stopped and went to the bathroom, and when I came out of the bathroom my mother was there at the door telling me that I should not have done that. Now it would be a problem, and I would not be able "to go" when I got to the doctor's office. At age nineteen, I was amazed at the things my mother still focused on and the amount of control she tried to impose on an adult, married daughter. Looking back on this day, I have to ask, "Why was she going with me to get the news of my baby instead of my husband?" She had a way of making me feel that she knew best and could dictate to me what should be done. My husband's job did not prevent him from meeting me at the doctor's office, but my mother had made it clear that she should and would be the one to go with me.

When I really analyze this situation, I see that I had a hard time telling my mother no or even explaining to her how I wanted things to be. She had a way of making me believe that her way was always right. And if I disagreed, I never felt it was worth the fight to speak up. I did not like to provoke a scene with her; I had learned from history to avoid this at almost any cost. I also felt some sympathy for her because of how bad her life seemed to hurt, and I did not want to make it worse. So I went along with her whether I agreed or not. It was just easier that way. It was not apparent to me then, however, the actual price I was paying for keeping the peace. I did not realize that I was losing myself in the pursuit of tranquility. Each time I denied what I truly felt and let her win just to keep peace and avoid her emotional outburst, I was actually burying my true self. But because of the experiences I had with my mother throughout my life, it was easier at the moment to keep myself tucked away and let her rule.

So on Wednesday, February 7, 1979, I sat in my living room (after my doctor's appointment) with my mother and little sister waiting for my husband to arrive home from work. When he came home, my mother was there to be a part of breaking some of the most intimate news a couple can share—it was doctor-verified, we had a baby on the way. The due date was September 23, 1979.

Chapter Thirty-Three

God Blesses Us with a Son

Experiencing pregnancy was one of the greatest joys and blessings of my life. God is merciful, and I experienced an overwhelming feeling of forgiveness when God allowed me to carry my baby to full term in spite of the bad decision I had allowed to taint my life. I knew for sure God had forgiven me and my husband for our wrong decision when the excitement and newness of life that comes with having a baby engulfed every aspect of our existence. Each visit to the doctor's office for checkups throughout the pregnancy was a blessing to experience as one of God's greatest miracles unfolded and grew right before our eyes.

Our baby was healthy, and everything about the pregnancy was normal. It was an extra thrill when we were able to hear the heartbeat for the first time. It was a rapid, loud rhythm that assured us our baby was alive and well. In 1979, there were no ultrasounds, but knowing our baby's gender was not as significant as the reassurance of a normal pregnancy and a healthy baby.

I felt the baby move for the first time on a weekend night in April when we were at the bowling alley with friends. The couple was my longtime friend Kim, from school days, and her husband, my college finance teacher. Kim was also expecting her first baby and was two months ahead of me. The feeling of my baby moving gave me a start, and my friend, who had been experiencing this feeling for a few months, confirmed that I had just felt my baby move. It was a most thrilling sensation, and this moment became an indelible memory etched permanently in my mind.

During the first four months of the pregnancy, I continued on with college and studies. In addition to working for Coca-Cola, Doug was now employed part-time at our local McDonald's restaurant. The plan was for the McDonald's job to end when we paid off our Sears bill. After the spring semester ended and with Doug working two jobs, I had a lot of extra time on my hands. I spent this time preparing for my baby. I found useful tips about body strengthening and developed a daily routine of exercises that strengthened my body and prepared me for the childbirth ahead. I worked outside in the yard and inside on our house. By staying busy, watching what I ate, and avoiding sweets and chocolate, I gained only eighteen pounds by the time I reached full term.

For several weeks during the pre-birth period, Doug and I attended Lamaze classes. I learned how to manage what was to come with breathing techniques that, I would learn later, really did work. One part of the Lamaze class I felt uncomfortable with was watching a film showing the actual birth of a baby. The film and touring the delivery department at the hospital made me nervous and created anxiety in regard to actual childbirth and the very near delivery date of our baby. I also had feelings of doubt as to whether I could actually give birth, but I reassured myself with the thought that millions of women had been through the experience and survived just fine. I mainly found peace with the inevitable experience I faced in prayer and Bible scripture. There is such a calm and genuine reassurance that comes only from prayer with God. Simply trusting Him for every need brings hope and comfort, which I really needed as the due date of my baby rapidly approached.

I went alone to my final pre-delivery checkup on a Wednesday. I was now nine months pregnant. I remember this day specifically because my baby's birthday was determined at this appointment. The doctor said I would deliver before the coming weekend was over. My decision to induce labor rather than wait for nature to take its course hinged on the doctor's opinion. My doctor would be out of town for the weekend, and I wanted only this specific doctor to deliver my baby. Therefore, it was decided that Friday would become a day to remember for the rest of my life. It would be the day I would give birth to my first baby—a long-awaited joyous and happy day. A special baby to take care of and fill the emotional emptiness I had felt all my life, a baby to attach to and love forever. A baby given to me by God who, in addition to God and my husband, would also be a part of my emotional healing process.

I left the doctor's office and found my husband working in town on his Coca-Cola route. I told him when Friday came, if labor had not fully begun, it would be induced. He was so excited to know for sure he would meet his baby in just two days. We rejoiced in our happy news that our first child would soon be born. I also wanted to share the news with my mother, so I hurried to her house excited to tell her the news, thinking she would be just as ecstatic as Doug and I were. This quickly proved not to be the case. Instead of showing happiness, her response was as always cautious, doubting, and very negative, coming with the comment of, "Oh, my gosh! You don't know what you are getting yourself into! It will be one of the worst experiences ever. Are you sure you want to do something like that?" This negative input came partly from her perception that I was a person exactly like her, and that just because she had a bad experience with induced labor, I certainly would too. She just never got the fact that I was a separate person from her, and just because she experienced something bad did not mean I was destined to relive her experiences.

When my brother was born, my mother had a long and hard labor, which she attributed to the one reason of labor being induced. Because of her experience, she believed I was surely destined to have just as horrible a time as she had. Her reaction to my joyful news about my baby's birth was, to say the least, terribly upsetting. I expected to rejoice with her, but I really should have been used to her lack of support and doubt with any decision I made on my own. If I wanted encouragement, support, and someone to share my happiness with, I should have known better than to go see my mother. I went to her house extremely excited, anticipating with joy the arrival of my firstborn. But my mother succeeded once again in throwing a sopping-wet blanket on my happiness. I cried for a while, but my tears seemed to make little impact on her resolve that I was doing the wrong thing. She still gave me no comfort, encouragement, or support. I soon left her house.

On my way home, I as usual started the process of regrouping my thoughts and feelings in relation to my mother's negative input. I was once again forced to rationalize and was trying to regain my perspective because of the inevitable, always predictable lack of support I had grown accustomed to getting from her. However, I was able to tell myself for sure that just because she had a bad experience with inducing labor did not mean I was destined to have the same experience. I did not even second-guess my decision; it was what felt right to me. I therefore disregarded my mother's input and, with my husband's support, stood firm on my decision … on Wednesday, anyway.

But when I woke up on Thursday, I spent most of this day with a headache and a general feeling of depression and confusion. That night, when my husband came home from work, he consoled me with positive words of encouragement. He gave me even more reassurance that we would be overjoyed the next day when he said, "By this time tomorrow, you will be holding our new baby!" That was a very happy thought. And my husband, as usual, was right! The man of my dreams, who always offers me his calming reassurance, was removing my doubts and fears again. And a day later, everything he said to make me feel better would come true. All I had to do now was get through the night and hope my headache went away.

Even though the next morning came slowly with very little sleep, it was a day to celebrate. Today was our baby's birthday! We arrived at the hospital by seven a.m. There were still no apparent signs of labor starting. The doctor visited me and started an IV of labor-inducing medicine around eight a.m. Labor began in full force after that.

My mother showed up at the hospital at some point during the beginning of labor. I had not even heard from her the previous day at all. She appeared this Friday morning acting as though the incident of the previous Wednesday had never happened at all, bringing her usual attitude of, "There is no sense in talking about unpleasant things, and we'll start fresh from this point on." Cover it up, deny it happened, and go on as if everything is normal and there is no emotional damage that might require healing or words of apology. After all, I was her child, and she could treat me however she chose to. She seemed to have wiped away all the unpleasantness from two days before. And just because she had, then I should have too. She may wish it would work that way, but the human psyche is just not programmed that way. You cannot deny hurtful things you have done to those you say you love and expect them to go on as robots with no damage done. Well, I had more important business at hand than to get hung up on another of my mother's uncomfortable episodes along with the emotional baggage it could bring.

My complete attention was focused on the labor process, which continued on normally with steady progress. Doug was successfully coaching me along, using the Lamaze techniques when appropriate that we had learned together. The labor pains increased in frequency and intensity rather quickly. It was about two-and-a-half hours from the first labor pain until I was ready to head to the delivery room. Doug was very excited and could not contain his enthusiasm. He was given the green light to don his delivery-room attire, complete with mask and shoe coverings. As he was displaying excitement for the moment, I was at the "don't touch me" point of labor. The baby had entered the birth canal, and I was uncomfortable, which was an understatement of how I felt at this moment. I was ready for this baby to be born now!

When I reached the delivery room, labor intensified even more. It seemed as though the labor and delivery process of a strong, intense pain and then getting in position to push went on for a really long time. But it could have been only one hour at the most when at last the final push resulted in the moment I had been working for, and I heard the long-awaited cry of my baby. Then, "It's a boy!" The doctor said he was crying because of who the president of the United States was at the time—Jimmy Carter, maybe? But I was overjoyed to hear the voice of my new son with the cry that sounded like music. This was one of the most thrilling times in my life. God had blessed us with a true miracle this day. Our precious baby boy was born at exactly 12:01 p.m., only three-and-a-half hours after my first labor pain. We named him Jason. I held him immediately as my husband lovingly looked on, standing by our side. Our eight-pound baby boy was healthy and perfect. I had a terrific experience with induced labor; it was far from unpleasant. My labor, comparatively speaking, was short, easy, and normal, with no drugs at all.

Grandma Ada, Aunt Judy, and my mother were at the hospital throughout the entire period of labor and delivery. There were many friends who visited, including the preacher who performed our wedding ceremony and my friend Dee. Doug's boss sent me a dozen red roses.

Doug and I celebrated this memorable day together in the indescribable bliss and thrill of it all. The date was etched in our memory forever, the joyful day when we became parents. Since I had abstained from chocolate for most of the pregnancy, it seemed appropriate to celebrate by having our favorite chocolate candy. Doug came back to my room that night bearing a large bag of peanut M&Ms. That became such a special memory that we have chosen to celebrate every birthday of our first son since that night with peanut M&Ms.

After I was married, the joy and love I experienced with my husband always overrode any problems, turmoil, or hurt my mother continued to bring into my life. At this point, I chose to focus on my husband and my new son and shove way back into the depths of my mind all the unpleasantness that my mother brought. I buried it in order to be able to live around her and continue on. I knew there was no point in trying to resolve the hurt she inflicted. It seemed as though she thought, as my parent, she had every right to behave just as she pleased, and I should take what she gave and go on as if it was nothing out of the ordinary. She never seemed to have a clue about the damage she was causing.

My mother never said a word to me about her behavior two days before my first son was born. However, she did state her regrets about the situation to my sister many years later. The hurtful thing for me is I do not seem to matter enough to her that she would talk to me about it. This did not concern my sister, it was about me. It would be nice to hear her say what she said to my sister. It seems her main goal in dealing with my life is to inflict as much pain as possible on me because that is how her life was, and I should hurt just as much as she did. I am supposed to ignore hurtful, damaging things and just go on living in denial, as if nothing happened.

But the facts are that these hurtful and ignored situations continue to mount up over the years with no resolution of any of the emotional damage. Then a trigger event happens that brings them all out at once, flooding into your mind. They all at once demand attention, and the past, previously buried in denial, can no longer be ignored. When this happens, it is impossible to rationalize just one hurt at a time; *all* the hurts are facing you at once. Then the past negative experiences must be worked through before your life can go on in a normal fashion. One day in the future, I would have to deal with emotional hurts when a trigger event would revive them all. This incident at Jason's birth was just one of many damaging events I would be faced with healing from decades into the future. God is the only one who is able to heal such wounds. I cannot change my parents, but I can find healing from the damage they inflicted in God's love for me.

Chapter Thirty-Four

Grandma Ada's Sixty-Eighth Birthday

The day Grandma Ada was born, January 6, 1912, also happens to be the exact date that New Mexico became a state. Grandma was even invited one year to the governor's mansion to celebrate her birthday along with the birthday of New Mexico's statehood. But for this birthday, January 6, 1980, we would be celebrating with Grandma on the farm. My baby and I traveled to the farm to be with Grandma for her special day. We went with my parents, my little sister, and my brother and his new wife. Doug did not go; he had to work. He now was an assistant manager at McDonald's and no longer worked at Coca-Cola. Also present for Grandma's celebration was my uncle and his family. It was a great day celebrating Grandma Ada's sixty-eighth birthday on the farm and being able to share this special time with my baby boy.

Going to Grandma's house was a nostalgic experience. It always felt like I was really going *home* when I went back to the farm. The passing of time had not changed my feelings. Grandma Ada was still the real mother figure in my life, and going back to the farm rekindled a wealth of fond memories and good feelings from an earlier time. There were so many positive, pleasant aspects to my childhood days spent on the farm with Grandma. The things I learned from her were being put into practice with a home and a baby of my own. Now I was especially grateful for the many things Grandma had taught me. Being with her was always a most wonderful time because of the emotional connection and special relationship we shared. And this day was even more significant since it was her birthday. We celebrated the usual way with birthday presents and a home-cooked farm dinner complete with birthday cake and ice cream.

Then, at the end of a beautiful day, we began the sixty-mile drive back home. For some reason, my baby was upset and cried the entire trip back. I tried feeding him, changing him, cuddling and rocking him; however, nothing worked. He was upset and thought everyone should know. My mother, sitting in the front seat between Dad and my sister, turned around, looked me in the eye, and said, "He's *your* baby," as if she thought that would be a revelation to anyone. However, what she must have meant was *take care of him—that is your job and don't look to me for any support, help, or assistance.* That is about all she said to me the entire trip home. It felt like everyone in the car was deaf and could not hear my baby's cries. It would have been nice to get a little supportive conversation at least. But as always in my parents' presence, I felt all alone emotionally with no help, understanding, or encouragement, as they continued to live in denial of reality.

When we finally arrived at my house, I was frazzled and went into the house crying but very relieved to be home. My husband met me at the door and wanted to know what was wrong. I went inside the house, put my baby in his crib, and continued to cry. I was not interested in talking at this time, so my mother gladly filled Doug in on her version of the situation. She said, "That is just the way new mothers feel, overwhelmed and crazy." I did not believe for a minute that this was normal. I desperately wanted for my mother to be a normal mother, instead of causing me to feel like she was some vengeful person who was trying to get even with me over something. I often felt as though she wanted to make my life harder because of how much her life hurt. I know for sure, I did not feel that my mother was on my side. I only wanted her to stop trying to control my life with her abnormal opinions.

Many times in my childhood, I observed that there had to be a crisis to get any sort of positive emotional response from my parents. There had to be a reason for them to react toward me; it was never just because I was a child who needed their attention. It usually took something out of the ordinary to provoke any sort of feeling from either of them, such as an emergency, accident, or emotional outburst. Otherwise, life was nonreactive in any area that could potentially create an emotional connection. Therefore, the emotional outburst, after I was safely home must have been another unconscious effort to communicate to them how bad I felt because of their lack of support. It had little to do with my parental responsibilities.

I frequently felt frustrated when trying to relate to my two childish parents. Thankfully, however, in the area of communication, my relationship with my husband was very different. With my husband, I could communicate and relate on an adult level in peace and truth. I was never afraid to tell him how I felt, and I never feared his reaction to what I shared with him. I could count on him to give me love, support, encouragement, and caring, no matter what. My marriage and life with Doug was completely opposite to the way my life had always been with my parents.

No real productive or meaningful interaction existed between me and my parents—there was no emotional connection. My mother just could not come outside of herself and relate in a normal fashion. Every conversation had to be turned into a battle of wits, and it felt as if she had to prove she was right and there was no other way but her way. It is no wonder, with the frustration building up on the trip home from Grandma Ada's birthday dinner, that I communicated my feelings with anger and dysfunctional emotion and crying. This was the only language they understood. It was the way I had been programmed to relate to my parents; that is how I witnessed them communicating with each other. It was all so abnormal. Interaction between me and Dad was little to none, and I felt helpless to communicate my feelings in a rational way to my mother. *Rational* and *normal* was just not a language she understood. An emotionally extreme display of feelings was the only way to break her emotional barrier and make her understand that there was a real problem present. I believe this is why she told my husband that my behavior was normal in relation to being a new mother. It was my mother's normal, because she could not understand calm, peaceful, and productive interaction. It took the extreme to get her attention. This is how my life had always been in relation to my mother, and it was really getting to be a drain on my adult life—especially since I had found the true normal way to interact with my husband in our marriage. I did not like the turmoil, control, and dysfunction that encounters with my parents brought into my life.

Even though I was now an adult, my parents' presence still stirred up the pain of my childhood past. In regard to the trip home from Grandma's, my built-up frustration and ensuing emotional reaction was *not* normal. My reactions, due to feelings of being overwhelmed with life and getting no support from my parents, were no more normal than my mother's abnormal fits of anger and rage. I was not born this way; it was abnormal. It was the effects of childhood emotional abuse surfacing. I was not weak because I cried and was frustrated. The underlying problem was that I had not learned how to cope with life normally. I had no functional example to follow in either of my parents. They also supported very little about me or how I wanted my life to be. They did not care how hard everything was for me. This was especially how I felt at age eight when I had the stomach ulcer. Both parents cared very little for me, and both made it all hurt more as they each cared only for themselves. Sadly, many years later, nothing had changed regarding my parents' behavior toward me in my adult life. With the programming I got from two childish parents, it is a miracle and an intervention from God that I was able to support and encourage my own children in their life's journey.

This trip to Grandma's convinced me that there would be no more traveling with my parents ever again without my husband along. And I kept that promise to myself; there was none. This trip became one more example of the dysfunction present, and it showed the same lack of support as when I tried visiting them alone, without Doug, after I was married. There was no doubt, being around my parents was just not something I should do anymore without my husband around. However, my son, who as a baby required much attention, would later become the one my parents wanted to see more than anyone else. He would become the link to keep me connected to my parents during his growing-up years. When he grew up and left home, this connection with my parents and the dysfunction they represented in my life would be severed. Years into the future, when my hurtful childhood past was brought to the surface, I decided my significance to my parents should not be dependent on the presence of my husband or my oldest son. I felt consistently that my parents were not interested in me personally—not as a child and not as an adult. Nothing had changed. This was how my life had always been. When no lasting attachments are formed and no real relationship is built between parent and child, there exists at best a fragile connection between them that is easily broken.

Chapter Thirty-Five

Continuing My Education

In mid-January 1980, I returned to college. My university had a branch campus in our city, making it possible to attend locally. Doug's mother supported me in returning to my studies and paid my tuition for the semester. I took one night class, Intermediate Accounting, a four-hour session that made for one long night at school. It was the one class known for weeding out the "wannabes" from the true accounting students. I would have preferred to take this important class on the main campus and go five days a week, but with a new baby, I had to do what was possible. And since the class met only one night a week, Doug could take care of our son while I was away. I finished the class with a 4.0 for the semester and needed no more classes with a Monday-Friday schedule to get my degree. I am very grateful to Doug's mother for caring and helping in my endeavor to continue my education. She made starting back easier after the birth of our son.

The following autumn, I returned to college full-time on the main campus. This meant driving out of town two or three days a week. I worked my schedule around my mother's school-bus driving schedule. This conformed to a family "should be" of life—allowing only family to babysit your children. But even though it was only a few afternoons per week, there still were issues to work through, because my mother was skeptical about how it would work for Jason to ride the bus with her these days. She seemed somewhat unwilling to agree, even though other drivers took their children, and Jason could ride the bus on these limited occasions without breaking any rules.

I have to wonder, in retrospect—did my mother not want to take care of my son, or was it that she did not support my further education? I believe the answer is *both*. My mother never said it specifically, but I felt she strongly believed my place was at home, not pursuing a college degree. Her attitude toward the university was plain when I took her with me to register. She did not like the school and thought I had enough education to do what I needed to. Being at the university made her feel uncomfortable, and she seemed to think I was supposed to feel the same as her. Therefore, I should not go to college; it was a stupid college, and the people made her feel out-of-place. I should not rock the boat and change the family status quo. I should feel lucky I graduated from high school, which was all I needed for what I would encounter in my life ahead. But I did not heed my mother's obvious wishes, because something inside me was not satisfied with just a high-school education. Therefore, I pushed on to achieve my goals for self-betterment and a belief in myself put there by God. God had a plan for me, and I knew with Him guiding, I would succeed.

I was determined to blaze new trails. I therefore pressed on, getting things in place to continue this part of my destiny in life, a college education. To get my mother's approval for Jason to ride the bus with her, Doug and I had to come up with a method of strapping the car seat onto the bus seat. We also had to show my mother how it was going to work by teaching her to strap the car seat in place. With persuasion and encouragement from my husband and me, my mother finally agreed to let Jason go with her a few afternoons per week. This worked well for me, Jason, and my husband, and it ended up being a good experience for my mother, even though she seemed to fight the idea in the beginning.

Jason got along well with the other bus drivers, and they enjoyed having him around to talk to and play with. My husband's perception of this experience was that it also grew my mother's affection for Jason and caused her to realize that spending time with Jason was something she could find value in. Her friends' interest in Jason seemed to magnify her significance to the group. She found acceptance with a group of people outside the family, and in some way it felt like Jason had helped her achieve that place. My husband believes this reaction from her friends was a positive experience that my mother did not expect. Therefore, it seemed to make her realize that this chance to spend time with Jason had turned into a positive situation and maybe she should enjoy this opportunity to get to know him.

Looking back, my husband and I do not believe my mother would ever admit to her initial feelings and reactions to this opportunity as problematic. Being at the place she is today, she also would probably never think of trading the time she spent then with Jason for anything. For my husband and I to have to persuade my mother to take on a responsibility she would later cherish seems to be another example of the dysfunction present in my childhood family. It felt like we had to reason with a child to get her to do what was in her best interest. But because of this defining time she spent with Jason, the relationship with her first grandson grew into something I had never known my mother to be capable of. Unfortunately, though, this brought another brand of dysfunction into my family life. Jason could do no wrong in my mother's eyes and was allowed to do whatever he wanted around his grandma and grandpa.

Chapter Thirty-Six

Overcoming Obstacles and Reaching Graduation Day

College attendance at the main university campus continued until my graduation ceremony at the end of the fall semester of 1982. I attended college when Jason was between the ages of one and three. Whenever my husband was not available, my mother took care of him, which sounds like a perfect situation. But even in this, my mother imposed her control and non-support, and Dad also contributed to the dysfunction I dealt with. During this period of returning back to college, their childish ways presented more problems for me to overcome.

When I would stop at my parent's house to pick up Jason, it would be a huge turmoil because he did not want to leave. Mainly he did not want to leave because my parents would let him do anything he wanted to; there were no boundaries. I would arrive tired from being out-of-town at school all day and get no help and support from my parents. My mother especially seemed to thrive on the attention and gloat because my son threw a fit when it was time to go home. This was an every-time occurrence, and I believe if my mother had not enjoyed the attention so much, she would have managed to make it easier for me to get my son home.

I also arrived each time to find toys thrown all over the room. I would have Jason pick up the toys before we left. I was trying to teach him to do the right thing. But looking back, because of the way things were, I should have just taken him and left the mess. My mother could have at least had most of the toys picked up before I got there, since the time I arrived did not vary much. It became a real exasperation for me, and I lost control at one point. I cried because of the distress and because it appeared my son was taking charge of me instead of the other way around. And I was still looking for my parents' approval—which, I had not realized yet, was something I would never get. But I had it all backward; I should have been angry with my parents for their lack of support and their encouraging Jason to disregard my direction. It became another of the many ways they succeeded in making my life harder. I also should have been very angry that both my parents were actively condoning my son's disrespect toward me. They did nothing to diffuse the unacceptable behavior and offered no support for me. It probably felt normal to them for my son to disrespect me because they had always disrespected me; nothing had changed. I feel that my mother wanted me to fail at getting an education because it was a threat to her for me to be better than the family status quo. Sure she was keeping my son, and that helped me, but she got plenty of reward for the privilege of spending time with Jason, which she was taking full advantage of.

These unnecessary episodes added even more stress to my already stressful life of taking care of Jason and pursuing a college education. Many times on our way home after I picked up Jason, I would tell him, "If you cannot cooperate better when it is time to leave, you will have to quit staying with your grandma." This method of handling the situation was another way that I had it all backward. Instead of holding my son responsible for fixing the problem that my mother was obviously creating, I needed to confront her and negotiate with her to reach the necessary changes to reduce the unnecessary stress. But as always, I avoided any kind of confrontation with her and continued living with the situation as it was … and allowing the frustration and resentment to grow. Denial and avoidance do nothing but damage everyone's emotional state. But this was the way I had learned to deal with unpleasant things in life from my parents—ignore, avoid, and deny. It was the normal family method of coping with problems.

So I endured the situation, which I felt helpless to change. Negotiating with my mother was not something I ever had any luck with. However, to endure, it helped to remember that my university graduation and degree were getting closer with every week, month, and semester. I made my college schedule with the goal in mind of minimizing the time Jason spent at my parents' house. And with the passage of time, graduation day finally came around. In spite of all the personal things I lived through and compensated for, I graduated with a double-major bachelor's degree in business administration and accounting. My final degree plan from the College of Business ended up at a 3.8 grade-point average.

On December 17, 1982, I graduated from Eastern New Mexico University in an evening ceremony. The man who spoke at the commencement was a famous news anchor from a widely watched TV station in Albuquerque. The commencement speech felt like watching the evening news, except the newscaster was there in person.

It was a great blessing to have my family present for the occasion. My husband and my son, Jason, who was three at the time; Grandma Ada; and my uncle and his family were there. Doug's parents, my parents, my little sister, and my brother and his family were all there with me to celebrate the momentous occasion. I was the first one on my mother's or dad's side of the family to graduate from college. After my son was born, my uncle had his doubts that I would indeed go on to finish my education. He felt it would certainly prevent me from having my diploma in hand at some point down the road. But I was determined to complete what I had begun, and Grandma Ada had told me I could do whatever I set my mind on. Also, I knew for sure it was God's perfect will for my life that I receive my degree. Graduating from ENMU and finishing the worthwhile work I had begun was part of a necessary process to bring healing from my childhood wounds. It made a huge difference in restoring my self-worth, and gave me confidence in my ability to accomplish something that really mattered all on my own. I now possessed an education that no one could ever take away from me. It was a healing gift from God, in addition to the gifts of a loving, supportive husband and a precious son who filled my life with joy and meaning. There were many more blessings in store for my future.

Chapter Thirty-Seven

1984

The year 1984 brought many changes into my life. However, those changes were nothing like the science-fiction imaginings of the George Orwell book *1984*—a book I had to read in high school about ten years prior. It is a story about futuristic assumptions that thankfully have never and hopefully never will take place. After reading that famous work as a teenager, I did wonder what would be in store for the future year of 1984. But as I said, life in 1984 was nothing like the book, and the changes in my life during this year had no connection to futuristic notions of prior decades.

Grandma Ada turned seventy-two in 1984. It's also the year my son, Jason, turned five years old and started school. The year began in the ordinary way, just like any other year. Spending time with Grandma and taking my son to visit her was something I did every chance I got. Then sometime in the early months of the year, Grandma began feeling as if something was not quite right. She thought maybe it was her heart causing the abnormal episodes. I took her to a heart doctor, and he ran some tests that showed Grandma had a healthy heart with no reason for alarm. But Grandma's discomfort continued, and the incisions from the heart tests were not healing properly. She saw many doctors and endured many tests throughout the summer, and no apparent cause could be determined for the way she was feeling. There definitely was something amiss, and Grandma was not herself. My uncle lived close by Grandma, and when he dropped in to check on her one night, she gave him a strange response when he asked how she was feeling. She said, "I feel like the queen of diamonds, or is it the king of hearts?" My uncle was puzzled by this response and knew there was a problem. Grandma had been playing her favorite card game of solitaire that afternoon, and some imbalance in her body caused her to respond to my uncle's question that way. In a few moments, Grandma came to herself and laughed with my uncle about her comment and assured my uncle that she was fine. He left that night very concerned about her condition, and she received more medical attention soon afterward. After many hospital visits, tests, and doctors, Grandma was sent to a specialist in Albuquerque. My mother would be the one to take her. Albuquerque trips were ones our family had made many times, usually for fun occasions and rarely for medical reasons. My mother and Grandma Ada set out on the journey with hope of finding a cure so Grandma would feel better soon.

After Grandma had seen the doctor, and he had diagnosed her condition, he asked Grandma what she needed from him. Grandma said, "I want you to give me something to make me feel better."

The doctor said, "Dear lady, I'm afraid there is nothing I can do for you; you will probably never feel better again."

This doctor had determined that Grandma had incurable, inoperable cancer, and it had spread to her liver. The doctors assumed that her cancer had to be somewhere in her body before it spread to the liver, but the cancer was found nowhere in her body but in the liver. This was hopeless news that hurt deeply. I believe Grandma was not totally surprised to hear the words because somehow, she probably already knew what her diagnosis would be.

I will never forget the phone call from my mother that afternoon in September 1984 telling me the reality of Grandma's condition. I fell to the floor and cried and cried for what felt like hours. Jason was home with me, and he got down on the floor with me and asked me what was wrong. I told him, and he hugged me, and we talked for a while about what this news really meant. I just kept thinking, *What am I going to do without her?* Grandma represented stability, comfort, and understanding; she was the mother figure I relied on as a child and now as an adult.

She was still the one I needed in my life. She meant more to me than I could express, and living without her in the world was not something I ever wanted to do.

The phone call with the grim news came on a Friday afternoon. Grandma and my mother were driving back from Albuquerque and would be at Grandma's house that night. It would be the last time Grandma would have to travel that road from Albuquerque. When Doug got off work that day, we picked up my sister and Dad and went to Grandma's house. I just had to see Grandma; my time with her was running out, and I wanted to go to her. When I saw her, I hugged her tight, and we cried together. She told me, "Don't worry; it should be an easy death. At some point, I will just drift off and kind of fade out. It all should happen pretty quick." That is how the doctor had described it to her. Grandma was strong and seemed to face death head-on. Her main response I remember was, "I am thankful I have a little time to prepare before I just keel over and die." She said, "It's a blessing; I will not be like your grandpa when he died—here today, gone tomorrow." And now, this night, Grandma was tired and needed to rest, so we all went to bed. It just felt good to be with her, in the same house. I remember trying to totally consume the feeling of still having Grandma present in my life. I could walk across the house and find her alive and in bed ... for now.

I mentioned earlier that my son, Jason, was school-age this year. Another of the changes I experienced during this time was sending my firstborn off to kindergarten. That was one of the most heart-tugging experiences I have ever lived through. But it was somewhat easier since Jason attended a Christian school run by our church. His teacher was a kind, gentle, caring lady, and I felt very comfortable leaving Jason with her. But this time in our lives could not feel normal and was even more magnified and emotional because of all that was going on with Grandma Ada. I also did not have fond, warm, happy memories of my early school years, and with that swirling around in my mind, it was extra difficult to take Jason to school and leave him there every day.

I know Jason was feeling some of the unrest in our home situation during this time, but with the exception of one incident, he seemed to do just fine with his adjustment to the school routine. Jason had been complaining to me about some of the kids in his class. They were bullying him and going out of their way to be unfriendly. One morning, I dropped Jason off for school and before I drove away, I saw Jason standing at the door watching me with big tears in his eyes. I could not leave him like that, so I went inside, hugged him, and asked him to tell me what was wrong. He said, "It's those kids again." We then found his teacher and talked to her. This visit with the teacher turned out to be just as much help to me as it was to Jason. God was watching over us and presented this opportunity for a good conversation with a Christian lady that gave both of us encouragement. Jason and I began by telling his teacher some of the things he was experiencing at school and who was causing him extra problems. She listened with understanding, and the problems Jason was having seemed to be fixed that day, or at least were not as hard to bear. Also as part of the conversation, I explained what was going on in our lives and that my grandma was dying of cancer. I told her how much Grandma meant to me and that I was spending my final time with her. The teacher already knew how hard it was for me to send Jason to kindergarten and realized that the added burden of Grandma's health was magnifying our family circumstance. She was compassionate, empathetic, and understanding; she promised to pray for us. This teacher is still a family friend, and we thank God for her being in our lives during this hard time.

One of the last family functions Grandma attended away from her house was Jason's fifth birthday party. The entire family came to our home along with several friends. The party was early in the evening and was over before nine p.m., but Grandma was so exhausted she had to go lie down in bed before the party was half over. She began looking very pale, and her energy level was very low. She did watch Jason open several presents and had cake and ice cream too, just not very much. I was very thankful and glad to have her there. It felt more normal to have her with us and made it easier to ignore the reality that we really had only a short time left to enjoy her company. After this party, Grandma traveled no more, and I saw her only at her home or the hospital in her hometown thereafter. During this time, my life consisted of getting

Jason to school and stealing away to Fort Sumner to be with Grandma Ada whenever I could.

In spite of the circumstances, there were some great family times. One of these was when Grandma's sister Ollie visited with two of their nieces. It was wonderful to see them all, especially Ollie. One of life's pleasures was watching Grandma and Ollie enjoy each other's company and laugh about all the memories they recalled together. Even with Grandma feeling so bad, Ollie brought some laughter into her sister's final days. Another blessing for me was that during Grandma's final days, I was able to celebrate my twenty-fifth birthday with her. I went to her house and was so thankful to be with her for one more birthday. She gave me some money for my present, which I have never spent. I just never could part with the actual money she gave me that day, because I knew it would be the last birthday present I would get from her personally.

In Grandma's final weeks, she had an episode where she cried out for reassurance that she would be going to heaven when her life was over. Grandma's destiny was no doubt heaven, but when you get down to the moment of dying, it is hard not to let doubt creep in. One night in the hospital toward the end of her life, Grandma began screaming and saying she was a sinful woman; she cried that she was heading to hell, which was not true—she had been saved for many decades. But to ease her mind, they called the Baptist preacher in to talk with her. I do not know exactly what the preacher told Grandma, but I believe he reassured her by reading from the Bible about the truth of salvation and helped her rest in the knowledge that she was saved years ago when she trusted Jesus to save her soul from hell and wash away her sins. In addition to reassuring Grandma of her personal salvation, he probably also reminded her that since she knew Jesus as her Savior, heaven would be her eternal destination. She seemed to have no more problems with doubt. Confidence and peace prevailed for her after this one night of unrest.

During Grandma's final months, I was privileged to spend some time with her again, just the two of us, like when I was a child in her care. We had some memorable conversations, but I regret not specifically thanking her for all she had done for me and all she meant to my life. I probably did not say what I needed to because it would be years before I would finally figure out exactly how much she did for me, years before I would grasp all the ways she made a positive difference and a real impact in my life. I believe she knew, but I still wish I could have spoken the words to her then.

Much of what was on Grandma's mind at this time was taking care of business and making sure things were as she wanted them to be left. One conversation I remember having with her was in regard to her most prized possession. It was an antique desk, approximately five-and-a-half-feet tall, with a large plate-glass door. The glass was rounded in shape with frosty etched decoration, and its appearance alone testified to its age of at least one century. As we were talking one day, Grandma told me, "I want you to have the desk, if you want it? You are the one in the family who became an accountant, and the family desk should go to the accountant." I could not believe that Grandma was actually leaving her desk to me. I excitedly said, "Thank you, Grandma! Of course I want the desk, if that is what you want me to have! I will cherish it always and continue to take care of it just as you have."

Many of my visits with Grandma were not focused on dealing with the inevitable future we faced. For some of those visits when it was just me and her, life felt hopeful, like maybe she would get better and things would become normal again. During these times, I decided it was time for my husband and me to have another baby. I could only hope that if I did get pregnant soon, Grandma would live long enough to meet another great-grandchild. I soon discussed these thoughts with Doug, and they became the beginning of a baby conceived very near to the exact time when Grandma would leave this world.

The next holiday on the calendar was Thanksgiving. My mother was exhausted from taking care of Grandma round the clock. In Grandma's final weeks, she stayed medicated with morphine; it was the only way she could endure the pain radiating throughout her body because of the cancer. Taking care of Grandma was our primary focus, and it was obvious under the current circumstances that Thanksgiving dinner would not get prepared if I did not do it. So I went shopping for the ingredients I needed to provide a Thanksgiving meal. I then cooked the dinner and transported it to Grandma's house on Thanksgiving Day. Our family all gathered at Grandma's house for the day. Everyone ate halfheartedly; no one was into feelings of celebration. Grandma was mostly incoherent, and I do not remember her even being able to eat. She was struggling, and it seemed she was barely hanging on. In fact, it was a blessing that she had survived the previous night and was still with us for Thanksgiving Day. At the end of the day, I did not want to leave, because it felt like Grandma's time was now down to days and maybe even hours. But Doug had to go to work; he had been the restaurant manager for several years now. The day after Thanksgiving was a busy day for McDonald's. He was needed there to run the restaurant for what was usually the busiest day of the year. So I reluctantly left with my husband and son, and we went home for the night.

Around three or four the next morning, on November 23, 1984, we woke up to a phone call. It was my mother informing us that Grandma was not suffering anymore. It was a relief to know her pain was gone from her now, but it was such an empty feeling to know I would not be able to be with her anymore. I knew she was in heaven and enjoying the peace, joy, and contentment you never feel on earth. And I cried because I would miss her presence in my life and her support, love, and encouragement. I knew from the previous day that Grandma could not hang on much longer, but I still was not ready to give her up and hear the final words that she was gone.

Losing Grandma Ada was one of the hardest things I had lived through. It unfortunately also was one of the most hurtful times in my life in regard to how my mother treated me. I had lost one of the most important people in my life. Knowing that Grandma was better off was the only way I could be all right with not having her in my life anymore. And as was the usual pattern of my life, my mother again made this time even harder for me. I know my mother was hurting too, but that did not mean she was the only one hurting and mourning because Grandma was no longer alive and with us. She never showed any compassion or empathy for how I was feeling. It never felt possible for my mother to share with me anything emotionally connecting in nature. Again it seemed to me that she could only shove me aside, care nothing about how I felt, and make everything about her and what she wanted and needed.

I talked to my mother on the phone the day Grandma died. She promised she would wait until I got there to go talk to the funeral director and make all the necessary decisions. I really had no specific input I intended to make. I just wanted to be included, hear the plans, and meet the man who would be in charge of taking care of Grandma. It would be the last time I could be involved in Grandma's life. But when I got to Fort Sumner shortly after noon that day, I arrived to find all the arrangements were already made and everything was taken care of. I reminded my mother that she promised to wait for me, but she had no explanation for cutting me out of the process. Years later, my mother came up with an explanation for her behavior—she now has said that the funeral director was pushing and urging them to get there right away because he had someone else he needed to meet with. My reaction to her flimsy excuse is, "Why did the funeral director's needs have to come before a promise you made to me?" She just could not value me or consider my feelings in anything, even when she had made a promise to me. But after all, she was in control. I was only the child; she was the parent, and in her mind she could do as she pleased. I, the child (now twenty-five years old), just had to take whatever she decided to dump on me with no regard at all for my feelings. Again, she seemed to think she was the only one who mattered, and I had absolutely no significance.

From my perspective, I had hurried to get everything together and get my family to Fort Sumner to be a part of the planning process. And I made sure to be there when my mother had requested. I now realized I had hurried for no reason at all. I asked my mother, "Why am I even here? You have taken care of everything, and you do not need me. I think I will just go back to Clovis and leave it all in your hands."

She said, "Oh, you can go and see your Grandma later this evening."

That is just what I had hurried to get there for, to go view the body that evening, just like any acquaintance could do. The frustrating thing was that my mother just could not understand why I was so upset and frustrated with her. She never seemed capable of comprehending how anyone felt but her. She was not capable of showing empathy. My mother could not grasp that she had made a promise to me, and her actions showed she had no regard for that promise. But this was only one of many times she had broken a promise to me, and whenever I would confront her about it, she minimized the situation by shrugging her shoulders as if to say, "What do you want me to do about it now?" She was so childish and proved to me over and over that I mattered very little to her.

One afternoon during this time of loss, a bus-driving friend of my mother's visited her at Grandma's house. It was interesting to see how she could welcome this lady and open up herself in conversation and feeling, but she had nothing like this to share with me. I was her daughter; I had lost my grandma, and my mother could care for other people but she had no time for me except to hurt my feelings so deeply that she might as well have stabbed me with a knife and twisted it hard.

The drama goes on. When the day of the funeral came around, I thought I could count on sitting with the family for the service, along with my husband and son. I knew that was how Grandma had planned Grandpa's funeral. Grandma even planned Grandpa's funeral so that everyone but the immediate family was seated and then the family walked into the service together. Well, my mother had planned for no one but her and her brother to be recognized as immediate family. My mother, dad, and sister sat in the front row with my uncle and his family, which included one of his daughter's friends. That filled up the front family row, and there was no other place for me and my family to sit but four rows back with Grandma's friends from her childhood days. These friends naturally asked why I was sitting so far back and away from the family. I had no explanation to give them at the time. My mother did not even know where I was during the funeral, but I am sure she did not care as long as she was in the front row. She was so unfeeling, uncompassionate, and oblivious to the hurt she caused in my life. In my opinion, her behavior toward me was inexcusable for one of the most emotionally traumatic days of my life. It just seemed that she had to prove she was the important one in Grandma's life, and I mattered not at all. I also wondered if the funeral director was so very inept, or had my mother never mentioned to him that there were several other family members to consider? My brother and his family also sat farther back with Grandma's friends.

After the funeral, the day settled down somewhat, and the family had gathered at Grandma's house. Doug and I were sitting together in the bedroom we were staying in. Doug loved my grandma too, and he was upset because she was gone. He was crying, and I was holding him as we talked about missing Grandma. The door was half-shut and my mother, like some dorm-monitor, stuck her head in the bedroom and said, "What is going on in here?" Then she looked at Doug and asked, "Why are you crying?"

I said, "Because he misses Grandma."

My mother's response was just, "Well, don't we all?" as she walked off. She offered no understanding or kind words; again, it was turned around to be all about her. It seemed she was saying, *I do not care or understand that anyone else is feeling pain too.* Maybe she thought she was the only one who had a right to cry.

Later that night, I was at the point where I did not care what happened, my mother was going to hear how I felt and about the things she had done causing me hurt on that day and a few days prior. I mentioned the funeral planning and the promise broken, the place my family and I sat at the funeral, plus the fact that it felt as though as long as she and my uncle were taken care of, no one else mattered to her. And also the way she treated Doug when he was mourning the loss of Grandma, when we were alone and she barged in on us with her irrelevant questions, offering no understanding for how we were feeling. And of course as always, when I confronted my mother with these emotional hurts, the encounter turned into an irrational reaction from her with no resemblance to a normal give-and-take conversation. She went into an emotional outrage and began raising her hands to the ceiling and repeating, "Dear God, dear God, what have I done to deserve this?" She became so out-of-control that I said, "Just forget it," and I walked off. She did not pursue and dropped it also. It became another bad memory that proved she did not care how I felt or how she hurt my emotions. She had no understanding of the pain she inflicted on my life; again, it was all about her. It seemed she was incapable of any feelings for me or empathy for how I felt. She is an emotionally detached individual with no ability to understand how anyone else feels; *her* feelings are all that matter. But many years later, there was one small glimmer of light when my mother commented to me regarding Grandma's death, "I guess you probably felt like you lost your mother too. You and her were so close." I just thought, *Duh! It sure took you long enough to grasp that truth.* But she still did not get the fact that all she did at the time of Grandma's death was to make a bad situation even worse for me. It was easier for her to deny the details of pain.

In spite of the hurt all around us, Doug and I had a secret that helped us through the tragedy of losing Grandma. I knew with little doubt before the day of Grandma's funeral that I was expecting another baby. God knew how hard it would be for me to lose my grandma, so He gave me a gift when He took her home. I did not know it until nine months later at my baby's birth, however, that I was carrying a daughter. She would be a daughter very much like my Grandma in many ways. God cared for my feelings, and when he took someone from me who I valued greatly, He replaced that void with the joy of a new baby girl to love and cherish and teach and raise like Grandma had done for me. It was healing for my emotions to know, even though my mother cared little for my feelings, God cared deeply for how I was feeling and what I was going through. God gave me a gift because He understood.

A few weeks later, it was Christmas. We all gathered at Grandma Ada's house as we had done every previous Christmas of my life—it just felt empty this time, since she was not with us this year to celebrate. But Grandma's presence was evident anyway, because everything we did was centered on the traditions she had incorporated into our family. She was absent in body, but her spirit was living on in each of us with the things we did together and in the many, many things she had taught to each of us. My grandma has a special place in my heart that no one else will ever fill, and part of her lives on through me. I also took this family gathering as an opportunity to announce that Doug and I were expecting our second child, to be born the following August. It felt empty that Grandma Ada was missing, but life continues on and we will meet up with her again in heaven one day. Oh, what a day that will be!

And that is how the year 1984 went for me.

Chapter Thirty-Eight

God Blesses Our Family Again

For many months after Grandma Ada died, life felt gloomy, and it was hard to get back to feeling normal and happy again. I guess it was a usual mourning process. But I felt like my sadness was affecting the baby I was carrying. Many times, my baby would go for days without moving, which was very different from before when I carried Jason. He moved and kicked for what seemed like most of the time; it felt as though he could be doing cartwheels. This experience was the opposite, and it even crossed my mind that my baby might not be alive. I had heard the old superstition saying, "Look into the face of death, and never feel your baby's breath." When my baby would be so inactive, this chant would randomly pop into my mind. And I would override that absurd thought with the truth I knew for sure, *God gave me this miracle growing inside me, and because I was pregnant at Grandma's funeral did not mean that my baby will not live just because I looked upon Grandma's dead face.* I also would quickly ask myself, *Where is your faith here? You have to trust God and believe this baby is healthy.* I also had regular reassurance from my doctor that my baby was developing normally and on schedule. The heartbeat was strong. My doctor told me there was no reason for alarm. This baby was just not as active as my first. Many times I would shake my bulging abdomen to encourage my baby to move. Most of the time it worked, and the baby would reluctantly move a little. I prayed for God to keep my baby in His care and for everything to be all right. I promised God that if my baby was born healthy, I would continue to do everything in my power to keep this young life grounded in His perfect will and teach it of Jesus' great love and power to save.

I also had more problems carrying this baby because of where it was positioned. The place the baby chose to rest made my back hurt, and it was hard to sleep. So my husband bought me a waterbed, which helped some. However, I seemed to be most comfortable sleeping on our couch. Again this time, my weight was in line; I gained only twenty pounds total. But otherwise it was a pregnancy unlike the first in almost every way.

During this time, I enjoyed spending time with Jason and helping with his homework. After school, we frequented many of Jason's favorite eating places. Being with my son and experiencing another pregnancy was a highpoint in my life that also brought healing during these months. When doing Jason's homework, reading was our main task. One of the schoolbooks contained many children's poems. There was a poem I remember in particular that contained one line as follows: "You are my pride and joy, my little boy." Jason read the poem, looked up at me, and asked, "Mommy, am I your pride and joy, your little boy?"

This was a very touching moment for me and I responded with a big hug and said, "Yes! You will always be my pride and joy! My little boy!" I have referred to him many times throughout the years as "my pride and joy, my little boy!" And he still is, now and always!

In May 1985, Jason graduated from kindergarten at a dinner graduation ceremony. Jason learned a lot during his first year in school and also made many Christian friends. It seemed he had a productive year in spite of the uncontrollable circumstances in our home life this year. Getting school over and having Jason home with me more was something I looked forward to, and this is when I remember beginning to feel hope again and that life was getting back to normal. Spending the summertime with him made life happier, and I was glad we did not have to think of school now, at least for a few months.

Also during the latter months of my second pregnancy, Dad went to a revival meeting one night and was saved. I was twenty-five years old when he finally made the decision that changed his eternal destination. I thought many times, if only he had made that life-changing decision years ago, before I was born. And not only made the most important decision of his life, but also determined in his heart to live the Christian life afterward. Then my childhood would have been so different and free of the unnecessary pain inflicted on our family led by an unsaved dad. Nevertheless, I was overjoyed that Dad was finally born again, and my son was present when Dad was baptized. There was a definite overall change in Dad's life for the better.

However, even today, there is little evidence that Dad has improved much in the area of selfishness and his attitude of "look out for number one." Our family was damaged due to this attitude. Even after Dad was saved, he never acknowledged the trail of hurt he imposed on his family. We were all expected to just go on and forget all that happened. Being saved did not seem to touch his heart and make him want to right the wrongs he had done for so long. Things he wanted to do were still his priority, but at least he was attending church now. I know salvation is a first step, and following that first step and changing a life takes effort to develop a relationship with God the Father. And I know from experience that my parents have a problem developing functional, healthy, emotionally connected relationships. This is an issue they have to acknowledge and choose to work on before God can bring the needed change. But Dad was now saved, an answer to a specific prayer of mine I began fifteen years earlier—a prayer I had made on Dad's behalf since I was saved myself back at age ten. I thanked God He heard my prayer and had answered it. And I also thanked God for His timing, in spite of the fact that I did not understand it. I know God's timing is always perfect; He knows best, and I do not have to understand why.

After many fun-filled days with Jason, enjoying the summer of 1985, we came to the memorable day of August 17. A day when strange feelings came upon me, soon determined to be related to the beginnings of labor. Almost six years earlier, my son's labor had been induced, and I had never experienced the actual beginnings of childbirth like this before. It felt as if I had a shot of something that was changing everything. Most of the day, I just watched the baby move; its activity had greatly increased. Jason sensed that something was different and kept asking me, "How are you doing, Mom?" I told him, "I'm fine." I really could not explain the strange sensations I was experiencing. That night, I did not sleep much, and Doug stayed by my side as I tried to sleep on our couch. Doug slept very little that night too. Then, early Sunday morning, before the sun came up, I knew for sure I was in labor. Doug helped me get things rounded up, and he woke up Jason. I had trouble standing, as the pains were intensifying. Doug made a few phone calls, and then we headed to the hospital. This time with labor, I was experiencing how it felt to have my baby when *it* chose the time was right. We got to the hospital and were checked in and ready to begin the labor routine around six-thirty a.m. I saw my doctor around seven a.m. He broke my water and said it would be a while, and then he left to play golf. That was a mistake!

After the doctor left, my labor became progressively more intense. Around nine a.m., the nurse on duty started to panic. She said she could not get the doctor on the phone, and she was not capable of delivering a baby by herself. She therefore spent most of her time coaching me to hold back rather than to push and have my baby. This process became more exhausting than actually continuing on normally. By the time the doctor finally arrived, I was too tired to push the way I needed to, and needed help from what the doctor called "the salad spoons"—also known as forceps.

Then, in spite of the more difficult circumstances, at 11:16 a.m. Doug and I welcomed our new daughter into the world. She was born crying loudly; I am sure her experience was painful too, and she had the battle scars to prove it. There were red places on her head from the "salad spoons." Her first cries were music to my ears and a moment I had prayed for regularly throughout the pregnancy. Then I realized that the doctor had said, "It's a girl!" What a blessing! She was healthy and normal, weighing seven pounds three ounces. She was so tiny, delicate, dainty, and fair. Her skin glowed with a beautiful pink hue. I loved my precious daughter immediately. Having a daughter brought enormous thankfulness and a heightened feeling of happiness. It was obvious that she was the apple of her daddy's eye. She made our world complete on this beautiful Sunday morning rich in God's blessings. We named our new baby girl Amanda. Amanda because it was a contemporary name allowing her to be Grandma Ada's namesake. The spelling of Amanda includes Ada. It was the perfect name for our daughter.

This little girl who had frightened me because she did not move much inside the womb grew into a bundle of activity. She was full of life and brought a great abundance of joy to our family. She loves to laugh, and her bright blue eyes sparkle with happiness. God blessed us greatly with our daughter, Amanda, a special fun-filled package of life and laughter. The sunshine she brought into our lives filled the void that Grandma's passing had left. Amanda brought special joy to Doug's life. She certainly has her daddy wrapped around her little finger. Doug is a father completely captured by the love he feels for his daughter. The Tim McGraw song "My Little Girl" is a good description of what I have observed through the years of their father/daughter relationship. Our daughter's zest for life added a special touch of happiness to our lives. I have wished so many times that Amanda could have known her great-grandma Ada, who also was a person known for filling life with joy, happiness, hope, and love.

Chapter Thirty-Nine

The Key to a Functional Family Life

I have heard people say, "Those Christians must be really bad people, since they have to go to church so much and repent of their sins." This assumption from the unsaved world is false; they just do not understand the Christian life. Going to a Bible-believing church on a regular basis does not prove that you are bad. However, it does mean that you are interested in learning how to avoid the pitfalls and traps of life that Satan lays for us all. The purpose of regular church attendance is more for preventive maintenance than for repentance of one's sins, with the ultimate purpose being to worship God with a grateful heart. Attending church is wise—it strengthens your foundation and grows your relationship with God and fellow Christians. When your major focus in life is to learn of God's ways, there are fewer reasons you will need to repent of worldly sin. Regular church attendance keeps you walking close to God. And walking close to God keeps you living a life that is pleasing to Him and yields a life of peace, contentment, and joy instead of strife, pain, and consequences.

When Doug and I got married, he had weak convictions concerning church attendance and worshiping God regularly. This was a crossroads in his life at which he could have chosen a wilder, bar-hopping lifestyle or a conservative lifestyle of Christian service and worship. Doug's decision depended heavily on me as his wife. Even though we both were born-again Christians, I was no more spiritually mature than Doug. But my desire was to serve God and please Him. Any lifestyle that pulled me away from God brought great unrest to my soul. So that is why we started out attending the church where I was saved at age ten. Doug's relationship with God did grow during our early years of marriage, even though he did not feel a connection to my church and was never motivated to join. That is because Doug's spiritual connection was not with my church; it was with God.

We continued attending the church where I was saved. Jason's first time at church, at only two weeks old, was recognized during the church service when the preacher introduced him to the congregation as the church's newest member. Later on, for several summers, Jason went to Vacation Bible School there, and Amanda also had some of her first experiences of church attendance there as well. However, since Doug was interested in finding a church that better suited him and our family, we visited several churches in a period of transition.

Then Doug hired a maintenance man for McDonald's who had been a missionary. This man had just returned with his family from Kenya, Africa. He was a member at a church that operated a Christian school where his wife was the principal, and he told Doug about the school. After getting some information, we enrolled Jason in kindergarten there. We also attended church there for several months while Jason was in school, but we did not join the church until Amanda was around one year old. I thank God that my husband led our family to join a church where we grew spiritually through the preaching of the truth from the King James Bible. Encouraging me to step out and make a change rather than stagnate at the same church I had always attended was a blessing in my life. God made this possible through my husband's choice to seek a better place for us to worship where we learned of God and grew together spiritually as a family. It was the right choice, and it filled our life with many great blessings in the future.

Our church, led by Pastor Stan White, became the place where we learned and grew, individually and as a family, in our relationship with God. It is where the strong, rock-solid foundation was laid for our lives. We were obedient to God, and our lives were richly blessed according to the promises God makes to His children in the Bible. This was the time in our lives when we learned the key to living a contented life filled with purpose. Weekly our faith increased, as did our desire to live a life pleasing to God our Father. We also made many lifelong friends to support, grow, and share life with. One unquestionable truth is that you will never find truer friendships than with fellow Christians. Sharing the bond of knowing Jesus as your personal Savior and sharing together your place in God's family as His child is the basis for the strongest, most dependable friendships you will ever experience. Our church is also where our family met an evangelist named Buck Hatfield, a man who would become an important part of our lives in the years ahead.

I also know that church was exactly where I needed to be because God was the only one capable of healing the emotional wounds I still carried from childhood. With every message of hope and every message that made Jesus real to me, I healed as I could have healed nowhere else. Building a strong spiritual relationship with Jesus my Savior and God my Father, in addition to all the wonderful friends I shared life with, made so many of the childhood hurts fade into a distant memory I rarely thought of unless my parents visited. My patience increased in relation to my household responsibilities. With Jason and Amanda, my feelings of love and peace also grew, changing me into the mother I desired to become. I was not perfect and still would, on rare occasions, get frustrated and lose my temper. But it was a different feeling and a different circumstance, because I felt Jesus was with me always. I felt that now I was really growing spiritually, and being enabled by the Holy Spirit made a difference in how I behaved. It made me stronger and wiser, and I was better able to think before I reacted.

The healing I was experiencing through church attendance and growing my relationship with God turned me into a more loving wife, mother, and person. My husband and my children were the ones I needed most to touch and love in order to heal my emotions and bring change into my life. God had given me the power to rewrite my future through the love and support of my husband and my children. With my family and the strength I received from my church, my future became brighter and life became more worthwhile, with renewed meaning and purpose. It was the exact prescription I needed to heal my emotional wounds, a task only God could accomplish. Without God, my family, and my church, healing for me would have been hopeless.

Another way my life was encouraged and healed was when Jason was saved in December 1986. He and Doug talked with Pastor White, and Jason realized his need for Jesus in his life and was spiritually born again, trusting Jesus Christ in faith. Jason was then baptized before the church, making his profession of faith public. Jason continued to grow spiritually, increasing his faith in his new relationship with God through Jesus Christ. At the end of his third grade year, Jason received the Christian Character award from the Christian school he attended. At the ceremony, two-year-old Amanda voluntarily went forward with Jason to help him receive his award. She too loved and supported her brother. It was said by several, "That proves he really deserves the Christian Character award—even his little sister supports him and thinks highly of him."

Worshiping together develops emotionally healthy families. Attending church as a family develops a common bond between family members. You learn together, grow spiritually together, worship God together, and all possess a life foundation built on a faith shared by each family member. The shared faith produces emotionally connected, healthy, caring, happy, and loving families. It produces family members who are on the same page and have the capacity to care, encourage, and support one another. Church life and God's presence also provides a safety net for the family when parents make mistakes. Since parents are human and will inevitably make mistakes, they need positive support to stay on track; a relationship with God and a church family provides that support. There does not have to be permanent damage from human mistakes with God's presence and protection over the family. Letting God lead makes a functional family and diminishes the chance for permanent emotional damage.

Communication is also improved when mutual caring for others is prevalent. Worshiping together with a true desire to learn God's ways and a heartfelt desire for self-betterment leaves no room for selfishness or the attitude of looking out for number one. Throughout my childhood, Dad often said, "Look out for number one; if you don't, nobody else will." Dad was right, *if* you live in a non-Christian world. But Christians, living as Jesus commanded, love their neighbor as themselves, which makes a world of difference for emotional health. When meeting each other's needs, a family is united with mutual empathy and caring for one another and other people, through a common faith in God and a shared belief in the truth.

Out of the numerous things Doug and I learned from Pastor Stan White, without a doubt one of the greatest lessons we benefited from was the importance of tithing. We thank God that Pastor White was not afraid to boldly share the truth with our church and us regarding this subject. It is sad that too many people are turned off by the mention of money and tithing and think that churches only want your money. If this is your thought process, you are allowing a stumbling block to prevent you from experiencing God's richest blessings in life. It seems when the thought of giving a portion of your income to the local church is disagreeable or offensive, the basic understanding that God owns everything is missing. God does not need your money. God made the world, and He owns everything in it, including your possessions. Whatever you are allowed to enjoy is only by God's grace. And God wants to bless you more when you choose to be obedient. Therefore, it is a small thing that God requires when he asks us to give back to Him a tithe, or one-tenth of the income He allows us to earn. To sum up God's plan for our money, taken from the website of Victory Baptist Church at *victorybaptiststephenville.com,* "… every Christian, as a steward of that portion of God's wealth entrusted to him, is obligated to support his local church financially. We believe that God has established the tithe as the basis for giving but that every Christian should also give other offering sacrificially and cheerfully to the support of the Church, to the relief of those in need, and to the spread of the Gospel (Gen. 14:20; Prov. 3:9–10; 1 Tim. 5:17–18; 1 John 3:17)."

You cannot out-give God. "So let each one give as he purposes in his heart, not grudgingly or of necessity; for God loves a cheerful giver" (2 Cor. 9:7 NKJV). In the Bible, God offers a promise related to tithing: "Bring ye all the tithes into the storehouse, that there may be meat in mine house, and prove me now herewith, saith the Lord of hosts, if I will not open you the windows of heaven and pour you out a blessing, that there shall not be room enough to receive it" (Mal. 3:10). Obeying God and giving your tithes and offerings to your local church does not necessarily mean that you will receive a monetary blessing in return. Life's blessings are not always related to money. Although increases in wealth can be a result of obedience, there are many far more important blessings that God can add to a life dedicated to serving Him. These blessings can also be in the form of relationships—such as a good, solid, lifelong Christian marriage to a person you genuinely love and care for and who loves and cares for you in return. The healthy and mutually beneficial relationships with your children or with friends who are a true blessing in your life. You and your family may enjoy physical health—that is a true blessing from God.

Another obvious blessing is that of raising functional, productive, responsible children. When raising children, you either put the effort and time into their lives when they are young and see your efforts grow into blessings, or you put minimal effort into their lives as children and then reap the pain and consequences in their adult life when problems come your way. It is another choice—you can pay now with your time and effort, or pay for the rest of your life when you have to deal with the undesirable outcome of raising your children in a dysfunctional home. Disobedience always leads to problems, but obedience brings blessings and the joy of a quiet spirit, free of turmoil. Other blessings come in different forms, such as when God chooses to prevent a tragedy in your life or warms your heart by giving you a dream you have always desired. There are many different forms in which obedience to God's law through tithing will bring blessings to your existence.

Also, when figuring a tithe, the 10 percent is to come from *gross* income, not *net* income. Gross income is actual earnings; net income is the money left from actual earnings after the government gets their share first. Therefore, be sure not to rob God by figuring your tithe from the lesser amount. At this point, some people say, "I can't afford to tithe." From my experience, no one can afford not to. The return is always over 100 percent with no risk. Where else can you find that in the financial world today? God is life's answer to every question. I am so thankful to Pastor Stan White for teaching my husband and me to tithe. And I thank God for giving my husband and me a teachable spirit willing to learn of God's ways through faith and trust, even when it does not appear to make sense in human or worldly terms. Tithing is a privilege. It is a way to give your life symbolically to Jesus. Money represents your life—it comes from time you spent using your life to earn a living. Giving a part of that earned money to God is one way to give your life to Him, just as Jesus gave His life for you. For my husband and me, our marriage and our life together is proof that you cannot out-give God.

When you live your life with a desire to please God in words, deeds, and actions, God will bless you richly as well as make you a blessing to others. Blessings manifest in many different forms: some are monetary, some are in relationships, some are in protection, and others are in prevention. When people truly live in God's truth and wisdom, they will not be prone to use their life to promote worldly thinking in opposition to God's principles. Instead, they will use their life to share God's truth with others, and when promoting God's way is their primary focus, it could prevent them from living in old age with a deteriorating mind. Prevention, protection, or any of numerous other blessings a Christian life reaps from God are always for good and come from God's love as rewards for obedience to His will.

I desire to serve God out of gratitude. I have placed my life into the care of the one who died for me. Jesus died on the cross for my sins and yours. Jesus sacrificed His perfect, holy life for all sinners. This was necessary to make a way for all mankind to have a relationship with the Holy Father, the One who is unable to look upon sin. Since God the Father cannot be in the presence of sin, sinful men and women are lost and without hope if they do not know Jesus. The shedding of Jesus's blood was a sufficient sacrifice to make it possible for sinful people to stand before a holy, righteous God. Thus Jesus, shedding His blood, is the *only* way to the Father. Unless you have trusted Jesus and are washed clean from your sins by His blood, you are unable to stand before God and enjoy heaven as your home. The simple truth is that without Jesus, you are lost and headed to Satan's hell of eternal torment. Jesus is the only hope to save any person from this fate. All you have to do is believe in the sacrifice that Jesus made for you; that Jesus is the only begotten Son of God; that Jesus died for all mankind and rose again after three days; and that Jesus did not remain dead, He is alive and is ready to save anyone who believes in Him and asks Him for salvation. I serve a risen Savior; not a dead powerless idol. Jesus paid it all—all to Him I owe. I serve Jesus out of a grateful heart. (See Appendix A.)

People avoid God and church attendance as if it would bring a plague into their lives or deprive them of something detrimental to their lives that they believe they must have even though it is harmful, such as drugs, alcohol, and illicit sex. But the real truth is that they are rejecting the greatest, most valuable treasure they will ever be offered, only because they perceive that a church life will cost them the worldly pleasures they desire. The irony of this thinking is that these pleasures are almost always the things that bring damage, hurt, and pain into their lives. These worldly pleasures result in suffering and death. But the greatest treasure people so quickly refuse brings only contentment, protection, provision, and ultimately the hope of everlasting life filled with peace. It is sad that so many searching souls will avoid and reject the only place they can find the truth and happiness that every human being seeks. The truth is found only in God and His Son Jesus. Any other road brings falsehood, misery, discontent, strife, pain, eternal suffering ... and dysfunctional families. Finding Jesus, obeying God, and attending a church guided by God's word, the Bible, is the point where a person really begins to live life at its best. For the sake of your eternal soul, stop running from God, let Him be your Father, and find your true purpose. The day will come when you will be eternally grateful that you did.

Chapter Forty

A Healing, Growing Period

After Amanda was born, my mother's need to control my life began to wane some. She seemed to focus more on driving her school bus and less on how my life should be. It also felt that she did not care to be around my daughter as much as she had needed to be involved with my son. She also mentioned a few times how my daughter did not look like babies she was used to. Jason had more of the Indian look with brown hair and brown eyes. Amanda had my blonde hair and her daddy's blue eyes. Anyway, I focused on my children, and they rarely stayed with anyone else during this period. Our young family benefited and grew through these years from the security of just being together. We experienced a feeling of unity and a shared common bond from regular church attendance and mutual spiritual growth. I was experiencing great emotional healing in my life during this period. I had a faithful, devoted, and loving husband who did anything he could to make my life easier. I was privileged to be the mother of two beautiful, healthy children and to enjoy the blessing of guiding their growth. And the greatest blessing of all was that we were thriving as a family under the shelter of God's wing. Psalm 91 is a beautiful description of God's protection and comfort from a hurtful world. I also felt that Grandma Ada's death had severed some link between my mother and me, and she did seem to back off ... at least for a time.

As my daughter grew, it became apparent that she possessed a personality full of life and vitality. She is open, emotional, and loving.

Our son being more reserved, analytical, and thoughtful made our two children so different in many ways. I had to learn to adjust as a parent. My husband and I are also more the analytical type. One of the ways I learned in wisdom how to relate to my lively daughter was found in some Christian resources I purchased. I learned a lot and had several revelations about parenting from *Hidden Keys to Successful Parenting* by Gary Smalley, a well-known counselor, speaker, and author. I discovered my daughter was operating from a different personality mode than I was. I needed to adjust my parenting of her accordingly, and I should encourage her to become her unique self. Just because she is my daughter does not mean she would live life just as I did. I did not want to repeat my mother's mistake and recognized early in Amanda's life that she was a unique individual, not someone exactly like me. Therefore, I chose to acknowledge her characteristics and encourage her to be who God made her to be. And I learned that it is a blessing to celebrate our differences.

I have always been very thankful to Dr. Smalley for the timely advice in parenting I got from him. It made a definite difference in my relationship with my daughter. That wisdom is probably part of the reason we have enjoyed a great mother/daughter relationship through the years and still do today, when she is grown and married. His teachings also helped me realize, by analyzing different personality types, that our daughter is actually more like Grandma Ada. Amanda's presence in the family brought to each of us her unique slant on life, filled with joy and love. We celebrated her personality and enjoyed immensely her laughter and ability to focus more on the sparkle and flame of existence than the serious side. One time when she was a teenager, she had her *serious* dad laughing so much, they were rolling in the floor and couldn't catch their breath. Then a few weeks later, when asked what they were laughing at, they couldn't remember what made them laugh, they just remembered that they did. The laughter was the memory!

One fond memory of my oldest son was when he chose to serve his dad and me breakfast in bed. Jason was about eight years old. Doug was home on Saturday morning, and this was cause to celebrate. As the restaurant manager ultimately responsible for every aspect of operating the McDonald's restaurant, he was almost never off work on Saturday. But on one of those rare Saturdays, Jason was thoughtful and got up before we did to cook breakfast. He then brought it to us before we got out of the bed. Jason did a wonderful job serving a delicious breakfast of perfectly cooked fried eggs and toast along with orange juice, milk, and even coffee! It is a memory etched forever in my mind of our thoughtful little boy carefully bringing a beautiful breakfast to his mom and dad in bed. Love was in every mouthful. Jason was such a considerate, sweet and caring son. He has always added his own special love, joy, and blessing to our life.

During this period of our lives, Doug and I celebrated our tenth wedding anniversary. As the perpetual planner and organizer, Doug put time and effort into making sure that our tenth anniversary would be perfect and memorable. About four weeks in advance, we visited a travel agent to find some place unique and special to go for the weekend. Then, after at least two meetings, we found the perfect getaway. We asked my mother if the kids could stay with her for that weekend in October 1987. She agreed at least two weeks in advance of our trip. So we made our plans and paid our money for the weekend in Cloudcroft, New Mexico, at a romantic, historic hotel called The Lodge. It was located in the Rocky Mountains by a ski resort and was also noted for its exceptional cuisine prepared by a professional chef. It all sounded terrific, and Doug and I looked forward to celebrating our tenth anniversary at The Lodge nestled in the mountains.

The Friday night came when Doug and I were to drop off the kids at my parents' house. We arrived with our kids and their packed bags, intending to leave them and be on our way. My mother started backing out by saying, "I am so tired. I will keep Jason but not Amanda." She said, "I just cannot keep up with her too." My mother had let me down again; it was just one more time she reneged on a promise she made to me. Therefore, my husband and I had to immediately adjust our plans. We had already paid for the weekend in advance; we would lose our money if we cancelled. Now we had no choice but to figure out how we could make our plans work and take Amanda. Maybe there would be somewhere in the hotel room for our two-year-old daughter to sleep too. Since we had never been to this hotel before, we could only hope it would work out.

After this episode, I would not personally ask my mother to babysit again. I got tired of her acting like it was such an imposition I was asking her to make. If our children stayed with her, my husband would ask. She did not behave this way when he asked.

Years later, when I brought up the situation of the tenth anniversary to my mother and told her how it made me feel, she claimed, "I said I would keep just one kid, Jason or Amanda, just one—it did not matter which one." But this is not the way my husband or I remember the situation. Jason could stay with her, not Amanda. That is why we re-planned a way to take Amanda. And my mother always had time for Jason whether she was tired or not. However, it never seemed she was interested in putting forth the effort to build a relationship with Amanda. My mother seemed to have a problem with the way Amanda would seize life with vigor, vitality, and happiness. She was too much of a livewire, and my mother was not interested in dealing with that. Amanda was not like her brother, but I chose to celebrate those differences rather than demand that Amanda fit into a preconceived mold and risk making her apprehensive about being herself ... the way my mother caused me to feel.

In retrospect, my husband and I are glad we took our daughter with us on our tenth-anniversary trip. It was packed even fuller of memorable moments with her along, and our walks in the woods are recalled with pictures of Amanda sitting on Doug's shoulders as together we walked the Osha Trail ("The Trail of Love") in the Rocky Mountains. Also, at the Lodge, in the den by a fireplace, stands a taxidermy version of a very tall grizzly bear. When Amanda discovered the bear, she came running to her dad, talking loudly in a very excited voice, "Daddy, there's a monster in there!" She had thought for a moment that the bear was alive. We found "the monster" and showed her that he was only a stuffed bear, and his claws or teeth could not hurt her.

Another thought I had later was that, if I could go back to that night when my mother refused to keep my daughter, I would leave her house not only with Amanda but with Jason too. If Amanda was not welcome, then we should not have left Jason either. I just wish I would have known then that it is perfectly okay and acceptable to set boundaries.

Chapter Forty-One

More Blessings than Pain

Emotional healing continued to be important during this period in my life. One of the things contributing monumentally to this healing was daily Bible reading. Pastor Stan White found a source that supplied the King James Bible in a version divided up into 365 daily readings, entitled *The One Year Bible.* We purchased copies of this Bible, and I finally accomplished a task I had always wanted to do: I read the entire Bible all the way through. After this accomplishment, daily Bible reading became a habit, and I have read the Bible in its entirety many times since. The Bible truly is a living word, and it meets different needs in your life each time you read the verses it contains. It is God's gift to us, His infallible word giving direction for life straight from God to mankind. I am blessed each time I read God's word and allow it to speak to my heart with messages relevant for specific needs at the time. Also, overall, I have been richly blessed through obedient determination to read the entire Bible. It is a source that guides my life. The Bible contains truth you will find no where else. If you really desire to hear from God, and you truly want to let Him lead your life to the purpose you were born for, listen with your heart as you experience God's word. Then get ready to begin your great adventure filled with purpose and meaning. A good nonfiction movie that provides tangible proof of what daily Bible reading can do to change a life is *The Secrets of Jonathan Sperry.* The Bible is powerful and life-changing. There is no other book that I love, respect, trust, and treasure more than the Bible. I have no other possession I hold more dear.

My church, Victory Baptist in Stephenville Texas, describes *The Holy Scriptures (The Bible)* as follows: "*The Holy Scriptures* of the Old and New Testament are the verbally and plenarily inspired Word of God. The Scriptures are inerrant, infallible, and God-breathed, and therefore are the final authority for faith and life (2 Tim. 3:16–17; 2 Pet. 1:20–21)."

At this time of Bible reading, church attendance, spiritual growth, and an abundance of family togetherness, baby steps had started the motion forward, stirring change in our lives of which we were presently unaware. It was a few years before the changes would become apparent and complete, but positive change had begun for our life and family. These positive beginnings would manifest in many areas of our life. And as usual, these abundant blessings were touched randomly with the negative presence of past childhood family dysfunction.

God blessed our lives materially and emotionally. Our finances were steadily growing with the raises Doug received as a result of his hard work and his exceptional work ethic. We regularly tithed 10 percent and more of the gross wages. We bought a new van that our children enjoyed greatly; the added room made traveling more comfortable for us all. We drove this van for about nine years and then gave it to a missionary family.

Throughout the years, Doug attended many McDonald's manager conventions in the summertime. At one of these conventions in New Orleans, he met some fellow managers who were planning to buy their own McDonald's restaurants. They had a goal and the training to make it happen. Doug began thinking along these lines for his future. He too was adequately trained and had been honored with numerous "outstanding manager" awards, which lined our walls at home. All he had to do was apply and tell the appropriate people of his desire. It did, however, feel like a long shot. Even though our finances were steadily improving, it felt as if there was no way financially to make this dream a reality. Even with the special financial opportunities available for managers of Doug's caliber, it was still a lot of money for a growing family to come up with. However, Doug continued to pursue this dream and talked to many owner/operators, including the one he worked for at the time, about the possibilities. He talked to many corporate contacts as well. Every conversation was positive and encouraging, supporting Doug's ability to succeed. The paperwork was filed, and Doug was approved to own a McDonald's restaurant of his very own. The next step was for Doug and me to meet with the licensing manager. At a McDonald's restaurant in Irving, Texas, we met with the man in charge of finding our restaurant. We had specified that we preferred a location west of the Mississippi and south of I-40. At this particular time, there were no restaurants available in this area. We were told to go home, save our money, and wait for "the call." This was March 1988.

A year later, there were still no possibilities, and we were still short on the cash needed to purchase the restaurant. It was obvious that the time was not right for us to become McDonald's owner/ operators. During this time in our lives, we were definitely learning a lesson in patience and believing that good things come to those who wait. Then, instead of keeping our life on hold and putting all our efforts into the dream of a restaurant, we decided to go back to living as if we were going to stay many more years where we were at. We were going to take the advice of Theodore Roosevelt: "Do what you can, with what you have, where you are." This thought kept us from living as though we could be moving next week and made life more peaceful. Doug continued taking the few classes he needed to receive his business degree from ENMU and as always put 110 percent into his job responsibilities.

There was a time during these years that I developed a very painful condition that centered around my monthly cycle. It caused unbearable, painful cramps, and it seemed to increase with severity each month rather than easing up. I saw my doctor for an annual checkup in December 1989. He said, "Without running in-depth tests, what you are probably suffering from is endometriosis. Considering your age of thirty, what I would recommend for a possible cure, if you and your husband agree, would be to have another baby." I told the doctor I was ready for that option but would have to get my husband's input. He told me that if we chose to have a baby and I had not conceived within six months, to come back and see him then. The doctor gave me a prescription for the pain, and I went home to discuss future plans with Doug. Doug was agreeable to this method of healing my condition, and he too was ready to try for another baby. So now we were working on conceiving a baby and still trying to get our McDonald's restaurant, which now was more on the back burner.

Somewhere in the process of applying for our McDonald's, it became known that I had a business degree with a major in business administration and accounting. The corporation was interested in me becoming part of the application process, and I had to provide my information also. It was recommended that I start the training process immediately so I would be ready to begin working when a restaurant became available. Therefore, I studied the training volumes and went to work with Doug randomly. Doug's boss even bought me some McDonald's uniforms to wear when I worked.

My training seemed to present a perfect opportunity for Amanda to spend time with her grandma before we moved. Doug asked my mother to keep Amanda while I worked some with him. It worked well for Amanda to spend about two to three hours with my mother while I worked the lunch rush two to three days a week. This schedule did not interfere with my mother's school-bus driving; I picked Amanda up before she had to drive her bus. I was not on the McDonald's schedule; I worked as an extra for lunch so I could leave when I needed to. This routine worked well for a few days, and then my mother decided she did not want to commit to a regular schedule of taking care of Amanda. Doug and I got an overwhelming feeling that she did not want to keep Amanda at all. The thought of babysitting Amanda seemed to bring so much strife to my mother that we felt it best for Amanda not to stay with her grandma.

My mother gave no reason for backing out other than she just could not commit. This made no sense to me. She was always complaining about how she could not spend time with Amanda and get to know her like she did Jason. We were trying to give her the opportunity before we moved, but something was becoming clear to me through this experience. My mother, although she protested loudly that she had no favorites, had a favorite grandchild, and that was my first son, Jason. There was a pattern developing here; she would not keep Amanda for our tenth-anniversary trip, and she would not keep Amanda for a few hours a week before we moved away for good. She talked a lot about how she thought things should be, but what she said and how she acted were totally opposite. She did not want to build a relationship with Amanda. For now, Doug and I decided it would be enough for me to study the training volumes to prepare for the time when we did get our own McDonald's restaurant. For now, I would work in the restaurant with him whenever we could work it out. This was another time in my life when I felt like my mother was trying her best to make things harder for me. And it was obvious that her wanting a relationship with Amanda was just talk.

In May of 1990, Doug graduated with honors receiving his associates degree in business administration and accounting. It took many years to finish; Doug had been taking classes at the local campus since before Jason was born. Getting a degree when you work full-time is very hard. But Doug made it to graduation day in addition to excelling at his very demanding job. And this degree, too, was a plus on the resume with McDonald's Corporation. As soon as Doug graduated, he and I went to Oklahoma City. We were required to meet with a McDonald's corporate accountant as part of the approval process. McDonald's had its own style of accounting, and I needed their accounting binder for a guideline when I became the accountant for our business one day.

It was sometime in May 1990 when I finally conceived. I was surprised that it took almost the entire six months the doctor allotted. The pregnancy was not officially verified during this month, but from what I was feeling, it was clear that I was expecting. I told no one of my suspicions except my husband.

May 1990 was also the month that my cousin, the "ring bear" in our wedding, graduated from Fort Sumner High School. Our family planned to attend the ceremony. The drive to Fort Sumner was sixty miles, and we were to leave after Doug got off work. I talked to my mother earlier in the day, and she promised to let Doug, Jason, Amanda, and me ride with her and Dad. We decided this because Doug was extra tired from work demands and had told me that he preferred not to drive this time. Well, it is probably obvious that another promise was about to be broken. My mother just did not place any significance in keeping promises she made to me. But she could give a good speech on why it is so important to be true to your word and quote the well-known fact that "a man is only as good as his word." In my mother's mind, it seemed these wise words regarding a promise applied only if the promise was not made to me—at least that is the message I repeatedly got from her empty promises.

My mother and dad drove up to my house with my sister and her husband in the car with them. There clearly was no room for me and my family—so let's disregard yet another promise made to me by my mother. I looked at her and asked, "How is this all supposed to work now?" She looked at me and shrugged her shoulders as if to say, *I do not know what you are going to do now.* My brother and his family arrived about the same time as my parents, and my mother said, "I guess you and Doug can take your van, and your brother's family can ride with you. That should work, right?" I just looked at her, walked off, and began getting everyone into our van. I was so infuriated with her, I was beyond words. I kept asking myself on the drive to the graduation, *Why do you keep on trusting this woman?* I also made up my mind that I might have the baby I was carrying before she would hear it from me that I was pregnant. I kept living through situations with my mother that made me feel like crying out to God and asking, *Why do I have to live through this all the time?* This was so abnormal and so far from the way my life is now with Doug and our children.

There was an extended period of time after this incident when I did not see my parents on purpose. I was so mad at my mother that I wanted nothing to do with them. It felt perfectly peaceful not having to deal with the childish behavior I experienced from them. Then, after a few weeks, Dad did one adult thing and called me. He wanted to know why he had not seen me and what I had been doing. I explained to him about the graduation promise broken, among many other broken promises before that. I told him I was tired of the way my mother treated me. That I felt she regularly catered to anyone else's needs but mine. That she routinely caused me to feel bad and then acted like she had done nothing wrong. He said, "I did not know you felt this way, and I will talk to your mother about what you have told me." Since Dad had called me, I did tell him I was expecting another baby. He seemed very happy to hear the news.

I guess when Dad talked to my mother, he also told her about the baby, because she came bringing me an abundance of maternity clothes soon afterward. It seemed she had ordered me one of each item from the JCPenney catalog. It was really more than I needed and more than I could wear in just one pregnancy. But that is how my mother says "I'm sorry," the way she shows her "love." The material things or money are supposed to show the love she cannot express with normal feelings and behaviors. These things did not fix my hurt feelings. This is a distorted view of love. Love does not equal gifts and money. Love needs to be expressed with words and given meaning through nonverbal gestures, such as hugs or touch or eye contact (the eyes are the window to the heart and soul). It should not be so hard to say "I'm sorry" or "I love you." These expressions, when used genuinely with actions, are necessary to heal emotions and to keep emotions healthy. But they mean little where no emotional connection exists.

It takes hundreds of positive actions to make up for just one negative, hurtful encounter. Therefore, both my parents are overdrawn and bankrupt as far as my emotional bank account with them is concerned. Emotional connection and interpersonal communication resulting in a healthy relationship cannot be replaced by money or things. My mother never brought up any of the things I told Dad regarding my feelings. I guess she denied all that away too.

Now Doug and I were expecting our third child. We had specific plans for our family and our children, many of which were already in place—plans to stop the dysfunction of our childhood past from tormenting another generation. Doug and I both had lived through the childhood hurt of our parents' divorce. Both our dads were uninvolved and detached from our lives. And both our mothers had told us of their hurt that was inflicted by an unfaithful husband. Therefore, we had determined particular preferences, goals, and objectives to protect our children from similar hurtful experiences we had lived through. We wanted our children free to experience normal and healthy emotional growth that would not require wasted time in their future recovering from unnecessary damage inflicted by abnormality and dysfunction. Their energies would not be diverted to soothing damaged emotions. Instead, they could totally focus on pursuing their dreams and growing into the successful individuals they each were born to become.

Chapter Forty-Two

How Life Would Be Different for Our Children

When describing the kings that reigned in Judah and Israel in the Old Testament books of the Bible, they are categorized in one of two ways. The king did "that which was right in the sight of the Lord," or the king did "that which was evil in the sight of the Lord." This description can be related to family life as well, with the father being the head or king of his home. As the leader of his home, a father can choose to do "that which is right in the sight of the Lord" and reap the rewards of a loving and functional family—or the father can choose to do "that which is evil in the sight of the Lord" and reap the undesirable consequences of damage and dysfunction. God gives man free will and the option to choose his own path.

After Doug and I were married and began building our family together, there was nothing from my childhood home that I wanted to emulate in our home. I had specific hopes and plans for our family and our future, centered in God's perfect will and free of the dysfunction I grew up in. With God's guidance and strength, my husband and I were able to provide that better place I dreamed of in which to raise our children. As a wife and mother, I failed many times, but God was there to lift me up when I fell and keep me on the path He had for my life. Without God, I would not be where I am today. Today I have accomplished much in many areas of my life, but only with God's enabling. I have been in a strong marriage with the same man for over thirty years. We have three successful children. My life is peaceful and content because I am focused on God's perfect will for me. I have experienced an adult life that most people only dream of. My relationship with God has been the source of countless blessings and miracles in my life.

Commitment to Avoid the Damage of Divorce

For my husband and me, our first commitment was that we would marry for life; divorce was not an option. We would work through what came our way together. We put our trust and faith in God to make this commitment to each other, and with His enabling we have found the ability to keep it. We pledged this to each other before we began planning our wedding, so we could begin a life opposite of what we each had experienced in childhood. Since we both were children of divorce, we neither one wanted to ever be damaged by divorce again. Therefore, any children we had together would not know the heart-wrenching, displaced feelings of rejection and abandonment when your parents tear your family apart and you feel lost in the world. The divorce magnified the feelings of abandonment and of being unwanted by my mother. It also was hurtful seeing Dad at this time and feeling even more strongly that he did not care for me anyway. It was an empty feeling I experienced too many times.

My husband and I did not want our children to feel the indescribable pain and the overwhelming impression that you belong nowhere on earth when you are forced to be with your dad and his dates. This abnormal situation is extremely difficult for children to understand. Dad dated haggy women, not nice girls. But I am sure Dad was not looking for an emotional connection with them anyway. The rejection I felt intensified when Dad's dates treated me like a lowlife and scum because I was not welcome in their relationship. My husband and I experienced enough pain of this nature to never want to pass this hurtful, damaging legacy on to our children. God did enable us to create a peaceful, secure home where our children grew in love and acceptance, and divorce was never a possibility because of God's presence.

A Defining Moment in My Life that
Strengthened My Commitments

Before becoming a mother, I made a commitment to myself that the things I had experienced in my childhood would never touch the lives of my future children. Only with God's enabling could I keep such a promise. This commitment I made to myself took on a more concrete form as a result of an interaction I witnessed between my mother and my brother when he was about eighteen years old. My brother was confiding in my mother about his plans and thoughts for his future, in addition to some things he was feeling. I watched on as my mother emotionally shot down everything my brother was telling her. It was her normal pattern of behavior to look for the negative and tell us why we could not do something rather than encouraging us and believing that we could succeed. Also, if anything we did was not pleasing to her, we were told that we should be ashamed of ourselves rather than receive neutral advice to help us think things through. I looked on as my brother melted into rejection and hurt. When I witnessed this episode between my mother and brother, I happened to be about six months pregnant with my first child. I had observed these scenes between them many times throughout the years and had experienced many of my own negative interactions with our mother as well. But since I was expecting my first child, this episode made a real impact on me. I remember during the interaction between them that I held my hand on my bulging abdomen where my little baby grew and thought: *God, help me to treat my child's inquiries with kindness and respect and honor my child's dreams with support and encouragement.*

Passing On the Faith

My husband and I determined to put God first in our marriage, our family, and our home. We would be true to the vows we made on our wedding day, including the words spoken in our home-dedication prayer. We would live true to the final statement in our wedding ceremony as we were pronounced husband and wife: "... to go forth upon your journey of life to bless the world and glorify God ..." We believed the best place to start this commitment was with our own family, through love and devotion to each other and then to our children who would join our family through the years ahead. We trusted God to guide us. In God's presence and through obedience to Him was the only way this promise could possibly be carried out to make a functional home for our children in such a sinful, dysfunctional world. Through our commitment to God and each other, our children had a home filled with memories of honoring God and of parents who loved each other. Our children grew up in a home completely opposite to the one I experienced as a child.

Guiding our children in God's ways would prevent a lot of potentially bad decisions in their lives made outside of God's will, resulting in problems and undesirable consequences. We would make it a priority that they knew what was right and best for them, giving them a firm Christian foundation to stand on. They would not have to make life-changing decisions based on the opinions of unwise individuals (teachers, schools, doctors) or parents' conformity to a harmful norm through ignorance. They would be protected because they would possess God's truth. They would know through life experience how important it is to obey God and would live the blessings that come to those who obey God.

In our home, God was honored through family church attendance and obedience to His word. Our children knew the joy of a personal relationship with God and Jesus. They grew up being part of a family whose God was reverenced and not shut out or rejected. Our children cherished the Bible and had two parents who prayed for their needs. Growing a real relationship with God through faith in His Son Jesus Christ is the first essential ingredient in a functional, loving, and contented home. Only through God can you find your true purpose in life. When raising children, however, it is important to remember that there is a fine line between demanding that your children go to church and creating a desire within them to go because they want to serve God. Parents must have the wisdom to achieve the proper balance, making the experience positive without making the children feel controlled. Demanding and controlling parents produce rebellious children who run from God, do not want to go to church, and will not go when they reach adulthood. But the right balance achieved through wisdom from God leads children to desire and grow in a lifelong healthy relationship with God, their creator. Growing in faith as a family gives a sense of belonging, worthiness, security, and connection.

It was especially important to me that these Christian values be passed on into the lives of my children because I know many things would have been different if my childhood family had honored God. My parents did not comprehend the importance of spiritual growth. If they had lived this basic truth, our family could have avoided much turmoil and damage. Without these basics in place, our family suffered the things that came our way because God was left out and pushed aside. My parents seemed to have no time for "those spiritual things." This made our family sitting ducks for Satan to come in to devour and damage. During their important years of child rearing, my parents just did not grasp that there is no peace and contentment in life without God and His guidance. I did not want my children to feel the gloom, frustration, and depression of living in a home where the family does not attend church together. Leaving God out causes an unnecessary feeling of emptiness and despair. This is how my parents' home felt when I was a child.

Children commonly desire something different from what they experienced in childhood. There were a few times when my children asked why they had to attend church. However, I would rather have given them a legacy of faith than be guilty of raising them out of church. As the passing of time has proven, our adult children are grateful for their church foundation and personal relationship with God. Raising children out of church without knowledge of Jesus's saving power will no doubt come with the realization at some point in their life that you failed them as a parent. The saddest thing that can happen is if children grasp this truth after they have died and are in hell.

Our Social Life Would Be Unlike My Parents' Social Life

There were many things I experienced growing up in a home without God that I never wanted my children to encounter. Dad's "friends" were regularly at our home, intruding in our lives. Dad would rather be with other people than his own children. He was more committed to his friends than to his family. There is one friend Dad has had over the years who knows Dad better than I ever will. Spending time with this friend was Dad's priority many times over the needs of our family. The people Dad brought into our house over the years are too numerous to remember, and most were only acquaintances and empty friendships. It seemed Dad preferred putting his effort into any dead-end relationship over building a real one with his family. The bottom line seems to be that Dad's responsibilities as a father were of little importance to him. I felt most of the time that he pretended we did not even exist. I wish Dad would have made me feel like I belonged in his life as much as his friends did. I wish Dad would have valued me as much as he valued his friends. Since I did not feel welcome in Dad's world and valued enough to participate in his life, a relationship never developed between us.

Throughout my life, Dad has never known me as a person or the things I am capable of, and he especially knew nothing of my hopes, desires, or ambitions as a child or as an adult. And sadly, I never knew him either. I made a promise to myself that my children would never feel this kind of rejection. Dad did not know God during my formative childhood years; he did not acknowledge God in his life and therefore lived a completely selfish existence. He was so busy doing what he wanted that there was no time for him to be a dad. There is nothing wrong with having friends and socializing, but it must be in balance or dysfunction will prevail. If my parents would have met my emotional needs, I would not have felt so abandoned when they socialized. If I knew that I mattered to them and they cared how I felt, these social weekends would not have been so damaging.

When I had a family of my own, I decided I would rather not have a social life at all than have one that interfered with my children's needs. Socializing was not such a priority in our life that it interfered with our children, causing them to feel rejected and abandoned. Another thing about my parents' socializing I did not want to carry into my own family was smoking and drinking. I never wanted my children to witness their mother drinking or smoking and have that picture forever etched into their memory. These activities are not part of our family lifestyle. When your life is on track, you feel God's peace, and these vices are not needed to stimulate happiness or provide a temporary haven from problems. In the long run, they only create more problems to deal with. I knew this for sure from my experience with Grandpa's alcoholic road to ruin.

A Marriage Void of Anger and the Sinful, Selfish Environment

Providing a secure environment for children begins with a stable, loving marriage. This does not describe my parents' marriage. They had a tumultuous marriage because Dad was disconnected and had no empathy for the emotional needs of his wife. He was unfaithful to my mother; therefore, my mother did not value Dad. A family environment where unfaithfulness exists fills a home with insecurity. A stable family home is not possible when this type of sin is present. Since my husband and I were both victims of unfaithful dads, we had lived the damage this brings to a family. We both pledged to each other our unwavering faithfulness. This became another promise we were enabled by God to keep.

Because of the unstable home I was raised in, another thing I experienced that I never wanted to touch my children's existence was violent anger. One of the main things that results in a family environment of sin and selfishness is anger that randomly erupts through a violent temper. This leads to a life contaminated by parental bickering, hate, strife, anger, and disrespect toward each other. In addition, there were many other attitudes and actions that consistently proved God was absent in my parents' home. Their marriage and our family were eroded by adultery, including the selfish, childish behavior of parents with narcissistic tendencies. It was a home filled daily with anger and frustration, led by parents who did not really want to be together and therefore showed little loving, respectful behavior toward each other or their children. I witnessed many episodes where my parents fought violently and verbally. Life had no peace—it was angry, tumultuous, loud, and uneasy. With a yelling out-of-control mother, there was no security to hold on to. I longed for peace and a life without the bitter, angry hurt that was a daily occurrence. I knew I had experienced peace in Grandma Ada's care; why couldn't my parents live peaceably? As a child, I wished many times that my parents could just get along without the yelling matches and without the hurtful damaging words, frustration, and anger, with Dad ultimately leaving the house many times in an angry rage, slamming the door behind him.

The anger between my parents in my early childhood could be attributed to many different things, and one may be related to their hasty decision to marry. In Dad's insistence to marry quickly with little forethought, he was acting impulsively in a childish manner. He wanted what he wanted, and he wanted to get married right then—no time for waiting. I believe from my childhood experience of living in their home that this impulsive decision to marry also happened before either of them were allowed to grow a friendship and build a foundation essential for a marriage to work. I say this after filling in the blanks with my parents' information to make my personal version of a quote by Paul Hegstrom in his book *Broken Children, Grown Up Pain*, a perfect summary of my parents' relationship: "The marriage relationship between my parents never seemed to develop into a real marital bond, and any emotional connection between them was lacking. It seemed that Dad used my mother for his needs and gave no attention to her needs or emotional state. Therefore, this relationship could best be described as having a sexual bond with no emotional connection. When the wife's emotional needs are neglected, her desires start to diminish after a short period of time. They therefore live more as roommates than in an emotionally fulfilled marriage."

It regularly felt that my parents were angry with the world and frustrated with each other. Most of the time, Dad would go his own way and my mother would go hers. For a great deal of their marriage, my parents have slept in separate beds. They were not a team focused on working together; we were never a family with shared goals and visions. It is sad, but I believe because of their backgrounds, neither of my parents was capable of getting through life any other way. Emotional wounds can render you incapable of building an emotional relationship with others. My parents were products of their pasts, and since they chose to deny their state and our family's state, there was no hope for anything to get better. And this is still their stance today; they say they are too old to change. But you are never too old to change and begin living your life in truth.

For my husband and I, with God leading our family, the fruit of the spirit (Gal. 5:22–23) prevailed in our home and the sinful, unfaithful behavior and the resulting anger were not things our children lived with. We believed change was possible and have lived the blessings of that belief throughout the years.

Parenting Focused on What Is Best—Not on Control

Because of my mother's past traumas, in addition to all of the things she lived with because of Dad and the fact that she was raised by a controlling father, she was a very controlling parent. I realize that parents must direct their children, and there should be a certain amount of control just because of the relationship between parent and child. However, this interaction should never be demeaning and overbearing with no reason other than, "I'm the parent, you are the child, and I will say how things will be." The problem I have always had with this is the way it felt more like extreme control than decisions made for my benefit and welfare.

One memory I have that explains the control perfectly was when I was a child and had a cold. My mother would put Vicks VapoRub all over my chest. My skin was tender, and it burned terribly. The burning was so intense that I would prefer to deal with the cold symptoms rather than live with the burning. I communicated my discomfort, but my mother said, "You will wear the Vicks and you will not take it off." She also explained, "That is what I was expected to do as a child, and you will too. It does not burn that much." How did she know exactly how I felt? There was no understanding, empathy, or negotiation; no amount of talking was going to change my circumstance. She was in control, I was just a child at her mercy, and many times I endured the pain of the VapoRub. It seemed that because of my mother and dad's backgrounds, most of the control and other things they dictated came more from their need to achieve significance. They needed to feel in control and would put little effort into making the *best* decision.

Another problem is that the control did not end in childhood; it has permeated many aspects of my adult life as well. God does not even control His children to that extent. This controlling stance dictates too much of life and does not allow for individual growth, which is necessary in order to find out who you are. I was not just like my mother, never have been, never will be. Parents who choose to control their children too tightly sometimes think the child is just like them and they know exactly how that child thinks and how they need to behave. This is stifling to a child's individuality and later on to the adult child. I wish my mother had realized that I am a person in my own right, both when I was a child and now as an adult. As a child, I was not allowed to be the unique person God made me to be because my mother assumed that I was another person exactly like her. She never got the fact that even as a child, I was "somebody," a unique individual made by God—*not* a possession to control.

Parents should celebrate the unique individuality God gives each child and not assume the child is a carbon copy of themselves. Experiencing this control made me determine to give my children the freedom to live their lives. However, this was one of the areas of parenthood I struggled with through the years. Being raised by a controlling parent made it hard to avoid being controlling myself. But since the trigger event forced all the childhood hurt to surface, it has been easier for me to stop my tendencies toward controlling behavior, because I have been reminded of how it feels to be controlled. That is a feeling I do not want to impose on my children. I am working now to find a middle ground—a place that is hard to find at times. I now find myself backing off too much.

Our Family Would Travel Together

One of the things I always longed to do as a child was travel to places I had never been before. Real family vacations were always just a dream, though. Traveling as a family was something we rarely did.

And dysfunction prevailed in the rare family outings. Mostly, all family vacations were planned around deer hunting or fishing, because that is what Dad wanted to do. There was the common excuse that we could not afford to travel as a family—even though it did seem there was plenty of money to do the things Dad wanted to do. There was money to buy the hunting essentials he needed to pursue his interests. He talked a few times about how we all could go on a family vacation via Amtrak; as a railroad employee, he got a discount on train tickets. But that was not a big enough priority to override his hunting and fishing expeditions. Dad regularly took his vacations during deer season, when my brother and I were in school. Spending time with his children was just not important to him. He never seemed to grasp that children are available to you for only a short period of time, and a father needs to enjoy them while he can. Childhood vanishes away quickly. I wish Dad had cared how it made me feel to be forced to go deer hunting and fishing. But as far as Dad was concerned, no one else in the family counted or had feelings but him.

One of these wildlife excursions turned traumatic for me. It was a deer-hunting trip when I was about nine and got lost in the woods. I could not find my way back to camp. Everything looked the same as I wandered around in the woods. I crossed a fence because it looked familiar on the other side, but it still was not right. I crossed back to the other side and tore my pants on the barbed wire. I was crying and yelling, hoping someone would hear me. Then, as I was walking along, getting close to camp, I saw Dad a long distance down the road in front of me. I also watched eight to ten deer run and jump the fence in front of Dad. Dad was walking along with bow and arrow in hand and did not even see all the deer run right in front of him. He was looking the other way. Dad's friend was watching in the distance too, and he laughed at Dad for not trying even once to shoot at all the deer running before him. I finally wandered around and reached the camp on my own. No one found me.

Then, rather than being glad I was back, my mother had nothing but harsh words: "How did you get lost? Why did you cross a fence? You did not cross a fence before you got lost, why did you cross a fence to find your way back?" I felt no empathy or understanding, just condemnation for being so stupid. She had a knack for making me feel this way. Then Dad lit into me for having the nerve to yell, cry, and scream in the woods and scare the deer. It seemed neither of them had any feeling for how scared I had just been; worse yet, neither seemed glad I was not lost anymore. One of my own personal thoughts about this was, *How could Dad be so mad about me scaring the deer if he had so many deer run just a few feet in front of him and he never even tried to shoot at just one of them?* Both my parents were always ready to pour out scorn and condemnation rather than love. Empathy was always missing; it was an emotion neither of my parents had the capacity to feel. It seemed more important that they look superior to their friends than to understand how I felt. It was more important to them to point out what a stupid thing I had done and that they did not condone my bad behavior. It seemed to matter little to them that I was lost and scared. Meeting emotional needs was not something my parents were capable of; it was the main thing missing in my childhood necessary for emotional attachment and for a relationship to form.

The outings I experienced as a child were in no way considered a *real* family vacation. And I wanted the family Doug and I had to go to fun places together and experience *real* vacations. And I was blessed that Doug shared my dream of family travel. Together our family made pleasant memories and experienced visiting new places. These were family vacations we planned together. A few of the places our family vacationed were Florida, New York, Arizona, Hawaii, California, Colorado, Minnesota, Washington, DC, and Okinawa, Japan. Our children grew up to become adventurous adults, not afraid to travel to new places and experience the beauty of God's world. Our family travels also provided shared experiences and emotional connection.

Our Children Would Feel Secure and Loved

It did not feel that I mattered to Dad or that he even cared he had a daughter. It felt more like he was comfortable forgetting the fact that I was alive and needed his guidance. He ran from his parental responsibilities and privileges. In his running and finding enjoyment in other areas of life, he frustrated my mother. That is partly why she was so angry a great amount of time, and I often felt her wrath. I believe since Dad was so uninvolved in my life, it touched the heart of God, and He showed compassion for my situation. Therefore, I was spiritually born again, and God became my Father. Then, God took care of me as no earthly dad could have.

Even today, I still feel like my parents have never learned to value me for the person I am. Because of their life history, they did not feel worthy and competent themselves and were unable to bring these necessary emotional attributes into my life. I believe they were too young to step into the parental role when I was born. They were not ready for the responsibility. Their actions, thoughts, and feelings toward me were cemented at this immature time in their lives and created habits that have never changed over the years. Neither of them has ever given me a feeling of confidence, assurance, and stability. I felt alone in this part of my life, not feeling a constant stability from adult parents who were there for me no matter what. They pushed me away when they should have been drawing me close, and I learned how to get along without them and get by on my own emotionally.

For our children, there was a concentrated focus on my part to keep their lives from hurting. I wanted to do everything I could to prevent them from feeling they faced life alone. They had a family they belonged to, that wanted them and loved them. They had security, stability, and support from me and their dad. They were inspired to follow their dreams in pursuing God's will for their lives and supported with encouragement of their ability to do so. We would strive to be parents they could count on to love them and meet their needs physically, spiritually, and emotionally. And by our actions, my husband and I conveyed to our children that we were there for them with behaviors, not just words. We worked hard to be parents they could count on to help with whatever came up in their lives. Our children were our priority, and we did our best to be there for them. With God's help, I had empathy for my children that I never experienced from my parents. I was not perfect, and I failed many times, but I believe now—because of all the things my children have accomplished—their childhoods were adequate in feelings of value, love, security, and belonging. Their emotional needs were acknowledged. They were treated with respect and encouraged.

All of us are able to make a conscious choice to make our lives better. Never believe you are stuck in a rut and your life cannot improve at any age. Just because things have always been a certain way does not mean things have to remain static. Positive change is possible when God is allowed to lead. Humanly, the kind of change I am talking about is impossible, but with divine intervention anything is possible. With God's presence, my husband and I consciously made a different life for our family.

The Power of Words

Meeting the emotional needs of your child is essential. Children must know that they are loved, valued, wanted, and important to the family. This must be heard, seen, and felt with empathy. Mutual respect is an extremely important part of family interaction. Valuing each other, caring, and expressing empathy are all essential for healthy emotional growth between parents and children. These elements are also essential between husband and wife. A spouse needs encouragement too and interaction between parents needs to portray the proper example for their children.

Words spoken unwisely and unnecessarily can damage your children as well as your spouse. Functional families focus on building rather than destroying. The things you say to each other can either damage or build. Saying what is on your mind is not always the best path to choose. While it is necessary to discuss important topics and talk things through to keep a balance or to bring healing, it is never appropriate to say whatever comes to your mind if it is said with the intention to hurt or belittle. These become the type of words that damage and destroy family life. Talking and saying what is on your mind for personal benefit without regard to how it may hurt someone else is not constructive communication. The Bible says, "A fool uttereth all his mind: but a wise man keepeth it in till afterward" (Prov. 29:11). Wisdom is found in considering the effect your words may have on someone else *before* you say them. Speaking without wisdom causes damage to souls, spirits, and emotions. The Bible says, "But the tongue can no man tame; it is an unruly evil, full of deadly poison" (James 3:8). No man can tame the tongue, but with God's guidance, one can speak words of health and hope. Just as in any other area of life, we can choose to use our words for damage or choose to use our words in wisdom, bringing health and peace to our families. According to the Bible, "For he that will love life, and see good days, let him refrain his tongue from evil, and his lips that they speak no guile: let him eschew evil, and do good; let him seek peace, and ensue it. For the eyes of the Lord are over the righteous, and his ears are open unto their prayers: but the face of the Lord is against them that do evil" (1 Pet. 3:10–12). This is the best reason to choose your words wisely and make sure they are uplifting to your family members whom you love.

Damaging words do not always come in one big episode; they can be small words spoken often enough to label and hurt the self-esteem of another. These words may seem little and insignificant, but spoken often enough, they can damage and ultimately destroy self-worth. To build a functional family, all members must be committed to believing the best in each other and encouraging the best in each other, no matter what. To accomplish this, choose uplifting words said in wisdom, striving always to be kind and selfless—never selfish. The words of Thumper in the Walt Disney movie *Bambi* are appropriate here: "If you can't say something nice, don't say anything at all." If you are guilty of using words to damage, you should ask yourself how you would feel if someone talked to you in the same way you talk to them. Usually people who use their words to damage have deep hurts and wounds themselves and would be destroyed if their behaviors were turned on them. Always treat others the way you want to be treated.

Nicknames can bring an emotional connection within a family. Each of our children had a special nickname. These promoted self-worth and built confidence. They were positive names that created a greater sense of belonging. However, sometimes the names children are labeled with can create damage and destruction to self-worth and do harm by diminishing value and belonging. Dad called my brother a "hoop-dee-doo feller" regularly throughout his childhood and into adulthood. Dad often used this negative labeling phrase to proclaim my brother's incompetence and shine superiority on himself. It seemed to say loudly, "Look at that boy. I am so much better than him. Why can't he do anything right?" This undermines confidence, self-esteem, and self-worth, and it had to have done damage to my brother's emotions and soul, especially when it came regularly from Dad. Carelessly spoken words can be very hurtful to others. This is another example of Dad's foolish ways. Words from a sermon I heard in our church on January 10, 2010 by Brother Russell White are appropriate here: "The fruit of a tree reveals the character of that tree, and the tree bears the fruit of the seed from which it was planted. So also, that which comes out of our mouth reveals the spiritual nature of our hearts. We must also beware of 'careless' words; phrases that have not been thought through completely. The words of our mouths will bear witness for or against us on that great judgment day."

I witnessed the effects of Dad's negative labeling on my brother's life. This highlighted another area I was determined would be different for my family and my children. My husband and I would use uplifting, encouraging words that positively impacted our children. The communication in our family did not tear down or destroy. It would be interesting to know how my brother's life would be now if he had been allowed to be himself without judgment; if he was encouraged to be who God made him to be and to let his unique self grow; if he was nurtured and allowed to mature comfortably in a loving environment. With no name-calling and without being labeled as the "hoop-dee-doo feller," I believe he would be more confident. He would also have a greater self-worth and therefore would live his life with less strife and more peace and contentment. Words are powerful tools capable of bringing hurt, health, or healing to one's emotional state.

Making Right Choices to Build a Strong Family

Proverbs 24:3–4 in the amplified version of the Bible says: "Through skillful *and* godly wisdom is a house (a life, a home, a family) built, and by understanding it is established [on a sound and good foundation], and by knowledge shall its chambers [of every area] be filled with all precious and pleasant riches." The family my husband and I built together with God is a *functional* family. However, I have been misquoted to have said our family is *perfect*. I am not naïve enough to believe that any family is perfect. But a family can be functional and free of much of the damage life can bring your way. The family my husband and I began together was not perfect, and it was not always free of things that can damage. But the one thing our family had that my childhood family did not was God. Placing your life and your family in God's care provides a safety net for your children at times when parents may fail. God will always keep your family on track, in spite of human failures, if you allow Him to lead and are obedient to His word. God can make things right that are set up to go wrong. My life is a living example of this truth. How does God give us this power? "If we have our hearts filled with the peace of Christ and the Word of Christ, then we will contribute to the joy and harmony of the home. If we live to please Christ first, others second, and ourselves last, we will build strong marriages and spiritual homes," as Brother Russell White said in his sermon of October 12, 2008. God is the only way to provide a functional family environment where children can become emotionally whole and grow into functionally productive adults. Because of my upbringing, my adult life was set up for failure. My childhood was full of things that make adult life unsuccessful. My parents did not seek God and focused mainly on their needs. Both of them were damaged adults, unable to connect to each other emotionally and therefore also unable to provide for the emotional needs of their children. But I thank God continually that He led me to a church where I found Him and my life was changed forever and set on a functional road the night of April 19, 1970, when I was born again.

The Indisputable Essential Elements of Emotional Health

In very concrete terms, the main difference between the home I grew up in and the home my husband and I provided for our children was the absence or presence of emotional connection and spiritual growth. All of us are the product of the many things spoken to us by many different people throughout our life. We also are the product of many nonverbal actions sent to us by others. These words and actions can bring health and well-being, or they can be destructive, damaging, and toxic. To quote a famous preacher, Dr. Charles Stanley, on the effects of these verbal and nonverbal communications, "Our sense of wholeness as a person is greatly affected by how we interpret those things that have been communicated to us." These words and actions have a direct effect on our emotional health. Healthy emotions are essential to living a productive life.

Dr. Stanley goes on to describe the three essentials of being a whole person:

1. A sense of belonging—a child is connected to a family that wants him or her. The assurance of belonging leads to the feeling of acceptance.

2. A sense of worthiness—a child is treated with value and respect. The assurance of worthiness leads to the feeling of love.

3. A sense of competency—a child is shown that someone believes in his or her ability to achieve and accomplish something worthwhile. The assurance of competency leads to the feeling of security.

Every person must feel these three essential traits in order to be emotionally whole, even in adulthood. For children to acquire a firm emotional foundation, they need to grow up feeling these essentials are present in everyday family life.

There are two places a person can find these emotional essentials: one is in family life and the other is in a relationship with God. God gives all of us the opportunity to experience emotional wholeness in our lives. This is where I found emotional wholeness, because it was not present in my childhood family environment. When God is part of your life, these essentials of emotional health are provided by Him:

Belonging. We find all the essentials for emotional wholeness in a relationship with God when we put our faith in Jesus for salvation and become a member of God's family. Being led by the spirit of God, we find belonging in God's family as His child. Without a sense of belonging to God, one will never be a whole person.

Worthiness. As Christians, we are worthy because we are loved in God's eyes. God sent his only begotten Son, Jesus Christ, to die in our place for our sins because He deemed us worthy, because He loved us.

Competence. When Christian believers are guided by the indwelling of the Holy Spirit, they are able to accomplish great things. With the guidance of the Holy Spirit enabling us, we are competent.

God provided a way for us to have a healthy, whole emotional being, but people damage His perfect plan with their words and actions. Ideally, children should get the essential ingredients for emotional wholeness from their parents *and* from a relationship with God when the parents make God and church attendance a priority in family life. But too often, these necessary feelings are void in family life, and therefore, a church life is nonexistent also. Under these circumstances, great damage is done to the soul of a child because of the reoccurring emotional abuse that is common in this toxic environment.

In my childhood, damage was done in the area of *belonging* because I regularly felt I was tolerated out of responsibility but never really wanted. My parents had many reasons for remarrying, but not one of them that I ever heard was because they wanted me. They consistently spent their time and effort in things other than being a parent to me.

Damage was done in the area of *worthiness* when, at eight years old, I was hospitalized for a stomach ulcer that I developed from living in my parents' toxic environment. I was told by Dad that I was costing him too much money just sitting in the hospital. He did not care how I felt, how I hurt, or about anything except the monetary cost of the hospital. I was not good enough for him to care about. I was not worth anything to Dad; I was just, in his opinion, an expense to the family. Dad's words also did damage in the area of worthiness when he told my brother and me at the dinner table, "I will be glad when you kids are grown and gone, so I won't have to feed you anymore."

Damaged was done in the area of *competency* when my mother would send the message that I was not capable, and she had to do things herself so it got done right.

These kinds of words and actions can destroy a person's future by inflicting pain leading to damaged emotions, causing feelings of rejection, inadequacy, and void of love—the very opposite of acceptance, security, and love. God never intended for us to have these destructive feelings, which caused the emotional abuse I endured as a child. It was a condition that *only* God could heal for me. I found healing for my life when I found Jesus Christ, who saved me. Then through Him I was able to build a relationship with God my Father and heal from the emotional hurt, pain, and abuse.

My husband and I provided a home where the emotional essentials were present for our children. And for the times we failed in our human strength, we had the safety net in place where our born-again, saved children found the emotional essentials in their personal relationship with God. Our children were never left alone to face the world without support, encouragement, and love; if Doug or I failed, God was there. Children need *both* God and parents who live according to God's will.

The God-centered Christian home my husband and I built is not perfect, but it is functional. We have three beautiful, successful adult children in spite of the sometimes controlling tendencies I acquired from my own dysfunctional childhood. They each have individually blossomed into the unique person God made them to be. My husband and I have always wanted and tried to encourage our children to follow their dreams. We endeavored to help them grow into the person God made them to be. God's will for our children's lives was our primary focus as parents. Watching, helping, and guiding them to find their own way and unfold their personal traits into individual uniqueness has been like watching a beautiful butterfly appear and fly off into the world, blessing the world with the real person God made them to be. (And flying off into the world is exactly what each of them did.) In spite of the distance between us, knowing they are in God's perfect will is one of my greatest blessings. I could not ask for anything more or for a better experience as a parent. None of it would have happened or been possible if our family had not found salvation in Jesus Christ and chosen to serve and obey God—and then allow God to live in and through each of our family members. God blesses when you "choose to do that which is right in the sight of the Lord."

Chapter Forty-Three

Our Family Becomes Complete

During this time in our lives, with the possibility of a baby on the way, owning a McDonald's restaurant became a lower priority. My husband and I anticipated the chance of experiencing parenthood for a third time with great joy and happiness. It was a thrilling time in our lives when almost everything was going well. A doctor's appointment the day after Father's Day officially confirmed that our third child was on the way—due the first week of February 1991. This made an extra special Father's Day for my husband. Our children were both so excited a new baby would be joining our family; Amanda was hoping for a sister.

A few months later, a second ultrasound was scheduled. Jason and Amanda went to this appointment instead of school. My mother also met us at the doctor's office. The ultrasound began; it was a thrill to see the baby, so small but easily identifiable. Then the technician performing the test discovered undeniable proof of the exact sex of our baby and said out loud, "It's a boy!" Amanda could not hold back her tears; she had wanted a sister so bad. Now a sister was just a dream, and in reality, she would have two brothers. Jason was pleased, however; he thought a baby brother would be great! Years later, when we recall this day, Amanda laughs and comments, "I am glad I have another brother; I probably really did not want a sister anyway. I can't imagine life without my little brother." Being in the middle, Amanda has been blessed to have a very special relationship with both her brothers. After the test determined our baby to be a boy, my mother's comment was,

"I just figured it would be a girl. I always thought your family would be just like mine—two girls and a boy."

Each doctor's visit came with good news. Everything was progressing normally; our baby was healthy and had a strong heartbeat. And again this third time around, it was a thrill to hear the heartbeat, so rapid and lively. I too was healthy; my weight gain was within normal limits, and I was experiencing another trouble-free pregnancy. I thanked God constantly for all the blessing He bestowed on our lives.

This was a great time in my life. I especially enjoyed this pregnancy because everything felt more stable this time. I had given birth twice before and was confident I could do it again. Our church life was on track. My days were filled with taking care of my husband and children. Since Amanda was in kindergarten, she went to school only half a day. I picked her up at noon, and we did many fun things in those afternoons together. One thing Amanda liked was playing dress-up, and sometimes I would fix her hair. A few years earlier, back when she was learning to talk, I would exclaim how beautiful she looked with her hair fixed and pretty clothes and jewelry on. She repeated "beautiful" in her sweet little two-year-old voice, but it came out "boosie." It was a nickname that stuck, and we still call her "Boosie," meaning *beautiful*—now a beautiful young woman. During those days when I was not feeling tired from the pregnancy, Amanda and I would do the things we had normally done throughout her preschool years. I love recalling those memories. Everything about this time for our family was a blessing, with the only exception being the ever present-issues from my childhood that I had yet to realize as the source of trouble that I experienced often.

But in spite of the turbulence my parents brought to my life, Doug and I experienced a time of great family togetherness and emotional connection with our children. Jason and Amanda were so helpful and caring. They each did what they could and were both a great comfort and support. Experiencing the special time with them was a blessing. They each randomly talked to their little brother and told him they loved him. They also often felt him move. Doug worked a lot but still managed to go to every doctor's appointment with me and was never absent when I really needed something. He always took his responsibility as a father very seriously. This wonderful family time of growth together was a blessing we all enjoyed, which was only possible because of God's presence in our lives. I also did not realize it at the time, but I was healing emotionally from my past in this family environment totally different from that of my childhood. God had given me the most wonderful husband and children, and I was thankful for each one of them every day.

During a doctor's appointment along about seven-and-a-half months, the doctor informed me that the baby I was carrying was no longer considered a fetus but had reached the stage at which he could function independently. Our baby would now be able to survive on his own with little danger if for some reason labor started early. This news felt good, because I knew the day was getting really close when I would be able to hold my little baby boy. It would be soon!

On January 30, 1991, I went to the hospital feeling as though I was definitely in labor. We got Jason and Amanda out of school, and then I checked into the hospital. Labor pains were coming frequently and intensely for a while. Then, with the passage of an hour to ninety minutes, the labor pains waned and completely stopped. After my experience with Amanda's birth, I was taking no chances with reliving that situation again. I wanted to be at the hospital with the doctor present when it was time. And because I was overly cautious now with my third pregnancy, I had finally gone to the hospital—for a false alarm. *Oh well,* I figured, *better safe than sorry.*

For the next few days, I continued to feel labor pains, but they were mostly random and noncontinuous. Then one day, real labor was clearly very close. I felt anxious and dropped to my knees, praying for God to help me through this impending engagement I faced. Prayer gave me peace and the ability to know everything would be fine. At a time when I felt I could do nothing, I had faith that God was taking care of everything. On February 6, I went to the doctor for my final predelivery visit. I was becoming more uncomfortable daily. With the doctor's advice and my preference for inducement of labor, he agreed it would probably be best to plan for delivery on Friday.

This time, I did not give my mother a chance to cause me despair. She knew the plan, but I gave her no opportunity to rain on my parade this time around. It was all matter-of-fact, and there was no room for discussion. I had personal experience now with inducing labor and knew for sure it was what I wanted to do. I spent the day before my baby's birth with Jason and Amanda as usual, and Doug planned some time off work. On Friday, our family went to the hospital together at seven a.m. When we arrived at the hospital, my uncle's wife, Judy, was there ready to wait it out with me one more time. I was taken to a labor room, and the labor-inducing IV was administered. This third time, my water broke naturally, not by doctor intervention. As the labor pains intensified, causing pressure, my water broke with a loud pop and then a flood. My baby had lost his cushion and began moving intensely. Doug was with me continually. Judy and my mother were in and out of the labor room until I went to the delivery room between eleven a.m. and twelve noon.

Once again with no medication, I endured labor and all that is involved with that process with complete consciousness and an unaltered sense of feeling. I intensely felt it all. I do remember getting extra tired this time from labor pains and the pushing that ensued. I thought, *I am getting too old at thirty-one for this to go as smooth as it did at nineteen and twenty-five.* But I endured, and once again Doug and I were blessed together with another miracle when our third child was born with a loud cry that was music to my ears! It is the most wonderful sound a parent will ever hear—her baby's first cry. And we now had another son, a beautiful little baby that we were privileged to love and care for. Our new baby boy was born at 1:23 p.m. and weighed seven pounds twelve ounces. We named him Jarrod. Jarrod is a name I got from a favorite western TV series, *The Big Valley.*

Jason and Amanda were allowed into the delivery room to meet their new baby brother. They both exclaimed how cute he was as they got acquainted with him. Then I was moved into a wheelchair, and Jarrod was placed in my arms. Jason pushed us from the delivery room to the nursery where Jarrod was to go, and he then took me to the room they had waiting.

Shortly after I got into the room, I talked to my uncle on the phone. He congratulated me, and I told him how beautiful Jarrod was! We had many visitors that day, including Pastor Stan White and his wife. But mostly Doug and I enjoyed the bliss of this special night together. It was also a night of good news nationwide; it was the date the Desert Storm war came to an end. I remember watching the news that night, and the end of Desert Storm was about the only subject covered on all the channels.

Very early on Saturday morning, I saw my doctor and was released to go home that day. So after a short stay in the hospital, we took our healthy newborn home to his family who loved and cared for him. A few days after we came home, Uncle Jim, Aunt Judy, and their family visited us. Judy said, "He sure is a lucky little boy to be born into this family." I will never forget her words; although few, they spoke volumes to me about how much she really thought of me. Her comment meant a lot. Most everything felt so good about this time. Having a new baby in our home was a joyous time.

Many times after we were home, my mother helped out by bringing food. We all appreciated the meals she brought, but there were dysfunctional situations even still that came with her visits. One afternoon when Doug and I were sitting on the couch, I was half-dressed while Doug was rubbing my back to ease the soreness I experienced from the delivery only days earlier. During this personal moment, my mother came barging into our home unannounced. She had a key she used for house-sitting when we were out of town, but she seemed to feel it was appropriate to use it at this time when we were home. She opened the door, and as I scrambled to get my clothes back on, she walked face forward, as if she had blinders on, headed to the kitchen. She pretended to be oblivious to the situation and made no apologies for barging right on in. It was the same old situation of "I'm the parent, you are the child"—even though I now was thirty-one. There was no mutual respect between adults. I was to put up with whatever she chose to do. And again, just as for every other uncomfortable situation between us, nothing was ever said, and we went on as if it never happened. This did not change the violation I felt, and more damage and hurt built up because she did not treat me as an adult. With her controlling demeanor, she had no regard for how I felt. I was not a child, had not been one for a very long time, and her behavior with no communication, no understanding, and no apology was destroying any relationship that might ever grow between her and me.

Thankfully, I quickly recovered from the birth of my baby and required no outside help to take care of my family. I saw my mother and dad very little, and I focused on all the things my children needed. It was an extra special time, and I get only warm, fond feelings when remembering back to the first months in the life of my third child. I loved everything about caring for our new baby. Jarrod's nickname was "Baby Sweet." Something Jarrod and I did together was share special moments listening to lullabies that I played and sang often to him as he drifted off to sleep at bedtime, in the middle of the night, or for an afternoon nap. I have never been known for any great singing ability, but Doug told me that I sang the lullabies very well. That was a real compliment coming from my husband, the singer! I also had no clue that the baby boy I was singing to would grow up one day to become a professional musician. The lullabies hold a special place in my memories, and Jarrod still likes hearing them even now as a grown young man. I had a nickname for Jarrod as a baby, but nowadays he is more appropriately referred to as "Dancing Fingers," since he becomes animated when playing the guitar.

After Jarrod's birth, our church life grew and was a part of our lives that brought spiritual fruit and abundant joy. Soon after Jarrod was born, we took him before the church one Sunday for a baby dedication. Jarrod was introduced to the church, and Pastor Stan White said a prayer dedicating our baby to the Lord and asking God to guide his life always. Then a few Sundays later, on Mother's Day 1991, Amanda was saved in Junior Church at age five. She came bounding out of the church that day with wide eyes full of joy and happiness. When she got into the car, she said "Mommy, I met Jesus today!" I could see something had changed, and she for sure had experienced the newness and great feeling that comes with salvation. Her face was absolutely glowing, and her smile was radiant; peace prevailed. I did not need words to know—I

could see the undeniable proof in the nonverbal evidence. My little
girl was saved. She became a child of God that day. And I had received
the most wonderful Mother's Day present ever. It was more valuable
than anything tangible I could have received boxed and wrapped up
in a gift. I will never forget the precious little face of my daughter that
day, a gift of great value. Soon after, in a public profession of her faith,
Amanda was baptized before the church. Now I knew for sure I would
spend eternity in heaven with my daughter, and she would also meet
her Great-Grandma Ada.

Our family had a struggle getting to church on that Mother's Day
1991. It was obviously a day when Satan fought extremely hard to
keep us away from church. Our family got into the van, ready to go to
church, but the battery was dead and it would not start. Then, strangely
enough, our Camaro would not start either. And that left only the 1972
Monte Carlo that had been sitting idle for several months. We had no
other option to get to church, and it never occurred to us to stay home.
So our family all piled into the very dusty Monte Carlo. When Doug
started it up, a cloud of dust filled the air and got all of us even dustier,
but we continued on. We made it to church in spite of the trials. Then,
at the end of the service, it was clear why we had been presented with
so many unusual obstacles trying to prevent our presence at church
on this Sunday. Unknowingly, we were fighting a spiritual war to get
our daughter to church and to a worship service that would ultimately
determine her eternal destiny. It was one of the most important journeys
we were to take, and thankfully our determination to prevail won over
the futile attempts of the devil. Following God is not always easy, but
it is always worth it.

These early months of Jarrod's life were full of happiness,
contentment, love, and abundant family togetherness. My husband and
children were the center of my world, and my family life was filled with
all the things that were missing in my childhood. I had a great sense
of love, security, worthiness, belonging, and competency, as well as a
tremendous sense of peace. Healing from past wounds was definitely
taking place. In addition to the emotional healing, I was also healed
from the symptoms of endometriosis. Those problems never returned;

having a baby really did heal me. Jarrod's first seven months were a great time to pause and enjoy the enormous blessings God bestowed on our family.

We were totally content with what we had, where we were. Therefore, we began building on and remodeling our small house to accommodate our three children. With the help of some friends, Doug began the task of making our house larger. The project was almost finished, and the additional bedroom for our oldest son was near completion. Then, on Monday, September 23, 1991, "the call" came. McDonald's had finally found a restaurant that we might want to buy. As soon as we let go and let God be in total charge of our dream, God made it a reality for us. Also miraculously, we had enough money to really consider purchasing our own McDonald's restaurant. The money came from many different sources, but when we added them all together, it was an adequate amount. I know without a doubt that adequate money was there because we chose, in obedience, to honor God with our tithes and offerings. Our dream was coming together, and it was clearly possible only because our dream was God's will for our lives and He worked out all the details. Also, being patient and waiting on God had brought more joy and blessings into our lives because, while we patiently waited for God's perfect will, He blessed our family with a precious baby boy. Now, for Doug and me and our children, life was about to change drastically.

Part V

Moving to Texas

Chapter Forty-Four

Our New Life Begins in Texas

At thirty-one years old, I still could find no freedom from my hurtful childhood past while continuing to live amid the family dysfunction. But God was actively guiding my life for the best. He knew of the control I had lived with since birth, and that I needed to be released in order to finally become the adult He created me to be. God's perfect will for me and my family was to move to a city found "deep in the heart of Texas." I would then be accountable only to God, my husband, and my children. The miles that would separate me from my parents would also greatly reduced the control I felt from their presence. Moving to Texas gave me freedom to finally live my life the way I was meant to. The turmoil from my parents, my mother in particular, calmed way down after the move. The ups and downs I had experienced all too often began to smooth out. It felt like I had finally gotten off the emotional roller coaster. This move and the freedom it brought from the family dysfunction was a gift from God. However, at the time, I did not realize this truth; it would take me years to understand how all this was working out for my emotional good. But I rested in the fact that God had always watched over me and knew what was best for my life.

A few days after we got "the call" on Monday September 23, 1991, our family headed to Las Colinas in the Dallas area where the McDonald's corporate office was located. We had a meeting with the licensing manager and the VP in charge of the Dallas office. By September 26, Doug and I were touring our potential restaurant. We discussed the financial side of the operation, which all seemed to be in line. That night, Doug and I went back to the restaurant. Since none of the employees knew us yet, we were able to watch them in action. There were issues we would take immediate action to fix if we did purchase the store, but nothing we observed was huge, and it all seemed manageable. There appeared to be no reason not to accept the challenge. We then began exploring the area. First of all, we visited a Baptist church that Sunday. We also looked at houses. Since we were unsure of the exact location we should live, we found a rental house to accommodate our family. For the first time ever, Doug and I became home renters.

We took possession of the restaurant on October 15. Our plan was for Doug to live in the rental house and run things alone until December, allowing our children to finish their school semester. Doug handled all the new responsibilities for about one month, and then it became too overwhelming. He called one night saying that we needed to change our plan. He needed me and the children to move to Texas immediately. Working in the restaurant with all the new employees and doing the accounting too was more than he could manage alone. So mid-November, I withdrew Jason and Amanda from the Clovis schools, and we moved to Texas. We took more of our things on this trip but did not sell our home in Clovis at this time. My mother seemed to have a real problem with us moving; Jason's comment to me regarding her distress was, "Why is she so upset? She never comes to see us anyway." I wondered too, but I told myself that we needed to keep the house for my mother's sake, because she seemed to have a hard time with our move. Keeping the house would make it all feel less permanent. But I later realized the real reason I did not want to sell the house was that I knew we would go back to Clovis often to visit. I did not want to stay with my parents when we did. My subconscious was at work here; there were too many denied hurts and traumas associated with staying at my parents' house. The thought of staying with them was the real reason I felt I must keep my Clovis home. We would sell the house in 2004 when more dysfunctional turmoil dictated the decision.

In transition, we made several weekend trips between houses. On one of these trips, my mother came with me and the kids. I had not seen Doug for almost two weeks and was glad to be with him again. The next morning, my mother was up with the kids, and Doug and I were in our bedroom with the door closed. We were just lying in bed talking. I am not sure why, but again my mother chose to barge into our bedroom, opening the door and asking, "What's going on in here?" I do not know if she thought we were having sex or what ... and if we were, so what? But as I said, we were only talking. It was another awkward moment she created, another time she did not treat me as an adult and seemed to believe that as the parent, she could be in charge of my home and still call the shots in my life. Doug and I both really resented being treated this way. We rationalized by agreeing that we would now live far away from my parents and would rarely have to deal with such things anymore. And once again, we did not say anything as we should have. But it is so hard to speak up when dealing with a controlling parent.

After Thanksgiving break, we enrolled Jason and Amanda in the Texas school system. One of the first problems we encountered was the inept employees of the school district we now lived in. Jason was in seventh grade, and policy was to give him an entrance exam before he could get a school schedule. After the exam, the lady who administered it said that Jason did not do very well. I questioned her results but thought maybe Texas schools were more advanced than New Mexico schools. But as time went on, it was obvious that the test results were wrong. Jason did not belong in the easier classes she had placed him in. The teachers he had were questioning why he was in such classes. An investigation revealed that the lady had used the wrong grading key for Jason's test. He scored way above her original report. The school system could not apologize enough for their inexcusable mistake. My son had also suffered ridicule because of the status these classes had given him. But he was then placed in classes he belonged in and given the privilege of being library aid because of the error. The woman who administered the test definitely had performance issues. This is one time I really wish I could do over. I would have stood firmer for Jason, because I knew for sure how smart he is. This situation only made the hardship of moving worse for Jason as the new student. Remembering this time brings sadness and hurt to me every time I think of it. I have told Jason how I feel many times. His response has always been, "Don't worry about it, Mom; it was a hard time, but it made me who I am today." This is exactly how we need to look at hard times in our lives. If it were not for hard times, we would all be soft and unthankful for all the good in our lives. Maybe there are specific reasons for some hardships to happen, and maybe there are also reasons we cannot go back and change the past. Positive things may sometimes come from the bad things, but only when we choose to learn from them.

For our family, changes for the better resulted from this unfortunate mistake. We felt it was best for our children to remove them from this school district. After renting for only six months, we bought a house in a small town located next to the bigger city where our McDonald's was located. Ironically, when we moved to another town, the drive to our restaurant was shorter than when we lived in the same town. It all worked out for the best. Our new house had four bedrooms and four bathrooms, a pool, a hot tub, almost 5,000 square feet of living space, and a huge yard. It was the only available home big enough for our family in the small town. Jason and Amanda began the next school year in a much better school district; it would be where they and Jarrod too would graduate from high school.

Our Church Life 1991–2005

Moving meant we had to find a new church where we could worship regularly, a decision essential to our primary goal of raising our children in a God-centered home. The task of selecting a church was not an easy one, even though the first church we visited was a definite possibility. We visited many churches in order to pick the right one. And after exhausting all possibilities, we joined the church we went to first. It was the church God led us to before we moved, and clearly it was the best choice for our family.

After about a year, our pastor resigned, and our church began the process of finding a replacement. A few weeks later, I received a phone call with unbelievably wonderful news. The following Sunday morning, the preacher speaking at our church would be Brother Buck Hatfield, a preacher we knew from our previous church in New Mexico. He was an evangelist who traveled to many churches doing revivals. We knew him to be an excellent preacher, guided by God and teaching Biblical truth. When he had visited our previous church, I invited friends to go along; it turned out to be a great spiritual experience where God was obviously working. And as it would turn out, Brother Buck Hatfield not only was a visiting preacher at our new church but also chose to be our permanent pastor. By a unanimous church vote, we had a new preacher.

This time we were given to learn from Brother Buck as our pastor was a true blessing and a privilege. We look back to this short, special time with great joy. One Sunday I remember in particular when Brother Buck and I had a conversation about things that make a church work and things that can tear it apart. He said, "Some churches can be torn apart by simply picking out a particular color of carpet. But one thing you really have to watch is how the preacher spends the money. Some pastors with good intentions can bankrupt a church. And the church has to have responsible members in place to keep those kinds of preachers in line, because they have no concept of handling money." This random conversation became a defining moment for me in years to come. It was as if Brother Buck knew I would need this information in the future. There were many times through the years when I thought back to this conversation and used it to help me understand and work through a position of church responsibility—a position I was given probably due to Brother Buck's recommendation.

In earlier years, Brother Buck had owned a restaurant in Sweetwater, Texas. It was a great blessing to have a preacher who could relate to things we went through as restaurant owners. He gave us insight in dealing with employees in a Christian manner. And he talked frankly about the everyday frustrations and responsibilities we were living through. He knew how to pray for our specific needs, and this was a special gift we appreciated.

The time we had with Brother Buck was packed with much learning from a man with great wisdom. We were and are so thankful that God blessed us with his leadership. He was our pastor for only about one year. After he had been with us for a few months, he began to have pains in his chest, which he felt merited a visit to the doctor. It was determined that his lungs had spots on them, and it was cancer. When it was discovered, he had only a short time to live. This was a very sad time for our church. However, even with the pain, Brother Buck kept preaching for as long as he was able. Before he left his duties at our church, he assisted in finding preachers he knew to fill the pulpit. By December 1994, Brother Buck was unable to preach anymore, and he and his wife remained at their home. We visited them, and even though Brother Buck was at a point where he did not know people too well and was not communicating much, he heard my voice when we visited and he called out my name. Then my husband and I went from the living room to his bedroom to visit with him. We had a short conversation; it was clear that he knew who we were. He told us he would be going home soon. That was the last time we saw Brother Buck; he did go home to be with the Lord in February 1995.

Our church retained a new pastor. Then, in May of 1995, the new preacher asked me to run for the office of church treasurer. I agreed and was elected unanimously. My husband already held an office as trustee. Even though neither Doug nor I needed one more thing to do in addition to running the restaurants, we gladly took the responsibility and made it a priority to do our best. This continued on in a productive fashion, and it was apparent that doing these jobs was God's will for us. I was thankful God gave me a job in His church that I was educated for. My husband and I continued to be elected and serve in our respective positions for more than ten years.

Our church life was also rewarding through the relationships we made with Christian friends. And there was continued evidence of our family's spiritual growth. Blessings abounded, with one extra special blessing on Father's Day 1997 when Jarrod trusted Jesus Christ as his Savior. It was a special Father's Day blessing for Doug. He knew for sure that Jarrod was a born-again child of God, a perfect gift more valuable than any material gift he could have been given. Jarrod was baptized soon after. This became another of life's treasures Doug and I enjoyed together. Now each of our children were spiritually reborn; they were all saved and bound for heaven one day. They each had been saved at a young age, and each would be protected and guided by God now and always.

Doug and I continued to serve in our church positions, which overall were fulfilling and workable. However, our current preacher was definitely the one Brother Buck had warned about in that conversation I mentioned. He lacked the ability to responsibly take care of the church's finances. In my position as treasurer, I had no decision-making ability; I could suggest, but this preacher did what he wanted for the most part. I basically accounted for things as told, as dictated by the preacher with little input from the trustees. I was rarely given the option to advise or share input. Also, the preacher seemed to indicate through random, subtle hints that he was not totally comfortable with a woman as the church treasurer. But the truth was that there was no man in our church capable, qualified, or willing to do the job I was doing. The books were a huge mess of disorganization when I took the job in July 1995. That was easily fixed with management, organization, and the establishment of a filing system. I therefore got the church books in workable order and cleaned up the mess I inherited. I counted it a privilege to do a job God had given me and help out the preacher too. I continued to serve, to care, and to do my best throughout the years, performing a job I was educated to do. It also was a job God had trusted me with, and that thought made it all worthwhile.

Our Life as McDonald's Restaurant Owner/Operators

Many times it felt as if our life had been turned upside down and things fell where ever they landed. I often referred to this time in our lives as a passing whirlwind. Looking back, I wonder now how we ever found the energy to accomplish so many necessary daily tasks. In the beginning, it had to be the sheer thrill and newness of it all, in addition to it being a lifetime dream come true.

Many people looking on assume that a business owner can choose to work daily or not. The reality, however, is that you work daily, nightly, and on weekends as well. There is just too much to accomplish to remain idle. First of all, Doug had left a restaurant with a competent, adequate staff of management and crew. That operation had gotten to the point of routine, and the daily tasks were well-integrated, so problems arising were minimal. But the restaurant we now owned had less than twenty employees total, and the ones on staff referred to as managers were greatly lacking in the skill and knowledge necessary to run an efficient operation. It was clear that training and people development was the first action to take, along with immediate hiring to attain an adequate employee base. With such a limited workforce, Doug was pretty much working round the clock. As for me in these early days, I was performing the accounting and office tasks in addition to getting our kids to school, picking them up, and meeting the 24/7 needs of our infant son. I spent little time training or working in our restaurant during the first year. We were just trying to adjust in the beginning and get our life somewhat stable after the radical change we had all experienced as a family.

Jason and Amanda helped their dad regularly at the restaurant. Jason had worked with Doug for several years and knew enough to be a big help. Amanda got in there and worked too. She cleaned tables and worked in the drive-thru serving customers. She could barely reach out the window at six years old to serve the food, but she did her best and the things she did were very helpful. People often asked us about child-labor laws—the truth is that if your family owns a business, your children are allowed to work in that business. Our children were blessed that it was a family business they wanted to be a part of, one where all the children wanted to go. When Jarrod got older, he also helped however he was able, and then I spent more time at the restaurant. When Jarrod was very young, he would give Happy Meal toys to children he made friends with. He began promoting the business at a very early age. Our life was extremely busy, but we were all happy and content just to be experiencing our once-in-a-lifetime dream together.

In October 1993 we opened another restaurant. It was one of the first McDonald's restaurants located inside a Walmart. At this point, we had owned our business for only two years, and just when things were settling down some, this new adventure came along to make sure we did not get too settled. Also, sometime near this time, we replaced the Playland at our main restaurant. That event made the front page of the local newspaper, complete with pictures and comments made by me. Our family also made a commercial that aired regularly on local cable channels, focusing on the new Playland. It was another unique family experience.

When Doug and I became business owners, our plan was for him to operate the restaurant. I would take care of our children along with doing all the required accounting involved in business ownership and in meeting McDonald's corporate requirements. But with my business background, I began getting pressure from corporate personnel to go through the training process and become an approved licensed McDonald's owner/operator in my own right. They said it would make our business stronger for both Doug and I to be certified, licensed, and approved. Therefore, I soon began working on the requirements to attend my first McDonald's training class. Sometime later, after tons of bookwork and managing restaurant operations, I completed three regional classes and five equipment classes, making the dean's list for them all. I was now prepared for national McDonald's training.

My completed McDonald's training up to this point opened the door for me to attend Hamburger University near Chicago, Illinois, in the suburb of Oak Brook. Many people I have encountered are truly amazed to learn Hamburger University really does exist. The technologically advanced school is real, and I have a bachelor's degree in hamburgerology hanging in my office as proof. It is not a degree in hamburgers but a degree in restaurant operations and management skills. Since I also have a bachelor's in business administration, I can attest that numerous things one studies in the world of business are directly related to the success story of the McDonald's Corporation. When I received my degree from HU, this time too I was on the dean's list. I also happened to know the dean personally, since he was the licensing manager Doug and I had first met with when we started the process of getting our own restaurant. I now was fully trained; all that was missing to become a certified, licensed, approved owner/operator was corporate approval from the VP in charge at the Dallas office. I had already met with this man on many occasions, and he was ready to seal the deal as soon as I graduated from HU. Doug and I met with him after graduation and got the paperwork in process. I received an official letter very soon after verifying my owner/operator status in the McDonald's Corporate system. A short time after I became a licensed approved McDonald's owner/operator I also joined a national group of women owner/operators known as WON (Women's Operator Network). I enjoyed the meetings at various locations across America. It became a good way to stay in touch with new things happening in the world of other female McDonald's owners throughout the country.

After receiving a Hamburgerology degree, we are encouraged to recycle through Hamburger University every five years as a process of continuing education. Doug was up for recycle and went with me to HU. Throughout the time Doug and I attended HU, our friend, the dean, watched our grades closely, encouraging us to compete against each other. And of course, Doug made the dean's list too. Doug and I were not in the same groups, but were in the same class of over two hundred students from all over the USA and many countries worldwide.

Hamburger University was a terrific experience for me. The entire training process I encountered with McDonald's, both regional and national, was completely positive. It too became a personal experience that healed and restored confidence in my abilities. The people I met were very supportive, encouraging, and caring. Back in the nineties, being part of the McDonald's system meant you had a group of people who cared about you and a place to belong. The classes were a safe place to learn and share. The focus was on people, the necessary element in running successful restaurants.

One special memory from HU made it personal for me. It was a final exercise our smaller, divided-up class of fifty students worked on throughout the time we were there. In the beginning, our teacher asked us to get to know our fellow classmates. We were to write down two things about everyone in the class and be ready to tell something about any of them, if asked. One of these two things was a fact that everyone would know and one was a fact you would know only if you talked to the person. The information we shared had to be facts; opinions were not allowed. As time went on, it seemed that they had forgotten to ask for the information we had all retrieved. But then, on the very last day of class, the teacher started calling on a classmate to tell something about another randomly selected classmate. It seemed she was never going to ask me anything about anyone, but she had saved me and Doug for last to give information about each other. I was ready to talk about anyone else in the class, and it now came down to what I wanted to share about my husband with them all. For the obvious statement, I said, "Doug is tall." That was an undisputable fact. Then, for the information no one else knew about Doug, I said, "Doug began working for McDonald's back in 1979 to pay off our Sears bill." And I said, "He has paid it off many times since then." Then it was Doug's turn. He said, "Debbie is beautiful." I said back to Doug, across the huge classroom, "That is your opinion, not a fact." He returned "No! That is a fact." Then the entire class including our teachers began clapping and cheering and agreeing with Doug by saying, "Yes, you are beautiful, and that is a fact." I was overwhelmed and all I could do was say to all my friends, "Thank you." The thing Doug shared that would be known only if someone talked to me was that I am an accountant. This class exercise turned into a most unexpected, positive experience, and one I will always remember. Through the years whenever I'm not feeling pretty and say, "I am ugly," Doug will retaliate with "You are not! And remember, I have fifty-plus witnesses to prove it." Doug was right, my HU friends from all across the country and around the world disagreed with Dad. This special HU experience healed a lot of the hurt Dad always brought into my life when he caused me to feel I was ugly in his eyes.

Eventually, Jason and Amanda would also attend Hamburger University. They both graduated with their bachelor's in hamburgerology, also on the dean's list; soon after, they got their high school diplomas. Jarrod trained some in the McDonald's realm, but he never got real interested in the training program. And as circumstances would have it, he did not have the same opportunity his brother and sister did to attend HU. However, he became a real help during his early teens and worked at the restaurant often in the summer and on school breaks.

During our life as McDonald's owner/operators, Doug and I both felt as if we were each working two or three full-time jobs at once. It was hard and even extremely difficult at times, but we knew we were in God's will, and it felt peaceful and right. Our family was working together on a specific goal. We had a common purpose that we all worked toward. Our children each developed a good business background from life experience and maybe partially due to osmosis. Owning a family business definitely gave each of our children a head start in the world of business and created a family emotional connection through a common interest that is rare and extraordinary.

Diminishing Dysfunction

Living in Texas was God's perfect will for me and my family. Being far away from Clovis, New Mexico, was a blessing because it made the dysfunction feel farther away too. But many times the old childhood feelings would surface through interaction with my parents. The turmoil was still there, and no acknowledgement of feelings, emotions, or problems was ever confronted. Denial was always the method of choice when hurts surfaced. There are hundreds of damaging emotional encounters I have lived through with my parents that I could relate. But I will relay a couple that seem most relevant and portray the denial present with an overall unwillingness to face the truth and problems as they arise.

There was one occasion when my mother called to say she and Dad were coming to our house for my birthday. I was not pleased to hear they were coming. So Doug called them back and said, "It would be best if you do not come." He explained, "I am only trying to keep the peace." My mother had an emotional reaction; she was crying on the phone and did not understand how I could possibly feel that way. From my perspective, I felt so overwhelmed with our McDonald's business; also, that weekend we had to attend a high-school marching band competition for Jason, and in between all that I just wanted to relax and enjoy my birthday weekend. I also simply did not want to deal with how they made me feel.

But I gave in and called my mother back. I told her, "Y'all should come if you want to. After all, my birthday is more your day of celebration than mine."

Her response was, "It is obvious we should not come, and besides, I have already unpacked my suitcase. So we will not be there." I felt both relieved and uncomfortable at the same time with this conclusion. But am sure it worked out for the best.

There was a similar emotional encounter when my mother stayed at our house. I got up one morning and walked by her without saying anything. I was thinking about something I needed to do, and it was totally unintentional that I did not speak. But my mother took offense and got all upset; she quickly packed up her things and left, crying, without saying anything. Both this and the previous example are so symptomatic of our family dysfunction. There was never any talking or facing problems. There was no digging, probing, or understanding— only denial, avoidance, and cover-up that led to more bad feelings. It was always just continue on in the dysfunction in an altered, compromised, emotionally disconnected existence. I believe now that it would have been best for me to ignore my parents' pattern of denial and address the situation. However, I knew from many uncomfortable experiences that talking to my mother about things she did not want to face could become even more emotionally charged. In dealing with my parents, I was frozen into her methods of denial; I did not understand at the time how very important it is to own up to the reality of the circumstances. It is imperative to stop living as if everything is fine, to stop continuing to swallow all the pain, and to stop ignoring the need to face the truth. I have learned from personal experience that this method will only lead to an emotional reckoning when too much pain has been consumed and falsehood has become the norm. Denial is an abnormal way to cope with life.

My mother denied many things, and one of them was that she had a favorite grandchild. It was obvious during phone calls from her and Dad. They would always ask about Jason but rarely asked about Amanda or Jarrod. Most phone calls would end without any mention of Amanda or Jarrod unless I volunteered information about them. But asking about Jason was always a top priority, especially for Dad. They seemed so connected to Jason but had little to nothing for anyone else. In fact, when my parents visited our family, Amanda and Jarrod would retreat to their bedrooms. I would tell them to come out and visit with their grandparents. But their reply would be, "They do not want to see me; they want to see Jason." I really could not disagree with that, so I let them get along however felt workable for them.

Chapter Forty-Five

Living a Genuine Miracle

One rainy autumn night, Doug and I were returning home from a day of shopping in Abilene, Texas. Traveling through the night in our new Chevrolet pickup, we listened to the first non-Christian CD we had bought in over five years. It was George Strait's newest music release containing the hit song "Carrying Your Love with Me." We were talking ... then my next memory was of quick turbulence and the thought, *If we could only make it to Coleman, we will be fine* (Coleman was a Texas town midway between Abilene and our home). I was thinking this while spinning around as if trapped inside a "squirrel cage" carnival ride. Then I knew without a doubt I was somewhere other than here on earth; my body was physically present, but my spirit had departed. I remember feeling a most heavenly, indescribable peace, and I have no earthly memories of anything afterward on this Tuesday night, November 11, 1997.

During the period void of earthly memories, I was in a place where I felt no pain, only complete blissful peace. It was as if I had been given an overdose of endorphins. I know for sure I was not spiritually present on earth, and the feeling I experienced was because I was in the presence of Jesus Christ, the Great Physician. I did not see white, bright lights, nor did I see Jesus's face or God. However, I felt Jesus's presence and the healing peace that it brought to me. If it were not for Jesus and His healing touch after the accident, I would not be writing this now. I would have been in heaven permanently from that night on. I had no concept of what I had just gone through.

Since I have no memories for a lengthy period, what I will relay now comes from Doug's personal account, which he has shared with me many times over the years. It grieves my heart even now to think back to the scene of the accident and imagine what Doug was living through. He called to my still, limp, lifeless body, covered in blood and glass; he got no response as blood oozed out of my wounds. The pickup had turned over and come to rest upside down. I was hanging inverted; the seatbelt held me suspended in place. My husband felt sure I was dead and gone from him forever. In hopeless despair, as Doug too was hanging upside-down beside me, he cried out to God in heaven to bring me back to him. He beseeched God to please return life to my body. The "won't let go kind of love" that Doug and I share was the provocation for Doug's prayer. He could not let go and knew God was able to change the hopeless situation.

The young teenager who ran the stop sign and hit us also believed I was dead. There was complete chaos at the accident scene, with people running to and fro calling for emergency assistance and helping however they could. Doug was able to release himself from the seatbelt and climb out the broken window on the driver's side of the pickup. He then slowly maneuvered his hurt body to my side and continued to pray. There was a point amidst all the confusion when a heated encounter occurred between Doug and the teenager responsible for the crash. Believing I was dead, Doug lashed out at him, demanding an answer for why he ran the stop sign. The young boy could only say, "I do not know." He offered no reason for not stopping and entering the highway from a crossroad without looking. He was not obviously hurt and was later treated and released at the medical facility. Tests revealed he was not driving under the influence of drugs or alcohol. It was just odd he could not explain his actions, since he traveled this road almost daily. He definitely had to be aware of the major highway there—why did he choose not to stop?

This young man had entered the highway we were on and crashed into us, hitting our front passenger-side fender. The impact stopped us dead in our tracks, which sent our vehicle rolling over. Our feeling of calm and security rapidly turned into sudden trauma filled with twisting metal, breaking glass, and the astronomical jolt of the impact that halted all forward motion. Then our vehicle became an uncontrollable rolling, turning ride, sending us in the opposite direction on the four-lane highway. Finally, the momentum created by the crash allowed gravity to take over and stop us just short of the traffic coming toward us. When the unrestrained ride ended, we were left hanging upside-down. A feeling of relief swept over Doug, but that feeling changed quickly when he realized I died during the rollover.

The impact caused glass and blood to shoot everywhere. Glass was embedded in my face, head, and hands. The wreckage was covered in blood. My clothes were soaked with blood. My blood-covered body had received great trauma from head to toe.

Many passersby stopped to lend assistance. One man lent Doug his cell phone to call whomever he needed to. This became a mixed blessing; the gesture was thoughtful, but Doug was in shock and operating solely on his concern for my condition. He called our home, getting our oldest son on the phone. My husband's words incited more anxiety and fear for our son than comfort and reassurance. Jason said after the conversation with his dad, he felt it was likely he would never see me alive again. My husband regretted calling with such a message of hopelessness. Doug felt he was functioning totally in survival mode and had no business talking to our son at that time. After getting the news from his dad, Jason called our preacher, and they both left for Abilene before midnight. It hurts to think what Jason must have been going through emotionally this night as well. I know it was not easy for someone so young, but he faced it all very maturely.

Throughout this heart-wrenching encounter, Doug continued to ask God for His presence and help. My husband ignored his own injuries and was concerned only for my well-being. Then, as Doug continued to pray to God, the miracle occurred: I began to moan, and then I spoke. Doug's prayers had fallen on the ears of God. The request of my loving husband had reached the very heart of God, and God responded in love to Doug's breaking heart. Being overwhelmed with emotion, my husband began thanking God for sending me back to him. But he was confused by the words I spoke—"Cut it." He soon understood I wanted free of my seatbelt, and he cut the seatbelt, freeing me of its grasp. A nurse at the scene helped Doug out until the ambulance arrived.

To the Hospital

I remember nothing about the actual wreck or anything about the scene of the wreck afterward. I felt no pain and have no memory of the ambulance ride to the hospital. Doug remained at the accident scene and watched the ambulance leave with me. I was told later that I informed the emergency team of my date of birth and social security number and gave coherent answers to other questions they asked me. It is a strange feeling to be unable to account for a lengthy period of time of which I have no memory. It feels like I have lost a part of my life.

When Doug got to the hospital, he was treated and released. He had cuts and bruises, and he was hit so severely that some of his bones were bruised as well. His hands were also hurt badly and would go on to give him pain for years. Later, when Jason arrived at the hospital with our preacher, he found Doug carrying around a multi-pack of paper towels we had purchased that day. Jason took them from Doug and said, "Dad, you don't need these right now. I will take them home for you." Doug does not know why he chose to take the paper towels with him from the accident scene. He was in shock—maybe he just needed something to hold on to. Doug would not go home that night; he chose to stay with me. He slept in a chair in the ICU waiting area near my room. Doug was hurt badly himself but stayed close by—a picture of love, faithfulness, and dedication. This was a hurtful time then, but remembering it now brings smiles of relief and always deep thankfulness because of the dire, life-altering circumstance our family survived together.

My Hospital Stay

After I arrived at the hospital, the emergency team mutilated my clothes—everything was cut off me, even my leather coat! Because of my injuries, they needed immediate access to review the bodily damage

I sustained. The first procedure necessary was to insert a chest tube to drain my right lung that was rapidly filling with blood and fluid because it had collapsed.

I had received a multitude of cuts and bruises. The gashes in my head required many stitches after being cleaned somewhat to remove blood and glass. Tests revealed the main problems to be broken ribs, which had penetrated my right lung, causing it to collapse. There was also concern about damage to my heart. Some findings were life-threatening, and others were not as urgent. The doctors said if my lung did not function as needed, I would require a lung transplant to live normally. I had no other apparent internal injuries, and my mind was functioning normally—even though I had no memory for days. After my injuries were assessed, I was hooked up to numerous tubes that provided various needs and medication. I still felt no pain.

It was a miracle that I was even alive, considering all my injuries. The force of the impact smashed my head into the passenger window, shattering the glass completely out. Yet I miraculously had no head injuries. I also was squeezed greatly by the seatbelt, which made my insides feel scrambled for months to come, but nothing was damaged permanently in my abdomen. My right lung was punctured by the broken ribs. A chest tube was inserted to release drainage from my deflated lung, a procedure done with no deadening to the area cut open to insert the tube. I have no memory of this procedure, which I am told is extremely painful. My husband said I was speaking to the doctor as he inserted the chest tube. It seemed that my heart was traumatized from the impact but returned to normal function.

I had just lived through an impact causing overall bodily trauma, which in many cases inevitably leads to sudden death. My doctors concluded it was a real miracle that I was still alive. The doctors were amazed at my overall condition. It became even more of a miracle that I would suffer very little permanent damage from it all. God is merciful, and He heard my husband's prayers. God answered his request, and I was blessed with the healing necessary. Therefore, I would live and recover, returning back to a normal, physically functional life.

During my hospital stay, I was in the care of several different doctors headed by one main doctor. A heart specialist, a neurosurgeon, and other doctors consulting about the condition of my lungs and broken ribs each told me there was no medical explanation as to why I was still alive and able to recover. They told me that I was a genuine miracle. They had seen many people die from a lot less damage than I had. These various doctors all having a part in getting my physical life functional again would randomly come by my room to check on me. When my memory started to return, the doctors came around acting like I should know them, but actually I would have no idea who they were or why they seemed to know me so well. When I inquired as to who they were, they would laugh and understand that I really had no memory of seeing them prior. They would fill me in on what they knew and give me a current update, and every one of them would also add how amazed they were that I was alive and recovering so well.

When my mother got the news the night of the accident, her thought process seemed to be one of talking herself into coming to be with me and my family. She had a dilemma between coming to Abilene or staying home and taking care of her job. She lingered and then told herself, "It was a wreck on a major highway, not an in-town fender bender; I should go." My mother drove a school bus and had a real problem with anyone driving *her* school bus except her. She hesitated to go be with her daughter who had almost died. (She never would accept the fact that I did die for a period of time.) Despite my mother being pulled between her job and me, she did choose to come to Texas. She arrived the next day in Abilene at the hospital. I was in the ICU, and my husband told me that at her first sight of me, she had to grab a chair because she almost fainted. I had tubes everywhere, and a lot of blood was still visible from the accident—it couldn't be washed off for a long period of time because of the injuries. My hair was also blood-soaked and full of glass particles. I still had no memory and do not remember seeing my mother at the hospital.

Doug described an intensely emotional encounter I had with my daughter. Amanda, only twelve years old at this time, was understandably very upset by our situation and my injuries. I am sure I looked very scary to her with blood and glass caked all over my hair, with cuts and bruises on all visible parts of my body, and so hurt that I could scarcely move, plus all the tubes and equipment I was hooked up to. She broke down and became emotionally distraught at seeing me in person for the first time after the wreck. Doug said that I helped calm her and told her all would be fine, I would be all right again. I comforted her and reassured her and told her not to worry and that I loved her. I held her as she cried. The fact that I have no memory of this emotional time with my daughter surprises me greatly. But even this is an event in my life totally erased from my memory.

Doug told me I carried on meaningful conversations with our children and with all the friends who visited me during the first few days. My uncle called to check up on me, and Doug said I also reassured him I would be all right again. I guess my mind was engaged, but memories were not stored. According to my husband, I seemed mentally functional, but I have no memory of what I did and said.

After several days, my consciousness vaguely returned; I had my first memory after the accident. I woke up and saw a large Peace Lily plant. After seeing the plant, I remember realizing I was in a hospital room in bed, and moments later, I had memories of excruciating pain. It was like I had returned, and this was my life now. Doug was there with me, and he began filling me in on events that had happened during my lapse of memory. Hearing details felt like I had been living in *The Twilight Zone*. I asked him repeatedly, "What happened to us?" and could not really comprehend why I was in a hospital in my current condition. I felt confused. As time passed, I remembered some things very vaguely. One memory is of feeling more intense pain whenever I moved. My consciousness was minimal, and the people and my surroundings where cloudy and unclear. Why was I here, and why did I hurt so badly? I continued to struggle with what had happened and had trouble grasping exactly why I was in the hospital in this condition. I could not conceive the reality that Doug and I were in a deadly car crash that landed me in the hospital.

The hospital staff and doctors made this unpleasant experience more tolerable. They were very empathetic and understanding, and they tried in every way to keep me comfortable. Although the physical therapist was caring, my memory of these sessions is only of excruciating pain. I could lift my right arm up only a couple of inches. The physical therapist explained to me that it was imperative I continue doing the exercises daily to regain use of my right arm. So I did the exercises, but one day I cried because so much about this experience was hard to live through. All the negatives about my situation were magnified by the pain of the exercises. It was all so frustrating, and I hurt so badly, even with medication. The physical therapy hurt, moving hurt, and I could not stand long enough to shower. I was hooked up to a catheter; my hair was still bloody and full of glass pieces and particles. I could only endure sponge baths, and that gets very little blood off your body or out of your hair. I cried, and the nurses and the physical therapist comforted. Their empathy and caring helped my emotional situation, but I still felt chained to the room. The only time I remember leaving my hospital room was to go for x-rays. Some of the x-rays I had were even done in my room, so I would not have to be moved. I was not able to walk the halls like most recovering patients do. This probably led to the crying scene too; I just felt so bad physically and emotionally, and there was no escape.

One vivid memory I have from my hospital stay was when the chest tube was removed. It felt raw and sore and hurt extremely badly when they pulled out the tube. Nevertheless, it was a time of celebration, because it meant my lung had inflated as hoped for. There was now no longer a possibility I would require a lung transplant. This too was a miracle.

Returning Home

After being released from the hospital only nine days after the crash, I finally headed home with Doug. Putting on a seatbelt was very painful, but in spite of the pain, I wore my seatbelt and endured the two-hour ride home. The trip was anxious, edgy, and painful. But however uncomfortable, it was worth the pain just to be back home again. It felt as if I had been away for a really long time. Our three children were home when we arrived, and it was a wonderful reception—one of heartfelt thankfulness and deep gratitude that we still could be together.

The first night at home was one of almost intolerable pain. I could not find a comfortable position; sleeping was not an option even with the strong pain medication. The pain was intense, deep, and raw. The throbbing ache all over my body penetrated every fiber of my being. Relief was not in sight. I had taken the dosage limit of my medication and could only endure the painful, sleepless night.

After a few days, the pain pills finally caught up and reduced the torture to a more manageable state. Sleep, although sweet when it came, was easily interrupted with a wrong move or the loud noise of a bone creaking. Learning to live through my current state was, to say the least, very frustrating. Things would gradually become livable, but for now, I could only exist. For many weeks, I was unable to do anything at all but attend to the basic functions of life, which too came with newfound ways to hurt. Have you ever coughed or sneezed with broken ribs? Extremely painful!

After I had been home for several weeks, I finally began to grasp the magnitude of what God allowed Doug and me to live through. The incident became clearer when Doug showed me pictures of our pickup in total wreckage. With the crushed metal and broken glass, it undoubtedly was a genuine miracle that we both were alive and still sharing our life with our children.

Living with the Pain: Steps in Healing

Six weeks later, I had a follow-up visit with the main attending physician who cared for me in the hospital. At this visit, he gave me a clean bill of health and said I could do whatever I felt up to. Also at this follow-up visit, it was repeated by my doctor that for me to even be alive was a miracle—a miracle still worth mentioning. And the fact that I suffered only minimal permanent damage was also miraculous. A miracle is just what had occurred! With God in control of my life and my husband praying, all that happened was no coincidence.

With time, I became able to lift my right arm over my head. However, still today, moving that arm repeatedly causes pain in my right side that no amount of physical therapy could do anything to change. The damage is permanent. My ribs grew back together unaligned, and my life was never to be as painless as before. But I choose to rejoice in the miraculous way I was healed overall and in the fact that mostly I am able to function as before. I could have easily ended up in a wheelchair for the rest of my days, or required a lung transplant just to live at all, or been damaged in many other ways permanently, or—worst of all for my family—ended up dead, permanently. God intervened on my behalf, and none of these terrible options came true. The pain I still have from living through this horrible accident I look at as a reminder of how God took care of me, healed me from a worse fate, and manifested His love for me as His child.

Several months after the accident, there was a point when Jason decided it was time for me to *do something*. So he came home one night and found me sitting in the hot tub with his dad. He announced that I needed to get out of the house, and he had come to take me for a ride. So he, his dad, and I got into his pickup and went for a ride around town. It was a nice change of pace, but just doing anything was still difficult—painful, to be exact. In spite of that, the outing was great, and probably what I really did need. Just getting out of the house and breathing different air can make you feel better. While driving around town, we ended up at the college campus Jason attended. The three of us went on a short stroll to some of the places Jason went every day. I enjoyed it very much, and Jason was right: I did need to do something different! This was a thoughtful gesture from my very caring son.

Around three months after the wreck, I tried going back to church. At this time, however, it was still a great struggle to get up, dressed, and ready to go anywhere. But when I got to church, I delighted in the many, many welcoming hugs from my friends. However, these hugs became very painful rather quickly because of the bruises and the damaged area around my ribs. Also, doing anything with a repetitive motion caused pain on my right side. But going to church was an uplifting experience. Everyone was very glad to see me, and it created quite a stir in the church since my return was unexpected. My husband's parents were visiting, and they decided it was time for me to go back to church while they were with us. It did work out all right; I made it through the day, but I knew I was not ready for regular church attendance yet. I guess my husband's parents thought three months was long enough to recover, but again, no one but Doug really comprehended the severity of my damage and circumstance. I was not purposely putting off getting on with my life, I just was not totally healed and ready to begin. I had no emotional problem attached to the delay; it was all centered on physical pain and damage not yet healed. During the healing period, I was asked many times, "Are you afraid to travel in a car again?" My answer was always the same, "No, because I witnessed God's protection, and I am not afraid to travel by car even now." I am certain and now know firsthand, through personal experience, of God's promise to take care of me.

After the wreck, I was checked and observed for brain damage. The fact that none existed also was miraculous to my doctors. However, eleven years later, when the childhood emotional abuse issues surfaced after the trigger event, my parents tried to blame brain damage from the wreck rather than face their responsibility in causing a real emotionally traumatic childhood for me to sort through. The fact is that I was healed after the wreck. God's intervention created circumstances of healing that baffled the medical profession. The doctors in turn chose to rely on faith in God's work as the most reasonable explanation for my recovery from such a damaging and potentially deadly accident. Then again, eleven years later, this area was examined by my Christian counselor, who found no pattern, substantiation, or reason to believe my parents accusations. My parents once again were trying to blame anything other than themselves for the repercussions they were now feeling, caused by the pain and hurt they had sown in my childhood past.

The Anger

It was several weeks or maybe even months before I completely comprehended what happened and how it happened. I became angry for all the obvious reasons. I hurt more than I had ever experienced physically in my life; the injuries were so numerous, so intense, and so concentrated. I could rest only on my back. I could not lie on my right side at all for several years afterward, and it felt as if I would never be able to sleep on my right side again. Any movement for several months caused a creaking, popping sound that only I could hear, probably due to my bones returning back to their normal position. I was angry because my husband's needs were overlooked after the accident; he was in shock and hurt too. He did not even rest in a bed that night after enduring the car wreck and sustaining injuries. I was angry for the entire emotional trauma my children lived through. I was angry because our new pickup was totaled, never to be driven again. I was angry because I could not run my business at all during this recovery period. Before the accident, my life was the equivalent of a faucet running full blast, turned up all the way—then suddenly turned completely off.

One of the things that added to my anger was a visit from a mystery woman while I was in the hospital. The irresponsible behavior of this mystery woman's son was the reason I had to live through all these things dumped in my life through no fault of my own. My family had suffered greatly. She visited me to ease her conscience and to take responsibility for the immature act of her son. This tells me volumes about why her son was irresponsible to begin with. She made it easy for him and did not make him face the consequences of his actions. The son should have at least come along to visit with his mother; he was physically able. I know for sure if either of my sons had been involved in such a situation, they would have visited on their own and faced their responsibilities. They would never have asked or let me go in their place. This circumstance could have been one I subconsciously related to Dad as an irresponsible teenager when his driving accident killed the woman. Maybe I mentally compared this woman and her son to Dad's unfortunate experience, but now I was the victim who died. And this teenager was avoiding his responsibility in the accident, just as Dad did when he moved away from home to evade dealing with his consequences. Then dad never talked about his incident through the years and only passed his pain on to me because he never healed emotionally.

However, during and beyond the entire recovery process, anger toward God was *never* something I felt. I did feel rejection, because

I had been able to experience His presence and then was sent back to earth in such a state of bodily disrepair. I felt more thankfulness, though, as time went on because of the mighty way God had chosen to use my life to make such a great impact on others. There was no doubt that God was getting glory from this time in my life when He walked me *through* the valley of the shadow of death. Multitudes of people were touched by this trial we went through—many just heard about it because they knew people we knew and others lived it with us. I have no direct confirmation, but I believe several souls were saved by knowing us and watching this miracle unfold. There were miracles all around, and God used *me* to bring glory and honor to His name. I did nothing spectacular. I only survived because it was God's will. The overall anger I mention here quickly dissipated when I realized more of the "big picture." God had used me in a mighty way, and the physical ailments and injuries were minimized with God's overwhelming peace because I felt totally comforted in His presence. Living life in the truth of God's hope brings no greater happiness and no greater peace.

Life Changes

After the anger was rationalized, I began to reflect back on November 11, 1997—the ordinary, routine day that became life altering. The place we ate and the pointless, stupid movie we saw were absolutely not on my list of last things to do before I died. Since this fateful night when everything almost abruptly ended on this earth for me, I have never watched another movie like that. The things I did this day were not my preferred last options. And looking at it this way gives new meaning to daily choices.

With additional analyzing, I also realized that just one small decision can change everything. Around ten p.m., with the rain drizzling down, Doug and I headed straight home without making our usual stop for coffee at McDonald's. If we had made our routine stop, the timing for the wreck would have been altered. It is strange to imagine how one minor decision could have changed the entire chain of events. But then I realize that one minor decision, capable of changing everything, was not supposed to be.

Five months after the accident, I attempted to get back into my previous routine by working in our restaurants. However, after struggling through the day, it became apparent I was not ready to resume the fast pace. Luckily, I was able to get back into the old routine gradually. But with the limitations caused by the permanent damage to my right side, I never completely regained the pace I had kept before. This caused temporary waves of discontent and helplessness. But when flooded by these feelings, I would remember to be thankful for all God had done for me; renewing my focus on that always made the bad feelings go away. This thought provided a ray of sunshine amidst the clouds of pain and recovery.

The Effects of the Accident on My Family

At this time, Jarrod was in the first grade. I learned from his teacher that Jarrod would put his head down on his desk and cry throughout his days at school when I was in the hospital. All the turmoil was terribly upsetting for a little six-year-old boy. His teacher talked to him and tried to help. She said his hurt was heartbreaking to her. But she said Jarrod was joyful and happy when I returned home from the hospital. Then, from a little boy's grateful heart, good things evolved between Jarrod and me from this hurtful, bad time. One was a ritual that lasted throughout Jarrod's school years—he would greet me every school morning with a hug and a kiss, and he would squeeze my hand and say "I love you." This was endearing and greatly cherished time for me; it came as a result of Jarrod's gratitude that I was still alive and part of his life. He was never ashamed to let me know how he felt, even in public, as he got older and then on into his teenage years. And at home, he still took the time every day, even when he was a little late getting to school, to give me these moments, continuing until May of his senior year. Now that Jarrod has graduated from high school and is attending college very far away from home, these daily memories of how sweet and giving he always was are even more precious to me. He still calls or regularly sends texts to me. Distance has not erased the connection built between us through this experience. Jarrod is very loving and caring and still shows me how he feels.

Amanda was twelve years old then and in the seventh grade. This experience hurt her deeply and unsettled her life for a time. She was emotional about the situation, and even though her actions were not as overt as Jarrod's, I know her love and support were present. She showed how much she cared by spending time with me while I could do and move very little. We talked, watched movies, and painted our nails together. She was always ready to get whatever I needed; she was my friend and companion during these months of recovery. Amanda as always also added her touch of humor and her love of life. It was an extreme joy and a tremendous blessing to spend time with her just talking about what was on her mind or what she was experiencing at school. I very much valued this time I spent with her. She always portrayed a loving and understanding spirit and was very patient whenever she helped me do something. The privilege I had of spending this time with Amanda brought emotional attachment to our relationship in a special way. I have always greatly enjoyed the uplifting presence my daughter adds to my life. With her, a smile or a laugh is always close by; she adds sunshine to any day. The time with Amanda during this tragic period brought emotional healing to us both.

Jason was eighteen years old at the time and a freshman at the local university. Although I know Jason was grateful that both his dad and I survived the accident, he appeared tough and unbreakable. Jason and I talked often during my recovery, but I never got a true feel of his actual emotional experience. Many times, I felt as if he blamed me for almost dying. He had the load of responsibility of running the restaurants in addition to living through his first semester in college. He came across with an attitude toward me that I should just get over whatever I was feeling and stop hurting. There were times when his position was less than sympathetic and caring. I guess he just wanted me better and did not know how to deal with an injured mom who was usually supporting him rather than needing anything from him. There were a few unpleasant encounters between us; they upset me and made me feel bad. Jason then at some point sent me beautiful pink roses with a card telling me he loved me. This meant a lot and smoothed over the rough areas, but as his mom, I understood he was having a hard time with all the things affecting our family at this time. I did not blame him, and I knew it would all return to normal sometime. I always knew Jason to be a sweet and caring young man. He was, is, and always will be my pride and joy!

Doug also experienced much emotional and physical pain, heartache, and torment from this experience we shared together. It has strengthened our marriage and our relationship. Every day, the reminder of how things could be makes us even more grateful and thankful to God for the life we are able to share. I probably cannot actually grasp the feelings of loss my husband experienced when he believed I was gone from him on this earth forever. But I know he has shown me, even more than he did before that night in November 1997, how precious our love and marriage are to him. His gratitude spills out regularly in the loving care that I am showered with daily. After the wreck, Doug had a bracelet made especially for me at our local jewelry store. It is an oval shape of smooth gold with the words *Lost Without You* engraved on it, and it is dated on the inside. I never go anywhere without wearing it. In addition to its simple beauty, its presence on my wrist has great meaning.

The Power of Prayer

The accident placed me in the same position Lazarus experienced in Bible times (John 11: 1—46). For me to live again, Jesus Christ would have to intervene—in a miraculous experience ultimately bringing glory and honor to God my Father. So through the prayer and faith of my husband asking God to hear and answer, God had compassion and responded. God chose to let me live again.

I survived a deadly accident and was healed because of prayers offered on my behalf throughout the miraculous ordeal. But I believe one prayer in particular was offered in passionate desperation. And when it reached the very ears and heart of God, God was moved with compassion for my husband's circumstance. This special prayer came from my loving, devoted husband, whose heart was breaking at the thought of facing life without me. I believe a major reason I am alive today is because Doug poured out his broken heart to God one rainy night on a desolate, cold, dark highway, and God heard his prayer. Then

God chose to let me live again. I believe my injuries were so severe that, without the time I spent in Jesus' presence, I would have been unable to live at all after the accident, much less expect a physically functional life again. I believe God gave me a hint of what it feels like to be in His presence. God was healing me as He was hearing my husband's prayer requesting Him to send me back. God made it possible for me to live without brain damage or heart injury, and to be able to breathe regularly without a lung transplant. He also allowed me to walk normally without need of a wheelchair the rest of my days. I was given a gift from God as an answer to prayer.

As born-again Christians, our efforts are not wasted in prayer to the one and only powerful God of the universe, Father of Jesus Christ. He alone is able to meet our needs; as born-again believers and His children, we are loved and cared for. My husband prayed for me to come back to him. There was also an abundance of prayers from people all over, after the news had been circulated of our accident. In addition to the numerous faithful prayers of our church, friends, family, and many acquaintances, there also were prayers of many people I did not know and had never met. They were touched by the news and prayed for me and my family. Prayer for my recovery was widespread throughout many different states and even in other countries. It felt kind of like the movie *It's a Wonderful Life*—so many caring and heartfelt prayers prayed on your behalf in a desperate time of great need. Prayer moves mountains and changes hopeless circumstances.

Compassion and empathy begin with *hearing* and *feeling*. There is a connection between the *ear* and the *heart*. Their shapes are even similar—both ears drawn together form the shape of one heart. God hears our prayers because they fall on his ears and then he acts on our requests because they touch His heart, leading Him to feel and answer. God cares for His children and hears our prayers. Answered prayer is proof.

In His Presence

Of all the times in my life I knew for sure God was with me, the car wreck was when I felt His presence the strongest. I saw evidence of how He takes care of me more plainly than ever before. Never have I felt more joy, peace, and serenity than during the death experience. I definitely know I was somewhere other than this world. This peaceful feeling was not possible without a heavenly presence. Even though earthly memories are nonexistent for several days after the impact of the collision, the feeling of indescribable peace is a vivid memory and a blissful reality for me. I was carried away to another place and was in the presence of Jesus, the Great Physician. This feeling could come from no other.

My physical injuries should have caused great pain. But my memories of pain are nonexistent for several days. My husband told me that in the hospital, I was hooked up to a pain machine that automatically dispensed morphine when a button was pushed. I do not remember pushing the button, and even if I had, no medication would have been given to me. The nurses thought all along that the machine was working but finally realized, after some time had passed, that the machine was not functioning at all. Considering the entire physical trauma my body had endured and the life-threatening damage I had incurred, feeling peaceful and pain-free for days after the accident would have been impossible without the presence of Jesus giving me peace and healing my injuries.

My husband was the only one who really understood the extent of what I went through. He lived it with me; he knew I was dead; he knew he prayed me back to life; he knew how much I hurt; he felt my pain and his too. Accurately describing my experience to family and friends was difficult. I never found adequate words to convey my actual experience, knowing I was dead and knowing how hurt and damaged beyond living I really was until God healed me. It was great comfort that my husband understood. He knew what a miracle had taken place for me to return to my family with mind and body intact and functioning normally. My husband knew this better than anyone else—he witnessed my death.

Since this heavenly experience, there are visions in my mind of colors—brilliant, uncommon, powerful, intense, alive, and vivid. On rare occasions, I can close my eyes and see these colors parading through my mind, an experience I never had before the wreck.

God healed me after the death-dealing car accident. I had been in Jesus's presence and touched by His healing hand. After the wreck, it became overwhelming how constantly I was told that I look a lot younger than I am. I have no explanation other than my injuries were healed by God, and His love is probably radiating from me. God's love is healing and can make a person appear young at any age.

I am sure that someone could try to come up with a logical scientific explanation for what I experienced in the days after the wreck. But from what I know, there is no human explanation for a genuine miracle from God. As is stated in the Bible, "For the wisdom of this world is foolishness with God" (1 Cor. 3:19). Some divine happenings defy human explanation.

After experiencing the peace and contentment of being in the presence of Jesus, I thought many times about why I had to return to earth. This really became a prevalent thought when the days of consciousness returned and the pain of all the injuries dominated my being. I asked God, "Why did I have to return? And can I go back to experience the blissful feeling I was privileged to experience for only a short time?" His answer was obviously always "No," and it came with a definite feeling that He had more for me to do on earth before I would experience being with Him again.

The truth is that once people are saved and have sealed their eternal destiny to be in heaven with the Father, they remain on earth to fulfill His purpose for their life. That purpose, in some way, spreads the Gospel message of salvation and brings glory to God and Jesus Christ. I believe I could have died permanently the night of November 11, 1997, if God did not have a specific purpose for my earthly life in the years ahead. I believe it is God's will that I share my experience so others can know Jesus is real. My encounter with the hereafter was no coincidence, and I look forward to going back when God is ready for me to. Without that healing time with Him, I would not have been able to continue living in my body any longer; there was too much damage done.

The indescribable peace I felt, which was not of this world, could have come only from being in the presence of Jesus Christ, the Great Physician. Some naysayers have given an opinion that when people have an experience with death and return to life, the "peace" they describe comes from the drugs they have been given. I can verify that in my case, the heavenly peace I experienced was not a result of any drugs taken. The peace I felt was immediate when the Tuesday night wreck resulted in life leaving my body. I had no drugs at the accident scene; I had no drugs during the ambulance ride; I had no drugs when they made an incision into my right side down to my lung to insert a chest tube (nothing was deadened); I had no drugs for a lengthy period of time in ICU when the morphine pump was not functioning at all. I felt nothing at all but divine peace, and there was no physical pain until my memories and consciousness began to return.

It was some time later before I was able to verbally express what I had experienced immediately after the accident. Even for months after my experience with death, talking about it with anyone was hard. I finally did discuss it with my husband. He understood because he was there. He knew I had died. When describing it to anyone else, I felt like I was being categorized as crazy to even suggest such a thing. But that is how I perceived their reaction, not actually how most people responded. There was one exception, however, with my preacher, when he quoted the Bible to me: "It is appointed unto men once to die, but after this the judgment" (Heb. 9:27). His intent was to tell me that in today's world, revival from death is not possible. The miracle Lazarus experienced was for another time. But I know what I experienced, and I know that Jesus is the same yesterday, today, and forever. Any miracle He could perform then, He could also perform now in the present time. To believe anything but this is to limit the power of God and His Son and limiting God's power does not enter into my way of thinking. Also, it is axiomatic that man dies once. However, exceptions do exist. Enoch and Elijah of the Old Testament never died but were carried away to heaven; all the saints who are alive at Christ's return will never die; Lazarus and others who were raised from the dead later died a second time. Reviving from death to continue on living your life is consistent with Biblical examples. However, no exceptions concerning God's judgment can be cited. There is no reincarnation. Every person gets one chance to prepare. After living through a deadly car accident, I like to think my middle initial L, now stands not just for Leigh but for *life* (or maybe even Lazarus) because of my life-to-death-to-life experience. I was revived from death just like Lazarus (John 11:43–44), and the purpose was to bring glory to God.

I know what I went through. I know it was real. It was not drugs causing hallucinations. I felt peace that did not come from this world, and I felt the "Master's Hand" healing me with love. My recovery defied medical explanation, and my being alive was an indisputable miracle.

When I tried to confide in my mother that I had died and God brought me back to life, her response was to throw her hands in the air and say, "I will not and cannot listen to such talk. I can't have the thought that you died." Once again, it was all about her feelings, and she could not even hear about the miracle God performed for me. And once again, I got no emotional support from her, which I really needed. She was there to provide for physical needs, but emotional and spiritual needs were as always pushed aside. Discussing all that happened to me could have been a very uplifting, connecting experience for us, but she has never been able to provide that kind of support. Maybe it is just too uncomfortable for her? But it would have felt good if she had tried for once to understand me rather than magnify her own needs.

When I had thoughts of wishing to return to heaven, I would remember my husband and his love for me and how much he must have hurt when he experienced my death. That thought made returning to the pain worthwhile for me. It is also a miracle from God to have another human being love you so much. That makes earth feel more like heaven—even though the peace and feelings I experienced cannot be found anywhere on this earth. Doug and I had just celebrated our twentieth wedding anniversary only thirteen days prior to the accident, and I was thirty-eight years old at the time. It seems like a young age to begin suffering from lifelong ailments. However, it was a rich experience, and maybe one I would not have fully appreciated at any other age. Sending me back to my husband was God's decision.

Knowing the glory this experience brought to God, I would do it again for Him, because He is faithful to take care of me in whatever I face. Returning for my children also makes the pain bearable and worthwhile. There is so much in their lives I would have been absent for if I had remained dead at age thirty-eight.

When I tell people of my experience of being in the Lord's presence, describe the overwhelming feeling of peace in such a circumstance, and convey that I believe I died when the accident occurred, I'm usually met with curiosity or a need for more information. There is often a probing interest rather than disbelief, and a statement that, "Anything is possible with God" or "That doesn't sound crazy at all." Jesus raised Lazarus from the dead, and He is completely capable of doing this same miracle on any day past, present, or future. The God I serve is not limited in His ability to perform miracles. He is not limited just because we do not live in ancient Biblical times. Jesus is just as real and capable now as He was then. I know because I experienced it.

There is a song by the trio known as Greater Vision that was released in 1998, the year following our car accident. The song is called "My Name is Lazarus." When I heard this song for the first time on the radio during my healing process, it grabbed my spirit and touched me with its message. As I have stated, the Bible story of Lazarus took on a very personal meaning to me because of my experience with death, and this song captured much of how it felt. The words of this great song that follow are copied with permission from singer-songwriter Rodney Griffin of Greater Vision.

MY NAME IS LAZARUS

Words and Music by Rodney Griffin, ©1998 Songs of Greater Vision, BMI.

Verse 1

One day, four men brought a crippled man to Jesus
Still and lifeless, he lay upon his bed
He had not moved since he was just a baby
Still he longed to become a normal man

Verse 2

Now we don't know much about the men that carried
The corners of his tattered bed that day
But if we may create an illustration
We'll see what these men might have had to say

Verse 3

Suppose that first man said, "I hate to doubt it"
"For Jesus touched my eyes when I was blind"
"He made me see and there's no doubt about it"
"But this man's needs are more serious than mine"

Verse 4

Suppose that second man said, "No need to bother"
"This man's condition will remain the same"
"Though Jesus touched my hand when it was withered"
"I don't believe he can heal a man so lame"

Verse 5

Suppose that third man said, "I hate to question"
"But no one here is more skeptical than me"
"Though Jesus cleansed me when I was a leper"
"This helpless man will never walk, you see"

Verse 6

Then every eye was turned to the fourth man
To see how he might criticize and doubt
But all three men were startled with amazement
When that fourth man stopped, and said his name out loud

CHORUS (twice)

He said, "My Name is Lazarus, could I testify?"
My name Is Lazarus. It feels good to be alive!
When I in chains of death was bound
This man named Jesus called me out
If you think your little problem is too big for Him to solve
Take it from the one who's heard the mighty voice of God
A living testimony of His death defying touch, My Name Is Lazarus!

Seconds before I was injured in the car crash, my last memories were of feeling turbulence and thinking about Coleman, a town midway between Abilene and our home. *If we could only make it to Coleman, we will be all right*, I thought ... and then began my Lazarus experience— dying and feeling God's healing presence. Over twelve years later, my husband and I made it to Coleman, Texas, to enjoy the music of Greater Vision as they sang "My Name is Lazarus."

On August 7, 2010, Doug and I were privileged to see Greater Vision in person and to meet and briefly talk to Rodney Griffin. There is no question God provided this opportunity. For Doug and I to drive only thirty minutes to a very small Texas town and experience the moving and awe-inspiring music of Greater Vision, the multitalented, award-winning, and very popular trio with national and international acclaim, was indeed a gift from God. It also was very timely and fit perfectly with the task God had given me of writing my life story. This visit is when I asked Rodney Griffin for permission to use his song in my book.

To quote Rodney's powerful song, "When I in chains of death was bound, this man named Jesus called me out." Death cannot bind when Jesus overrides. Jesus provides the only hope of coming through such a physically and emotionally damaging experience and remaining functionally intact. Doug and I survived the car accident only because God was present, watching over us, and healing us in the days afterward. Without God, our future would have been hopeless, but with God we came through victorious. Through the accident, death came to my body, but with God's presence, I was revived. I became "a living testimony of His death defying touch"—these words from the song "My Name is Lazarus" had real personal meaning to me. Unless I experience the rapture, an end-of-time Bible prophesy when the saved are taken from this earth to meet Jesus in the air, I will die again due to the passage of time. But either way, through death or the rapture, I will be transported to heaven to live eternally with my Savior, Jesus Christ and my Father, God.

I believe there are more people alive today than we realize who have experienced death and been given the miracle of life returning to their earthly body. This is no doubt something that should be awe-inspiring, but there is a greater miracle the world looks on with too little significance. That miracle is when a lost sinner comes to Jesus in faith, realizes their lost condition, repents of their sins, and places their trust in Jesus—the one and only way to life everlasting. This too is a time when a person experiences life when they are dead. Being lost in sin means people are spiritually dead, doomed for hell eternally after they die. But when saved by the blood of Jesus Christ, they become spiritually alive, no longer dead to the wonderful life-giving existence that only God offers through His one and only begotten Son, Jesus Christ. When sinners are saved by grace through faith in Jesus Christ, they become alive spiritually because they also have "heard the mighty voice of God" bestowing newness and giving them the greatest gift ever offered.

Final Thoughts Regarding this Life-Changing Experience

I survived an automobile crash because God intervened on my behalf. Many times you hear in the news that someone was in a car crash and lived. I believe it is normal to think the survivors are lucky just because they did not die. But actually living through a wreck gives new meaning to the entire circumstance. When you live through a tragedy of this magnitude, you realize that it will be something you carry with you the rest of your life. It is a continuous process that is concentrated in the beginning and wanes throughout the years to come. But when it is something so huge, it never really goes away. It is normal to ask, "Why did I live?" or "What should I be accomplishing because I am still alive and did not die?" Maybe just being content to go on living each day the best you can is enough. It definitely is a gift to make the most of. Maybe there is unfinished business God has for you; if so, He will make it clear. One thing is for certain: no one is promised a tomorrow, all any of us are guaranteed is right now. That is why the *present* is a *gift*.

Even though I will never be as I was before, the pain I live with is minor in comparison to what it could have been. Maybe God left some pain so I never forget the wonderful miracle He performed for me. In this life, some of the things we go through are so damaging and deep—both in the physical realm and in the emotional realm—that coming through them untouched and totally renewed would not be feasible. Scars of wounds received can be a helpful reminder to be more compassionate and understanding toward others. They also serve to remind us of the pain we all face when walking through this life. When Jesus died on the cross for every human ever born, He received scars on His hands and feet that are an ever-present reminder of the pain He suffered and the agony He endured for every person. I believe when the born-again are reunited with Jesus in heaven, we will see the scars He bears on our behalf. And maybe we will be proud to show Him the scars we have accumulated during our walk on earth, because hopefully our scars were used as a part of His perfect plan for our lives that have brought glory to God in some way.

A Life of Contentment Is Yours for the Asking

Everybody has one of two choices in life to make. They can choose to *accept* Jesus Christ and the gift he freely offers to every person ever to exist. This choice comes with an earthly life of joy and contentment, experiencing the gift of the fruit of the spirit. Then, after death, the born-again children of God live in blissful peace with their Father in heaven. Those choosing to *reject* Jesus Christ will live out their earthly life in strife, pain, and discontentment that includes constantly occurring consequences coming your way due to a lifetime of bad choices. Worst of all, the ones rejecting Jesus will die and face their eternity in the torment of hell. Hell is where souls exist forever who have chosen to live their earthly days in disobedience to the one and only true God and have rejected Jesus as their Savior. Living life outside the will of God and rejecting Jesus Christ is dangerous and foolish; it causes pain every day you live on earth, with even more guaranteed torment in the hereafter. The existence of hell and Satan is not a fairy tale, as so many people are deceived into believing. Satan and hell are real; if you choose to test this truth and die without the salvation God offers, then you will know firsthand they exist because hell will be your eternal destination of torment.

I praise God that I can know for sure the horrible doom of hell is not my destiny. I know heaven is my eternal destiny because I am saved by Jesus. Also, because of the fatal car accident I experienced, I got a tangible glimpse of the eternity I am destined for in heaven. It was an awesome experience, more wonderful than words can convey. I know Jesus is my Savior and indescribable peace and contentment are waiting for me when I draw my last breath. I hope and pray that souls who do not know the saving grace of Jesus will seek the truth of a blissful, peaceful, eternal destination waiting for anyone who will choose to have faith and believe in the word of God for salvation. God is God, the creator of everything that exists, and nothing can change that fact. A person's choice of disbelief does not alter or override the truth that God does exist.

Another fact is that Satan is in a war for the unsaved soul who has yet to believe. He fights against God who created your life and soul, hoping to win. But Satan can only win by your choice to reject Jesus Christ; this one choice will condemn you to Satan's hell forever. If you allow this to happen, then Satan has won your soul, giving you no way out. He will laugh at you throughout eternity for believing his lie. Please do not be deceived by Satan's lies. A peaceful eternity with God and Jesus in heaven is true; I have felt it for myself through a brush with death. Satan will never win the battle he has waged with God, and he knows that. That is why he will stop at nothing to deceive and win the lost. Hell is Satan's destiny, and misery loves company.

Satan can also try to make the life of a Christian tougher, especially those who are living a life that makes a difference for God. I believe a possible cause for the wreck was that Satan was fighting against me and my husband, and he wanted us dead because we are both children of God living in obedience to God's will and for His purpose. God is always more powerful than Satan and can override anything Satan does. Even though Satan tried to bring about my death permanently, it did not happen. God had a purpose for me to live. My life is in the hands of God and in His power; only He can choose when I die. Even though this period was a difficult time in my life, God's guidance, provision, and healing power made it a time that possibly accomplished the most.

Even though this may sound impossible, this time in my life was also one that felt wonderful, both spiritually and emotionally. Through it all God was with me, filling me with His spirit and comforting me with peace like I had never felt before. It brought glory and honor to God, my Father and was noteworthy to the world because God's presence was evident and indisputable. God brought me back to life and healed me in ways that medical doctors considered to be impossible. My survival was a true modern-day miracle.

Despite the evidence otherwise, there were a few judgmental people who suggested I was being punished by God for doing wrong in some way. However, I know through personal examination, I was living the way God wanted me to. God does not punish with car wrecks. People who think this way do not really know God at all.

For me, praising and thanking God throughout this ordeal made it a rich experience. Without God, it would have been unbearable. Although God did not plan the wreck or cause it to happen, it was a tragedy God turned into good for my life and the lives of others I knew. "And we know that all things work together for good to them that love God, to them who are the called according to his purpose" (Rom. 8:28). From my perspective now, if I would have known what was ahead on November 11, 1997, by continuing on down the highway that fateful night, I am sure I would have proceeded anyway. God used me to bring glory to His name, and that means I was able to fulfill my ultimate purpose in life. This experience also made it very real to me that as I live, God is with me; when death comes for me, I will instantly be with God in heaven, forever, living in a mansion He has prepared just for me.

There were physical, spiritual, and emotional changes in my life because of the accident. The pain of damage that will never heal is one physical change for me. Especially at times when I do more than I am now capable of, I can expect to hurt like I never did before. A friend jokingly told me that I can blame my pain on the wreck instead of age as I get older. Another change for me is in how the thought of death affects me now. I know death will be a peaceful, wonderful experience, and even visiting graveyards does not bring the foreboding feeling it used to. Graveyards actually bring more comfort than fear and anxiety. It is interesting that through experiencing the accidental death of an eighteen-year-old young man when I was only four years old, the irrational fear of death was introduced into my life. And then, in 1997, the irresponsible act of another eighteen-year-old young man gave me total peace with death. In Hebrews 2:15, the Bible says, "deliver them who through fear of death were all their lifetime subject to bondage." Jesus conquered death, and Satan has no power over anyone's life as long as Jesus is their Savior.

Physical death is a fact of life, not to be feared—*if* you are a born-again Christian confident of your salvation and eternal destination of heaven. However, if you do not know the salvation that Jesus Christ offers on a personal level, then death should be what you fear the most in life. That is because hell will be the definite eternal destination for the unsaved. Satan is a liar. He wants to steal our joy and replace it with hopelessness and lies. He does not want unsaved people to grasp the truth of their eternal destination but wants as many as he can deceive to blindly follow him into hell. Your eternal destination is *your choice.* Life with God is an endless hope; life without God is a hopeless end. Luke 16:19-31 is a story of hell's torment.

My home is in heaven with my Father, and my Savior Jesus Christ. I will go back there someday when my purpose for God is finished here on earth. I pray you will join me at the greatest place ever to exist. The peace is indescribable, and I've read the view is beyond human comprehension. The company is also incomparable to anything you have experienced on earth—there is none better. Your ticket is already paid in full; all you have to do is accept it by putting your faith in Jesus to save your soul. If you are not a child of God, you too can be saved. Jesus died for you so He would not have to live without you. In the Bible, salvation is found for anyone with the faith to believe and not blinded by Satan's lies. Refer to Appendix A to accept Jesus now and experience the peace that only Jesus gives.

Remember that no one's sins are too great to keep them from experiencing the saving grace that Jesus Christ freely offers to *all.* Jesus Christ died for *all.*

If you have just welcomed Jesus into your life as your Savior, I encourage you to find a Bible-believing church where you will find fellow believers who will rejoice in your decision. A church of born-again Christians is the place to find acceptance, encouragement, friendship, and love found nowhere else on earth. I too would be privileged to know of your decision and pray for your growth in a strong relationship with God, your Father. Please e-mail me at the address found in this book or at deborah.leigh@live.com.

Chapter Forty-Six

The Peace that Comes from Knowing God

Our family had survived a life-changing ordeal, and each of us had been changed in some way by the car accident. But we all got through this challenging time intact, only because of our faith in God. Placing our trust in Him enabled us to continue on emotionally healed and functional. Our family continued to grow spiritually through this time and throughout the years ahead. God's peace and contentment prevailed in our lives.

Our children advanced and matured, and our business grew in a big way. I tolerated my parents' visits because it was what I was supposed to do. I knew being around them felt mostly abnormal, but I really had no idea what was at the source of it or how to start figuring it out. It was an intangible mystery. Denial and repression were so prevalent, I could not recognize a real problem existed that needed to be acknowledged. My parents still caused the occasional waves of turbulence, but the only way I knew to deal with it was endure. And rather than ponder much about it, I chose to focus on my family and my business. Besides, denial was how I had been programmed to cope when there was something really big that proved to be uncomfortable to face.

In our family, Doug and I continued to experience a very different side of life. God blesses greatly when your children grow in their own Christian life, becoming productive, successful, and accomplished adults. Our children all grew in their relationship with God, and God enabled them to succeed as caring individuals of high moral character, going on to accomplish great things. As a parent, the blessing of watching and being a part of this process and growth filled my life with peace, contentment, and happiness. That is because I know my children are who they are only from living God's way, raised in a Christian home. Each milestone in their life brings joy, not sadness, whether it be graduations, marriages, or moving to a place far from home. After experiencing the wreck and death, I am thankful to be alive and a part of all they do. Knowing my children are following God's perfect will is all I need to find happiness in the inevitable changes that come with life. God has blessed each of our children in a big way because they seek His will for their life.

Jason had graduated from high school only a few months before our car accident and then went on to college. Since age sixteen, Jason had dated Mandy, who was a support to our family during the wreck time. They would continue dating off and on for several years. Jason being a busy, focused young man, he possesses great motivation to continually accomplish more and work hard to live his dreams. He is also a young man of high moral and Christian character. Deep inside and on the surface, he is a person of great courage. He is caring, loving, and genuine—I see the true person he is when I look into his eyes. Through his hard work and dedication, Jason graduated magna cum laude from college with a bachelor's degree in animal biology and a minor in history. Soon after that, we all rejoiced when he was accepted to the University of Texas Health and Science Center at San Antonio (UTHSCSA), where he would study to become a dentist.

Soon afterward, Amanda graduated from high school. At this point, with Jason and Amanda we had lived through many proms, school plays, honor-society ceremonies, drill-team performances, band competitions and performances, dates, driver's licenses, car purchases, parking-lot fender-benders, insurance rates skyrocketing … the list goes on. Right before graduation was Amanda's senior high-school prom; her date was Daniel, a boy she had been dating for only a few weeks. Daniel would later tell us what it meant for him to date Amanda. He said she was a girl at school with an impeccable reputation. She was known as the Christian girl who did what was right. And if you were planning to do anything questionable, you did not want Amanda to be with you, because she would not approve and something would happen to mess up your plans.

Soon after the prom came graduation day for our daughter. Facing this time with Amanda was no different from the way it felt when Jason had graduated before. I remember thinking back to when they were small. I thought in those earlier years that there would be no way I could live through Jason's or Amanda's graduation and all it would mean emotionally to me—the thoughts and memories of childhood left behind when moving into a world of adult responsibility. Graduation Day meant they were grown and off on their own adventures. It is amazing, however, when you actually come to that day and even though it *could* be overpowered with sadness because of the inevitable change, it all feels so different from what you imagined. I was so proud of my children and their accomplishments, and I knew they had a bright future ahead of them. It was a time of celebration. The imagined thoughts from years earlier of sadness and emotional inability to cope with the milestone all faded away in the joy of the moment. Coping with the graduation they each had worked so hard to earn was no problem at all. I believe this example is why we are not aware of what our future holds. What may seem impossible today will most likely be completely different from what we imagine. Our feelings and perceptions change when we are prepared by the passing of time, but more importantly, it is easier if we are also changed by growth in God's wisdom. We get to a different place and enjoy the future moment we currently dread or fear because of positive growth and change that we allow. Only God needs to know what tomorrow holds, and since He knows that, I will trust Him to prepare me to be ready to face it. It also helped that I still had one child at home when Amanda graduated.

Amanda would also go on to accomplish much in her life after high-school graduation, and she continues to spread sunshine where ever she goes. Amanda helped me remember how to laugh. She brings joy into my life. She does not believe in taking life too seriously. I admire her for this. She reminds me of Grandma Ada in so many ways. Amanda is a young woman of high moral and Christian character and does not hesitate to share her faith. Amanda works hard too, but all with a lighter view of life—laugh throughout life and do not get too stressed out.

When Amanda graduated from high school, Jarrod was in middle school, and his independence was still work in progress. Doug and I had a definite plan in this area, and Jason and Amanda had proven that it worked well. We had learned it was best for our children to experience small steps to independence as they continued to grow and mature under our protection. As they would respond responsibly, wisely, and maturely, we gave them more freedom. And as the parents of two adult children, we knew the wisdom in letting your children go. We would give them our blessing with freedom to be the person God created them to be, adding no sense of guilt when they left home. We would give our love, support, and encouragement with no strings attached. Holding on too tightly and controlling when inappropriate brings strife into the relationship with your adult children. "A bird in a cage forgets to sing"; freedom is important to allow a person to become who God meant for them to be. We would also learn to give advice mainly when they asked for it and to be available when they needed us. Above all, we emphasized that while they were on their own now, they were still accountable to God now and always.

I also had much to learn from Jarrod as well. One of the important things I see with Jarrod is that he chooses to believe the best of people. He does not judge by outside appearance and learns to see beyond the outside to love the person inside. Jarrod is a very loving and supportive young man. He cares deeply, and he too possesses high moral values, Christian character, and faith that guides his life. He is a genuine friend. When Jarrod was only ten, he made a random comment to me that I will always remember. He said, "Reading makes your life easier." That was a simple piece of wisdom I have carried forward and quote often. Jarrod also is a talented musician, and watching him play his bass guitar and hearing his music permeating our home is a great privilege and blessing that I cherish. Jarrod went on to study music and develop his talent and skill as a professional musician.

Knowing my family remained in God's care and protection daily continued to be a heartfelt desire I had, which became even stronger after the car accident. I knew the world was full of evil that could bring harm, hurt, and destruction to life. I find comfort in praying to God that He would keep my family and me in a protective bubble as we traveled through life. This image I envisioned was of being surrounded by God's impenetrable protection, manifested in human terms as a clear bubble. While I am in the world, harm cannot reach me because of God's invisible bubble of protection. It is similar to a child with an immune deficiency who must live his life in a bubble, void of contact with contagions. But the bubble of protection that I pray for allows normal contact with the world around us. It just adds for me a real and tangible image of Godly protection, which is present with me and my family everywhere we go. I ask God often to provide His bubble of protection. It is something I have prayed for regularly for many years, probably since the time of the car accident. This was a time that I felt God's presence and protection most powerfully. During that time, I felt as though I was shielded inside an invisible layer of protection. And since then, I have desired to remain inside the bubble.

Amanda and Daniel's Wedding Day

Our next big milestone was when Amanda married Daniel in November 2005. This too was one of those events in the future I thought I would have trouble living through when it actually came around. When Amanda was that little "Boosie" girl, I thought about the future day she would marry and became overwhelmed with emotion. Of course, then I was not prepared to even comprehend participating in a wedding day for my daughter. But many years into the future, I was almost emotionally ready to join in the festivities of our daughter's wedding day. I liked Daniel from the beginning; he was always respectful to our family and of me and Doug. But most importantly, he obviously loved and cherished Amanda.

Planning my daughter's wedding was a wonderful, once-in-a-lifetime experience that I will always look back on and greatly treasure. There were times throughout the planning experience when I cried and when Amanda and I cried together. It was a huge emotionally connecting time for us. And crying beforehand was good because when the actual wedding day came, I was all cried out and filled with joy the entire day.

The church our family attended was small, so we rented a large church in order to accommodate the very big wedding we had planned. When we arrived at the church on the wedding day, it was beautifully decorated by Daniel's grandmother, who he calls Gram. Gram owned a florist shop and had made everything in this area of the wedding above-and-beyond special and beautiful. Since Daniel was a Lance Corporal in the United States Marine Corps, he had many Marine friends attend the wedding in full uniform and participate in the ceremony. When Amanda was ready and everyone and everything was in place, Jason and Jarrod both walked me to my seat. It was now time for the wedding to begin. It started with a PowerPoint presentation that Amanda and Jarrod compiled with pictures of Amanda and Daniel from birth to the present. Wow! That was an emotional experience for me. If I had not seen it several times before the wedding day, I could not have held back the tears.

Then came the moment for Doug to walk our beautiful daughter into the church and give her to Daniel. When they arrived at the altar where Daniel was waiting, Doug answered the standard question of "Who gives this woman to this man to be wed?" by saying, "Amanda's mother and I do." But before this exchange took place and Amanda went with Daniel, Doug had a speech of his own to deliver. When Amanda began her teenage years, Doug had bought her a necklace with a heart on it; the heart had a key accompanying it. At this time, Amanda made a pact with Doug and me that the necklace and key would be symbolic of purity, love, and watchful care. Throughout her dating years, Doug wore the key as a tie pin; it was a symbol that he kept watch over Amanda's heart. Amanda wore the necklace as a symbol that her dad's love protected her. It also was a promise to remain pure until her wedding day, when Doug would give the symbolic key to her husband. As Daniel waited to take Amanda from Doug and walk together to the altar, Doug took a moment to explain the meaning of the key he was passing on to Daniel and added our prayer for them both to "... unconditionally love each other from this day forward, renew their love daily, keep God in everything that they do, be obedient to God, and seek and stay in God's will." Then Daniel took Amanda to the altar, and Doug joined me in the church pew.

The ceremony was exquisite, with all going as planned. It was a very joyous time for all. The ceremony honored God and included prayer asking for His blessings on Amanda and Daniel's newly formed marriage union. When the newlywed couple exited the church together, they walked out the doors and down the porch stairs. The stairs were lined with Marines holding out their swords in an arch, which Amanda and Daniel walked under. Then, as is customary with a new Marine wife, the sergeant at the end of the line gave her a quick swat on the behind with his sword and welcomed her to the United States Marine Corps family.

The wedding party moved to the reception at the beautifully restored train depot a short drive from the church. It was an extravagant reception complete with a caterer, abundant food, wedding cake, punch, a DJ, and dancing—an event of great expense. Doug and I wanted it to be everything our daughter had dreamed of. And there was *no* alcohol. Since alcohol is damaging, it had no place at the beginning of a marriage destined to last a lifetime. For something unique, in addition to the catered food, McDonald's hamburgers and cheeseburgers were served. Our employees delivered them regularly to keep them hot and fresh throughout the reception. The guests really enjoyed this special touch. Everything went as planned—with one exception.

For the start of the reception formalities, there were a few designated tables for those who were participating to sit. One table was designated with our family name for Doug and me, our sons, and their dates. When Doug and I arrived at the reception, *our* table was occupied by my parents and some others they asked to sit with *them*. This left Doug and me with no place to retreat when others were speaking; it left us both feeling very awkward. For me, this was frustrating and brought flashbacks of grandma's funeral, when my mother did not care where I sat. Now again she did not care about the inconvenience she caused—not one person sitting at our table had the same name as the card designated. But for now, it was not appropriate to cause a scene over seating.

Again, my feelings stem from my dysfunctional parental relationship. I should have been comfortable and secure in telling my parents how things were set up regarding the seats. But I just defaulted to old ways of keeping silent, adding more unresolved feelings to deny. This entire incident would probably not even be remembered if my mother was not so controlling and had not treated me as so unimportant all my life. Needless to say, this is the *only* unwelcome memory I have from my daughter's fairy-tale wedding day. Luckily, the reception felt more comfortable after the formalities, when the dancing began. The reception continued on in a great celebratory fashion; it was a wonderful experience for family and friends, but mainly for Daniel and Amanda.

As things began winding down, I had made it without crying through every phase of the wedding, even the wedding ceremony. But when several guests had left and it was time to leave the reception, Amanda, Daniel, Jason, Jarrod, Doug, and I made a lifelong memory of an emotional family meeting in the ladies powder room. It was time for our family to move to another level and let our daughter and sister go off to begin a new life with her new husband. It was an emotional, tear-filled time of saying good-bye to a much-loved era we all cherished and saying hello to a new era to come. The words spoken many times were "I love you, and I will miss you," complete with an abundance of hugs and overwhelming love flooding the room. Then, after a lengthy period of time, when our daughter felt emotionally ready to face her guests, she dried her eyes and left with Daniel. They departed arm-in-arm, walking through the bubbles blown into the air by the waiting guests wishing them well. They entered Daniel's decorated pickup truck and drove away to begin their new life together as husband and wife.

Chapter Forty-Seven

Always Put Your Faith and Trust in God—Not Man

An incident Doug and I encountered with our preacher is included here because of its relevance as the emotional trigger. This is not intended in any way to put down or discredit a man of God. But it is necessary because of the role it played in bringing my childhood dysfunction to the surface. Without this encounter taking me back to a time and place I had long denied and buried, I would not have seen my need to face the truth of the childhood emotional abuse I endured. I have no intention of bringing hurt to our ex-preacher, who in times past was a true friend. But I want to point out that as born-again believers, saved by grace, we must focus our worship on our Savior and Lord, Jesus Christ. Jesus Christ and God the Father are why we attend church and serve, and focusing on that is necessary if or when a preacher lets you down so your faith will not be shaken. You can identify the problem as *human* and continue on in your faith in God, knowing He will never let you down. Although preachers, in a place of God-given authority in the church, must be respected because of their position, we must never place our faith in a preacher as we would in God. Keeping things in perspective, preachers are men, and men are only human. When a preacher becomes dictatorial and controlling in the name of God, it causes hurt and damage to relationships. With your faith and focus only on God, your Christian foundation is firm and does not change because of human circumstances with a preacher. You can continue on, knowing your personal relationship with God is intact no matter how inappropriately a human preacher may choose to behave. "Your faith should not stand in the wisdom of men, but in the power of God" (1 Cor. 2:5).

Sometimes life closes in, causing someone to behave in irrational and inappropriate ways. I have learned from a pivotal experience in my life that some preachers are no exception to this unwelcome behavior. Even though they are in a God-given position of responsibility in church leadership, they are still only human. Preachers, too, can get off track when they choose to ignore God's guidance.

Christmas Day 2005 was on a Sunday. We went to church, and afterward I performed my treasurer duties as I normally did. Before the preacher left for the day, he came back to the office to check on the finances. My husband stood in the hall but was still involved in the conversation, a circumstance that was not unusual. Also according to the norm, I explained to the preacher that the money for this day was not adequate to pay all the bills. I paid the ones I could and left two unpaid—two of the preacher's extra bills. This financial scenario too was not unusual. The preacher had no reaction to the situation and then left the church that Christmas Day. We had no indication that there was a problem of any kind.

The next Sunday was January 1, 2006. Our entire family attended church together. The preacher seemed to avoid talking to me this Sunday and did not check on the finances, but I did not think anything of it because he had done this before. During the sermon that morning, our oldest son noticed an odd statement by the preacher, which he mentioned to us later. It was in reference to how the preacher would do what he thought was necessary in running the church because he was the one accountable to God for the church and not the workers. Our son thought this statement was very out of place in the sermon and was odd coming from the pulpit with the tone used. But we still had no indication a week later that there was a problem or that the preacher's particular problem was with me and my husband. We later discovered the preacher did not want to stir things up with us this particular Sunday since all our children were with us at church. He also said later that he looked at our children and hoped it would not damage his relationship with them—"it" apparently meaning how he was about to treat their parents. I have wondered how "it" could *not* affect his relationship with our children, especially since all my husband and I had ever done was support, help, and pray for this preacher. His anger was irrational and continued to grow unchecked for another week. He was reacting on assumptions, and the direction he was heading in was dangerous since it had no basis in truth.

Throughout the first week of 2006, the preacher did not reconsider his stance but only stewed in his anger, self-inflicted fury, and boiling emotions for another week. Then he finally decided to blast Doug and me, letting his angry emotions fly. That Sunday began normally; we went through the entire service, and then I went to the office as usual to make the deposit and pay the bills. When I arrived at the office, I found the preacher was already there waiting for me. This was unusual, since he normally talked to the congregation after church. He was obviously extremely agitated and very angry. I asked him what was wrong, and he said he would prefer to talk about it whenever Doug got there. My husband was detained by a friend and did not show up right away. My youngest son was in the office with me for a time, and he felt the tension that was so thick, you could cut it with a knife. He became very uncomfortable and went to find his Dad to speed up his arrival. During the wait, which felt like an eternity, the preacher would only blow air like a mad bull with fire in his eyes. I was trying desperately to think what could possibly be wrong with him. I asked him if his son, who had been sick, was doing okay. He emphatically replied, "My son is doing *just* fine." I said nothing else until my husband finally arrived.

With Doug present, the preacher verbally tore into me, accusing me of treating him disrespectfully and rudely on Christmas day, two Sundays before. He also accused my husband of lurking in the hall and cooking up something against him, because he had been standing in the hall on that Christmas morning. We were both so shocked that it took us several minutes to grasp what he was saying to us. He also accused me of not caring about his needs and putting off his bills and paying the electric bills instead, which were not even due that day. I thought *yes, I know they were not due on Christmas Day. But if I had failed to mail it that day, it would have arrived late, resulting in a late fee.* I was simply doing my job responsibly; I was in no way trying to do anything against the preacher. His angry, explosive outburst was irrational, and there was absolutely no reason for him to act that way, much less treat me and my husband in this disrespectful way when we were doing jobs that made his life easier. However, he made it clear at this particular point in time that he did not appreciate the job I was doing as the church treasurer. But I did know, even in the midst of this heated encounter, that this was strictly his opinion, and there was nothing inadequate about the job I had performed for over ten years. If the preacher was not in such an angry state of emotional rage, he knew it too. His emotions were out of control and were the reason he was speaking and acting so irrationally. From my perspective, experiencing the preacher in such a fit of rage made me question whether I wanted to work under his direction at all. His angry outburst prompted my comment, "If you feel that way, then maybe I should resign."

He replied by saying, "I think that is best."

I told him, "Okay, if that is what you want; but you need to know that whatever consequences come because of this decision are your responsibility, and they rest on your head, not mine." I made it clear that I was doing a job God wanted me to do, and I was doing that job where God wanted me to be. This statement caused the preacher to pause and think.

During this confrontation, things got very emotional. I listened intently at first because I needed to hear what was causing the preacher to behave so irrationally. When it became clear that all of his rage, wrath, and anger were targeted at me personally, I became emotional. Being accused of something so untrue with the venom of the preacher's wrath made crying extremely hard to avoid. When I had to speak, tears came with the words. It was incomprehensible that he thought my husband and I were out to harm him. We had considered this preacher to be a good friend and ally; we never expected him to treat us so badly. We were terribly hurt and wounded by his irrational behavior and unfounded accusations. My husband's first reaction was anger, and that we needed to talk when the preacher could be calm and not so engulfed in anger. My husband said, "We need to leave. If you choose to be this way, I do not want any part of it." But the preacher continued to talk—probably realizing that he must get a handle on his reactions to continue with the conversation. There was a point at which I had to leave the room to calm down some and dry my eyes. The entire encounter was extremely emotionally charged.

The preacher's inappropriate behavior was verified when, during the confusion, his wife came into the office. She was crying and begging her husband to stop acting like this. At some point, he realized how upset his false accusations had made us and how obviously upset his wife was as well. He seemed to finally grasp that we really had no bad feelings toward him and never had, and that all his accusations were completely false. He then did admit to it, saying, "I let the devil get a hold of me, and I should not have behaved this way." We told him that we had known him for almost eleven years, and he should have known all the things he was imagining were false and unfounded.

After he finally let his temper cool down and the atmosphere got more comfortable and rational, he realized he had made a mistake with his accusations and assumptions. He was ready to let it go and let me continue on with my job as church treasurer. But after hearing all the feelings he had let fester for two weeks and hearing him verbalize all he had imagined about me and my husband, I was uncertain if I wanted to continue on with the job as church treasurer where he was the pastor. Furthermore, I was unsure if we should even continue to be members at this church. We had witnessed an entirely different side of this preacher, a man we had trusted for almost eleven years to spiritually guide our lives and family. This preacher really had let the "devil get a hold of him." He acted with hate and vengeance, and that should never be part of anyone's life when they truly allow God to lead and guide them. Everything about this unpleasant experience was disappointing and ugly. Also, one of the things that frustrated me the most about this episode was that my fourteen-year-old son had witnessed our preacher acting like a madman raging out of control. He witnessed our preacher behaving so childishly and hurtfully, giving no consideration to the harm he was inflicting on people who cared for him.

The reality of Christian life is that if this preacher had done what God commanded and followed Biblical advise, he would never have gotten so out of control. The devil would have never gotten his foot in the door of this preacher's life if he truly had been letting God lead him. The preacher's first mistake was not talking to my husband and me when he first became upset. He should have communicated his feelings at that time and settled the issue with us when it began. The second mistake was letting his anger grow for two weeks into something he could not manage. His unfounded perceptions caused his anger to develop into rage. The situation only became worse, with more potential to cause damage. It damaged his testimony, and he became a bad representative for God. He was destroying rather than building. By a preacher's words and actions, you can tell if he is letting God guide him or if he is going his own way. It seemed that this preacher was frustrated and angry because he was choosing to control more than God intended him to.

After much prayer and thought, twenty-three days after the incident with the preacher, my husband and I met him in his office to resign from our church positions and gather our belongings from the treasurer's office. At this point, the preacher still offered no apology for his behavior and just said he wished things could be different. We could no longer see him as a trustworthy shepherd leading the church by Jesus' example.

The preacher's behavior was full of wrath and rage, accompanied with a bitter attitude he allowed to eat away and erode any wisdom he may have possessed in regard to this matter. His behavior caused me to feel that I was in terrible trouble, but I had no idea why. This preacher, responsible to lead and teach God's way, had been angry for two weeks over something he only *perceived*; his assumptions were not true at all. And rather than face what irritated him when it happened and get over it then, he chose to harbor his anger and then release two weeks worth of pent-up rage on me for something he had only imagined. There is a reason the Bible warns in Ephesians 4:26—27, "Be ye angry and sin not: let not the sun go down upon your wrath: Neither give place to the devil." This preacher cannot possibly comprehend all the actual damage he is personally responsible for, damage that transpired as a direct result of his inappropriate actions and his choice to behave in a way incongruent with Biblical guidelines.

During the heated minutes of the preacher's unbridled rage released with fury on me and my husband, I was returned to the tumultuous days of childhood when my mother would pour out her wrath. I was seated at my desk in the church treasurer's office, and the preacher was standing over me and attacking with all his might, releasing all the anger he had accumulated over the previous two weeks. Even though the majority of his anger was directed at me, he also focused on my husband when he had trouble looking at me. Maybe that was due to how outraged he was, or maybe it was just because I am a woman. I had previously felt he had a problem communicating with me because of my gender.

Since the very nature of a preacher's job is dealing with people a majority of the time, this preacher should have been more adept in basic people skills. In management or any other profession that involves dealing with people, there is one common and constant rule: attack the *problem,* never the *person.* There are ways to communicate without tearing a person apart. The preacher, however, chose to disregard basic people skills, etiquette, and common decency, and administer an attack on me personally. He let his anger rule, and in the end he had to admit, by his own words, "I let the devil get a hold of me." I could not have summed it up better. To put it nicely, his unfounded assumptions had left him with egg on his face.

The preacher did let the devil get a hold of him because he was concerned about only himself and what he needed; it was a selfish display. He had been mad for two weeks, holding in the anger that stemmed from selfish thoughts. His concern was only for *his* financial situation. Therefore, since I was the church treasurer, he let all his unfounded anger discharge on me. He could not possibly have allowed himself to work through a rational thought process, because if he had, he would have easily known that I spent the money only as he directed and tried to pay the bills in a timely fashion. It also seemed he blamed my husband and me for not giving extra to cover the church deficit. We always gave more than the minimum tithe required by God and did not know why he would logically expect that our McDonald's restaurants should support the deficits in church funds.

In my opinion, this preacher was a man reacting irrationally to a burden he faced. He lashed out to attack the closest person he perceived to be involved in causing his pain. This was somewhat out of character for him. It seemed that during the later years of our membership at this church, the preacher was changing. Doug and I knew and worked with this preacher for many years, and he was not always so difficult to work with and hard to get along with. It seemed that somewhere along the way, he lost the spirit of compassion and caring and became someone fighting to survive. It has been suggested that his health may have caused the change. He dealt with cancer and survived. It seemed, though, that rather than being thankful and sweeter, he was more bitter and hard. Some have thought he might have a brain tumor because of the difference in personality. Most of the time, I had enjoyed helping the preacher because in every area other than finances, he was kind, caring, empathetic, and understanding. He did strive to do what was best for the congregation as a whole and for individual needs as they arose. He preached true to the Bible, and he became our friend. He baptized Jarrod, was Jason's friend, and had often prayed specially for Doug and me and our family. He performed the marriage ceremony for our daughter the day she married Daniel. Looking back, it might have worked out had we not been responsible for anything connected with church finances. This seemed to be the area where the preacher had problems coping—this definitely was the preacher Brother Buck Hatfield's warning applied to.

And now this preacher was experiencing financial burdens and was not the person I had known and worked with the previous ten-plus years. He was not the person who went on a two-hour trip out of town with our oldest son in the middle of the night when my husband and I had the car wreck. He was not the preacher who prayed and cared for our family over the years when burdens arose, or as our children grew up, or when they attended church camp. He was caving under financial pressure, and I, in the position of church treasurer, was the closest one he could blame for his money problems.

The irrational display of behavior, out of line for any preacher to exhibit, made it impossible for our family to continue as members in a church under his leadership. We could no longer in good conscience stay at a church led by this preacher—especially when it was proven to us that he preached one thing and lived another. It was very apparent that he was not living by the Bible he preached. We have other friends he has treated in unacceptable ways just because he wanted to control and did not tolerate any open thinking that opposed his self-imposed rules. We have witnessed other families leaving the church because of his dictator-like style in running God's church, complete with rage, anger, and an uncontrollable temper. These families also chose to leave without causing a scene. The Bible describes this situation from our perspective: "Many pastors have destroyed my vineyard, they have trodden my portion under foot, they have made my pleasant portion a desolate wilderness" (Jer. 12:10).

This preacher is great when things are going his way and people obey him. He gets ugly at the slightest hint of opposition—a real Dr. Jeckyl and Mr. Hyde situation. My husband and I have experienced both sides of his behavior. For the most part, the church members who continue to follow him have not experienced the extreme bad he is capable of.

I hold nothing against this preacher. People can change for the better, but only with God's help and intervention. For change to happen, though, the person has to be willing to acknowledge there is a problem and that they genuinely want to fix it. I pray he has the wisdom to see his need and a desire to do something about his inappropriate behavior as a church pastor. My husband and I pray for this preacher; we forgive his inappropriate actions and wish him no harm. My life has only gotten better since the unfortunate incident with him. For my husband and me, God also knew what was in our future, and that we would soon sell our McDonald's restaurants. In the overall picture of our life, it was best for us to move on from this church. God also knew that when we sold our restaurants, our tithe from that sale would be significant. We believe God wanted that tithe in hands that were more financially responsible.

This unfortunate event with our preacher was significant in surfacing my dysfunctional childhood past. This preacher's angry outburst in a direct attack on me revived those old childhood feelings from long ago that had been locked away and dormant for decades. This happened because his actions and behaviors were so similar to my mother's outbursts of anger and rage when I was a child. It took me back to the pain, helplessness, and feelings I had denied for so long. Today, I could look at the preacher's attack with bitterness, anger, and hate, or I could choose to view it as a growing experience that has made me better. I believe God wants me to see it as a stepping stone to a better life filled with more of His blessings. The preacher will have to answer to God for his behavior. However, even in the bad things—which God does *not* cause but sometimes allows—He is faithful to His word. God truly will turn all things around for good for His children. Just as God said in His word, "And we know that all things work together for good to them that love God, to them who are the called according to his purpose" (Romans 8:28). I can see the incident with the preacher as a catalyst to reveal the childhood hurt and trauma I had denied for too long. The healing process that followed, although uncomfortable, painful, and undesirable, has brought me to a better place because it has been all about facing the truth. It has also revealed and magnified the many ways God has watched over me since the beginning of my existence.

Since our ex-preacher had proven that he lacked control over his own life, we did not want him leading ours. We ended our membership at this church, which we had attended for almost fourteen years. My husband, youngest son, and I would soon after join another church more suitable in every way. This new church is led by a man who is spirit-filled and God led. He is gifted with speaking skills and runs the church with wisdom. The wisdom he possesses is gained only by walking daily in a close relationship with God. However, even with the tremendous blessing of such a wonderful preacher, the best advice ever is to always *trust God* first and foremost. God will never disappoint you. "Always remember that man is not capable of doing what only God is able to do."

Chapter Forty-Eight

The Trigger Revives Old Emotional Trauma

The unresolved traumas of my childhood were locked away, awaiting the day when the precise emotional episode would bring them to the surface. It was like a dormant volcano just waiting for the necessary conditions to erupt. I was unaware that the emotional residue of my dysfunctional childhood past was just sitting there, percolating in my subconscious, waiting for the right opportunity to be revived. I felt in control enough to believe that it was all dead-bolted away, and I had left it in the past where it belonged. It is hard to face the past of a dysfunctional childhood filled with shame and neediness due to being raised by childish, emotionally disconnected parents. However, it was clearly God's plan to confront the past because locking away unpleasant things is not facing the truth. A relevant Bible quote from Psalm 33:4 says, "...For the word of the Lord is right; and all his works are done in truth." God is truth, and He knew it was best for me to face the hurt of the past in order to experience His complete healing. Up to this point, I believe God had protected me from the past until His perfect time came to put it in the proper perspective. I could find healing from the hurts and then live on without the ugly pain of it all for good. It also would provide the perfect opportunity to glorify God for all He had been and is in my life. He sheltered me from the badness my hurtful experiences could have led to.

The trigger event happened when a preacher acting in great anger and wrath verbally attacked me. I had not experienced these old familiar feelings from emotional abuse and trauma since I was a child at my mother's mercy. Although I did not immediately realize the true affects this confrontation had on me, it became apparent during the months of counseling that this had been the trigger event responsible for reviving bad feelings from my childhood that I had denied for so many years. This one trigger event was all it took to bring the past hurts to the surface—all of them at once. It was a lot to face and would require wise counsel to embark on such a God-led journey of healing. Seeking counsel, however, was something I fought at the time, but only because I did not understand that it was best for me and my family.

The preacher's irrational behavior opened doors I never intended to open again and unburied emotions I thought were better left buried. It was a catalyst to reveal things I needed to face in order to truly become the whole person God intended me to be. I discovered the truth of my emotional circumstance, and with God's help, I have been led to a better place today. For many months afterward, I could not see that the incident with the preacher was the perfect emotional episode necessary to revive my dormant childhood trauma. While I was experiencing the preacher's anger, old feelings of childhood helplessness surfaced. I had not been in a position since childhood of such vulnerability due to another's anger and rage while being confined in a small room from which escape was hindered. The preacher raged, and it was a direct personal attack on me. No one had treated me in this emotionally abusive way except my mother decades before. The old painful childhood feelings were creeping out of the closets of my mind. At age forty-six, a time in my life when I had two grown children and another rapidly reaching adulthood, these long-forgotten childhood memories of emotional abuse came rushing back forcing me to deal with the past rather than keeping it under lock and key any longer.

After the subconscious locks were removed, releasing the old harmful memories, visits with my parents became torturous to endure because their presence was a living symbol of the damaging past. Things they would say and do continually brought back toxic memories of my childhood to feel and relive the pain of again. These unpleasant visits happened routinely from January 2006 through May 2007. In May 2007, my oldest son graduated from dental school. This was the last so-called "normal" visit I had with my parents, or at least that is how the family perceived it. For me, most visits before that had felt very abnormal. After the graduation, I knew I could no longer put myself through the torture of pretending everything was normal. I eventually avoided visits with them completely, as each visit would bring out a deluge of unpleasant buried memories flooding forth. It came to a point where I did not want to feel the past of hurt and denial they had always represented to me anymore.

Because of the way my childhood was, a real relationship between me and either of my parents never developed. Any relationship between my mother and me is symbolic of an old dilapidated house, barely standing. One good windstorm could cause the house to fall. The trigger event with the preacher became that one good windstorm that blew through, causing the house to fall, revealing all of the problems, hurts, and traumas that truly existed. As far as a relationship with Dad, the house was never built. Any relationship between me and my parents would be described as dysfunctional because it was comprised more of hurt, trauma, and rejection than any warm, fuzzy childhood feel-good memories.

Part VI

Life After the Trigger

Chapter Forty-Nine

Many Normal Life Changes

The emotional encounter with the preacher in January 2006 revived my entire hurtful past. Then soon after, I began dealing with a flood of childhood memories randomly surfacing from closets of denial in my subconscious. Because of the incident with the preacher, we no longer had a permanent church home, and that created a huge gap in our lives in general. This situation, along with many other circumstances, caused 2006 to become a year of great changes and challenges for our family. And throughout all this change, I experienced hurt and intense pain from every visit with my parents. Also, as it would happen, their visits increased in frequency during these months of transformation.

Daniel's Deployment

Orders to Iraq came for Daniel, which brought additional emotional distress to our family life. Prior to deployment, Amanda had to read and sign military papers giving her power of attorney over their affairs. This included discussing the possibility of Daniel not coming home alive. This was a big load for a twenty-year-old, newly married bride to deal with. It was an extremely emotional and taxing situation that one can only face confidently by placing her faith and trust in God. After deployment preparation, the day quickly came when Amanda had to say good-bye to her newlywed husband, walking away and leaving him on a military plane destined for the battlefield of Iraq. It took great courage for Daniel to leave, and it also took great courage for our daughter to continue on that day and in the months ahead. Amanda and Daniel had been married less than three full months when they had to experience a mandatory separation for seven months. It was inescapable, because the USMC required Daniel's presence on the other side of the world. He left the day before Valentine's Day.

During their military enforced separation, Daniel and Amanda were able to talk on the phone often, and they also wrote letters. But there were many times when communication was blocked on base shutdowns where Daniel was stationed, due to security reasons. There was one time in particular when Amanda dreamed that Daniel had died in battle, and she understandably was having a hard time functioning until she was able to hear his voice again. This dream happened to come at a time when Daniel was unable to communicate. Amanda shared her feelings with me during this time and could only text by cell phone because speaking her feelings through words was not possible because of the flood of emotion involved. I tried to comfort my daughter; needless to say, this became a hard emotional time for me as well. I just wanted Amanda to feel secure and not hurt in her present circumstances. Doug and I were there to support our daughter however we could. We made ourselves available for whatever she needed.

During Daniel's deployment, Amanda was pursuing her bachelor's degree. She was a full-time student enrolled in very difficult core-requirement science classes. Also during this time, she had been attending a very supportive and caring church in the same town as the university she attended. She and Daniel worshiped there often before he was deployed. Since we had no church home, Doug, Jarrod, and I attended church with Amanda. Attending services together and praying for Daniel's safety with church friends was an enormous comfort for Amanda and for us during this time of great challenge and sacrifice.

Selling Our McDonald's Restaurants

In March of 2006, Doug and I decided, with God's direction, that it was time to sell our McDonald's restaurants. The McDonald's Corporation was pressuring us to either remodel or rebuild our existing main restaurant. That meant basically signing up for another ten years of McDonald's life in order to once again get to the point of break-even and start realizing a return on our investment. After over twenty-five years of McDonald's life to date, we very prayerfully decided it was best for us and our family that we sell our restaurants and do something different with our lives. It was a perfect time to sell since our restaurants were paid off, and we were free of debt. Our sales were at an all-time high; we had increased our total sales over 2.5 times above our beginning figures during the fifteen years we operated the restaurants, even with the Walmart location being more of a drain on our business than an asset. The McDonald's corporate focus had changed drastically since the year 2000. They were more interested in stock-market earnings per share than the daily trials of the local owner/operators. In my opinion, the new corporate direction cost them their emotional connection with customers, leading to a loss of their hometown charm. New corporate leaders and a new corporate direction were very unlike many of the original McDonald's roots founded by Ray Croc. With all that considered, but mainly with God's direction, Doug and I made an appointment with our corporate office and discussed selling our restaurants.

It can take months or even years to find a qualified buyer with enough funds and a background to achieve corporate approval. But we knew for sure this was the direction God was leading us when a fellow owner/operator we had worked with for years wanted to purchase our restaurants. He talked with the appropriate people and voiced his desire; the selling process happened relatively quickly after we agreed with him on a selling price. Our family business was turned over to a new owner on June 30, 2006.

My parents were visiting when we sold our restaurants. Our McDonald's corporate contact at the time was a man I had worked with for about two years. We built a good business relationship and for the most part enjoyed working together. When we parted that day, he gave me a hug and voiced his feelings about how he would miss working with me, which included many kind words. Dad observed this interaction. Later, Dad said to me, "Man he sure seems to like you." Dad's words sounded like he could not believe anyone would enjoy knowing me and working with me. Dad's tone of surprise caused me to feel devalued, again. But Dad would not have been surprised if he really knew me.

Jason and Mandy's Wedding

At the time we sold our restaurants, we were in the middle of planning Jason's wedding. Our friend and the new owner of our restaurants agreed to let us have enough hamburgers and cheeseburgers to serve at Jason and Mandy's wedding reception just as we had done at Amanda and Daniel's wedding. Doug and I were also very involved with the wedding plans for Jason and Mandy. We helped out with many aspects, including our part as the groom's parents of hosting the traditional rehearsal dinner.

I spent time with Jason and talked with him often before his wedding day. He said he had one request for me, which was not to cry at his wedding either. He asked me to be just as I was for Amanda's wedding. I told him of the pre-wedding time I had spent with Amanda and how it prepared me to get through the day. I confided in him that I cried with Amanda a lot before her wedding, getting me ready for the wedding day when it came. If he did not want me to cry at his wedding, we would have to prepare and cry together before that special day came around. He agreed, and the time we spent together before his wedding day talking and planning and crying (mostly me) was more than wonderful and special. Jason was very understanding and showed great empathy for my feelings. He is a caring, loving gentleman—just like his dad! Back when Jason was small, I thought forward to how his wedding day might feel. I knew this time would take place one day in the future, and back then my feelings of reaching Jason's wedding day were wrapped up in questioning how I would ever cope with the actual event. It was a future event I needed many years to prepare for, and just like Amanda's wedding day, I made it through Jason's tearless.

Jason and Mandy's wedding was a beautiful, big wedding in a large local church. Jason's preacher from San Antonio came up to perform the ceremony. Mandy planned a gorgeous reception and dance that followed the ceremony at the same renovated train depot we had rented for Amanda's reception. Jason made a point to put specific name cards at each chair to avoid someone else occupying the place Doug and I were supposed to sit. He did not want that same problem again. This event too was catered with abundant food. Mandy's cake was beautiful, and appropriately, the groom's cake was in the shape of a tooth as a symbol of Jason's profession. The event seemed perfect; Doug and I feel that we helped to make Mandy's wedding everything she had always dreamed of.

At this point in my life now, with two married children, I was very thankful for Daniel and Mandy joining our family. Mandy had spent a lot of time with our family throughout the ten years she and Jason dated. When she was only sixteen, we took her with us on a family vacation to Corpus Christi, a place she was very familiar with. Mandy showed us things we would not otherwise have found without her expertise. It was a joy to hear the excitement in her voice as she told us of her family's outings and adventures in this part of Texas. There was something about Mandy that I liked from the beginning. It also was clear, through the trials of dating, that Jason loved Mandy above all the other girls he dated—even before he would admit it to himself.

Our family wished Daniel could have been with us to share the joy of Jason and Mandy's wedding too. Being a newlywed at the wedding without Daniel present was very hard for Amanda. She naturally missed him during every wedding detail she experienced. Serving in the military creates heartache when there are life-changing and once-in-a-lifetime events you must be absent for because duty calls.

Daniel's Homecoming

But in September of 2006, it was a joyous and long anticipated occasion when Daniel returned home from Iraq. Doug and I were privileged to be present in Yuma, Arizona, for the well-publicized welcome-home reception for the returning Marines. We woke up that morning to the radio announcement declaring a group of military servicemen would be returning home that day from Iraq. It felt good to know that announcement referred to Daniel's return. On the Marine base, the airplane hangar was filled to capacity with anxiously waiting family and friends who had not seen their loved ones for many months. The plane was delayed several hours, which increased the tension. Among all the patriotic decorations and the multiple American flags positioned throughout the building, there were babies crying and mother's pacing. Our daughter, waiting to be reunited with her husband, was overcome with anticipation for the moment when she would be blessed with that first glimpse of her Marine, her love, her husband. Then, after what felt like hours of endless waiting, the plane finally landed.

There were more minutes of waiting as the plane unloaded. Daniel was a designated flag-bearer for his platoon. Amanda spotted him immediately and could hardly hold back the urge to run to him. Then, after the military formalities, she was free to run to her husband for that long-awaited kiss and hug as she leapt into his arms. Daniel being the strong, physically fit Marine, held his flag and Amanda firmly as they were at last able to embrace. The joy all around from all the families who had sacrificed and missed their loved one in longing anticipation for this day were finally satisfied with the presence of their returning Marine. It was a very emotional experience; there were buckets of joyful tears cried this day at the Marine Corps Air Station in Yuma, Arizona, when this group of Marines returned to their homeland to a waiting crowd of Americans grateful and thankful for their sacrifice and safe return home. And Amanda's heart-wrenching time without Daniel present in her life was now over; he was home again! There were television crews present to tape the event and televise the reunion of family and Marines later that night. Daniel and Amanda's friends said they saw Doug and me in the crowd on the TV news broadcast that night in Yuma.

This deployment to Iraq was just one of many bonding experiences Doug and I shared with Daniel. It was clear Daniel was truly and deeply in love with our daughter. We are thankful that he is our daughter's husband and a member of our family. I also continually became aware of his rural country roots. In talking with him and getting to know him, our shared connection with country life was obvious. For me, it was like going back in time to the farm and remembering the old way of life that meant so much to me. It rekindled feelings of the way things were when I lived with Grandma Ada. Being around Daniel's grandparents also felt like I was with people so familiar to me; they felt like people I knew as a child on the farm. I loved exploring this realm of my life and remembering the part of my childhood that felt so good—an era I had left in the past. It was as if Daniel had brought to me a wonderful revival of a part of life I had buried with the pain of the hurtful years.

When Daniel was in the USMC boot camp in California, I sent him a CD by Craig Morgan that included the song "Almost Home." It represented a country connection we shared then that still continues to grow. Daniel had brought to me an awareness of the country life that I had loved so much and left behind. As Doug's wife, I also experienced the definite city side of life through all the things I encountered in life with him and, later on, with our McDonald's business. I therefore have concluded, with Daniel's input, that a well-rounded person is comfortable in living both the country side of life and the city side. There are abundant joys found in each way of life to embrace and celebrate.

Realizing the Need to Face the Dysfunctional Past

Reconnecting with the country part of my past was a real blessing. And I was doing just fine coping with all the changes our family was undergoing. But then, after the trigger event with the preacher, each visit from my parents caused an increase in intense emotional feelings that I did not understand, know how to fix, or believe I could avoid. There was a "should be" in place from childhood programming, and I felt obligated to spend time with my parents. It was expected, no matter how I felt or how it was damaging my emotional well-being. So I did my best to continue on as before, in spite of the childhood feelings, hurts, and old wounds I now experienced as raw and resurfaced.

Something positive about this time was when Doug and I traveled to San Antonio and Jason practiced his newly acquired dental skills on a few of our dental needs. This was a special and wonderful time, to be our son's patient and a part of his new profession in action. Doug and I both were patients for some of Jason's major tests, which he passed with very high grades. I also now have beautiful gold crowns on two molars that are the handiwork of my proficient son, the dentist. Jason also got little brother Jarrod in his chair a couple of times. It was a time when our family looked forward to going to the dentist!

Jason said it seemed that the turmoil in my life appeared after we sold our McDonald's restaurants, because without McDonald's keeping me busy, I had more time to think. This is a viable assessment. However, I know that God wanted me free of McDonald's. It was His perfect will to accomplish my life's purpose. After the trigger event, my ability to perform at McDonald's as before was compromised, since dealing with the past interfered with my work. Being free of McDonald's and work responsibilities enabled me to deal with the past, face the truth, and find healing and freedom—freedom from a childhood that for too many years had imprisoned the person God made me to be. I found a renewed purpose in life and was guided there through God's gentle leadership.

Ironically, my first step in facing the past was probably rooted more in denial than in facing reality. At first I tried to ignore the nagging feelings that came with a resurfaced past, a past that was raw in emotional pain. I tried to do as I had always done—ignore, bury, and deny the things that were too painful to face. But after the trigger event, this did not work at all. Then I decided to do what I thought was expected of me, and that was to spend time with my parents. So I tried to face the past head-on and planned a trip with my parents. I thought that maybe spending time with them would make all the feelings of pain and upheaval go away for good. It seemed like the perfect time, since I had no business obligations. I had free time on my hands. Why shouldn't I spend more time with my parents? Maybe then everything I was feeling would just dissolve away. So in the summer of 2006, shortly after we sold our McDonald's restaurants, Doug and I took a trip with my parents to a country inn located on the Paluxy River in Glen Rose, Texas. The river was beautiful as it flowed past the huge, centuries-old oak trees that stood in the abundant green grass on the hill serving as the river's banks. We sat in white Adirondack chairs, talking as Dad waited to see the turtles and fish when they visited the surface of the river. It was a nice peaceful environment conducive to good conversation.

Overall, this trip was pleasant, with no notable encounters. It was, however, very difficult to relate to my parents, something I tried to understand but would not grasp until some time later. This trip served to reveal that the pain my parents represented in my life could not be resolved in casual and cordial visits. I felt no different after this trip to a peaceful retreat. I realized that, with the unpleasant memories of childhood in the forefront again, spending time with my parents was even more unsettling and continued to damage.

After our excursion, many things in Jason's life also led to my parents visiting more often. The Inn on the River trip was right before Jason married Mandy, which would be a reason for them to visit more. Also, Jason needed patients to practice his dental skills on. Dad needed dental work and was happy to let Jason practice on his teeth. These dental visits for Dad were also a reason for more visits. Even though I do not remember any single, huge emotional problem that happened during this time, there were plenty of unpleasant things I felt. My parents' presence brought back hurts I had not experienced for decades. The trigger event had made all those old feelings raw and new, and my parents' behavior had not changed much from the years of my childhood. They still interacted in the same old dysfunctional ways, things I guess I had just overlooked and ignored since I had moved on and buried the past. But now, the things they said or things they did, how they interacted with each other, or things they said to me personally all hurt so intensely, which in turn revived things I did not want to feel again. It was clear that just being around them, after the past had been triggered to the surface, was hurtful and sent me to a place I did not want to be. It became apparent that what my parents really represented to me was pain and damage. There were no warm, happy memories to draw from creating a connection between us. I had arrived at a place in my life where I must face the truth and find healing from the hurtful, damaging childhood legacy my parents had passed on to me. But it would still take some time for me to figure out how to begin repairing the damage.

The next big family event was Jason's graduation from dental school. He would be graduating as a doctor of dental surgery (D.D.S.). I told him in jest, "You did not have to study so hard to become a DDS. You have always been that—with DDS meaning *Doug* and *Debbie's Son*." Jason accommodated me with a small laugh. He knew that I was so proud of him and of the fact that this time DDS meant certified and competent doctor of dental surgery. The date was May 20, 2007, a day Jason had worked extremely hard for. He experienced a day of great celebration with family and friends present. It was a very proud moment for Doug and I as his parents to witness Jason's graduation and see him hooded as a doctor and presented with his doctor of dental surgery diploma. I could not help but momentarily think back to that New Year's 1979 weekend and remember when the hope of his birth was only an unknown. But now God was revealing a part of the great extent of those blessings He had in store for us. The years of blessings as Jason's parents, plus now the parents of Jason as a DDS, all began on that snowy trip Doug and I took twenty-eight years before.

But now, sadly, I was feeling great emotional turmoil. The day would have been perfect without the uncomfortable feelings brought on by the presence of my parents. There were plenty of uncomfortable moments I experienced during this day, a day that should have been totally joyous. I was frustrated by the clinging feeling I got from my mother. It felt like she was trying to consume me and take over my space. For too many times, beginning in Jason's early years, my parents seemed to feel and act as though Jason was their son instead of mine. They both have a dysfunctional attachment to my first son that brings me an uncomfortable feeling. And along with the past dysfunction, revived from the trigger event, this increased my distress this day. My parents' presence intensified the old hurts and the damaged emotions as they poured out, reaching the surface of my feelings. The newly surfaced pain continued to grow in intensity with them around—the denial was gone, and the pain it served to cover up for years had returned. I got through my son's special day by focusing on him. I consciously stomped down and choked out the way I was really feeling so that there would be no chance of ruining the moment he had worked so hard to achieve. Jason's dental graduation would be the last time I would see my parents at all until my mother insisted on a visit in October of 2008.

Jason joined the United States Navy in the summer of 2006. He now had graduated from dental school, and it was time for him to begin naval service as an officer. He always has been my pride and joy, and now on top of that he was "an officer and a gentleman" as a lieutenant in the US Navy. The first step was to attend OIS (Officer Indoctrination School) in Rhode Island. Then he would be deployed to Okinawa, Japan, where he would begin an "advanced education in general dentistry" residency. This was another deployment that would bring great sacrifice to our family. I have thought that maybe having Amanda and Daniel's and Jason and Mandy's wedding reception at a renovated train depot may have served as a symbol leading to all the traveling in their futures. But it was just a passing thought, probably no real connection. Nevertheless, in July 2007, Jason headed to Okinawa, Japan, to serve overseas in the US Navy.

Chapter Fifty

Ending the Denial and Facing the Past

Sometime during the autumn of 2007, sensing the presence of a problem that I needed to deal with, I began to write about the past, one situation at a time. I realized quickly that there were many painful experiences I had to work through. My writing began when I heard a sermon by Dr. Charles Stanley on the subject of rejection. This sermon became the catalyst revealing to me the real problem in my life that had always brought pain. I knew I needed to find healing for the emotional abuse I had experienced. Around this time, I read a book by Jennifer Rothschild entitled, *Self Talk, Soul Talk,* which also led to recognizing my need to fix a problematic past. The damaging self-talk became magnified after the trigger event and was destroying my self-worth. This was the result of years of negative parental programming and an inability to trust my capabilities. God used a famous preacher and a Christian author to show me how I needed change and restoration. This was the time in my life when I began to write profusely. The things I wrote were not always book-worthy, but they served the great purpose of getting the pain out and dealing with what was damaging my life. The more I wrote about things I did remember, the more previously buried memories also abundantly surfaced. I cried rivers of tears when I wrote as the pain was released. This process made me aware of even more things I desperately needed to heal from. The tears flooded as the memories of the pain of a damaging childhood past returned from the cloak of denial. Then continuing to repress the past was no longer possible, as years of denied hurts were coming forth in torrents.

Because of the raw pain the healing process brought, I avoided seeing my parents for months. The thought of being around them brought great emotional stress. And no one in my family pressed me to see them. But because of their attachment to my first-born son, I knew it would be difficult to exclude them when he came home for Christmas. It always felt they thought it was their right to be included in my family despite the emotional abuse they were responsible for throughout my life. Just because that hurtful past was revived for me and I did not want to see them, would be no reason for them to stay away. After all, Jason was the one they desired a relationship with, and he was returning home from Okinawa, Japan. I knew they would expect to join our family celebration. My feelings, which I shared with Jason, were difficult for him to understand. He knew little about my dysfunctional childhood past that was now resurfacing. I did not fully comprehend what was really happening either at this time. Even though Jason did not understand my stance, he offered a solution by agreeing to meet my parents in another town. I could stay home and not be involved. That compromise made me feel better, except for Jason's comment that "Grandma and Grandpa would have gladly come to our home if you would let them, and I would not have to drive out of town." This made me feel bad, but I could not give in and let them visit. For once in my life, avoiding the inevitable pain was more necessary for me than giving in. I also knew that the grandparents Jason knew were different people than the parents I knew. And I did understand why he had trouble with my new protective boundaries.

During this time, I had trouble emotionally functioning and rationalizing. I felt bad because of what this seemed to be doing to my relationship with my oldest son. I felt bad that I could not completely celebrate his holiday homecoming, since he had come so far to be home. I also was frustrated because I knew the feelings I experienced were because of my childhood past and a dysfunctional pair of parents who for many years had wanted a relationship with my oldest son but not me. And that damaging past took on a living, breathing pain with my parents' presence. The past had surfaced, and feeling all the hurt my parents' presence represented to me was more than I could face at this time.

I had trouble coping emotionally with normal routine events. The morning came to celebrate Christmas together—Jason, Mandy, Amanda, Daniel, Jarrod, Doug, and me. I felt so emotionally drained, unworthy, hopeless, depressed, and lost that I could not join our children for Christmas. I truly did not understand what was happening or why I felt this way. I really felt like giving up and not continuing on. I even asked God if I could just come home now and feel His presence like I did back when I was in the car wreck. I never had anything resembling a suicidal thought, but I just longed for a period of time that brought emotional relief. It felt as if I was losing my oldest son because of my parents. I wanted nothing to do with my parents and the pain they represented to me. All the repressed childhood feelings and pain that I had denied and buried for too many years was now demanding that I recognize and face it to find truth, healing, and peace. And I felt as if everything would be okay if I could only help Jason understand what I was feeling and if I knew for sure he would not expect me to see my parents.

I needed support and understanding from Jason, but it felt like he was more into pulling away. All this upheaval was confusing for him. Considering his history with his grandparents, it really could not have been any other way. Therefore, due to my dysfunctional childhood surfacing, our comfortable family life had suddenly become very uncomfortable. These changes in my emotional state had caused my children to feel my problem too—a problem that had always been there but they knew very little of. To put it in their own words, it felt like they were walking on eggshells to be around me during this time. They were unsure of what to say or how to say it. I too was wary of communicating with my children because I did not know for sure what they were thinking and feeling about this situation.

When these old hurtful memories began to take a prominent place in my life again, I became less sure of myself, less confident; the old tapes of self-destruction and magnified rejection began to loudly play once again on a regular basis. I felt as if for this period of time, I had gone back to the very early childhood years of feeling worthless, intensely rejected, and without a place to belong. The strong, confident mother my children knew me to be all their life had gone away, and this weak person had replaced her. This happened when the trigger event returned the denied and buried emotional trauma and a multitude of hurtful memories sprang to life. Just as physical injuries require a healing period, so do emotional injuries. And I would learn that this would all get worse before it got better.

Needless to say, our Christmas celebration did not happen as planned. Doug had to explain my absence to our children. After the explanation, Mandy went to her parents' house to pack for a trip they had planned later that day. Jason, Amanda, Jarrod, and Daniel came to my bedroom to talk to me. We talked about what I was experiencing and how it was affecting our normal family existence. Doug stayed away and prayed. I shared with them many of the painful experiences from my childhood past that were now causing great emotional stress. I got only love, support, and tears from my children, including Daniel. I was reassured; it helped tremendously to know my children understood, cared, and wanted to help however they could. This opened the door to talk about the subject and deal with it in truth. Also, I mentioned to Jason a visit his dad had with our doctor earlier that month. I told him I had an option to take antidepressant drugs, and Jason's response was that I should do whatever it took to make me better. He just wanted me well again. I had a real problem with the thought of taking that kind of drug, but it helped to know that Jason just wanted me as I was before, whatever the method. Talking to my children became a first pivotal step in the healing journey I was destined to begin in the coming New Year of 2008.

After my children and I talked for what felt like hours, they had to leave for the New Year's excursion Jason and Mandy had planned for them. This left me and Doug alone, with no children, for the first New Year's Eve since before Jason was born. It became representative of the healing journey ahead for us in the New Year of 2008. It would be a healing road that Doug and I would travel together. Doug was my number-one advocate and support for the journey back through the childhood pain, always listening, caring, protecting, and helping however he could. He never let me down.

This journey was necessary and was God's will for my life. God is a God of truth, and when you live in denial, you deny the truth. Although my life was functional in every way except in the relationship I experienced with both my parents, the bad part was now messing up the good part because of the presence of falsehood and denial. Where my relationship with my parents was concerned, I was not living in truth. Therefore, facing the hurtful past became necessary so I could live every aspect of my life in truth and live a life pleasing to God.

Chapter Fifty-One

Seeking Professional Help

After the holidays, it was apparent to Doug that something needed to happen for our family to return to the way it was before. At some point in early December 2007, Doug had visited with our family physician regarding the things I was experiencing. It was an action Doug took completely out of concern for my welfare. Our doctor told Doug that he could help me feel better within weeks by prescribing some medication. However, he also told Doug that he could do nothing until I had come to the point where I chose to seek help for the emotional upheaval.

I was still in the "deny the problem" mode of thinking. I thought, *Why get someone else involved? I will handle this problem by myself!* I caused Doug to feel bad for asking for the help, which I really needed. Although Doug felt bad that he had visited with our doctor about me without my knowledge, it did not change his stance that I should go talk to our doctor and get help with what I was experiencing. I fought somewhat, but I did not fight too hard because I knew I needed some relief for what I was feeling. I trusted our doctor too; he is a caring, understanding, empathetic, and committed Christian physician. I knew he would help or know what I should do next. So the question became, when would I be ready to go get help?

In mid-January 2008, I came down with a very sore throat that required medical attention. Doug went with me to the doctor. I asked Doug if he was going to bring up the emotional situation with our doctor. He said, "No, if it gets brought up, you will have to be the one to do it." So I went with the thought of getting medication for my throat and asking a few casual questions about my emotional condition.

I began by asking our doctor about the medication he told Doug about and how that could help. He explained it would balance chemicals in the brain to help achieve an emotional balance and gain a better outlook on life. We then talked about some specific problems I was experiencing with regard to my childhood wounds. Then, looking into his sympathetic and caring eyes, I could not hold back the tears and proceeded to divulge many specific instances that hurt deeply. He and Doug both held me as I cried and let go many of the things I had held in for years. This became the longest doctor's visit I ever had, but it also became the most healing overall.

When the emotions calmed down, our doctor's comment was, "Something has happened to cause all this to surface at once." He also said, "Short of a miracle from God, you will not be able to work through all this on your own without some professional counseling." Before Doug and I left, our doctor gave me the name of a Christian counselor he believed could help, along with some samples of and a prescription for an antidepressant drug. I discussed my concerns about taking the medication and decided I would not take any drug that would alter my perception of completely feeling what I was about to experience. I did not want anything fake about my reality at this critical time. My doctor said, "That's fine; just take the samples in case you get into the process and change your mind." He also warned me, "This will all get worse before it gets better." And truer words were never spoken.

This doctor's visit had brought me to another pivotal point in my healing process. My husband and my doctor both helped me get to the very important step I had been avoiding, which was seeking help from a Christian counselor. I am thankful to God for blessing me with such a caring doctor and friend, and I will always remember with gratitude this day when our Christian family physician helped me see my need to face my dysfunctional childhood past.

On January 22, 2008, I had my first visit with Athena H. Bean, M.Ed., LPC, a professional Christian counselor. Doug went along for support.

Chapter Fifty-Two

Working Through the Dysfunctional Childhood

The way of a fool is right in his own eyes: but he that hearkeneth unto counsel is wise.—Proverbs 12:15

There were many pieces of history from my past that I began putting together. Understanding this history revealed the truth and made clear the real picture of my life up to now. I found pieces that fit together perfectly. And then there were other pieces I had to search for and work on in order to grasp their purpose, significance, and place. Talking with Athena felt comfortable, and I began to open up like I never had before and talk about things I never even wanted to acknowledge much less say out loud. It was a safe place to find answers, help, and direction. It was a place I finally felt free to gain an understanding of all I had experienced that did not feel right and normal. The nagging and turmoil turned into peace as insight into my situation increased.

One of the things I needed to understand was why my life felt so normal in every aspect except where my parents were concerned. This was a multifaceted area to explore. I eventually realized that the main thing that had kept me on track was my relationship with God, which began when I was saved through faith in Jesus Christ at age ten—and then also, the many new, healthy relationships I formed with people God brought my way. I learned how the parenting styles of my mother and dad were mostly damaging and dysfunctional and were the reason I still had problems being around them. In the beginning of my counseling period, I had no idea what the trigger event could be that brought forth the flood of unpleasant buried memories from childhood, but through much work I got answers to that question as well.

I will now detail a few of the many things I learned through God's guidance, a lot of prayer, reading the Bible and other relevant books, and exploring it all with the functional guidance and direction of my professional Christian counselor and friend, Athena.

The first meeting was mostly a time to get acquainted and tell Athena about myself and my family. I told Athena of my accomplishments in life, of my three children and their achievements and goals, and of my fairytale marriage to Doug, which I have always been extremely thankful for. She then looked at me as if to say, *So what's the problem?* We then talked about some of the emotional turmoil I had been living with. That led to talking about my childhood, the relationship I had with my parents, and how that regularly brought pain into my life. Athena's comment to this was, "Isn't it funny that after thirty years of love, acceptance, and support from your husband and children, it still matters so much that your parents treated you with rejection and unworthiness?" She said the need for acceptance from parents is very strong in children and becomes a real problem when parents treat their children badly. Athena also said, "All this has been building and growing most of your life with no resolution, and something has triggered it to the surface." I realized that no matter how successful you make your adult life, the pain of childhood can still cause problems. The things I was dealing with were repercussions of my parents not getting help with their problems. They did not deal with their pain; instead, they passed it on to me. Athena said that my parents needed counseling more than I did, but getting them to realize that fact would be the hard part. Athena said writing was good therapy, so I should continue to do that to release the pain. I should also consider writing letters to my parents, one to both of them and one to each of them separately, explaining how I felt as a child, things they did that hurt me, and what I wished they had done. She said I may or may not feel like mailing the letters. She also told me again the same words my doctor had told me before:

"Working through the past will get worse before it gets better." With Doug being the exception, I found this to be true, especially in relation to those closest to me. It is hard to find the truth when denial has been allowed to cover it up for years.

One of my concerns was about the way this emotional turmoil might be affecting my relationship with my own children. Therefore, Athena suggested I make it a point to talk to each of them about any problems that could be present. They at least needed to feel comfortable talking to me about the things I was working through. Athena gave an interesting example of counseling: "Think of a mobile that you hang over a baby's crib. When the wind blows, it does not move just one object, it moves them all. That is how counseling is. It affects the person getting counseling and all the people close to that person."

From my experience, it is worth mentioning that those close to you may begin to question the kind of counsel you are getting when things begin to change and get uncomfortable. During the part when things get worse before they get better, you may have to deal with comments like, "Is this really doing you any good?" or "Should you be trusting that counselor?" or "I am wondering, is this really for the best?" or "Why are you letting that counselor fill your head with falsehoods?" From my experience, it seemed normal for those close to me to question the process, because there were a lot of changes going on for me. However, my constant was Doug. He attended every session with me and knew every aspect of the change I was experiencing. He knew it was all positive, and he never questioned its validity. His support was extremely valuable in my healing process.

The changes I was experiencing were positive and drawing me to a more functional place. I was rebuilding my confidence and becoming more emotionally healthy and comfortable after the trigger event had brought the past flooding forth. I was finally facing the truth of my childhood. I also was doing some things differently, like drawing boundaries for my own well-being. These were changes I had needed for a long time. One change specifically was that I needed to be free of my parents during this time in my life so I could heal without all the toxicity they represented to me. They did not agree with healing and positive change, so their presence became contrary to my goal of emotional healing. For the family as a whole, this created a very uncomfortable situation. But it was what I had needed for years. The decision to set this boundary was *not* done because my counselor advised it; it was done because it was what I needed to do. From this, my brother got the mistaken idea that Athena advised me to have nothing to do with my parents, which was absolutely not true. Athena was a support and an advocate; she never told me what to do. If there was something I needed to do differently, she gently guided me, but she never told me to do anything specific. She told me that for my entire adult life, I had needed to know how to draw boundaries and be comfortable doing so, but she never told me where to draw them or for what reason. I figured out what and where the need was for me by gaining more functional thinking and an understanding of my situation through counseling. In every step of my healing journey, God was leading me to the truth and away from denial and repression.

Athena suggested several things of relevance to my situation and that of my family during our first meetings. One of those things was "the elephant in the living room," a common reference in counseling. No one sees the elephant in the living room. They all walk around something so huge as an elephant and do not see him standing there, consuming the living room with his enormous body. Family norms have been to ignore the elephant and deny his presence. No one wants to acknowledge the elephant's presence or do anything to remove him from the room. They go on living in denial and pretending everything is normal and fine as they continually adjust their lives to move around the elephant. I could immediately see how this was a good comparison to the life my parents were living. Always deny and do not face anything unpleasant, because acknowledging it would mean you had to react and that thought was uncomfortable and probably even unbearable. Deny the elephant's presence so you do not have to figure out how to remove him from the room.

Athena also told me I was extremely resilient to have survived all the things I had. I am resilient because I went on to make a normal and functional life as an adult—a life that was even way above average in many respects. I did not use my past as an excuse to blame and to fail. Athena told me that it is typical for people living through fewer traumas than I had experienced to be on their fourth or fifth marriage by my age. They were also commonly addicted to drugs and/ or alcohol. Basically, their lives were in shambles, and they usually had accomplished little to nothing. They just wallowed in self-pity and did nothing to change their course. With this information, I could only praise God for undeniable proof of how He had healed my wounds and the obvious way He had taken care of me and brought me through it all. God gave me the resilience I required. God helped me cope and survive. For me to go on and live a productive life, void of all the pitfalls common to those experiencing a lot less than I had, was a miracle. It was a miracle that I was mostly unaware of until it was explained in this way. When we choose to live in God's protection, our reality many times is comprised just as much of the things we escape as the things we know for sure.

Talking to Athena was safe, and it felt good to finally face the past and stop running from it. I had found a good counselor; she was my advocate when talking through the years of emotional pain. Athena provided acceptance of me as a person without judgment. I felt free to tell her whatever I needed to. Her advice came more in the form of gentle guidance than shoulds and rigidity. She presented better, functional ways of dealing with common life circumstances. We discussed normal behaviors in building healthy relationships. She helped me understand why many things I experienced in childhood were dysfunctional and damaging and not a normal way of life, as I was taught. It helped me to change for the better and incorporate functional skills into my life in a way that felt uncomfortable before. Athena's advice was congruent with Biblical direction, and God's way was mentioned regularly throughout each session. I prayed for God's presence at each session and asked Him to guide our words each time. Each session flowed together to meet the current need. Input was timely, necessary, and harmonious as we met in God's presence to attain the desired result. In many sessions, Doug also found help and healing from his childhood past. He gained insight and a positive perspective on hurts he carried with him for years. Finding the truth and healing from a hurtful past is also finding freedom from bondage.

There are reasons to seek counsel. Biblical guidelines are available for finding the right counselor. When life's experiences become too much to handle alone, God instructs us to seek Godly counsel. Any professional counselor can give helpful advice for many of life's common problems. But real healing and real answers for repairing emotional damage has to come from counselors who choose to trust God to guide the advice they give to others. Knowing God and obeying Him is the beginning of wisdom, and seeking counsel is wise when life becomes overwhelming. It therefore follows that in order to get the best advice, a counselor you choose should also be grounded in God's wisdom and living a life obedient to His way. "Without counsel purposes are disappointed: but in the multitude of counselors they are established" (Prov. 15:22). Counsel that is void of God's guidance can be dangerous and could potentially do more harm than good. This type of counsel can lack the essential element of spiritual insight.

Spiritual insight is necessary to find genuine healing; otherwise, the problem will continue to be present. Without spiritual insight, the present problem is a life-altering circumstance that is not permanently healed but temporarily mended and still there. "There is a way which seemeth right unto a man; but the end thereof are the ways of death" (Prov. 14:12). I have read many books about counseling experiences. I believe a temporary fix is what happens when people with emotional damage receive counsel without spiritual insight. They end up spending countless hours talking to and getting advice from a counselor. At certain points, there seems to be real progress, but then the person gets discouraged and quits the counseling sessions. They then revert back to the way they were before, just as if they never went to counseling at all. Some even get discouraged, quit, or commit suicide. In other cases, they never even get started because the kind of change that must take place with emotional damage is just too big to face without God guiding it all. "Counsel in the heart of man is like deep water; but a man of understanding will draw it out" (Prov. 20:5). The Bible's book of Proverbs has much to say about the wisdom of Godly counsel.

I did mail the letters I wrote to my parents, but the response I got was far less than I needed. Rather than take responsibility for the damage and feel remorse, repentance, or empathy for the hurt they inflicted in those years, my parents chose to blame me in various ways for the pain they passed on to me through their dysfunctional lives. After communicating my feelings of childhood wounds to my parents, my mother accused me of making it all sound hateful. I had not made anything hateful; my parents made it what it is. I was just telling how things happened and how it all made me feel, without embellishing or diminishing facts and details. There are some parts of it that can sound no way but hateful. I am not trying to be hateful, but many times the truth can hurt, especially if it has been denied for decades and is nothing they wanted to hear. My mother has a great need to control, and I believe denial helps her control the pain. But it seemed that if she would try to understand her past better, the need to control would fade away with a renewed awareness of why she is controlling. She could also find that many of the things she did to hurt me were not necessarily her fault. They came from generational dysfunction, passing on hurts that were not healed in generations before. But a person has to realize her need to understand and choose to change a hurtful family legacy before healing is possible. It seems my mother chooses to look at life through rose-colored glasses of denial. Therefore, she does not recognize the truth or reality of my childhood and the real hurt that was present. That makes the truth seem hateful, because she prefers to see everything as rosy when it was not.

During my healing process, the mode of communication I preferred to use with my parents was writing. So I wrote numerous letters to them explaining many different areas of my childhood that hurt and how I believed they had not tried to help me but only made things hurt more. My mother did write several letters, but all of her responses, with the exception of one, were only justifying why they could have done nothing different. There was one letter that felt like my mother was trying to show some feeling for what I went through as a child, but for some reason, that brief period of empathy was suddenly gone and replaced with more justification, scorn, and defiance. It seemed that Dad had said something to get her out of the empathetic mode. Basically, both my parents still refuse to take responsibility for their actions that resulted in emotional abuse and damage during my childhood years.

Dad's strong stance was, "I do not write." So if all this were left entirely up to Dad, I would have gotten no response at all. As a child and again now as an adult, I have never felt any real love from Dad, and I truly believe that he would have been happier if I had never been born. He has never stepped outside of his comfort zone to do anything for me ever. Any positive actions from Dad were for the family as a whole; there was never anything just for me because he desired a relationship with his daughter.

Although I got absolutely nothing from Dad and very little understanding from my mother, Athena helped me come to terms with the pain of my childhood and get a healthy perspective on my life. Even though I cannot change my parents or the past, I can live independently of the pain and all my parents still represent that hurt and damaged my emotions. I also learned to shake off the old falsehoods and gain an understanding that just because my parents treated me as though there was something wrong with me, that did not make it so. The truth of my life, grounded in facts and undeniable evidence, is that there is nothing wrong with me. I have overcome the past and have lived a functional, successful life on my own since I left home at age eighteen. My thoughts and self-talk will no longer give my parents power over how I perceive myself. My parents' dysfunctional past will not pass forward to me. I will leave the things that tried to drag me down out of my life, out of my existence, and out of my children's future. All these revelations and determinations are completely unattainable without God's enabling. I can do all things through Christ who strengthens me. With God's presence, I do have the power to change and leave all the baggage far in the distance. It will no longer be something I carry with me into the future.

Counseling has been nothing short of a positive, tremendously helpful experience for me. Athena helped me understand that the things I was experiencing and feeling were normal reactions to the dysfunctional things I had lived through. This helped me to feel comfortable continuing on with the healing process and to know my feelings were not dysfunctional or irrational but expected. Understanding is sometimes all you need. It is sad but true that the negative stigma in our society about counseling and mental health is what keeps people trapped into living with their emotional pain. People must realize that seeing a counselor does not mean you are crazy; in fact, it means the complete opposite. It takes wisdom to see when counseling can be beneficial for a problem in life. We all have problems to live through, and some are much bigger problems than others. When the bigger problems overwhelm, distort your reality and truth, or interfere with normal daily functioning, it is wise to get outside help. Seeking professional help for emotional pain should be just as commonplace as seeking medical attention for a physical ailment. There is a lot of truth in Gary Smalley's quote that "Only wise people seek counsel." He quickly qualifies that to say, "The counsel you seek must also be Godly counsel for it to help." It is just as wise as getting a doctor to mend a broken leg. In both cases the person is healed and once again capable of functioning in a whole state. Damaged emotions need healing just as much as a damaged body.

Through this thought process, if I had to choose between a physical and an emotional injury, I would choose the physical injury. The bruises, wounds, and scars are evidence of what happened to you. The people around you expect that a healing process (both physical and emotional) must take place from physical wounds caused by physical abuse or physical trauma. When you experience emotional abuse, it is invisible, and there is no expectation that healing of any kind is necessary. Emotional abuse only hurts from the inside, and few people seem to understand the magnitude of pain involved. Just because there are no visible wounds, it is assumed that nothing of significance happened. Physical wounds heal eventually; emotional wounds may never heal because they are not considered real wounds since you cannot see them. That makes it difficult to recognize the damage done or to get help and support for the necessary healing process to take place.

However, the severe emotional stress I was experiencing as a child in the early elementary-school years eventually manifested into a physical condition in the form of a bleeding stomach ulcer. I believe this was my body's reaction to a very toxic, unhealthy environment, and was a plea for help before death was the only alternative. The result of living a childhood in an emotionally abusive home is death in one of two forms—physical death or a death of emotional health and well being. If physical death does not result, the real emotional you is forced to die in order to survive living through the turmoil. You revert to a survival mode.

Emotional wounds are similar to physical wounds. The physical wounds I received from the extremely bad car accident were extensive—a car accident that took only seconds to happen. In comparison, the emotional abuse happened over many years, causing suffering on the inside due to the pain and emotional wounds I endured as a child. The pain of the emotional abuse far exceeded that of the car accident. It also came with more permanent damage. But there were no visible wounds, no obvious pain, nothing clearly present that required healing at all. Toxic, dysfunctional family patterns, although old, familiar, and sometimes comfortable, must go—giving way to a healthy emotional life without all the doubt, distrust, hurt, and pain. Therefore, just as time for physical healing is necessary, time for emotional healing is also crucial.

Chapter Fifty-Three

Making Sense of the Past and Discovering the Truth

Through counseling, I realized how much Doug had done to make my life feel normal. Since he understood the hurts inflicted by his own biological dad, he also understood what I needed help with and protection from. Doug was guided by God to protect me from the pain. There have been many times throughout the healing process where Doug has felt like Jesus to me. The love he gives seems supernatural at times, and the way he cares and gives feels as if it comes from a spirit completely able and available to love. Doug totally portrays the Bible verse from Ephesians 5:25 that says, "Husbands, love your wives, even as Christ also loved the church, and gave himself for it." An explanation of this verse from the Nelson KJV Study Bible is, "The marital responsibility of husbands is to love your wives. The Greek word rendered *love* is agapao, which denotes the willing sacrificial giving on the husband's part for the benefit of his wife, without thought of return. As Christ gave himself for the church, so there is to be no sacrifice, not even the laying down of his life, that a husband should not be willing to make for his wife." Since I married a man who loved as Jesus commanded, my marriage provided the healing, loving, accepting, nurturing environment I needed and would become a place to feel safe and live as the person God created me to be.

Therefore, on my wedding day, I began a new era in my life. I had survived my hurtful childhood and looked forward to leaving all of that behind. My husband loved me unconditionally. He was a real boost to my self-worth because he made it clear that his life was incomplete without me in it. I had never felt such a sense of belonging or worth before. We grew together and healed each others' childhood wounds. We made a commitment to each other that our marriage was for life, and this brought security and stability to each of us and our home. We also promised each other that our home would be a place very different from what we both had experienced as children.

Our marriage was held tight through our faith. This made a triangle of strength consisting of God, my husband, and me. Our marriage became unbreakable and permanent because it was bonded by the glue of God's protection. God's presence in the relationship strengthened the love we shared, which allowed it to grow stronger day by day. When God is included in a marriage, it can weather any storm and will only grow stronger and better through the years. God also brings peace and contentment to a marriage and provides protection from many of life's pitfalls that otherwise result in turmoil and strife. My husband and I have experienced this divine protection because as part of our wedding ceremony, after we said our vows, we dedicated our home and our marriage in prayer on our knees before God in His church. We then continued to live our lives together honoring God and faithfully serving Him.

My marriage anchored my life to something meaningful. My husband's love and God's presence gave me confidence in myself. I finally believed I really had a purpose and had become a significant part of someone else's life. Therefore, this enabled me to overcome my past and leave the unpleasant childhood memories *mostly* buried and forgotten. I became successful in every area of my life as an adult. I had a happy, loving, and contented marriage. My husband and I had three beautiful, healthy children who we were also raising in church and teaching of God's ways. In addition to my marriage, the relationships I had with each of my children also brought special emotional healing. I had attended college and graduated at the top of my class. We owned and operated a successful business, making a living that provided everything we needed in addition to an excess of wants. Everything in our life worked and brought joy and contentment to our family.

However, the one thing in my life that was not and never had been right was the dysfunctional relationship I had with my parents. I had never learned to cope with the trauma and hurt they brought to my emotional existence. Through the years after I married, their sporadic presence would bring old hurtful memories to mind. Old memories and feelings would surface, usually one trauma or hurt at a time, but would quickly retreat because God had anchored my life to my husband and children. They made life normal and concrete. The past was easily forgotten when my days were filled with their love and acceptance. My husband's support through the years and my children's presence were how I survived the "bubble up" incidents.

Even after I had been married almost thirty years, my parents had not changed their old hurtful methods. They related to me in the damaging ways they used when I was a child. They still could not convey that they valued me. One of the many ways they devalued my self-worth was to minimize or ignore my accomplishments or even give credit to others for things I did. This interaction between them during a visit at my home revealed this truth. I have a teacup with the words on it "million dollar accountant." Dad asked my mother, "*Who* does that cup belong to?" With this question, Dad proved his ignorance of my profession and the work I actually did. My mother's answer was, "Well, I guess it's Debbie's?" Her response too was questioning. Watching this interaction between them proved again what I had always felt from them—they did not know me at all and had no understanding of my abilities. Dad especially seems incapable of knowing the real me and appeared clueless regarding my profession and education. That is because he does not care or believe I am capable of doing anything worthwhile.

When I was a child, my mother oftentimes diminished my feeling of worthiness by saying, "I'm bigger than you, so what I say goes." This caused me to feel very insignificant and unimportant. What I felt and thought mattered little to my controlling mother. But in spite of how unworthy and devalued my mother caused me to feel, I now realize

I have an obligation to be the person God created me to be—*not* the person my mother tried to force me to be through control.

The relationship with my parents had always been abnormal; everything was all about what they expected with no consideration for my feelings. It was a confusing relationship because of the dysfunction present. My parents seemed to believe that just because they were my parents, they had the right to control my life, even when I became an adult. Many times it felt that just because they possessed the parental link, they also had a right to intrude in my adult life however they saw fit. They also always seemed to view me as someone they created, not the person I truly was and am. Because this abnormal dysfunction had always been present, I was too close to the situation to identify what was really happening.

The circumstance was too ambiguous and clouded, making it difficult to pinpoint the real problem and draw boundaries that I had every right to set as a grownup. I did not have to live with the dysfunction if I chose not to. If they had loved and valued me as a child, and even if I felt they loved and valued me as an adult, it would have been normal to want an adult relationship with my parents. But with all the emotional abuse I endured as a child in their home without God, when I reached adulthood I was ready to flee from them and the way they made me feel. I also did not like the influence they still tried to exert on my emotional well-being.

After I had silently endured a dysfunctional parental relationship for too many years, the trigger event brought it all out in the open. It was time to stop the denial. I would finally find freedom and truth when the buried past was triggered to the surface. Then I learned through wise Christian counsel that I could draw boundaries in my life to protect myself from the pain of the past. I could make rules for my life, and they did not have to be consistent with my parents' dysfunctional expectations. It is normal and functional to set boundaries. I finally realized I did not have to feel controlled by abnormal parental expectations any longer. Many things about the past began to make sense, giving me an understanding that ultimately allowed me to let go of the hurt and enabled me to begin living free of the past and its baggage and burdens. Why should parents expect to exercise control over their children's lives well into adulthood? Even God does not control our lives—God always gives us freedom to choose.

Understanding My Mother

My mother's main loyalties were to her parents and brother. She longed for the place she left; her heart was always with them and her childhood days. I am sure my mother's life with Dad hurt plenty, and she was seeking a time and place that felt better. During my childhood years, I often was aware, from my mother's direct words and actions, of her desire to be back on the farm. She did not hide her preference to be back *home*. The old saying "Home is where the heart is" explains my mother's priorities. Her heart lived back in her childhood days with her parents.

For this reason, I never felt comfortable telling my mother how Grandpa caused me to feel. She believed I had a great relationship with him, only because she would not face the truth. She never allowed a negative word to be spoken about her dad. Ironically, however, my mother talked negative plenty about my dad.

The family my parents started together never felt significant to my mother the way it should have. She did not show that she loved Dad and did not honor him. Maybe he did not deserve her love and honor, but she married him, and a real commitment was lacking between them. I also felt her words and actions conveyed that her children were not as important to her as we should have been. I believe this was both from the lack of respect she had for Dad and because of her misplaced loyalties. My mother often told us how wonderful her daddy was; it was as if he was some sort of deity. He could do no wrong; my dad could do no right. My mother obviously would rather have been back on the farm with Grandpa, Grandma, and her brother than live with the burden of making our family her priority. Many times her brother's family seemed to take priority over our own family. I remember my ninth birthday was pretty much a non-event because on the day before, my uncle's first child was born. That became the overriding news at the time and was more important to my mother than my birthday.

I had a healthy relationship with Grandma Ada, which caused another form of dysfunction between my mother and me. I got strong feelings throughout my childhood that my mother disapproved of my functional relationship with Grandma. It felt more like my mother and I were sisters, and she was the big sister competing with me for Grandma's attention. This created great confusion for me since I was her daughter, not her little sister. It never felt like she could put my best interests before her unmet needs. It would have seemed more normal for my mother to be happy I had attached to Grandma Ada and was eager to be with her. This would have been more functional, especially since my mother was absent for most of my very early childhood years because she was either unavailable or living in another town. There had to be something missing in my mother's life for her to be reacting to my relationship with Grandma in this way.

During my preteen and teenage years, I had a best friend who came to our house on occasion. I have talked to her in recent years about my childhood. She has one prevailing memory from being around my family. She remembers how my mother threatened to leave our family and go back to the farm. She said she always thought that was a strange thing for my mother to say, but she never wanted to tell me then what she thought about the things she heard.

As a child, my little sister must have picked up on the abnormal situation also. She has told me that she feared abandonment when she was small. I believe it was because she sensed our mother's priorities and thought she might just leave one day and go back to the farm. I also felt this insecurity, but since my mother had already abandoned me at an earlier age, it was not something I feared. I knew from experience things felt better when our mother was somewhere else. That was mainly because her control and raging temper were not present.

The Bible says in Colossians 3:2, "Set your affection on things above, not on things on the earth." My mother definitely set her affection on her parents and not on Jesus. She also seemed frustrated by her husband and her children. It always felt like we were something to deal with, not someone to love.

The Bible also says in Matthew 6:21, "For where your treasure is, there will your heart be also." It was clear my mother's treasure was found in her parents, not in Jesus. She seemed to view her treasure as the home she was brought up in—not first in Jesus, then in dedication to the home she was supposed to be building for her husband and children.

After Grandpa's death, my mother was devastated. She said many times, "No one ever understood me like my daddy did." That is probably because my grandpa and mother both grew up in generational rejection. Rather than see Grandpa as the real source of her insecurity, rejection, and pain, she connected with him because of the similarities of their dysfunction. Therefore, through this shared connection, she believed and felt as if he understood her situation better than anyone else.

Another relevant Bible verse: "No one can serve two masters; for either he will hate the one and love the other, or else he will be loyal to the one and despise the other" (Matt. 6:24 NKJV). Of course, Jesus should be the only master in the life of every born-again Christian. But since my mother was not serving Jesus during the early years of my childhood, she had a dilemma. Her conflict came because she had a family of her own she did not seem to love, revere, or respect as much as her parents and brother. There were many times in my childhood when I felt despised by my mother because her heart and loyalties were with the family that reared her. It felt as if she blamed me, my brother, and Dad for making her leave home. It seemed that she thought that, without us dragging her away, she could have continued to live where she was happiest. And she always seemed happiest on the farm.

As I have said, my mother behaved childishly in many ways. Maybe she just could not face being an adult, especially considering the fact that Dad also behaved childishly and really gave her no support. Maybe she was just seeking the only place she thought possible to find comfort. She did not realize that the only real comfort is in God's protection and guidance. God was always there, ready to help her make her life better and her family stronger. But she rejected Him as a source of strength and help. When she was only thirty-one years old, her dad died. That was when she began attending church, even though she said she had been saved since her early teens. However, my mother's behaviors changed little, even at this point, especially in the ways she related to me and our family.

Understanding the Anger

Understanding anger has helped me get a more healthy perspective also. Anger is a weapon. Just like any weapon, it can be used productively or it can be used to damage. Anger can be used in a positive way as a catalyst for needed change. It can also create motivation to accomplish greater things when one becomes frustrated with the status quo. Anger is an emotion that can prompt us to work through a situation, fix a problem, and improve. It is meant to be a useful and temporary part of life, not a way of life.

When people use anger regularly to cope with everyday life, they are *not* using anger for its intended purpose. This type of anger damages and destroys. God never made anyone with a temper to use in anger and rage throughout daily life. Anger should be temporary, to be felt and used when necessary, not as a normal mode of coping with life. We all expect two-year-olds to react with frustration due to their budding independence. It is temporary and not a behavior we would say they inherited. Claiming anger as an inherited family trait is just as absurd as claiming that crying is inherited and someone cannot stop crying because they come from a family of criers and therefore cry all day. Both crying and anger are normal emotions when appropriate but are not to be frequently used as coping devices in everyday life.

Unproductive anger used by adults at inappropriate times is more likely evidence of their underlying arrested development and/or inability to cope functionally with life. When people choose to believe God made them with a temper that flies off the handle at the slightest provocation, they are only compensating for their childish behavior and excusing it away with false beliefs. When these people become parents, their anger is destructive, traumatic, and damaging to their child. The child acquires lifelong wounds that may never heal. And if healing does happen, it may take a very long time to overcome the damage inflicted. When a family chooses to believe that anger and temper are just family traits one inherits and something to be expected, anger is allowed to become a damaging way of life. Families that choose to accept the dysfunction, instead of seeing it as emotional damage requiring healing, perpetuate generational emotional abuse. The wounds inflicted by anger are passed on to children rather than passed back to the parents. Without acknowledging the true problem, there is no hope for healing.

The family I was raised in excused anger away by saying that anger defined who they were. They would say anger and temper were family traits. During my childhood, my mother used to say in reference to her family, "That's just how we were born—angry with a temper. My dad has a temper, my brother has a temper, and I have a temper, and that is just how we are." They would get mad, take the Lord's name in vain, throw things around, yell and scream, and make those around them feel completely frightened and helpless—always justifying their behavior by saying it was okay to do these things because that was the way they were made.

This is false thinking and should never be used as permission to act in inappropriate ways. God's word says not to give way to anger and to practice self-control. A Bible verse gives direction in regard to dealing with angry people: "Make no friendship with an angry man; and with a furious man thou shalt not go; Lest thou learn his ways, and get a snare to thy soul" (Prov. 22:24—25). God always knows best. I know for sure how I was damaged by my mother's anger. When children witness a parent losing her mind in bouts of anger, it changes who they are and damages them for life. This kind of damage is hard to "love away," because the security in the children's world is shattered by the person they rely on to provide safety—their parent. My mother's anger became the storm in my young life.

Facing the Truth

The trigger event made the buried, hurtful childhood past prevalent in my mind again as an adult at age forty-six. It returned old thoughts and self-talk, which screamed in my head that I was of no value, no good, damaged, and unwanted. These unpleasant thoughts resulted from messages sent repeatedly through verbal and nonverbal communication by both my parents. My parents may or may not have consciously sent these messages; all I know for sure is that I received damaging communication from them both. I believe because of childhood trauma of their own, my parents were incapable of giving any form of normal emotional parenting that promotes emotionally healthy childhood growth. All of this shame-based thinking had been repressed far back into my mind; I never wanted to retrieve it again. Each time the hurt from my parents' actions would strike me, I would repress it. Then the trigger event brought all the repressed memories pouring forth. The memories flooded out over a period of several months, demanding that I face the truth, heal from the damage, and become emotionally whole.

Repression was a protective way to cope with the reality I did not want to face. It gave me a way to move on and feel mostly functional. But after the hurt was triggered by the episode with the preacher, the time had come to confront the past. There was no peace until I did. I had been ignoring the truth, and God wanted me to live in complete truth. I needed to face the pain of my childhood once and for all and then put it to rest. Because of hurtful experiences that damaged my emotions, I reacted to my childhood with shame—and shame deteriorates the very core of a person's being. I was afraid to even speak the words and tell anyone else about my unpleasant history. I was living in survival mode, programmed to avoid rejection that *might* happen if I allowed anyone to know specific things about my parents' behaviors or admit to the emotional damage I had experienced along the way. I was operating on the false belief that there was something wrong with me, a presumption instilled in me by my parents' dysfunctional behavior.

Shame is a tool used by Satan to destroy us and cause us to feel we are unworthy, damaged, and useless. This thinking process offers no hope and no way out. For over four decades, I carried around many different experiences that caused shame in my life—repressed but still present underneath. Shame can be such a huge destroyer because children cannot make the distinction between hurtful actions directed at them and the person they are. Their experiences tell them that bad action means they are a bad person, and it causes them to feel responsible for things beyond their control. Children are just not equipped to deal with the emotions that accompany traumatic situations. If something bad happens causing trauma to children, they are incapable of separating their value as a person from the incident that happened. Therefore, they conclude that the person they are is bad and take responsibility for something they had no control over. When parents are the source of these feelings, it brings more damage. Parents suffering from arrested emotional development are not capable of meeting a child's emotional needs and therefore easily bring shame into the life of a child.

My mother was very controlling, angry, frustrated, unhappy, and unfulfilled. I believe these characteristics are signs of the emotional condition responsible for inflicting emotional abuse on her children. These things were present in her life due to her past pain and her denial of it. She had a great need to always feel in control. My mother also in my early years frequently gave me the feeling that I was just not as good as she was. She often pointed out—as if addressing breeding stock—that Dad did not have the best DNA. He was the one responsible for passing on all the problems that cropped up in her children, such as bad eyesight, migraine headaches, weak stomachs, and so on. These undesirable traits were not in *her* family, and her comments also led me to believe that I was just not up to standards and never could be. It caused more shame for who I was and pointed out that I was not and never could be adequate like my mother and her family were. Her comments made me feel shut out and totally unacceptable. This damaged my sense of belonging, worthiness, and competency, all of the core traits necessary to develop a person's emotional well-being.

I felt responsible for my mother being so mad when she yelled at me and raged out of control. I felt liable for what was happening. Feeling like there was something wrong with me because my presence seemed to trigger these episodes, I was enveloped with shame. I felt rejection intensely, as though my mere presence was a burden causing all the unrest my mother displayed. Dad brought more shame because, through his lack of interaction with me, it was clear he would rather I was not around. He was a neglectful parent and showed no joy or love toward me; it felt more like he played make-believe that I was not there. I felt bad around my parents. I believe it was this way because of the trauma they each experienced earlier in their lives. There is a root cause for the type of anger my mother depicted. She was not born that way, with "the family temper." My parents' development was arrested, and their emotions became unreachable. They were not capable of functioning in a normal way to be the parents a child needs. All the things I should have been experiencing with them never happened; they were both so wrapped up in their own pain, they had nothing to give.

The shame I felt came from being rejected by the ones who were supposed to love me the most as a child—my parents. It created a great sense of inadequacy and worthlessness. Rejection is the most damaging emotional abuse a child can endure. I felt I was not good enough; after all, it was my parents' actions and words that caused me to feel so rejected by the world. The many different ways my parents rejected me included anger, raging, wrath, looks, exclusion, divorce, abandonment, and neglect. My parents were so childish that neither of them knew how to build a healthy relationship. Their actions were always damaging during my childhood years.

My mother has said many times through the years that Dad would never grow up; he would always be a little kid. She probably never knew or understood the enormous truth her statement revealed. It contributed in a big way to the family turmoil and childish dysfunction we lived with through the years. Dad's inability to face life as a mature adult, include God in every aspect of family life, and provide the leadership, stability, and love our family needed provided a breeding ground for family dysfunction. Although my mother did not obviously behave as childishly as Dad, she too reacted to life in very childish ways. In the early years of my life, I remember Dad as very narcissistic, and my mother was angry and tried to make everything be about her. With the many other childish behaviors they exhibited, I conclude that they did not behave as mature adults able to cope with life as stable parents.

Through research, I have learned that there are psychological and emotional reasons for people to continue to exhibit childish behavior throughout their life. As a point of clarification, there is a difference between *childish* behavior and *childlike* behavior. *Childish behavior* is acting selfish, as though you are the center of everything and everybody. *Childlike behavior* is trusting, loving, and forgiving. As is written in the

Bible, "When I was a child, I spake as a child, I understood as a child, I thought as a child: but when I became a man, I put away childish things" (1 Cor. 13:11). God is pleased with childlike behavior; this attitude is how we are able to come to Him. God says when we become an adult, there is still a place for childlike behavior, but there is no longer a place for childish behavior.

However, those with childhood wounds and emotional damage will continue to exhibit childish behavior into adulthood. It is not simply because they want to be the perpetual child; it is because they have been wounded somewhere in childhood. In the book *Broken Children, Grown-Up Pain*, Paul Hegstrom defines *arrested development* this way: "The wounds of our childhood hinder our emotional development. We grow physically and chronologically yet remain like children, holding on to our fears and rejection." This produces a person who is grown up bodily, appearing to be an adult, but acting and reacting to life in childish ways. These childish actions should not be dismissed by simply saying, "This is just how I am" or "This is how I was born" or any other number of excuses one can come up with. Any person reaching adulthood who continues to display childish behavior must face the reality that something is amiss. These individuals need help to get over the pain and emotional wounding in order to become the person God intended them to be. There are devastating consequences of continuing to live in denial of your real circumstances. For your sake and for your spouse and children, face reality. This is how healing and maturation begins. It is also how to accomplish the goal of every born-again believer, and that is to become more Christ-like. When you acknowledge your reactive behaviors, you face the truth. When you live in the truth, you are set free, and the burden you carry from arrested emotional development is released.

Living in a state of arrested development is like living under a mask, suppressing and repressing the real you, hiding the beauty of God's creation. This fake existence also damages all the people close to you. The people you live with are the people you hurt. It is natural for people you do not live with, such as acquaintances, friends, and other family members, to think your life is mostly well-adjusted and normal;

they rarely see a reason to believe otherwise. But you are frustrated and angry because you fight to hide the real you, the person who is struggling to step forth. To the world, you put on a false front. Your actions display this without question to those you live with. In fact, all of the childhood wounds I have previously described in my life were the result of my parents living with their pain rather than healing from it. They chose not to break free of the burden it caused. But breaking free would have been the adult thing for them to do—and doing the adult thing was not usually something they did. With both of them living underneath this façade, they were unable to be loving, compassionate, empathetic parents connected to the emotional, spiritual, and social needs of a child. I suffered because of their emotional state up to age ten; that is when I went to church and was spiritually born again. God was my Father thereafter. This is when my healing process began, and God's protection was something real I could lean on. My parents did not change, but God became very real in my life, and He was my strength to live through what I faced.

There are many ways a child can experience arrested emotional development. It is impossible for me to pinpoint the source of my parents' pain or to know at what point something of this nature might have happened to either of them. But living with them for eighteen years and being around them randomly for another twenty-eight years, I am confident that something did happen in both of their lives at a young age to cause the problems they still live with and will not face. As their child, I was forced to live through and deal with the effects of their trauma. Because of this, I too have lived with some form of arrested emotional development because of my early childhood circumstance. Since my parents have never dealt with their own pain, they cannot recognize the severity of the wounds they have inflicted or the enormous effect it has on their children's lives. This became a family legacy passed from my parents to me because God was absent and no healing was allowed to take place.

Individuals who have experienced early wounding will deal with life's problems in various ways. One of those ways is to "project the problem"—they blame someone else for things that happen to them.

They find it hard to take responsibility for their own life. This is a childish way of coping with life rather than being adult and taking responsibility for one's own actions, thoughts, feelings, and behaviors. Dad is very good at blaming others for his problems. When I started dealing with the pain of my childhood, Dad blamed me in various ways. Rather than facing how he behaved when I was young and how he treated me as a child, he blamed me by saying there was something wrong with me. Again, he ran for cover rather than face the music.

Another dysfunctional method of facing problems is to "ignore the problem." My mother is good at ignoring problems by pretending they do not exist. She freezes her emotions; this leads to the anger and rage. Another way I witnessed her coping was by "playing the martyr." She often played the suffering hero. One example was when she would cook dinner and say, "I am so tired from cooking that I just have no energy to sit with you all and eat now." She then retired to the living room, and this caused the rest of us to feel guilty for eating without her. She also used to mention often how we would all miss her when she was dead and gone; she was so tired. I used to deduce that I was the reason she was so tired since, as my mother, she was supposed to take care of me.

My parents were both more caught up in their own problems and had nothing left over to give their children to satisfy emotional needs. They just did not seem to know how to communicate to us that we were loved and we mattered to them, or provide an environment where we felt safe and secure. Therefore, dysfunction bred dysfunction and rejection bred rejection. Since the arrested development in my parents was never acknowledged and healed, it was present to pass on to their children from generation to generation. Hurt people, hurt people. But this was not a family legacy that I wanted to continue.

Paul Hegstrom gives the following statistic in *Broken Children, Grown-Up Pain*: "We have found in 25 years of research that close to 98% of the issues couples deal with are rooted in childhood wounds each of them suffered below the age of 11 that should have been dealt with and healed before having a first date with anyone—much less each other." My parents have had plenty of major issues to deal with pertaining to their marriage. They both appear to be unable to bond emotionally with each other and are more like roommates than a healthy, emotionally bonded married couple living in love and mutual respect as God intended. From my memory, my parents were not loving toward each other in a consistent, normal way. They slept in separate bedrooms and seemed happier apart than together. My mother was more calm and peaceful when Dad was not around. She also fought any attempt Dad made to show physical affection, such as a hug or a kiss. Her response was invariably, "Don't touch me!"

My parents needed to face the reality of our family situation. There were reasons they behaved the way they did, but that was no excuse to continue living with the dysfunction it was causing and the hurt it brought to their children. It is sad to suffer from an illness your entire life and not even realize you are sick, therefore also not realizing your need to heal and recover. My parents are not responsible for the wounds they received in their childhoods, just as I am not responsible for the wounds both my parents inflicted on me. But they both are responsible for the reactive behaviors that came from the childhood wounds that they dragged into their adulthood—just as I am responsible for how I chose to deal with my childhood wounds by electing to change the behavior pattern at the root and reveal the source of a lifetime of pain. The greatest power within a person is the ability to select change. This kind of change is only possible with the help of the Holy Spirit to bring the necessary change from within.

Understanding how arrested emotional development happens to a child and recognizing that it is most likely the reason for my parents' childish behavior makes what I experienced easier to forgive and put to rest. After working through the past, I feel healed from my childhood wounds. God has been the source of my relief from the pain and healing from its effects. The turmoil I still experience, however, is in dealing with my parents directly. It remains an unsettled issue and will continue as such until they stop their denial, face the truth, and stop blaming me for exposing the truth and ending the pain in my life. I need to know that they understand, acknowledge, and feel remorseful and repentant for the damage they are responsible for in my childhood and the effect it has had on my adulthood. They also need to stop trying to prove there is something wrong with me and that what I experienced is all my fault. Only by God's help and strength have I been able to overcome the wounding of my childhood, and there is nothing wrong with me. I had to be a resilient survivor to overcome the dysfunction I lived in as a child.

Obviously, I am unable to change the past, and I surely cannot change my parents, but I can choose the process of emotional healing for myself to benefit me and my family. Selecting this path for my life is not dependent on whether my parents choose to change or not. Also, it is easy for me to find healing through changes in behavior because I know it is God's will for me to live in truth and freedom instead of falsehood and bondage. And because it is God's will, He enables me to succeed. Christ called us in Matthew 18:4 to humble ourselves as a little child, which means to be trusting, lowly, loving, and forgiving, *not* childish. As Paul Hegstrom, PhD. writes in *Broken Children, Grown-up Pain*, "When we seek wholeness and healing from the wounds of our past, we can begin to give up the traits, habits, and undeveloped character we cling to and restart our growth by developing the character of Christ."

Chapter Fifty-Four

Fitting the Pieces Together

Throughout counseling, I read many books that helped in the healing process. One book helped most of all: *Broken Children Grown-Up Pain* by Paul Hegstrom. On many pages of this book, it felt as though I was reading about my childhood family. The turmoil I lived through was present due to generational dysfunction that passed from one generation to the next—from Grandpa to my mother to me. This dysfunction was never acknowledged or healed, just passed on. Therefore, the greatest help I found in this book was the way it made a direct connection between childhood emotional wounds and the healing process. It clearly showed how recovering from this type of wound was only possible through God. True healing and hope are found when God is allowed to repair the damage done by emotional abuse.

Arrested emotional development happens with exposure to traumatic experience at any time during preadolescence. A percentage of the population, probably as many as three-quarters or more, suffers from some form of arrested emotional development. It can be insignificant in some cases, having effects categorized more as a mere nuisance. Or it can be dangerous and damaging, causing normal everyday functioning to be impossible. However, it seems that most cases lie somewhere in between.

God never intended for children to suffer trauma at all or be faced with things of the adult world before they were grown up enough to handle it. This is why God gave everyone a mother and a father; parents are present in a child's life to nurture, protect, guide, and provide a safe environment. That environment should be free of damaging experiences that traumatize and lead to arrested development. But sadly, too many times the parent or parents are the source of the trauma and abuse because of their own arrested development. They are too self-absorbed in their survival to be a real parent, available to meet a child's needs. Paul Hegstrom states, "When we look at our families, often we'll discover that our parents have never dealt with their own pain and therefore cannot recognize the severity of our wounds and their effect upon us."

There are several experiences that cause arrested development to occur. The most devastating and harmful is rejection, especially when it is the parent causing the rejection in the child's life. The child then has nowhere to turn for the security and developmental encouragement she requires. In my childhood, since both my parents were responsible for the rejection I experienced, there was no one I could count on to relieve the bad feelings, except for the occasional visit from Grandma Ada. Those visits did a great deal to bring some normalcy into my life and were what I lived for between the ages of five and ten.

I found more answers in Dr. Charles Stanley's sermon on rejection. Hearing this sermon helped me understand that the things I experienced as a child were very abnormal in God's eyes. It was damage I suffered as a child and was not something I should just get over and forget about. And it was very likely something I needed emotional healing from. Life in my parents' home was more about rejection, unworthiness, and feelings of incompetence. Experiencing these regularly from each parent caused suffering and a painful existence. After exploring the past, I gained an understanding of my parents. Because of arrested development and pain of their own, my parents had problems building emotionally connected relationships and were unable to emotionally connect with me. Therefore, they provided a home life filled with rejection.

According to Paul Hegstrom, in addition to rejection, there are many other ways a child can experience emotional abuse, such as suffering verbal or physical abuse; being part of a dysfunctional family;

experiencing trauma; learning the process of shame; living with fear, anxiety, and insecurity; and lacking a value system that could have brought support and healing at the point of trauma. When any one or more of these things happen in a child's life, it causes arrested development. Unless healing is allowed, the child will, from that point on, live a compensating life, usually displaying reactive behaviors with varying degrees of childish traits. I experienced all these forms of emotional abuse at some point during my childhood. It causes damage that can be healed no other way than through God's divine intervention bringing healing to a life injured in childhood.

Arrested development is not in God's plan. It is a tool Satan uses to defeat and hinder people so they are not whole, rendering them unable to live their life as God intended. Arrested development causes narcissistic, self-centered, childish behavior to surface. It causes a person to reach adulthood with limited coping skills. Therefore, the person as an adult functions emotionally at the age they were when the trauma occurred. Their actions portray childish, self-centered behavior because they never grew up emotionally from the point of trauma—that's why it is called *arrested* development.

A Bible verse relevant here is from Matthew 18:6: "But whoso shall offend one of these little ones (children) which believe in me, it were better for him that a millstone were hanged about his neck, and that he were drowned in the depth of the sea." The perpetrators causing the arrested development in children need to take heed to this verse, because damaging innocent children is not behavior pleasing to God. From my perspective, I believe arrested development is an epidemic in our society today; it is very likely the reason our society is referred to as the *me* generation. People in general are so wrapped up in their own needs, they are incapable of stepping outside of themselves long enough to empathize with other human beings, even their own children. Arrested behavior is how Satan has so subtly gotten his hooks into people today. As a result, people are so worried about *me* that his plan is working beautifully to accomplish his ultimate goal—to own the souls of as many as he can. However, *me*-centered, selfish thinking is totally opposite to what God expects from us. God commands us to "…

Love thy neighbor as thyself" (Luke 10:27). This cannot happen when a person is consumed by narcissistic thinking. Self-centered behavior usually leads one far from God. The real truth is that people in this state have no hope of healing when they have no personal relationship with God. They desperately need God to heal and repair their wounds, but their self-centered, prideful sin nature continues to keep them far away from God.

In my life, God healed my wounds because I trusted in Him. God began that process by providing what I was missing emotionally in my life when I was saved at age ten. He gave me a sense of belonging and love because I was now God's child. I felt a sense of worthiness because Jesus died for me personally. I was given a sense of competency because the Holy Spirit enabled me to accomplish God's will for my life. When I obeyed to God's will, He continued to heal my emotional wounds. I desired to be an emotionally whole person, free of the burden of childhood damage. I wanted God to guide me through a healing process necessary for my improvement. I trusted God to make me aware of the causes and effects of past traumas on my emotional well-being and on my life. I choose to be the mature adult God intended me to be, living life in a way that pleases Him. It is my choice to live a life that will make a difference and bring glory and honor to God, my Father and to Jesus Christ, my Savior.

To live the best life possible filled with contentment, purpose, and peace, it is essential to allow God to lead and guide, and to live obedient to His will. When God is not allowed to lead, families are vulnerable to Satan's attacks. Too often, the worst cases of arrested development, childhood trauma, and all forms of child abuse occur in homes where God is left out, not honored, not recognized, and not served. And also, any Christian family can leave themselves vulnerable if they become lax in steadfastly living for God. Even in families where the father's profession is a church pastor—they too can be tempted by Satan and go astray. Sometimes preachers, being only human, allow Satan to use them in ungodly ways. One must never forget to "be sober, be vigilant; because your adversary the devil, as a roaring lion, walketh about, seeking whom he may devour" (1 Pet. 5:8). God is the hope for all mankind, and when He is left out of family life, Satan is given free rein to abuse and destroy. It is like asking the worst, most perverted pedophile to be your babysitter. Satan will devour human souls, but God and Jesus will love, care for, nurture, and save souls. It is not a hard choice to make; God's way brings peace and emotional health. Why do so many people choose to leave their homes and children vulnerable to Satan's devices? Homes require God's spiritual protection and guidance in addition to the presence of earthly parents choosing to live obedient to God daily. God will not lead families or individuals astray. There is no doubt that if my parents had chosen God's way, I would not have experienced many of the damaging things I did as a child. Even on occasions when there were inescapable hurts common to life, the environment with God's protection would have been nurturing instead of one that caused the damage to multiply. Support would have been available to heal from traumatic experiences at the time they happened instead of leaving me alone to find my own way.

Part of the problem in finding healing is in realizing the true condition of a damaged life and then recognizing the need to heal. Emotional damage often leaves one in bondage, living in the prison of the past. The prison comes from an inner bondage placed there from past trauma and hurt—bondage from emotional and/or spiritual damage, or maybe from some other form of psychological damage. It is not God's will that we live in this emotional bondage. The dysfunction comes when we choose to willingly accept the past hurts and allow those past hurts to define who we are. This false resolve is not acceptable to God, and at some point He will bring us to the truth and cause us to search out the real person we were born to be in Christ Jesus. This process is God's way of prompting His children to stop living a compensating life because of past pain and move toward changing the beliefs that brought on the lies we have swallowed about ourselves. The traumatic, painful past must be acknowledged with a willingness to respond to God with an open heart and mind ready to heal and to change.

This healing process is beautifully summed up in a quote by Dr. Charles Stanley in *The Life Principles Bible*: "If you are willing to allow God to surface the inner rubbish of your life, and if you are willing to change what needs to be changed, you will emerge from adversity closer to Christ, more mature as His child, and with far greater potential to reflect the love of God to the world around you" (Life Principle 29). You will no longer live a compensating life due to the pain of your past but will live a life of meaning that truly reflects God's light and love to everyone you know and meet. You will finally be at a place where your life will bring all the glory to God it was meant to.

Things happen in your life that may seem bad, but they can be turned around for good. When you turn it around for good, you may even greatly benefit from the bad you lived through. My childhood was mostly bad, damaging, and hurtful, but now I would not change it because of all the good it has brought into my life. The main benefit is that it brought me to God, and I believe I have experienced His love like I never would have without the pain, making me closer to God my Father than I may have ever been otherwise. And I believe the abundance of blessings and miracles I have experienced has come because of that early relationship I began building with God. There is so much to thank God for. But the most important thing is *not* the material possessions, *not* the worldly wants that are satisfied. What really matters in the life of a born-again Christian are the relationships you build along the way. The difference you make in the lives of others is what matters most—just as long as that difference points their soul to heaven and shines the light on Jesus as the way.

Another bad I would not change if I could is the wreck Doug and I lived through. This bad experience afforded me the awesome privilege of feeling God's presence, and while in His presence to also feel and know God's peace. That was worth all the bad I felt at this time. It became an experience that made my life forever better.

Another bad experience I would not change is the experience I had with the preacher that triggered memories of the past. It was very uncomfortable and caused me to face enormous pain, but it presented a positive opportunity. I could finally do something worthwhile with the trauma, pain, heartache, and rejection I lived with as a child. It became a way to give God the glory for transforming the bad things into good and helping me find the truth and overcome the denial. I also know

God's timing is perfect in every way. It accomplishes His perfect will in our lives at the appropriate time. Even though it is sometimes easy to wonder why things happen when they do, there is no doubt that God is always on time for whatever He is doing in our lives.

Chapter Fifty-Five

Ending the Compensating through True Healing

I have spoken often of a compensating life one lives because of arrested emotional development. A compensating life happens when living in denial of the truth. When refusing to live in truth, everything in life becomes distorted. A person compensates in their thinking, actions, and behaviors to find a sense of alignment or make their altered thinking fit into an unaltered world.

I offer an example that everyone should readily relate to: the time changes in the spring and in the fall. I especially dislike the spring time change. I have thought about *denying* it happened and refusing to reset my clocks. But this would set me up for a life of compensating during the next six months. And just because I refused to acknowledge the time change did not change the fact that it happened. Since the time changes twice every year, living in truth would be to acknowledge the time change and set your clocks accordingly. But people who choose to deny the truth because they do not agree with changing the time will decide not to reset their clocks. Every day, they will have to compensate because their time is not aligned with the world outside. In choosing to deny the truth and not go along with the standard practice recognized by society as a whole, they have to compensate to live in real time and get anywhere they need to be at the appropriate time. They are forever living a compensating life because of their denial of the truth—adding or subtracting an hour to make their time line up with reality.

This is how people with damaged emotions and arrested development live life. They deny their true needs and the truth. They then are forever living a compensating existence because they refuse to face what is real. They have a desperate need to heal from the emotional damage they have sustained. They need God in their life to find true healing from the pain, but choosing to deny their hurts only magnifies the pain, which continues the trail of damage as they live a compensating life.

Simply because a person chooses to deny that the time changed does not change the fact that the time did indeed change. Choosing to deny the need for emotional healing does not change the fact that healing is needed. People can choose to believe that God does not exist, but that choice does not make it true. The true facts always remain—God does exist; the time does change twice every year; and the need for emotional healing through God is the reality for many people living compensating lives. A time always comes to stop the denial, stop compensating, and live in truth for the emotional welfare of present and future generations.

When emotional abuse has happened, your thoughts, perceptions, reactions, and interactions are all compromised due to the underlying tragic event you refuse to face and heal from. The real you in your real world is constantly covered up and living an altered existence that takes you far from the real, normal, functional way you were created to be.

Finding the truth of your situation and ending denial is a necessary part of getting over the compensating. Become an authority on your past and present life. Gaining insight of your past helps you interpret who you are, why you think the way you do, and why you react and behave in certain ways. Knowing and discerning past truths of your life, with a willingness to make positive changes, can tremendously affect your future for the better. Live in truth; truth sets you free.

Finding Healing

Childhood emotional abuse creates a bottomless pit of need and an inability to give and receive love. This problem happens oftentimes because of the refusal to face the truth. Through God's guidance, the truth can be found, which allows healing to take place. God is the only way to bring genuine healing to damaged emotions. That is because God is the only one able to fill the unquenchable need that results from early trauma and bring healing and function to a damaged life through understanding and truth. God's healing presence in these experiences can be enhanced through the help of a Christian counselor. A qualified, neutral, unbiased Christian counselor can help by guiding and bringing understanding to the denied reality and revealing the root source of the pain. This healing process provides the knowledge that allows understanding. Understanding leads to the repairing of a damaged life, thus restoring normalcy where dysfunction prevailed. Throughout this time of healing, thought processes and patterns engrained through dysfunction and compromised by survival techniques begin to mend. This process opens doors that only God can open, bringing hope to a hopeless situation.

The first step to find genuine and true emotional healing is that, if you are not already, you must be born again. Receiving Jesus as Savior means a person is born again by the Spirit of God, redeemed by Jesus Christ to now live a life of obedience, seeking the Father's will. It is the most important choice a person can ever make during life on earth. "Born again" means experiencing a spiritual rebirth—you become born from above. The spiritual rebirth results from the regenerating work of the Holy Spirit (see Appendix A). You are then enabled by the Holy Spirit to live a life pleasing to God and a life of concern for your fellow man. You will also be enabled to raise Godly children in spite of the falsehoods filling the world in our godless age.

When you become a born-again child of God, healing from emotional wounds is now possible. Knowing God and building a relationship with Him through Bible reading, prayer, and regular church worship brings healing to a damaged life. It also replaces hopeless despair with contentment, peace, and happiness. Peace is the main element of happiness. Peace can best be described as freedom from conflict and turmoil. A state of happiness is impossible to achieve where peace is absent. And a universal fact, too often overlooked, is that there is no peace in life without God. One must know one's creator to ever experience true peace and happiness. A Christian experiences all the fruit of the spirit listed in the Bible in Galatians 5:22–23: "… the fruit of the Spirit is love, joy, peace, long-suffering, gentleness, goodness, faith, meekness, temperance …" Having these present in one's life can bring overall healing to any situation.

Healing through God is possible even when emotional wounds are scabbed over with repression and denial. Until God is allowed to heal damaged emotions and the pain of the past is acknowledged, revisited, and resolved, it is ever-present. This pain is similar to a wound that a person suffers from and constantly carries around. The person lives with the hurt but has no hope or remedy to heal the wound. The wound may scab over through repression or denial, and as long as one doesn't think about it, it may feel as though the wound does not exist. However, the wound is still present, affecting a person's emotions, behaviors, and actions. Until healing takes place from the emotional abuse, pain, and trauma, the wound is ever-present, just scabbed over. There is always a possibility that something from the past could trigger a memory or emotion that would rip the scab away, causing the old hurtful feelings to flood back. This is possible because the emotional wound has always been present, and now with the "scab" of denial and repression ripped away, it is open, raw, and bleeding profusely with a flood of damaging memories. This is why facing past traumas and pain is so very important—bad things can reach an emotionally healthy conclusion, and one is not left vulnerable to emotional triggers.

Without true healing, an emotionally damaged person will continually experience the symptoms of the emotional wound. You can temporarily find peace by using antidepressant drugs to numb the pain, but this method is not for the long haul of life. When you avoid facing the root cause of the emotional turmoil, the real problem will never be healed. There is a choice of two paths: you can permanently fix the root problem and be free of the emotional roller-coaster, or you can choose to temporarily relieve the symptoms with drugs and know that the root problems are only masked for a time.

Even when the wound is healed and the emotions are more normal, a scar from the wound may remain, because experiencing some bad things in life leave behind permanent damage even when the wounds are healed. Scars may be thought of as having been acquired from unfortunate circumstances. The wounds are healed and a place has been reached where the past has no power anymore to cause pain, but the battle scars from the experience never go away.

The Healing Power of Music

Healing came to my life many times through music. Throughout my journey of revisiting the past, it has become apparent that music played a major role in my emotional healing. My earliest memories of music are with Grandma Ada, playing her records as we sang and danced. It seemed to bring a carefree feeling to life among all her daily responsibilities.

Through the damaging, hurtful years, music brought healing to my emotions whenever I listened to Glen Campbell, B. J. Thomas, or numerous others as they sang to music that felt good. However, the most powerful effect of music on my life was when I began attending church at age ten. Many of the songs we sang in church and the special songs I heard others sing were spiritually uplifting. Christian music brought emotional connection to God in a personal way, which also brought healing to my life. God was repairing me through music I enjoyed as well as sermons I heard. Throughout years of attending church services, there have been numerous times when the spiritual message conveyed by special music and song has touched my soul deeper than a most eloquently delivered sermon.

In addition, music played a big role in my teenage years of adolescent freedom. Even now, many times just hearing some of the songs from 1974 to 1976 will take me back to that time and a feeling of high school, friends, fun, and dating. This time frame is probably strong because it was a time of newness, change, growth, and independence. It was an important time to gain new direction; a time that offered the promise of moving on into my own life.

When I began dating Doug, music was very prevalent in our lives. Since Doug was performing with a band regularly, listening to music and being involved with his musical performance was a large part of the time we spent together then. He sang to me often, and we had many songs that were special to us and our relationship. Music was a definite part of the romantic connection I experienced with Doug.

Another time in my life when music brought healing and hope was after the car accident. Music drew me closer to God when life hurt so badly. I had many favorite Christian songs that I listened to often. Listening to music brought healing in a special way during this time when I could do very little.

My youngest son, Jarrod, is a professional musician attending McNally Smith College of Music in St. Paul, Minnesota. Their motto is "It's All About the Music." Music is healing, calming, motivating, teaching, and emotionally connecting. It connected me and Jarrod when he was a baby and could not speak. The lullaby music soothed and comforted and then brought him peace and sleep. Music has the ability to reach inside a person and release feelings. It can change your mood or motivate. Music has the power to lighten burdens, and it touches emotions in ways ranging from provoking tears to bringing happiness. Music is a universal language that can connect people whether or not they speak the same language.

I choose to listen to the type of music that builds rather than destroys, music that is productive and meaningful rather than wasteful and negative. Your life can be influenced greatly, either good or bad, by the kind of music you choose to listen to—it can be uplifting or depressing. There is power in music, and just as in any other area of life, there are choices to make.

Chapter Fifty-Six

Tangible Proof of My Survival through Faith in God—The Functional Legacy Begins

God brought many functional relationships into my life, beginning with Grandma Ada and my uncle Jim. Then the healing process began when I was saved by Jesus Christ and spiritually born again at age ten. I prayed to God often, and I have no doubt that He heard every prayer. At this point, my life changed drastically on an emotional level and definitely for the better. Looking back, I know for sure it was God's guidance and presence that made the difference in every area of my life through the years. I trusted Him in faith to take care of me; He did then and still does today.

God has blessed my life richly. My best decision ever was when I became a born-again child of God through faith in Jesus. The next best decision was when I married Doug. I found a great treasure of enormous value in my relationship with Doug—a true gift from God, my Father. Being married to Doug, a dedicated Christian, husband, and father, is like heaven on earth. Doug and I were blessed with three amazing children who also live Christian lives and have been blessed greatly by God. Getting an education and being a successful wife, mother, and business owner are usually only unattainable dreams for someone coming from a background such as mine, because we do not usually believe in ourselves enough to be successful. But again, I give glory to God for all I am, all I will be, all I have, and all I have enjoyed.

My main goal is to obey God and seek His perfect will for my life. I strive to live a life pleasing to God and bring glory and honor to His name. When you live this way, from the heart, God will shower your life with abundant blessings. Through God's enabling, I have accomplished much. I received diplomas and college degrees in business administration, accounting, and management. Getting an education was God's will for my life, which I followed despite the many hurdles and roadblocks I experienced along the way. During my first few months of college, Grandma Ada talked with me about my education, giving me her perspective on my goal. She said, "I admire you for going to college, and I believe in you. I believe you can accomplish whatever you choose to." She also told me, "Your grandpa would never have allowed me to pursue an education, because it would take me away from the household chores." She then told me she was so proud of Doug and the support he gave to my dreams. She added, "There just aren't many men around like Doug. Take care of him." This talk may have been part of the driving force that kept me going when it was difficult to balance school responsibilities and family obligations. I also believe that my mother's lack of support may have in some way come from Grandpa, just as so many other dysfunctional notions had.

God continued to bless our family through the years as Doug also received an accounting degree. We owned and operated our family business, which opened up many opportunities in our lives. And through the years, our children grew into adults who also accomplished much in their lives. In addition to the things I have already mentioned that our children have accomplished through God's guidance, there is much more. Throughout my period of counseling and writing, our family continued to excel and achieve, which is a great blessing from God. In May 2008, Amanda graduated *cum laude* with a bachelor's degree in biology. Doug and I were proud and thrilled as we watched our daughter cross the stage and receive her college diploma. She had worked so hard, and it was a day filled with happiness. Daniel was there too, providing loving support for his wife. Amanda was basking in the joy of the day and in her accomplishment. Doug and I gave Amanda a graduation party at our house, and Jarrod assembled his band to play for the occasion.

During Amanda's graduation party, Jason called from Okinawa, Japan, to inform the family that he and Mandy were expecting a baby at the end of December. Our first grandchild, a baby girl named Averie, was born in Okinawa Japan in January 2009. It was a bittersweet experience. We rejoiced in the news that Averie was born and was healthy, but Doug and I felt empty that we could not be present for the birth of our first grandchild. We chalked it up to more military sacrifice.

In May 2009, Jarrod graduated with honors from high school. The following August, Doug and I loaded up all his belongings in a U-Haul and drove him north to St. Paul, Minnesota, over 1,200 miles from home, to begin his new adventure. Jarrod had been accepted to McNally Smith College of Music through an auditioning process. He is majoring in a performance/production degree. It was very difficult to leave him so far away from home, but we knew for sure it was where God had planned for him to be, and that made it easier. Jarrod thrived in his new environment and managed just fine in his new life in the city. Doug and I returned home from St. Paul to an empty house, and we now were officially "empty nesters." We settled comfortably into our new lifestyle that came with a new sense of freedom from responsibilities that had been a part of our lives for thirty years, since Jason was born. Doug and I miss Jason, Amanda, and Jarrod everyday but we find great satisfaction and comfort in knowing they each live happy, contented, and productive lives in God's perfect will.

Amanda graduated again in November 2009. Doug and I once again were filled with joy and pride as we were privileged to see our daughter receive her diploma and certification as a medical laboratory scientist. She now works at a major hospital in Fort Worth, Texas, in a lab that takes up one entire floor. Amanda makes a difference everyday assisting doctors in diagnosing patient illnesses.

In the summer of 2010, Jason, Mandy, and Averie returned from Okinawa. They are now stationed in Bethesda, Maryland, where Jason is working on an endodontics residency at the President's Hospital on a US Navy base in Maryland. In April 2011, Jarrod graduated with a degree in bass guitar performance. He will continue his studies pursuing a second degree in music production. God blessed Doug and I with children who seek God's will for their lives. They in turn are blessed by God through their achievements and accomplishments, advancing them on through life to help others.

Our newest blessing was anticipating the birth of our second grandchild. Amanda and Daniel were expecting their first baby, and we welcomed our newest family member in June 2011—another grandchild to love and pass the legacy on to. Our first grandson was named Samson.

My life proves that there is hope for healing from emotional damage. It can be overcome with God's healing power. I survived my dysfunctional childhood only by God's presence and grace. No one has to surrender to the emotional pain and live a life of despair and hopelessness that accomplishes little to nothing. God took me from a life of hurt and damage and gave me an effective life that fulfilled every emotional need I had been lacking. I survived only because God led and protected me through vulnerable years and then blessed me with a husband who truly is the love of my life. I have overcome and left the turmoil and abnormality far behind. I am nothing like either of my parents. Doug and I provided a Christian home for our children that was nothing like the one I was raised in. Because they grew up in a functional Christian home, our children had the necessary foundation to trust in God, believe in their abilities, and go on to accomplish much. They began their adult lives emotionally healthy, without the baggage and bondage of emotional wounds to overcome. They were able to spend all their energies functionally working, within God's will, toward their goals and dreams rather than spend time healing from and overcoming dysfunction too. As for me, I have overcome and survived through God's guidance. I have a solid relationship with God my Father, one where the fruit of the Spirit (Gal. 5: 22–23) abounds for me and my family. God enabled me to build a new life with Doug, a life totally opposite to that of my childhood years. Doug does everything to encourage me, support me, and make my life easier. I have worth, value, and belonging in my life with him. And I also find great emotional health and support in my relationships with each of my children.

God filled my life with healing in many different ways after I was spiritually born again and redeemed by the blood of the Lamb. My story is one that God wants me to tell. I know this for sure from experiences through my writing years. Every time I would get discouraged and think of quitting or question the purpose of writing, God would speak to me in some form. God would always encourage me to continue on with the task, which is His will for my life. At these times when quitting felt easier, I would get clear nudges from God to continue. These nudges ranged from sermons or radio programs I heard, to daily Bible reading, to just hearing that still, small voice when I stop to listen or pray. It also would come in things I heard someone say. One day when I was especially discouraged, Doug asked me to listen to a "Focus on the Family" program. Someone was telling a story that was very similar to mine. The program ended by encouraging others who had a story to share it. They emphasized the importance of doing so. I understood that telling my story was a way to give God the glory for all He had helped me live through and for adding to that His blessing of a functional adult life. After hearing this broadcast, there were still a few times when I would try to stop writing because telling my story felt like a frightening thing to do. But every time I tried to put my writing on hold, God stepped in and encouraged me to continue on. God's message was always crystal clear: "This is your story, guided by *Me*, and it is a story *I* want you to tell." So to avoid the risk that Jonah took by ignoring God's voice and direction, I chose to obey God and continued to write my story. Ending up in the belly of a whale or something worse was not a risk I wanted to take. I chose to take the advice of a wise preacher I have listened to often since the late 1980s. Dr. Charles Stanley says, "Obey God and leave all the consequences to Him." Obeying God has always been a safe haven for me. I know God has an awesome use for my life story and is counting on me to share it.

Part VII

A Future Free of the Past—
A Future Lived in Truth

Chapter Fifty-Seven

The Power of Forgiveness

Jesus Christ is the only perfect one ever to live on this earth. Humans in their imperfect state will make mistakes resulting in hurt, damage, and pain to others. Things will happen that cannot be changed, and words will be spoken that can never be retrieved. Sometimes the damage is permanent; sometimes it is minor. Sometimes it is life-changing; sometimes it will be forgotten before tomorrow. Whatever the wounds, a spirit of forgiveness must be present to prevent bitterness, anger, scorn, and hate. Many circumstances cannot be forgiven immediately—some things are so damaging and harmful that it may take a long time to get to a place of forgiveness. But whatever the wrong, whatever the damage or whatever the trauma involved, it is always best for a person to work toward forgiveness. The act of forgiving is not something you do only for the other person, it's also something you do for yourself.

Forgiveness can be an ambiguous word and hard to grasp without a proper perspective. What does it really mean to forgive? I believe, as in every life circumstance, that God is the only real answer to life's questions. *Total* forgiveness without God's enabling through a Christian perspective is impossible. Forgiveness occurs when the injured party gives up the right to hurt, get even, or cause pain and damage to the victimizer. Forgiving someone in no way says that what was done to you was right, it just releases you from the pain that can result from living in an unforgiving way. It then places the matter of revenge and consequences in God's hands where it belongs. It restores peace to the person who received the damage. In my life, I have witnessed many times that letting God handle the revenge for me is much sweeter than anything I could do to someone who hurt me. Working to get even on your own will only cause more stress, turmoil, and grief.

Even though I have plenty of reason to feel unforgiving toward my parents, I honestly never have. I definitely wanted to get away from the hurt they caused me, but I never wished them harm or hurt in any way. I never wanted revenge in any form, and I never wanted to do anything that would cause them strife and hurt to compensate for the way my childhood was. I could see throughout the years that their life hurt plenty without me inducing more for them to deal with. I have wished thousands of times that they would change and let go of their own bitterness, but I have never felt vengeful or wanted to hurt them because they hurt me. I feel more love toward them than anything else. It is sad to me that their lives have been so void of real joy, peace, and contentment. A loving, mutually beneficial, Christian marriage is something I have never observed my parents experiencing. Their inability to emotionally connect and build real relationships prevents them from truly enjoying life without pain. The pain of the past that they each carry, causes them to live a compensating life. The anger and frustration they display are all too often the outward sign of the pain that has been bottled up inside for a lifetime. When this spills out, emotional damage occurs and creates an uncomfortable atmosphere. I also know I cannot change my parents; they have to change themselves. I have tried to make them see there is a better life than the one they have been living. They say, "We are too old to change."

I do believe that, at the root of my parents' bickering, arguing, and anger, is a deep-seated stance of un-forgiveness that has produced a spirit of bitterness. For too many years, the hurts between them have been denied and buried but continue to seep forth in anger and an unquiet spirit. I do admit that the things Dad did to my mother were inexcusable, uncaring, and inappropriate. They were in no way the acts of a husband obligated to love and protect his wife. It seems that my mother believes this has given her unbridled permission to make Dad's life hurt every day he lives. I also believe that many of the things my siblings and I experienced in childhood could be traced back to the big ugly monster of un-forgiveness ever present in and constantly destroying my parents' marriage, their lives, and our family—preventing true emotionally connected relationships to grow.

For many years now, both of my parents have claimed to be born-again Christians. My mother is quick to preach the need to forgive others, but I look on and really wonder, can she see what is happening in her own life? Has she really forgiven Dad, or does he not count in that forgiveness statement? As Christians, we have Jesus as our example. He commands that we forgive each other. The example Jesus lived out on the cross when He asked His Father to forgive those who nailed Him to the cross is the example we as Christians must try our best to follow. There is great peace in letting go of our need to make others pay for their mistakes. God gives us grace to follow His lead. I still pray that my parents will see their need to let go of the pain and live free of the burden of un-forgiveness and bitterness. I pray that God will bless them with a renewed outlook on life based on the truth. I also know that my parents are childish because of emotional hurts they each endured decades ago. Forgiving is an adult action. People unable to forgive are childish. Un-forgiveness is narcissistic. The mature, adult Christian understands how to forgive and why it is necessary for a healthy life. Being stuck in a state of arrested emotional development does not allow a person to live as a real adult or have the ability to fully obey God's commands.

Part of being born again is changing from old damaging ways and repairing hurts you have caused. I have paraphrased the following notes from a sermon I heard by Stan Roberts at Victory Life Church. These notes explain how someone can be born again but still cause emotional damage—again, it is all about personal choice:

When people become children of God, saved by grace through faith in Jesus Christ, they can still continue to reap the consequences of their previous sinful life. This happens because they do not choose to change their behavior and continue to live with the pain of their actions. Repentance is part of finding salvation from sin and putting their faith and trust in Jesus Christ as the one who died in their place and paid their sin debt in full.

Repentance is a lifestyle and also a three-step process:

1. The sins committed must be confessed.
2. We must stop doing what we are doing.
3. We must determine to change our mind.

As this point, we are saved, not perfect; but we can continue on to live a mature Christian life. One way some Christians fail to reach their potential is that they accomplish the first two steps but do not get to the third because they make no real change in their personal behavior or make no choice to acknowledge and repair the pain their sins have caused in the lives of others. When this happens, it can be compared to a convict doing time in prison. They admit they broke the law (admitted they were a sinner); they then stop doing what they were doing because they are in prison, but no real reformation occurs because they do not change their mind to live differently. This requires a conscious action, not just an emotional reaction. Without this change of behavior taking place, they will not reach the full potential of who they were meant to be in God's perfect plan. This conscious action to change behavior is necessary because doing good is what it takes to choke out the damage of the past. They must communicate to the people they have hurt that they empathize and understand the damage their previous behavior has caused. And that now life will be different and the same old patterns of behavior will be extinct. You cannot expect to do damage in the lives of those close to you and go on with life pretending it never happened. This is the ultimate disrespect to those you say you care about.

Honor Thy Parents

I believe that God's commandment "Honor thy father and thy mother" (Exod. 20:12) must be mentioned. I believe this is God's commandment, and living by God's law is always for our own good. I also feel and truly believe that I have never dishonored my parents in the past or now by telling *my* story. My counselor verified to me that in all the things we have discussed from my past, I have never dishonored my parents in any way through my journey of understanding my childhood. Rather, through the years, I have tried to be a friend to them, take care of them, share my life with them, and do whatever I could to make things better in my relationship with them. But I guess deep down I have always known the truth, that my parents were unable to connect emotionally, and their actions said loudly that I mattered very little to either of them. I just would not let myself face it. I wanted our family and my relationship with my parents to be different—like a loving, functional family—but it was not. I denied the truth because it was easier to pretend my parents loved me and that our family life was normal. Also, denial was easier because that is how my parents dealt with unpleasant things. I had witnessed this from them all my life—just cover it up and go on while you die emotionally and the pain grows. I could go into many more examples of how each of them hurt my emotions, but I have already given enough examples to suffice.

It is time to face the truth. I never felt genuine, unconditional love from either of my parents. They are not emotionally capable of showing real love because of their own emotional condition. I have pleaded with them face-to-face to change, but they reply by saying, "We are too old to change." They do not want to change, and until they face their desperate need to change, they never will. I cannot change them, and my doctor told me that I should not spend my time trying. However, I believe that caring and wanting things to be better for them is honoring them. When I communicated to them how my childhood felt, I felt like I was exposing my hurts to people who were drawing from an emotionally empty well. They have nothing to give me and do not care how they damaged me emotionally. Instead, they blame me and will not acknowledge the hurtful, dysfunctional family lifestyle they provided for their children and each other. Instead of giving me empathy and understanding, or trying to feel anything for me, they tell me I should be glad things were not worse. I therefore feel that for my own emotional health, until they choose to face the truth and repent of the real damage, I am at the end of the road with them.

My parents' selective relationships with their grandchildren and great-grandchildren are pretentious, since they were unable to provide adequate parenting for their own children. They cannot just move on into a functional future without acknowledging and repairing their dysfunctional past. It feels like my parents are trying to take part of something they did not build. Trying to live this way only causes more pain because they cannot pretend to be someone they are not. The people my parents present themselves to be are not the people they were as parents. They live in denial of the hurt they caused. This is not a healthy way to live and only devalues even more the ones they hurt. To me, my parents will always represent emotional disconnection, hurt, and pain until they face the damage they are responsible for bringing into my life as a child. In addition, they need to show genuine care, empathy, and understanding for how they made my life hurt, display true sorrow for their inappropriate parenting, and learn to respect me as a competent, worthy adult. Maybe then we could start fresh and move forward in some form of relationship—but, of course, only with appropriate boundaries drawn.

I have no doubt that the journey through my past was led by God to bring healing to my emotions. I know God was not pleased with my parents' reaction when I shared with them the pain of my childhood. They are closed emotionally and do not even try to understand any of it. It is easier for them to live on denying everything. But God, through my counselor, has shown me that I do not need my parents' involvement to heal from a damaging past. As long as they choose to deny the reality of our family's past, I have peace from God in knowing that He allows me to protect myself from the emotional turmoil by not seeing my parents. Choosing to change and feel repentant for the past is something they will have to decide to do for themselves, on their own. The truth is that you cannot get over the bad things in life until you take responsibility for your part in them. When you choose not to, the hurt remains as a part of your life forever.

Through God's grace, I have found ways to be grateful even for the childhood hurt I endured. It has brought me closer to God and given me a story to tell that reveals how God gave me the protection and strength to survive. I have honored my parents despite the pain they brought to my life.

Now I want to offer a few thought provoking questions for those blessed to grow up in a loving and emotionally sound home. Did you have Christian parents who made you their priority and provided for your emotional needs? Were you blessed with parents who proved their love to you through actions that gave you a sense of belonging and a feeling of self-worth? Did you have parents who encouraged you and gave you confidence in your abilities? Did your parents support your life as a child and then continue to support you as an adult? If so, you need to thank God for the tremendous blessing you enjoyed. Remember to thank your parents for the legacy they gave you through hard work and sacrifice. And thank God too that you will never feel the dysfunctional childhood pain that you escaped because of a functional upbringing. God is always pleased when we are grateful in everything, whether it is for the good things we can feel and know *or* for the bad things and pain we are blessed to escape.

Chapter Fifty-Eight

What Is Your Family Legacy?

Is your family legacy focused on the money and possessions you will leave behind when you die? Have you thought at all about the emotional and spiritual legacy you are passing on to future generations? I believe it is much more important to pass on a sound emotional legacy and a solid spiritual legacy based on Biblical principals and a relationship with God and Jesus Christ. These have eternal significance. Money is elusive—here today, gone tomorrow. An abundance of money has no importance if your spiritual and emotional heritage is not secure. A legacy entirely of money where God is rejected and no relationship with Him exists is a useless legacy leading to wasted lives void of purpose.

Doug and I were determined to pass on to our children a functional family legacy centered around God and the Bible. We did not want our children to experience the hurtful feelings we had lived through as children. Doug and I both knew firsthand how bad it felt to live through your parents' divorce. We made a choice that our children would not experience those feelings of abandonment, rejection, and turmoil. We would provide a home where our children knew they were loved and felt a sense of belonging, worthiness, and competence.

All three of our children are born-again Christians, saved from the bondage of sin at very early ages ranging from five to eight. They all have built a strong relationship with God which defines the people they are. It has put them all on a functional road of life, to feel the constant abiding peace that comes from trusting God for every need and circumstance, to live in contentment and know for sure that, when they die, their eternal destination will be heaven. They were raised in a Christian home where God was welcomed and honored by a mom and dad who clearly loved each other and loved them too. For Doug and I to accomplish this for our children and our family legacy, we had to be enabled, strengthened, and led by God every step of the way. These kinds of changes, especially considering our backgrounds, are only possible when God is in our midst—working on us both, healing our wounds, and transforming the old dysfunctional thoughts and behaviors into new Christ-like ways. We were two lumps of clay asking God to mold us into parents He could use to make a difference for our future and our children's future.

The legacy Doug and I passed on to our children is more valuable than all the money on earth. That legacy is faith and a personal relationship with God the Father—a relationship established through salvation and belief in Jesus Christ, a relationship that grows through church attendance, daily Bible reading, and prayer. The Bible is the greatest treasure on earth, more valuable than gold, silver, precious gems, or pearls. It is the very word of God giving guidance for life. The Bible contains a wealth of wisdom and knowledge and offers the opportunity to live life at its best with purpose and direction. People spend their time searching for great treasure and wealth but never realize that the most valuable treasure is easily attainable. God's word is readily available for those wise enough to seek a true treasure. Born-again Christians living their lives guided by God's word are living the greatest adventure life has to offer. Anything else is unfulfilling and drab. My Bible is the most valuable treasure I own.

When you get to the end of your life, the legacy you leave to your family has very little to do with money or material possessions. It has everything to do with the relationships you have made and the bridges you have spent your life building between your heart and the hearts of your spouse, children, family members, and friends. You can take your children to heaven with you, but you cannot take money or things with you when you die. A life focused on building loving relationships and sharing God's way to heaven is without question a life well spent. As a parent, if you give your children everything money can buy but you do not teach them of Jesus and his power to save their souls from hell, you have failed as a parent. During eternal life after death, your children will thank you more for the legacy of a saving faith in Jesus Christ and their home in heaven than for anything monetary you may pass down.

Parents have a great deal of power. People seek great power but routinely minimize the power they possess as the parent of a child. A parent's actions mold children either positively or negatively into the adults they eventually become. Some parents abuse this power while others seize it and make a difference for their children and themselves. One of the ways that Doug and I passed on our legacy to our children was to talk to them often and spend the time required to build a healthy relationship with each of our children. There were many long nights we would talk to each of our children individually way into the early morning hours. It was usually not about anything in particular, just a time to listen and talk about what mattered to them. These talks happened regularly when our children were teenagers and had lots of things to explore and discuss. Even though there were plenty of times when Doug and I would get very tired, our children were always more important than sleep if they needed our undivided attention and a long chat. Looking back now, it is a great memory that I treasure and cherish, a time I love to remember. Jarrod being the youngest had been aware of these talks with Jason and Amanda. When they each had grown up and moved away, Jarrod began asking for us to talk to him like we had done with his brother and sister. It had become such a family routine that when Daniel joined our family, Amanda would tell him, "Okay, Daniel, time for a family meeting, in my bedroom. We are going to talk with Mom and Dad for a while."

Previously, I mentioned our family's military sacrifice when Daniel was deployed to Iraq soon after he and Amanda were married. Our family endured more military sacrifice when Jason and Mandy were stationed in Okinawa, Japan. It was hard enough having them fifteen time zones away for three years. The real hardship came when our first grandchild was born during that time, and we were not able to be there. In January of 2009, Doug and I became grandparents to a beautiful baby girl named Averie born so very far from home. Jason and Mandy had no family there for support, and our granddaughter was almost four months old before we finally got to meet her and hold her. That was a difficult time for us all, not to mention all the other family events Jason and Mandy had to be absent for. Many times military service goes unnoticed, and I believe our country as a whole should know, understand, and above all be thankful for the many obvious sacrifices our military personnel make for us all. And may we also not forget the many sacrifices families endure that are not apparent to the outside world. We all need to thank God for our country, our flag, and those brave and courageous military individuals who serve to preserve all that America stands for. We all enjoy the legacy of freedom that comes with America's military but sometimes do not comprehend how extensive the sacrifice is for those who serve in military life. They provide freedom for America, allowing all American families the ability to pass on their family legacy.

For Doug and me, our family legacy was passing into another generation with the birth of Jason and Mandy's baby girl. When we finally met our granddaughter, watching how involved Jason was as a father was a blessing for me. Since I had no relationship with Dad, it is extremely healing for me to witness Jason being such a good father to his daughter. It makes me feel that I really did survive my dysfunctional childhood and go on to make a real difference in the lives of my children and grandchildren. Dad always stood firm on his excuse that his job prevented his involvement with family responsibilities. But with Jason's example of fatherhood, Dad is left once again with an empty excuse that in no way justifies his lack of involvement in my childhood. Dad's job was in no way comparable to Jason's when considering job demands. Jason is a US Navy Lieutenant and a dentist currently doing an endodontics residency at the President's Hospital in Maryland. He eats, sleeps, and studies—seven days a week. He has no time for anything outside of his residency. But Jason still finds time to stay connected with his daughter. There is more of a relationship between them already than I ever had with Dad my entire life. And Dad's excuse was work—that excuse holds no water with me. As I have always known, it was all about what Dad wanted to do, not what he needed to do. But it is also healing to know that Jason got a large part of his determination to be the dad he is from the example Doug set as a dad to him.

Healing comes to my emotional wounds as I watch my children live out their faith in God. It is good to witness a functional, healing family legacy being passed on in the way Jason is a father to his daughter; to witness Jason and Mandy live in faith through their difficult times of sacrifice. And it is a blessing that Mandy is teaching our granddaughter to pray and be thankful to God and Jesus. It is healing to witness Amanda and Daniel grow in their relationship with God together as a married couple, attending church regularly and growing spiritually in faith to strengthen their Christian lives and marriage. It is also healing for me to know how very important Jesus's guidance is to Jarrod while he is working out his path in life, standing on his faith for direction. Watching as our children rely on God for guidance in their daily lives is one of life's greatest blessings as a Christian parent. In my particular circumstance, this is an extra special miracle. Despite my dysfunctional roots, Doug and I have made a normal and meaningful legacy for our family, one we are privileged to watch as it passes on to our children and then into the next generation—our granddaughter, Averie; our grandson, Samson; and all the grandchildren to follow. That is what makes our life worthwhile. It is a valuable family legacy that brings healing, function, and peace to future generations.

Chapter Fifty-Nine

Our True Reality

One night when Jarrod was in second grade, I had a dream. I woke up the next morning crying, and I had a terrible feeling of foreboding. It was as if I had been warned that Jarrod should not leave the house that day. I ignored the feeling and tried to rationalize. It was just a dream, and Jarrod would be fine at school. But the more I tried to ignore the feeling, the stronger it became that Jarrod should stay home this day. I told Doug through tears about what I was experiencing, and he said, "Well, I trust your judgment. I will tell Jarrod that he can stay home today." Jarrod stayed home that day, and it never became apparent what he may have avoided by doing so. But I believe it is always best to listen to warnings that come through a small persistent voice and know that God is keeping watch over all. Through faith, I believe not knowing what Jarrod avoided is much better than living through what could have been. I also believe a person's reality is just as much about the things they have avoided as it is about the things they know for sure. Sometimes, the things we avoid are known only to God. I trust God to take care of me, and listening to His warnings is part of that protection. I believe whatever we avoided on this day was not good. I am thankful it became something we escaped rather than a bad reality. God's protection was obvious that day.

A positive family legacy is something to be thankful for. But just as in many other areas of life, it is hard to appreciate blessings you do not fully understand. It is easy to be thankful for what is real and tangible and harder to be thankful for things that are intangible. When you have not personally experienced or known of the previous sacrifices and determined choices that make your life and world better, you may not be fully thankful for them. If you have not lived in a dysfunctional home without God, you may not fully appreciate the Godly functional home you have experienced. Our reality is just as much about the things we have escaped from as it is the things we know, feel, and have experienced for sure.

People who have gone before have sacrificed and made right decisions to pass on a way of life. Their sacrifices and decisions have changed your reality. People's choices from the past have shaped your environment for better or worse. Our lives are full of benefits directly related to positive actions of others who have gone before us, allowing us to follow in a world made better because of what they did.

Christian parents mold reality into function and a life of blessings because of their decisions to make your family life better than theirs was.

American servicemen have died so Americans can live free. You do not usually know these people who sacrificed on your behalf, but you enjoy the freedom that comes from their sacrifice to mold your reality into a life of American freedom.

Jesus Christ died on the cross as an ultimate sacrifice for all mankind. He chose to die in our place so our reality would be a home in heaven, and we could escape hell. For all Christian born-again believers, hell will be an unknown torment that we will escape, and heaven will be our reality that we live and know for sure. This is true because Jesus made a choice, sacrificed, and created a way for our true reality to be in God's presence. Jesus' sacrifice provided a way to escape eternal damnation in hell.

We need to spend time pondering the things we have escaped so we can be truly grateful for the reality we have. All Americans enjoy freedom—freedom that came from great sacrifice. I believe if we thought more of how living in bondage might feel, we would quickly become more thankful for the freedom that is ours to enjoy. Many times we are not as thankful as we should be because we have not lived on or experienced the other side.

When children are born to dysfunctional, ungodly families, they are born in bondage even though their home is in the free country of America. Souls that do not know the saving grace Jesus Christ offers continue on, living in bondage even though they are privileged to be Americans. The reality for the life lived without God is a life of dysfunction and bondage, headed for hell. But for those whose lives are saved by Jesus Christ and lived for God, their reality is a life of function, true freedom, and a reassurance in knowing their final, eternal destination is a home in heaven.

Freedom is born from adversity. Soldiers die so our country can be free. Jesus died so all people everywhere can find true freedom for eternity from the bondage of sin. Because Jesus sacrificed, died, and lives again, a dysfunctional home can be a reality that one escapes. My childhood was a reality of godless dysfunctional bondage; my children's childhood was a functional home led by God, free of the bondage. When families rely on God for guidance, protection, and hope, many of life's trials will not become their reality, but something they escape because of God's presence, just as God's voice warned me for Jarrod's protection. Life is never perfect, but when God is present, everyday trials do not become life-damaging. Wherever God is, hope is there also.

Chapter Sixty

Why Some People Believe
There Is No God

God will take care of His children and provide for their needs. God will feel close by when His children choose to abide in His love. But no one can expect to receive God's blessings when they choose to live like the devil and reject the salvation that Jesus offers when He died for their sins, in their place on the cross. Anyone willfully rejecting Jesus and living a sinful life of disobedience will inevitably feel like God is far away or that God does not exist.

People often ask the question, "If there really is a God, then why is there so much suffering in the world today?" Those who really feel and believe this are only testifying to the world their lost and hopeless condition. People create their own problems through disobedience and then choose to put the blame somewhere it does not belong. You cannot expect to feel God's love and presence while living in disobedience to His will. The world suffers because people ignore God and His instruction book for life, the Bible, and then continue to expect God's blessings to shower their lives and fix their problems.

There is a loving, caring God. He is Holy, and perfect, and He cannot look upon sin. Therefore, He has provided a way for all people in their imperfect sinful state to become clothed in righteousness and washed clean of their sin in His sight. This happens when people place their faith in Jesus Christ. He is the only way to God the Father. God has given all people the opportunity to become His child by trusting Jesus to redeem them from their sinful condition and save their soul.

Too often, humans in their sinful state choose to ignore God's way and believe they can make it just fine on their own. Then when they make a mess of their life and reap the consequences of their actions, they choose to blame God for their unfavorable circumstances. In their undesirable self-induced state, they look for somewhere to place the blame and even proclaim the false statement that there is no God. While drowning in a personal pit of regret created by their own sinful choices, they believe falsely and proclaim loudly, "There is no God, because if there were, He would not allow this to happen to me." But the undeniable truth is that when choosing your own way without God, you also chose the undesirable consequences that follow. Believing there is no God is the ultimate denial of the truth and proof that one is choosing to live without Him.

Simply put, some people are disobedient to God's plan for their life. With this choice, a person's connection to God is corroded with sin, leaving this individual to feel that there is no God. The experience of knowing God, feeling His love, and receiving His blessings is available to everyone. Every person has the God-given opportunity to personally know God is real and God does exist. The first step to find God is to take care of the sin problem that separates you from God and start doing it God's way (see Appendix A). Then be willing to obediently work on building and growing a personal relationship with God, your creator. When people choose to seek God His way, He will be found. Then there will be no doubt or question that God exists, because you will know and feel it is true and that He is a loving, caring God.

My childhood was filled with emotional abuse because it was a family life without God. As an adult, I have lived with my Christian husband in our Christian home where God is honored and obeyed. Our home is a place where our relationship with God has been allowed to grow and flourish. I know from personal experience that it is foolish to face the world without God helping and guiding you through every day. My parents wrongfully thought they could live just fine without God, but my childhood was living proof that they could not. I lived through a childhood of pain, rejection, and turmoil. I know for sure that finding a life of peace and happiness without God is just not possible. When you choose to live without God's presence, you will know a life of strife, pain, discontentment, and unhappiness—a life that most likely could make a person falsely feel that God is unloving and nonexistent. Life is all about the choices one makes. Someone's disobedient choices and their feelings that ensue do not change the indisputable fact that God does exist and He does love His children.

Chapter Sixty-One

How Emotional Abuse Affects Us All

People today want the blessings that come with being an American but choose to reject God. Not seeming to comprehend that God is the one who gave America her greatness and blessings, they foolishly try to abandon God, or serve a false god; yet they still want to enjoy God's gifts. They covet what the USA has to offer and push God out. The fact remains bold and true that without God in America, there are no blessings to enjoy. The prosperity, the freedom, and the American dream melt away with the sin brought into our country by godless people choosing foolishly to disregard God's law and impose their ignorance on a God-fearing nation. America became a nation that would be blessed and would achieve worldwide greatness only because her leaders willingly determined to honor God first with reverence and respect even before the date of her birth in 1776. The fact is, for those who want a godless America, you cannot have your cake and eat it too. There can be no prosperous, free, and true America without God as her guide.

This problem began with the breakdown of the family. Families failed to produce devoted, dedicated Americans who cared for one another. Loving God, country, and your fellow man are qualities of character and integrity resulting from being brought up in a Godly home. Problems appeared when people began to kick God out of homes, schools, and every aspect of life that they could. They chose the path of gloom and despair when they should have made God, their creator, the foundation of their lives. The result of rejecting God was that childhood homes began to experience divorce, family turmoil, anger, rejection, and adultery. These homes possessed no security, stability, or comfort to enable children to grow into productive, caring Americans devoted to God and country. Instead, these children focused only on survival and their lives, due to arrested emotional development, became narcissistic. They cared little for others around them, so they could not grasp the concept of devoting their lives to any cause greater than themselves. They turned out self-centered and made their lives all about self-gratification, seeking to fulfill all their selfish wants and needs, thinking little about fellow citizens much less the country as a whole.

Healthy emotional development is a critical part of children's upbringing. When these needs are not met, the results can be devastating. It causes damage and becomes a wound that only God can heal. When God is not allowed into our lives, there is no hope for healing or prevention of emotional damage. Then, through narcissistic behaviors, the damaged lives multiply, creating uncaring individuals incapable of parenting their children any different from their emotionally damaged selves. Families suffer through divorce, rejection, and turmoil because of self-centered individuals seeking their own significance and giving nothing emotionally to their children. This does not produce strong, stable, secure families or caring, loving individuals. It is a costly road our country is on, and today too many Americans are victims of Satan's lies. As long as Satan can damage a child's emotions and that child has no hope of healing from God, Satan rules the person, the family, and ultimately the country. It becomes a subtle takeover of the mind, leaving the victims of arrested emotional development helpless to overcome a condition they do not even realize they suffer from.

God is the only hope for individuals, for families, and for our nation as a whole. There is nothing else parents will ever do that will matter as much or have a greater impact than teaching their children to obey God and live for Him. Leading their children to a saving knowledge of Jesus Christ is the single most important responsibility of any parent. Parents failing in this one task will contribute to the destruction of our society and the destruction of America as we know it. God is the one to turn to; He alone is the hope for healing, survival, and the preservation of the individual and the family, which ultimately will lead to restoring America to the greatness that true Americans know and love.

How It All Fits Together

I began life feeling rejection and pain from both my parents in their world of turmoil and strife. I lived in this dysfunctional lifestyle throughout most of my childhood. At age ten, I accepted Jesus as my Savior and was born again. I then experienced the beginning of emotional healing and a totally different outlook on life. However, I was still a child in my parents' home where God was rejected; even though my circumstances had not changed, my emotional outlook was very different.

For many years after I was saved, ignoring my true circumstances became a protective shield. God was restoring my emotional health, and it was not the appropriate time to face the truth. I rarely thought about the things that hurt, and most things I experienced outside of my family home were positive. I had been taught to deny and cover up, and it felt mostly as though all those hurtful things from before did not exist during this time. From age ten to seventeen, I grew in my relationship to God. He brought many different people into my life who had a positive impact on my emotional state. God was healing some of the emotional damage at this time through new relationships.

At age eighteen, I married Doug. Emotionally, my married life was completely different from my life as a child. Doug valued me and loved me unconditionally. I had started the most significant relationship I would ever experience with another human being. Then our three children were born, and they too would be significant, positive relationships in my life, also bringing healing to my emotions. After marrying, all aspects of my life continued on in a positive manner, with the only exception being the dysfunctional relationship with my parents. They would often bring unrest and discontent into my life, but since the damage of the past was buried in denial, I did not understand why I had these feelings toward them. I continued to spend time with them, but something was just not right. Even though I had no conscious bad feelings toward my parents, it seemed that parenthood had begun to stir up some of the pain of my childhood days.

In 2006, the incident with the preacher provided the perfect emotional trigger. It became the catalyst for a flood of buried hurt and damage from prior decades. My parents had hurt me years before, and now my preacher hurt me in a similar way, inducing hurtful feelings similar to my childhood past. It became the defining incident that tied the emotionally damaging past to the present and made it necessary for me to seek help and healing.

I learned that caution should be exercised when putting your trust in human beings—even preachers who claim to be following the Lord. This episode with the preacher made it perfectly clear that people will let you down, no matter who they are. The preacher, my mother, my dad, and my grandpa were all people I should have been able to trust, but each made emotionally damaging mistakes that affected me personally. Therefore, it is necessary to put your complete trust only in Jesus. I knew from years of experience that Jesus had never let me down—not once. And I know He will not start now. Jesus is completely trustworthy; He will not hurt but will only heal my emotions.

When people in your life let you down, it is important to work on forgiving them. Forgiveness may be very difficult, but there are two thoughts that make it much easier. One is that you seek to understand the other person. Many times just understanding the background of a person can bring you to forgive. And two, when I think of the awesome wonder and the magnitude of what it means that God has forgiven me and adopted me as His child to live with Him forever in heaven, forgiving someone on earth is not nearly as hard. I remember that God forgives me every time I ask Him to; He has forgiven me many, many times over the years for little things as well as big things. I am thankful that God forgives me, and I choose to have a forgiving heart. Some things are hard to forgive and may take time and effort, but one should always work toward forgiving others, with *total* forgiveness being your goal.

The journey I began with God as my guide brought understanding of the dysfunction I lived with in childhood. I also vividly saw how God's presence and protection over my life had made everything work out for the best. I have been given an explanation for why my childhood hurt so much. My childhood hurt because my maternal grandpa's childhood hurt. Then my mother's childhood hurt because Grandpa hurt as a child. Neither found healing from God for their emotional wounds. My mother passed on her unresolved hurt to me. Although I know very little about Dad's hurts specifically, I do know from patterns of childhood emotional abuse that Dad shows plenty of symptoms that he too possesses hurts from long ago—hurts he has covered up for a lifetime, hurts he chooses to deny rather than acknowledge and heal from.

When people choose to live with their emotional wounds and seek no help and healing, the emotional damage just multiplies. It goes on to hurt and wound even more innocent people in future generations. Since my parents both had experiences that caused them some degree of emotional damage, they passed on an abundance of emotional pain as their family legacy. Our family environment was toxic because of unresolved emotional baggage brought into my childhood by both parents. God was left out, and the emotional pain only became more destructive. Dad destroyed the love my mother felt for him. She then focused on making him pay for his actions. Bitterness, anger, wrath, and un-forgiveness entered our lives. With all this turmoil going on between my parents, they had nothing to contribute for the healthy emotional growth of their children. Our family life continued on a destructive path, causing extreme damage with no hope of healing because God was left out of every aspect of our lives.

I wanted to bury my past, leave it behind and never remember it again. Many things about my childhood hurt like nothing I have ever experienced before or since. But living in denial of the things that hurt and damaged me was not living in truth. Just because I chose to ignore the past did not change the fact that it was an ever-present part of my life that changed the person I was born to become. I did not realize through the years that I was only living in false security with my hurtful, damaging past locked away and out of any conscious thoughts. In fact, my real state was one of insecurity because all that was required was one perfect emotional encounter for all the buried past to flood forth at once. This left me in a very precarious position emotionally, one of which I was totally unaware.

Any experience that damages emotions and/or results in emotional abuse needs to be acknowledged and understood so a place of healing and resolution can be reached. It should never be denied, buried, ignored, or put away without allowing healthy emotions to be restored through healing.

God is a God of truth. Since I was ignoring my past and denying the existence of the things I had buried, I was not living in truth. When I experienced the trigger event that caused the buried past to flood forth and fill my conscious memory, it became clear it was time to face the pain from years before. It was time to face the truth, put the hurt in the proper perspective, and find freedom from the compensating it was causing me to live with. This was something I could never accomplish without God's presence and guidance. True and lasting emotional healing comes from God alone. Wise, Godly Christian counselors are an integral part of God's healing process. Real emotional healing is not possible with counsel void of God's wisdom.

All through the years, I have never felt animosity, hatred, bitterness, un-forgiveness, or anything else in a negative way toward my parents. I always held out hope that things would get better, that the anger, bitterness, turmoil, and neglect in my parents' lives would magically disappear. I dreamed that they would be replaced by two parents who loved and valued me, made me feel like part of the family because they wanted me there, and believed I was capable of doing something worthwhile. I did not realize this was chasing an elusive dream because with their damaged emotions, neither of them was capable of feeling the way I hoped. They also would never get in touch with their emotions and heal from their damage unless God was allowed to bring the necessary healing they needed. They were not acknowledging their need or looking to God for healing.

My mother was enslaved by un-forgiveness and bitterness toward Dad in a way that she could not even recognize. Her constant ranting and raging at dad for things he did was both toxic and damaging emotionally. There was and is no peace between them as long as un-forgiveness of Dad's past constantly shadows their lives. A definition of un-forgiveness is holding onto your animosity toward someone and unjustly believing you have a right to make someone pay for your pain. Looking at the way my mother interacts with Dad, it is clearly evident that un-forgiveness still clouds their life together. It therefore is a life void of the fruit of the spirit (Gal. 5:22–23) and abundant in the turmoil of the flesh. Dad has done many things he never should have, but with my mother still trying to make him pay for his mistakes, more conflict and strife result. I also think it is possible that my mother's behavior toward Dad has been going on for so many years, it now is just habit for her, and she may not even realize what she is doing. In these circumstances, we need to let go of any perceived right to hurt and let God administer the consequences. In the Bible, Jesus says, "For if ye forgive men their trespasses, your heavenly Father will also forgive you: But if ye forgive not men their trespasses, neither will your Father forgive your trespasses" (Matt. 6:14–15). Revenge is God's, and we need not waste our lives away living in un-forgiveness.

Even with the entire damaging past revived and unburied, I choose to feel only forgiveness toward my parents. After exploring the past, I can better understand the roots of their pain. I understand their behaviors are only reactions to hurts passed on to them. Through understanding, I have learned to look past my childhood pain to see my parents' pain. I pray that they too will find understanding of their past and see their need for emotional healing and change. I pray that they will find a better place through the restoration of healthy emotions; that they find true forgiveness for past wrongs so they can be released from the bondage that un-forgiveness inflicts; and that they will recognize and let go of the baggage and live in real love for once, open to experiencing all the things I have witnessed them missing out on. I truly wish for them peace, contentment, happiness, and the gift of living out the rest of their days without all the turmoil and strife they have always known.

However, forgiving my parents and wishing a better life for them does not automatically open the door to them, restoring access to my life. Understanding where they come from makes it easier for me to see them as they really are: hurt people who hurt me. Understanding also makes forgiving them possible, because I know they really could not have behaved any other way due to their own emotional damage without proper healing by God's intervention. But forgiving and understanding does not mean I want to be around them and spend time with them. They have not faced or tried to understand the dysfunctional past, and therefore are no different from the way they have ever been with me. They continue to come from a place that brings turmoil, hurt, and emotional pain into my life. Being around them adds more emotional damage because of the way they have always related to me; nothing has changed. When a person learns that fire burns, she does not expose herself to be burned again.

I realize I cannot change my parents; only they can do that. Dad has done absolutely nothing to repair the damage he is responsible for. He only continues to blame me with ridiculous accusations that have no basis in truth. My mother has tried to do something, in her very controlling way. But she is still so entrenched in denial, she will not let herself see the truth and looks for ways to blame me too, rather than take responsibility for the damage she caused. She also wants to fix everything her way and ignores my feelings. There is no empathy from her. I know it is easier for them to blame me for the dysfunctional childhood they provided, which I had no control over. My parents are facing this situation just as always. They run for cover like children rather than face the music and take responsibility for their actions as an adult would do. Both my parents need healing from their emotional damage of prior decades. I pray they will recognize their need and seek God's emotional healing power.

Conclusion

Some things in life God asks us to do can be difficult, uncomfortable, and painful; many times they are things we just do not understand. This is because we do not have the vantage point on our lives that God does. Writing about my hurtful childhood was one of those difficult tasks in life that I did not understand, but God required of me. Why was God asking—many times insisting—that I write down the hurtful history? Why did I need to revisit that past by recalling my vivid memories of the turmoil? It became a time of reliving much of the pain I had buried long ago. But I knew God had a purpose, and I knew from experience that it is always best to obey Him.

Revisiting my childhood has shown how damaged emotions can harm. If healing is not allowed to repair the damage, emotional dysfunction will continue on into future generations, causing the damage to snowball. In my story, I share through true-life examples how emotional abuse damages lives. This kind of damage was so great in my childhood because family life was void of God's presence, protection, and leadership. My purpose in telling about my past is to show how vital it is for parents to meet their children's emotional and spiritual needs. I hope that sharing details of my childhood wounds will be used by God to heal people who also hurt from emotional damage and abuse—or even better, will prevent future hurt through awareness. I hope my parents will be included in those it helps. Telling about the pain of my childhood is not done to get even or to cause my parents pain. Understanding the problem can bring healing and prevent future damage. I do not blame my parents; I forgive them. I know that ultimately, "… all things work together for good to them that love God, to them who are the called according to his purpose" (Rom. 8:28).

Without the pain, I would not have started to write. The details of my life are my story to tell, written completely in God's leadership and guidance. It is not just a story of my parents. It begins with the bad things I endured during my childhood years in their care. Those tumultuous years are what provoked me to begin the healing journey and the writing. But throughout the writing and healing process, I came to understand that my life story is even more about how God healed and cared for me as only a father can. This magnified the other side of my story, which is the blessings God gave me and all the good I have experienced in life as an adult with my loving husband, Doug, and our children. I shared my discoveries and hope my story will bring help and healing where there is need and ultimately bring glory and honor to God, my Father.

With God's help, it is possible to prevent emotional damage through understanding. When parents comprehend their ability to damage and destroy their children emotionally, they can parent to build emotional wellness. By being aware of the emotional damage incorrect parenting can cause, loving parents can choose to let God enable them to unconditionally love, support, and encourage their children. Parents can choose to provide a functional home for their children and determine not to pass damage on into another generation. Life is all about choices, and everything can be better when you determine to pass on a functional emotional legacy. The day will come when you will be glad you did—whether it be here on earth now or later when you face eternity.

My journey back has given me peace with the past. I gained an understanding of what caused my childhood to hurt and now have a future free of that pain—a future where I can truly be the person God created me to be, free of the burdens of previous programming to falsely believe how life "should be." Just as before, I will continue to completely trust God to lead me forward in His will for my life, but now with renewed resolve to always live in truth after being set free from the baggage and burden of denial of childhood wounds and damaging relationships.

No one has to live a compensating life, weighed down under the burden of past emotional damage. There is hope in Jesus Christ for healing and freedom. In a born-again, *personal* relationship with God, you can break free of the dysfunctional baggage that damages and distorts. God alone offers the hope you seek. Only God can heal the hurts inflicted by living in dysfunction.

A Final Thought

I hope by reading my life story, you not only know me better but also, more importantly, you know God better. If you were not saved before, I hope you are now, and you feel God's infinite love for you as His child. God is the single source providing hope to overcome any form of emotional damage, and He alone has the power to change a dysfunctional family legacy. Only God has the power to give a heart the ability to completely forgive those at the source of its pain.

I now finish with one final thought, giving God the last word. This is one of my favorite Bible verses; it strengthens my life and promotes wisdom.

> *"Trust in the Lord with all thine heart; and lean not unto thine own understanding. In all thy ways acknowledge him, and he shall direct thy paths."*—Proverbs 3:5–6

Plan of Salvation

If you died today, do you know that you would go to heaven?

The Bible says that we can know. 1 John 5:13: "These things have I written unto you that believe on the name of the Son of God; that ye may know that ye have *eternal life*, and that ye may believe on the name of the Son of God." (*Eternal life* means to live with God forever in heaven.)

The Bible says that all are sinners. Romans 3:23: "For all have *sinned*, and come short of the glory of God." (*Sin* is breaking or disobeying God's law.)

The Bible says that all need a Savior. Romans 5:8: "But God *commendeth* His love toward us, in that, while we were yet sinners, Christ died for us." (*Commendeth* means He proved His love.)

The Bible says that all must confess. Romans 10:9: "That if thou shalt *confess* with thy mouth the Lord Jesus, and shalt believe in thine heart that God hath raised Him from the dead, thou shalt be saved." (*Confession* simply means to "agree" that Christ is the sinless risen Savior, and you are a condemned sinner.)

If you believe and are ready to receive Christ as your personal Savior, then pray this prayer and mean each word as your own as you speak to God: "Dear God, I know that I am a sinner, and I believe that Jesus died on the cross and rose again to pay for my sin. Please forgive me of my sin, and save me right now. In Jesus's name, Amen."

The Bible says if we will believe and call upon God for salvation, then we can know by God's promise that we truly are born again. Romans 10:13: "For whosoever shall call upon the name of the Lord shall be saved."

Further Information on Salvation

Salvation: Salvation is the gift of God brought to man by grace and received by personal faith in the Lord Jesus Christ, whose precious blood was shed on Calvary for the forgiveness of our sins (John 1:12; Eph. 1:7 and 2:8–10; 1 Pet. 1:18–19).

Eternal Security: All the redeemed, once saved, are kept by God's power and are thus secure in Christ forever (John 6:37–40; and 10:27–30; Rom. 8:1, 38–39; 1 Cor. 1:4–8; 1 Peter 1:4–5). It is a privilege of believers to rejoice in the assurance of their salvation through the testimony of God's Word—which, however, clearly forbids the use of Christian liberty as an occasion to the flesh (Rom. 13:13–14; Gal. 5:13; Titus 2:11–15).

The Eternal State: We believe in the bodily resurrection of all men, the saved to eternal life, and the unsaved to judgment and everlasting punishment (Matt. 25:46; John 5:28–29 and 11:25–26; Rev. 20:5–6, 12–13).

We believe that the souls of the redeemed are, at death, absent from the body and present with the Lord, where in conscious bliss they await the first resurrection when spirit, soul, and body are reunited to be glorified forever with the Lord (Luke 23:43; 2 Cor. 5:8; Phil. 1:23; 1 Thess. 4:16–17; Rev. 20:4–6).

We believe that the souls of unbelievers remain, after death, in conscious punishment and torment until the second resurrection, when with soul and body reunited they shall appear at the Great White Throne Judgment, and shall be cast into the Lake of Fire, not to be annihilated, but to suffer everlasting conscious punishment and torment (Matt. 25:41–46; Mark 9:43–48; Luke 16:19–26; 2 Thess. 1:7–9; Jude 6–7; Rev. 20:11–15).

The Godhead: We believe in one Triune God, eternally existing in three persons: Father, Son, and Holy Spirit, each co-eternal in being, co-identical in nature, co-equal in power and glory, and having the same attributes and perfections (Deut. 6:4; Matt. 28:19; 2 Cor. 13:14; John 14:10, 26).

The Person of Christ: We believe that the Lord Jesus Christ, the eternal Son of God, became man, without ceasing to be God, having been conceived by the Holy Spirit and born of the virgin Mary, in order that He might reveal God and redeem sinful men (Isa. 7:14 and 9:6; Luke 1:35; John 1:1–2,14; 2 Cor. 5:19–21; Gal. 4:4–5; Phil. 2:5–8).

The Person of the Holy Spirit: We believe that the Holy Spirit is a person who convicts the world of sin, of righteousness, and of judgment; and that He is the Supernatural Agent in regeneration, baptizing all believers into the body of Christ, indwelling and sealing them unto the day of redemption (John 16:8–11; Rom. 8:9; 1 Cor. 12:12–14; 2 Cor. 3:6; Eph. 1:13–14).

Information printed with permission from the website victorybaptiststephenville. com.

Relevant Quotes by Deborah Leigh Alexander

You lose what you abuse.

The family legacy and inheritance has little value if it is only monetary and void of emotional and spiritual connection.

No matter how hurtful, damaging, and uncomfortable things in your past have been, it is those times of turmoil and pain that turn you into a usable vessel, able to carry out God's purpose for your life.

Just as some physical ailments cannot be healed without the aid of a physician, some emotional ailments cannot be put into the proper focus and healed without the help of a Christian counselor and God's presence.

Just like our spiritual life, our emotional life must be connected to God in order to be healthy, functional, and purposeful.

Don't live your life backstage in the shadows; live it center stage in the leading role with God as the director of every scene and the final authority for every decision.

Living life without God is like traveling without a destination, purpose, or direction.

No human being will ever reach their full potential without God's enabling power and presence in their life.

The unsaved world looks upon the Christian life and chooses to condemn and criticize a miracle it does not comprehend.

Just because an atheist chooses to deny the existence of God does not change the fact that God exists.

Where faith grows, fear is choked out. Just as where God is worshiped, dysfunction disappears.

What you do is not the same as who you are.

Money is not needed for happiness; it is needed for survival.

Knowing which teams played or which team won the Super Bowl will be meaningless when your time comes to die. Spend your life on things that truly matter.

Living in denial is a lonely place; it conceals the truth and robs one's true identity.

It's crazy to live in denial. Truth brings healing. Truth is where hope lives.

Acting selfish is easier to overcome when you recognize the childish roots it evolves from.

Believing and living by false assumptions creates more false assumptions and lies. These false beliefs or lies lead to further separation from God, since God is truth.

Always remember that man is not capable of doing what only God is able to do.

At times in my life when I can do nothing, I know God is taking care of everything.

Be patient—God is working.

Trust God's will to guide your life. If God has brought you to it, He will see you through it.

Choosing to live life without God never works. It is like trying to put a huge puzzle together when most of the pieces are missing.

Living life without Jesus is like living life without a home; you have no shelter for protection. Jesus provides shelter from the storms of life.

Positive working relationships are built on love in action. Simply existing together does not build sustaining permanent, loving relationships.

A person choosing to live life outside of God's sheltering wing chooses to live a life wasted and without purpose.

As God's children, we have an abundant life waiting that is filled with the fruit of the spirit along with every other good gift God promises to us. Enjoy God's goodness as you live a life obedient to His will for you.

A child of God should never play with the devil.

God's truth does not shift with popular trends or change in cultural whims.

Relevant Quotes by Others

Reading makes your life easier.—Jarrod (my youngest son)

A life devoted to something greater than themselves.—US Marine Corps billboard

Sin does not start with the act; it starts as the thought.
Watch your thoughts; they will become words.
Watch your words; they will become actions.
Watch your actions; they will become habits.
Watch your habits; they will become character.
Watch your character; it becomes your destiny.—Anonymous

Sin will always take you farther than you wanted to go; keep you longer than you planned to stay; and cost you more than you intended to pay.—Pastor Stan White

Sin will take you to unpleasant places. And just as you do not have to live the experience of sin to know of its damaging effects, you do not have to go to the sewer to know it stinks there.—Pastor Stan White

You are never a victim of your circumstances, for your sovereign God has determined to use everything that happens to you for your blessing and His glory.—Dr. Charles Stanley

Anything you hold too tightly, you will lose.—Dr. Charles Stanley

You reap what you sow, more than you sow, and later than you sow.—Dr. Charles Stanley

Obey God and leave all the consequences to Him.—Dr. Charles Stanley

Guilt breeds suspicion.—Joyce Meyer

The evidence of God's presence far outweighs the proof of His absence.—Joyce Meyer

Jesus died for you so He would not have to live without you.—A bumper sticker and a Facebook page

When God is all you have, He is all you need.—A quote from a sermon

It's hard to be an earthly dad without a heavenly Father.—A church road sign

Mindless worship is meaningless worship.—A church road sign

Jesus is Lord. Eternity is too long to be wrong.—A church road sign

A person of character possesses a series of virtues or values. These are courage, compassion, generosity, temperance, persistence, and friendliness, among others. But the most important value in determining the depth and strength of your character is integrity. It is integrity, living in complete truth with yourself and others, that most demonstrates the quality of your character.—Brian Tracy

Little value comes out of the belief that discipline and punishment go hand in hand.—Eric Harvey

The style and tone of your communications are messages in and of themselves.—Eric Harvey

Let go and let others be themselves.—Karen Casey

We are not here to merely make a living. We are here to enrich the world, and we impoverish ourselves if we forget this errand.—Woodrow Wilson

Commitment is what transforms a promise into reality. It is the words that speak boldly of your intentions. And the actions which speak louder than the words. It is making time when there is none. Coming through time after time after time, year after year after year. Commitment is the stuff character is made of; the power to change the face of things. It is the daily triumph of integrity over skepticism.—Abraham Lincoln

A house is not a home unless it contains food and fire for the mind as well as the body.—Benjamin Franklin

Hurt people, hurt people.—Bill Cosby

And then the day came when the risk to remain tight in a bud was more painful than the risk it took to blossom.—Anais Nin

Dare to dream of your great success. Become intimate with those things which deeply motivate you and regularly work toward the realization of that mission.—Mary Anne Radmacher

As we express our gratitude, we must never forget that the highest appreciation is not to utter words, but to live by them.—John F. Kennedy

Change allows us to exit the comfortable and enter the improved.—
David Cottrell

Appendix C

Definitions of Related Terms

Anger is an emotion given to prompt us to work through a situation, fix a problem, and improve. It is intended to be a temporary part of life, not a way of life. Anger is abnormal when used as a constant coping device when faced with life's frequent frustrations.

Arrested emotional development is caused by an exposure to a traumatic experience in childhood that hinders emotional development. A person grows physically and chronologically yet remains like a child, holding on to fears and rejection.

Childish behavior means acting selfishly, as though you are the center of everything and everybody. This is living narcissistically in a self-centered way, which is often a symptom of emotional damage due to arrested development.

Childlike behavior occurs when a person is trusting, loving, and forgiving; this is behavior pleasing to God.

Compromised means yielding to and living in partial truth. Compromised people hang the truth to fit what they feel and believe, living in denial of what's really true. Emotional damage causes one to live a compromised life.

Denial is refusing to accept the truth even when overwhelming evidence proves otherwise. It is an altered way of thinking, living in compromise. When living in denial, one refuses to face the truth.

Dysfunctional interaction between people involves abnormal communicational modes, whether verbal or nonverbal, that inflict hurt and damage, causing emotional harm. It is highly probable that families become dysfunctional when they leave God out of family life.

Forgiveness happens when injured parties give up their perceived right to hurt, get even, or cause pain and damage to the one who hurt them. Forgiving someone in no way says that what was done to you was right; it just releases you from the pain that can result from living in unforgiveness.

Functional means useful and adaptable; working in order to accomplish a designated purpose; acting according to a primary basic of design; fulfilling normal behavior modes conducive to healthy emotional development. A functional family is one that honors God and obeys His commands, loves each other, and works together for the mutual benefit of all. Emotional damage is minimal in functional families.

Generational dysfunction is a dysfunctional lifestyle passed on from one generation to the next. Dysfunction perpetuates when no emotional healing is sought, and God is disobeyed and continually left out of family life.

Generational rejection happens when a parent suffers from rejection and, unless they find healing, passes on the rejection syndrome into the lives of his or her children. Without proper healing, generational rejection becomes a vicious cycle of unnecessary pain and turmoil until the chain is broken through God's intervention which may include Christian counseling.

Repression forces thoughts from the conscious mind into the unconscious mind. It is a defense mechanism by which unacceptable or painful impulses, emotions, or memories are put out of the conscious mind, their energy or effect remaining in the unconscious, where they influence personality and behavior. Repressed emotional trauma can often lead to outbursts of anger or other unacceptable emotional behaviors.

Resilient people are able to withstand or recover quickly from difficult conditions. Being resilient helps one survive emotionally abusive circumstances.

Suppression is a conscious knowledge of painful feelings, thoughts, memories or experiences that are subdued; kept secret; or refrained from disclosure. Suppression tactics are often used when a person has experienced emotional trauma or abuse.

Truth is that which is in accordance with the fact or facts; fixed established principle or law; and proven doctrine. God is the beginning of all truth and wisdom. Truth is the opposite of denial.

Total forgiveness means giving up one's perceived right to cause hurt or get even. Feelings of resentment are replaced by prayers of blessings for the person you were hurt by.

Unforgiveness means holding on to one's animosity toward someone in a willful, deliberate manner, unjustly believing you have a right to make them pay for your pain.

Useful Lists

Basic Needs in Relationships:

1. The need for good will from others.

2. The need for emotional support.

3. The need to be heard by others and to be respectfully responded to with acceptance.

4. The need to have your own view, even when others disagree.

5. The need to have your feelings and experience acknowledged as genuine.

6. The need to receive a sincere apology for the behavior from others that is devaluing, such as belittling remarks or episodes of anger toward you.

7. The need for clear, honest, and informative answers about what affects you.

8. The need to live free of accusation, interrogation, and blame.

9. The need to live free of criticism and judgment.

10. The need to have your work and your interests respected.

11. The need for encouragement.

12. The need for freedom from emotional and physical threat.

13. The need for freedom from angry outbursts and rage.

14. The need for freedom from labels that devalue you.

15. The need to be respectfully asked rather than ordered.

16. The need to have your final decisions accepted.

17. The need for privacy at times.

Steve Hein version of "Basic Needs" posted on Emotional Abuse website by Steve Hein

Characteristics of Emotionally Abused People:

1. They can only guess what healthy behavior is.

2. They may have trouble completing things.

3. They may lie when they don't need to. Lying might have been a survival tactic in the home. Perhaps the child learned this from parents who lied to cover up problems or avoid conflict, or simply used it to avoid harsh punishment or get needed attention. As an adult, this tactic is no longer appropriate, but has become a habit.

4. They judge themselves without mercy.

5. They have trouble accepting compliments.

6. They often take responsibility for problems, not successes.

7. Or maybe they go to the other extreme and refuse to take any responsibility for mistakes while trying to take credit for the work of others.

8. It is hard for them to have fun since their childhoods were lost, stolen, or repressed.

9. They may take themselves too seriously or not seriously at all.

10. They may have difficulty with intimate relationships.

11. They expect others to *just know what they want*. They cannot express it because they were so often disappointed as children that they learned to stop asking for things.

12. They might overreact to things beyond their control.

13. They constantly seek approval and affirmation.

14. They feel different from others.

15. They are extremely loyal, even when facing overwhelming evidence that their loyalty is undeserved.

16. They are either super-responsible or extremely irresponsible.

17. They tend to lock themselves into a course of action without giving serious consideration to alternative behaviors or possible consequences. This impulsiveness leads to confusion, self-loathing, and loss of control over their environment. The result is that they spend much energy blaming others, feeling victimized, and cleaning up messes.

If you suffered emotional abuse, some or all of these may be familiar things you struggle with.

Information from the work of Janet Geringer Woititz found on "Emotional Abuse" website and posted by Steve Hein.

Bibliography

Hegstrom, Paul. *Broken Children, Grown-Up Pain*. Kansas City: Beacon Hill Press, 2006.

Nelson, Thomas. *The King James Study Bible*. Nashville: Thomas Nelson, 1988.

Scofield, C.I. *The Scofield Study Bible, King James Version*. New York: Oxford University Press, 2003.

Smalley, Gary. *Hidden Keys to Successful Parenting*. The Gary Smalley Seminar, 1988.

Stanley, Dr. Charles. *Life Principles Bible, NKJV.* Nashville: Thomas Nelson, 2005.

The Amplified Bible. Grand Rapids, Michigan: Zondervan and the Lockman Foundation, 1987.

The One Year Bible: King James Version. Carol Stream, Illinois: Tyndale House, 1987.

Sermons Quoted

Stanley, Dr. Charles. "Release from the Bondage of Rejection." Sermon given on *In Touch Ministries*, Episode 522, November 11, 2007.

White, Russell. "A Family Affair." Sermon given at Victory Baptist Church, Stephenville, Texas, October 12, 2008.

White, Russell. "The Power of Words." Sermon given at Victory Baptist Church, Stephenville, Texas, January 10, 2010.

Unless otherwise indicated, all Scripture quotations are taken from the King James Version of the Bible.

Suggested Reading

Covey, Stephen R. *The Seven Habits of Highly Effective Families.*

Engel, Beverly. *Healing Your Emotional Self.*

Farmer, Steven. *Adult Children of Abusive Parents.*

Farris, Michael. *What a Daughter Needs from Her Dad.*

Kendall, R.T. *Total Forgiveness.*

Kennedy, D. James. *Turn It to Gold.*

Leman, Kevin. *What a Difference a Daddy Makes*

McBride, Karyl. *Will I Ever Be Good Enough?*

Meeker, Meg. *Strong Fathers, Strong Daughters.*

Moore, Beth. *Breaking Free.*

Moore, Beth. *Get Out of That Pit.*

Neuharth, Dan. *If You Had Controlling Parents.*

Rothschild, Jennifer. *Self Talk, Soul Talk.*

Secunda, Victoria. *When You and Your Mother Can't Be Friends.*

Smalley, Gary. *Hidden Keys to Loving Relationships.* (Video and Book)

Stanley, Charles. *Our Unmet Needs.*